WAIMH

HANDBOOK OF
Infant
Mental Health

VOLUME THREE

Parenting and Child Care

WAIMH
HANDBOOK OF
Infant
Mental Health

Joy D. Osofsky and Hiram E. Fitzgerald / Editors

VOLUME THREE

Parenting and Child Care

WORLD ASSOCIATION FOR INFANT MENTAL HEALTH

John Wiley & Sons, Inc.
New York • Chichester • Weinheim • Brisbane • Singapore • Toronto

Library of Congress Cataloging-in-Publication Data:
WAIMH Handbook of infant mental health / World Association for Infant Mental Health ; edited by Joy D. Osofsky and Hiram E. Fitzgerald.
    p.   cm.
  Includes bibliographical references and indexes.
  Contents: v. 1. Perspectives on infant mental health — v. 2. Early intervention, evaluation, and assessment — v. 3. Parenting and child care — v. 4. Infant mental health groups at high risk.
  Other title: WAIMH handbook of infant mental health.
  ISBN 0-471-18988-X (set : alk. paper).— ISBN 0-471-18941-3 (v.1 : cloth : alk. paper) — ISBN 0-471-18944-8 (v. 2 : cloth : alk. paper). — ISBN 0-471-18946-4 (v. 3 : cloth : alk. paper). — ISBN 0-471-18947-2 (v. 4 : cloth : alk. paper)
  1. Infants—Mental health Handbooks, manuals, etc. 2. Infant psychiatry Handbooks, manuals, etc. 3. Child psychopathology—Prevention Handbooks, manuals, etc. I. Osofsky, Joy D. II. Fitzgerald, Hiram E. III. World Association for Infant Mental Health. IV. Title: WAIMH handbook of infant mental health.
  [DNLM: 1. Child Development. 2. Infant. 3. Child Psychology. 4. Parenting. 5. Early Intervention (Education) 6. Developmental Disabilities—prevention & control. WS 105 H2363 2000]
RJ502.5.H362 2000
618.92'89—dc21   99-11893
                                               CIP

Contributors

BETTY ANN ABLON, MS
The Child Care Group, Dallas, Texas

KATHRYN E. BARNARD, RN, PH.D.
Parent-Child Nursing Center for Human Development and Disability, University of Washington, Seattle, Washington

SONYA BEMPORAD, MSW (deceased)
The Child Care Group, Dallas, Texas

LISA J. BERLIN, PH.D.
Center for Children and Families, Teacher's College, Columbia University, New York, New York

MARC H. BORNSTEIN, PH.D.
Child and Family Research, National Institute for Child Health and Human Development, Bethesda, Maryland

JEANNE BROOKS-GUNN, PH.D.
Center for Children and Families, Teacher's College, Columbia University, New York, New York

JUDE CASSIDY, PH.D.
Department of Psychology, University of Maryland, College Park, Maryland

MICHELLE DEKLYEN, PH.D.
University of Washington, Seattle, Washington

GREG J. DUNCAN, PH.D.
Institute for Policy Research, Northwestern University, Evanston, Illinois

ELISABETH FIVAZ-DEPEURSINGE, PH.D.
Centre d'Etude de la Famille, Prilly, Switzerland

FRANCE FRASCAROLO, PH.D.
Centre d'Etude de la Famille, Prilly, Switzerland

CAROL GEORGE, PH.D.
Department of Psychology, Mills College, Oakland, California

CHRISTOPH M. HEINICKE, PH.D.
Department of Psychiatry, University of California at Los Angeles, Los Angeles, California

WADE HORN, PH.D.
National Fatherhood Initiative, Gaithersburg, Maryland

TAMA LEVENTHAL, PH.D.
Center for Children and Families, Teacher's College, Columbia University, New York, New York

MARVA LEWIS, PH.D.
School of Social Work, Tulane University, New Orleans, Louisiana

ALICIA F. LIEBERMAN, PH.D.
Child Trauma Research Project, San Francisco General Hospital, San Francisco, California

ROSINE LOB-IZRAELSKI, MA
Centre d'Etude de la Famille, Prilly, Switzerland

Contributors

Margaret McKenna, Ph.D.
University of Washington, Seattle, Washington

Hanus Papoušek, M.D., Dr. Sci
Institute for Social Pediatrics, Munich, Germany

Arietta Slade, Ph.D.
Center for Children and Families, Teacher's College, Columbia University, New York, New York

Susan J. Spieker, Ph.D.
Parent-Child Nursing & Center for Human Development and Disability, University of Washington, Seattle, Washington

Joanne Solchany, Ph.D.
Parent-Child Nursing & Center for Human Development and Disability, University of Washington, Seattle, Washington

Judith Solomon, Ph.D.
Judith Wallerstein Center for the Family in Transition, Corte Madera, California

Contents

Contents

Contents

Foreword

Yvon Gauthier

I had the privilege to participate in the first international congress of the World Association for Infant Mental Health, then the World Association of Infant Psychiatry, held in Portugal in 1980. There was a very special feeling throughout this congress, a feeling that researchers and clinicians from several countries were for the first time putting together their observations about infants, and discovering their importance. Most probably, these people knew one another's writings and had met before in other situations, but there was, in their presentations and discussions an emotional tone that I personally felt intensely. And I often heard others talk about it in similar terms over the years. Can we say that this was the beginning of an infant mental health movement? We evidently need more historical facts before answering this question. But as I look back on it, this 1980 congress stands in my mind as a historical mark in terms of an international beginning of knowledge transfer in the infant mental health domain. The publication of

this WAIMH handbook 20 years later is an international attempt, sponsored by WAIMH, to mark the progress made during those two decades, and to propose important directions in many areas of this most dynamic field.

In many parts of the world, ideas and practices concerned with infants and young families are gaining in importance. We may note that Spitz's and Bowlby's early works gradually had an influence on practices of institutional life and adoption all over the world, and that foster homes have become standard practice in many countries, in spite of their frequent inadequacies. Attachment-exploration phenomena are being studied in several countries, with findings that show cultural variations in infant care (see Bretherton and Waters, 1985; Waters, Vaughn, Posada, & Kondo-Ikemura, 1995). Can we predict that this movement will continue to have a considerable influence all over the world, particularly in less developed countries? It is very interesting and important that several chapters of this handbook develop cross-cultural perspectives in infant mental health, showing that this movement has already crossed several frontiers. Prepared by specialists in their own countries, they demonstrate the variety of approaches used to understand and help families who are dealing with problematic infants and young children, while taking into account culture-relevant elements involved in understanding and intervention.

Several theoretical currents are influential in infant mental health, but psychoanalysis, clinically and theoretically, holds a special place in our field. We may remember the importance that psychoanalysis has given to infancy in its theoretical development. Of course, for Freud, infancy meant the verbal child, and more specifically the 3- to 6-year-old during the Oedipal phase. Melanie Klein placed emphasis on earlier phases, though in doing so she attributed to the very young infant very destructive imaginary strivings and projections that she reconstructed from her treatment of older mostly psychotic children.

We know how much Bowlby questioned some of these psychoanalytic hypotheses. His observations of very young children in situations of separation, among other influences, led him to develop his theory of attachment, which has come to play a crucial role in research and clinical activities. With the contributions of Mary Ainsworth, Mary Main, and many others, attachment concepts have become central to research and clinical activities in many countries and have opened the way to a deeper understanding of both normal and psychopathological development. Infant mental health is deeply influenced by the attachment paradigm.

We also have to note that family systems and family therapy are closely tied to attachment theory (Byng-Hall, 1990; Stevenson-Hinde, 1990); and thus also are very useful in infant mental health practice. Fundamental research done on the early father-mother-baby interactions (for instance in Lausanne, Corboz-Warnery, Fivaz-Depeursinge, Bettens, & Favez, 1993) is also bringing an interesting contribution to our practice.

It has almost become a postulate in our field that early intervention frequently leads to symptomatic and internal changes within the parent-child dyad or triad. More research is needed, but already significant results are available (Cramer et al., 1990; Landy et al., 1998; Robert-Tissot et al., 1996). Stern (1995) has developed the idea that early intervention for which there are many possible "ports of entry," has a good chance of mobilizing a system that has great mobility and offers true opportunities for change at this stage of life. This mobility has been well demonstrated all through this phase of life, from early pregnancy to age 2 to 3. We can now really talk of perinatality as a phase of life where an intervention, even of small proportions, can move the system in a durable manner (Gauthier, 1998).

There is an important corollary to this appreciation of the importance of early intervention: Several disciplines are involved in the care of infants, young children, and their families and must be aware that their role is essential. First-line workers, whatever their original discipline—nurse, midwife, child care worker, obstetrician, pediatrician, etc.—have to be trained in a truly systemic orientation. Examples of different types of training in this direction are reported in this handbook, opening the way to an essential transfer of knowledge between disciplines.

It also becomes clearer as we study infants and young families that parenting, mothering, and fathering do not start at birth, but are present as soon as a child is expected. Therefore, professionals have to become involved even during pregnancy, for there is evidence that even before birth the child becomes invested with affects and images that may influence development. Bydlowski (1997), Raphael-Leff (1993), and Molénat (1993), among others, have described well how this developmental phase is often marked by a "permeability of the unconscious" that often allows significant therapeutic work.

From a similar perspective, Fraiberg's clinical studies opened the way to the concept of intergenerational transmission, which finds interesting confirmation in recent research on transmission of attachment patterns (Benoit & Parker, 1994; Fonagy, Steele, Moran, Steele, & Higgitt, 1993). Important changes are being observed in the responsibilities that parents assume in the care of their children, just as greatly differing societies and cultures are developing new ways of socializing the infant and the young child. This handbook will bring us up to date on such issues.

Research on brain development shows the importance of the early years and the essential role of the environment in its development (Schore, 1994, 1996). Early intervention is essential for all, but particularly for high risk populations, since we now know that poverty and psychopathology are intricately connected, and that early intervention is essential to avoid repetitions and reach parents' desire for a new experience, one different from their own childhood, with their child. We also know that several situations constitute a risk for the coming child: Prematurity, substance abuse, depression, adolescent pregnancy, death of a previous child, and traumatized childhood are all conditions that call for early preventive intervention from professionals who are naturally in contact with mothers and fathers.

This handbook is an unusual sharing of knowledge from experts in several disciplines and all parts of the world, whose work focuses on infants and young families. It expresses the conviction, which has gradually come to all professionals working in this area of infant mental health, that early intervention is the best way to prevent the severe difficulties in the development of children and adults that often lead to psychopathology. Although such early intervention may be costly, it is certainly less so than later psychopathology is to societies. Let us hope that this major effort will be much read all over the world, so that it influences, in all parts of our global environment, the development of social policies that encourage and support an early involvement with infants and families.

References

Benoit, D., & Parker, K. C. H. (1994). Stability and transmission of attachment across three generations. *Child Development, 65,* 1444–1456.

Bretherton, I., & Waters, E. (Eds.). (1985). Growing points of attachment: Theory and research. *Monographs of the Society for Research in Child Development, 50* (1–2, Serial No. 209).

Bydlowski, M. (1997). *La dette de vie: Itinéraire psychanalytique de la maternité* (Le fil rouge). Paris: Presses Universitaires de France.

Byng-Hall, J. (1990). Attachment theory and family therapy: A clinical view. *Infant Mental Health Journal, 11*(3), 228–236.

Corboz-Warnery, A., Fivaz-Depeursinge, E., Bettens, C. G., & Favez, N. (1993). Systemic analysis of father-mother-baby interactions: The Lausanne triadic play. *Infant Mental Health Journal, 14*(4), 298–316.

Cramer, B., Robert-Tissot, C., Stern, D. N., Serpa-Rusconi, S., De Muralt, M., Besson, G., Palacio-Espasa, F., Bachmann, J. P., Knauer, D., Berney, C., & d'Arcis, U. (1990). Outcome evaluation in brief mother-infant psychotherapy: A preliminary report. *Infant Mental Health Journal, 11*(3), 278–300.

Fonagy, P., Steele, M., Moran, G., Steele, H., & Higgitt, A. (1993). Measuring the ghost in the nursery: An empirical study of the relation between parents' mental representations of childhood experiences and their infants' security of attachment. *Journal of the American Psychoanalytic Association, 41,* 957–989.

Gauthier, Y. (1998). Du projet d'enfant aux premières semaines de la vie: Perspectives psychanalytiques. In P. Mazet & S. Lebovici (Eds.), *Psychiatrie périnatale. Parents et bébés: Du projet d'enfant aux premiers mois de vie.* (Monographies de la psychiatrie de l'enfant). Paris: Presses Universitaires de France.

Landy, S., Peters, R.DeV., Arnold, R., Allen, B., Brookes, F., & Jewell, S. (1998). Evaluation of "Staying On Track": An early identification, tracking, and referral system. *Infant Mental Health Journal, 19*(1), 34–58.

Molénat, F. (1992). *Mères vulnérables.* Paris: Stock/Pernoud.

Raphael-Leff, J. (1993). *Pregnancy: The inside story.* Northvale, NJ, and London: Jason Aronson Inc.

Robert-Tissot, C., Cramer, B., Stern, D. N., Serpa, S. R., Bachmann, J. P., Palacio-Espasa, F., Knauer, D., De Muralt, M., Berney, C., & Mendiguren, G. (1996). Outcome evaluation in brief mother-infant psychotherapies: Report on 75 cases. *Infant Mental Health Journal, 17*(2), 97–114.

Schore, A. N. (1994). *Affect regulation and the origin of the self.* Hillsdale, NJ: Erlbaum.

Schore, A. N. (1996). The experience-dependent maturation of a regulatory system in the orbital prefrontal cortex and the origin of developmental psychopathology. *Development and Psychopathology, 8,* 59–87.

Stern, D. N. (1995). *The motherhood constellation: A unified view of parent-infant psychotherapy.* New York: Basic Books.

Stevenson-Hinde, J. (1990). Attachment within family systems: An overview. *Infant Mental Health Journal, 11*(3), 218–228.

Waters, E., Vaughn, B. E., Posada, G., & Kondo-Ikemura, K. (Eds.). (1995). Caregiving, cultural and cognitive perspectives on secure-base behavior and working models: New growing points of attachment theory and research. *Monographs of the Society for Research in Child Development, 60*(2–3, Serial No. 244).

Preface

Joy D. Osofsky and Hiram E. Fitzgerald

In 1996, anticipating our 6th World Congress, we recognized with the Executive Committee of the World Association for Infant Mental Health (WAIMH) that our next World Congress planned for July 2000 would not only mark the beginning of the new millennium, but also, for WAIMH a celebration of our 20-year anniversary. Thus, the WAIMH Handbook of Infant Mental Health was "conceived" as a tribute to that occasion. We agreed to undertake the editing of a series of volumes that would present a comprehensive review and integration of work in the area of infant mental health from around the world. From the initial idea, with the help of our editors at John Wiley & Sons, we decided that four volumes were needed to truly represent the area covering the breadth of programs and approaches that would best describe the field including: I. Perspectives on Infant Mental Health; II. Early Intervention, Evaluation, and Assessment; III. Parenting and Child Care; IV. Infant Mental Health in Groups at High Risk. We were committed to making the book in-

terdisciplinary and international to reflect the vision of WAIMH.

Many people have been very helpful and encouraging in bringing this major effort to an excellent conclusion. First, we want to thank the Executive Committee of WAIMH including Yvon Gauthier, Peter de Chateau, Tuula Tamminen, Elizabeth Tuters, Miguel Hoffmann, Antoine Guedeney, and Bob Emde who encouraged us from the outset. They thought it was an exciting and very worthwhile undertaking, and have been extremely helpful in assisting us in bringing many chapters to completion and editing others when we needed their help. Second, we are very appreciative of the vision and foresight of Kelly Franklin, first our editor and now publisher, who brought us to New York to discuss how Wiley could play a role in advancing the field of infant mental health. We hope that you will agree that her encouragement of us to develop the *WAIMH Handbook of Infant Mental Health* and her saying, "You can do four volumes!" was fortuitous.

We each have individual people to recognize and thank. I (JDO) want to thank my colleagues, especially Martin Drell, Head of the Division of Infant, Child and Adolescent Psychiatry at Louisiana State University Health Sciences Center who not only were available and supportive of this work, but offered inspiration as well. Through the Harris Center for Infant Mental Health that I direct at LSUHSC, I am constantly exposed to the excitement in our faculty and trainees as they learn more about and provide better interventions and treatment for infants and their families. In such an environment that values making a difference in the earliest years of life, the development of this publication has been encouraged and valued. My support staff for this book, including some who have moved on to complete their graduate education, have included Bridget Scott, Ana Linares, and Angela Black. I am appreciative of their careful record keeping and help with organizing this project. Of course my family, as always, has been very patient with me and encouraging as I spend endless hours in front of the computer writing and/or editing. Perhaps the best part of that support is seeing how my three growing and grown children have learned to value education, writing, and helping others. My husband, Howard, has always been there for me with encouragement and pride as such a major project has come to completion. I thank him for always providing a "secure base" and for his love and steadiness for all of us.

I (HEF) too have many individuals to thank, starting with my wife Dolores. Not only has she been a steadfast companion for the past 37 years, but she actually holds her own place in WAIMH's history (as Paul Harvey might say, see Volume 1, Chapter 1, page 20 "for the rest of the story!"). When writing and editing there is no more treasured commodity than time, and my colleagues at Michigan State University, Rachel Schiffman, Ellen Whipple, and Holly Brophy-Herb helped to release some of that by sharing responsibility for administering the interdisciplinary graduate programs in infant studies. I learned a great deal about infancy by participating in the rearing of three individuals each of whom has blossomed into a caring, compassionate adult who values education, children, and family life. Being a grandparent, however, provides insights into infant development and parent-infant relationships not afforded to parents as they play out the daily routine. So, thanks to Sean, Ryan, Mara, and Mallory for refreshing and renewing my opportunities to view again the truly wonderous early beginnings of human devleopment.

Finally, we want to thank the many infants, toddlers and families who have really "taught us all we know" about infant mental health. Without them, we would not only be less knowledgeable, but also, we would never have had the opportunity to appreciate the magic of human development. Combined we have probably directly sampled a small portion of the lifecourse of thousands of infants and their caregivers. The diversity of human development, the resilience to adverse outcome, and both the compassion and inhumanity of humankind, each, in its own way, challenges infant mental health specialists to hone their scientific and clinical skills, and to participate in advocating for policies that enhance the quality of life, especially during the early years.

These volumes are a beginning, not an end. They are intended to provoke discussion about the field of infant mental health and to frame a definition of that field. They unambiguously join scientific and clinical perspectives and boldly speak to public policy issues. We invite each of you to join this effort to help shape a perspective, one that will play out across disciplines, across national boundaries, and across the full spectrum of human development.

Joy D. Osofsky
New Orleans, Louisiana

Hiram E. Fitzgerald
East Lansing, Michigan

1

Child Care,
Parenting, and
Public Policy

Betty Ann Ablon and Sonya Bemporad

1

Introduction

As America approaches the end of the twentieth century and the beginning of a new millennium, there are few areas that indicate as clearly the profound difference among Americans, the diversity of opinions and passionately held beliefs, and the complexity of the problems and issues facing America as child care. Who should take care of America's children? How should they be taken care of? What should that care look like? What constitutes quality care? Who should pay for it? These are fundamental issues inside a heated child care dialogue. The robust economy has generated an increasing demand for child care by parents of very young children who are returning to work while their children are at increasingly younger ages. This is creating what has been called "a hidden revolution" that reflects a major shift in the way American families care for their very young.

With America's unemployment at its lowest level in 29 years (Bureau of Labor Statistics, 1998), America intends to maintain a healthy economy based on high productivity and high corporate profitability. This is the major force behind an ever-increasing demand for child care for very young children. What is different about this economic boom when compared to others, however, is that the traditional benefits of economic prosperity for working people—greater spendable income, job security, more benefits—are not present. This is another major force behind the demand for child care. For most Americans, it now takes two incomes to keep a toehold in the middle class. The Census Bureau's publication, *We, the American Children* (September 1993), reports that the chances of a child having a "comfortable, prosperous, or high" family income depend on the amount of time that his or her parents work. Ninety percent of all children with both parents working full-time experience at least a comfortable standard of living compared to 65 percent of all children with only a father working full time, a 25 percent difference. Although Americans see the late 1990s as a time of prosperity, studies of real wages in America indicate that wages are falling. Workers in the middle and lower income brackets (where the vast majority of families with dependent children fall) have, in fact, suffered a long-term wage decline (Hewlett & West, 1998).

The public debate concerning child care, which continues to lurch onward as it has for most of the twentieth century, rarely, if ever, focuses on what it means to America's children that by the year 2000, 70 percent of all children under the age of six will be cared for by non–family members while both parents work outside the home. While the birthrate in America is dropping, the number of children with working mothers is increasing (Goldman & Lewis, 1976).

What is at risk to very young children, their parents, their extended families, the greater community, and America when the preponderance of young children's waking hours are spent away from their primary nurturing figures rather than with them? What are the potential long-term consequences? What kind of child care needs to be offered to protect development in the absence of the loved parents who are away all day at work?

Emotional Development in Young Children

Winnicott (1965, p. 39) teaches us "there is no such thing as an infant, meaning of course, that whenever one finds an infant one finds maternal care, and without maternal care there would be no infant." From birth, the self emerges within the baby-parenting relationship. A baby without a parenting person could not, does not, survive. From birth, the quality and nature of this primary baby-parenting relationship is the center of optimal development. For parents, the birth of a child is a profound, intense, complex emotional experience that will alter their lives forever as individuals and as a couple. Suddenly and unalterably, the family focus must change to providing for and meeting the needs of a helpless, dependent baby.

For the infant, the voyage from total dependency to increasing independence, from conception and birth to libidinal object constancy, requires a focused and intense commitment on the part of the parents to the child. For children to thrive, parents need to have available vast reservoirs of altruistic love as well as the ability to postpone the gratification of some of their own needs for the immediate benefit of their child. Parents need to fall madly in love with this child and offer an unending supply of intense, available "irrational attachment" (Bronfenbrenner, 1990).

Winnicott (1965, p. 85) states that the "primary maternal preoccupation" with the baby lays the foundation for the parents to develop close bonds with the baby and for the baby's capacity for intimate relationships in the baby's own later development. The experience of primary preoccupation is when parent and baby connect to one another in deep and positive ways.

From the very beginning of life, intimate moments of interaction between parents and the baby not only determine the physiological self, but also the psychological self. How the baby is comforted, how hunger turns to satisfaction, how bodily discomfort turns to bodily comfort, how the ministrations of the parent give feelings of pleasure and success to the parent, and how they give organization and pleasure to the developing baby all determine the success or failure of the beginning relationship and all subsequent relationships. The self develops through the relationship with a constant, responsive, loving parent who is attuned to the needs of the child, responds to alleviate the infant's distress by offering comfort, and mirrors back to the infant what is being experienced. The qualities that make us human—the capacity for intimacy, empathy, interest in the environment, desire for learning—require these earliest experiences of loving, caring, consistent, and reliable care.

Margaret Mahler's work describes the infant's process of development in a clear, usable way beginning with a symbiotic relationship with the parent, moving to the hatching period, through the period of separation and individuation that includes the subphases of practicing early and practic-

5

ing proper. Rapprochement, the final crisis, if resolved, will result in the child's ability to achieve object constancy (Mahler, Pine, & Berman, 1975).

The three years of life during which the process Mahler observed is taking place is an intense, complex, challenging period for what Winnicott (1965, p. 145) terms the "good-enough" parents as well as for their child. Parents' emotional and physical resources, from sleep deprivation, to dealing with a two-year-old's activity level, to the ambivalence experienced concerning their child's continuing ability to take on those self-care tasks, once the sole province of the parents, are often seriously tested.

But what if this good-enough parent is forced to return to work because of economic necessities before the baby and parent have had enough time to connect with each other? What if a good-enough parent, actively available and integrally involved with the baby through this process, exists but has limited time to be with the child? What if the emotional and financial stability required for the family to be able to sustain itself and for the parents to sustain each other is fragile? What if the care available to the baby in the parent's absence is offered by a parade of indifferent, undifferentiated caregivers?

According to the National Institute of Child Health and Development's (NICHD) recent report (NICHD Early Child Care Research Network, 1997), at the end of their first year, most American infants will have experienced more than two nonparental care arrangements. This 1997 study also reported a very rapid reentry by mothers into the workforce, resulting in longer hours for the infant to be in child care than had been previously postulated. Finally and most damning, it reported a great instability in the child care arrangements for these newborns.

Because of the way most child care is organized and because of child care's unstable workforce, the young child can expect to have five different caregivers by their third birthday. In another study of child care in America (Cost, Quality, and Child Outcomes Study Team, 1995), only 14 percent of child care for all age groups was considered adequate, with the percentage of adequate care being even lower for infants and toddlers.

What will this mean to children's emotional development? What is at risk for the parents, children, and America if the main ingredient necessary for children to develop a self is missing most of the day because parents and children are away from each other? What will it mean if the child rearing done by others is primarily custodial and neither designed nor practiced to protect a child's relationship with the parents or attend a child's development of self?

The work of Sigmund Freud, Anna Freud, Melanie Klein, Margaret Mahler, Heinz Kohut, D. W. Winnicott, and others all reflects a systematic approach to understanding and codifying infant development. Regardless of the specific system, their work describes development as, in its largest sense, predictable and uniform within a specific culture as opposed to random and idiosyncratic. Development, for example, is perceived as cumulative with each stage building on the stage that preceded it, regardless of where in America that infant is living.

This rich body of scholarly research from child psychiatry and child psychology is now being strongly validated and supported by new imaging technology that allows direct study of the brain. Some of the results of this research clearly indicate the long-term effects of inconsistent, nonresponsive care on the infant's developing brain. What it means to a child to be in a nonresponsive, nonnurturing environment that includes the lack of a constant caregiver in child care can now be seen on a scan.

Why has this critical, profoundly important information that includes physical data on the attending risks when infants' needs for nurturance are not met not created a major course correction in the way America cares for its children? Why has government not been besieged by a cohesive, united coalition of parents, professionals, and children's advocates demanding that significant changes take place in the public policy arena? Why have they not demanded that America take the kind of care of its children that results in healthy, functioning adults by paying for the quality care that addresses as primary the emotional needs of children upon which all healthy development depends?

Child Care in America

Part of the answer concerning the fragmentation of child care's potential natural constituency lies in its past history. Child care did not arise from, nor is it rooted in, the public sector in the same way that public education is, nor does it reflect the same philosophical commitment to the education of the young. Child care began as a service to the poor. An increasingly industrialized America offered employment to poor women in its cotton mills (Secrest & Bergman, 1986), in its shoe factories, and in the homes of the wealthy as washerwomen, kitchen help, and servants. Child care was the link that made this possible. Often these women were "the resourceless mother, the poverty-stricken wife or widow, or the deserted woman without relatives or friends, who was compelled by circumstances to make unfavorable child care arrangements" (Tyson, 1924, p. 18, cited in Cahan, 1989, p. 15). They were new immigrants or young women driven to the city by the poverty of rural areas.

Early nineteenth-century America had a short flirtation with "infant care" for all children. For the poor, it was thought to be the means of moral instruction to the very young, and as a result of this instruction, poverty would be eradicated. Trustees of the Infant School Society of Boston, founded in 1828, indicated that children "would be removed from the unhappy association of want and vice, and be placed under better influences. . . ." (Infant School Society of Boston, 1828, quoted in Cahan, 1989, p. 9). Infant schools for the affluent, although fewer in number, existed to provide very young children the same educational opportunities available to the poor that, it was felt, could not be provided within the home.

Of significance to us today is that the decline of the infant schools is partly attributed to the rejection of the idea of incorporating infant schools into the public system of primary education. Care of infants and young children was not to be seen as a public responsibility. Whereas there were concerns about the poor's ability to provide for the moral upbringing of their young and the belief in the potency of early education as a tool for lifting children out of poverty, these concerns were greatly outweighed by the fear that the sanctity of the American home would be compromised and the family's responsibility for the young child's care and moral and intellectual development eroded. While its benefits were clear and accepted, the preponderance of concern regarding child care involved the potential of child care as a means of coddling the poor and allowing such families to evade their obligations to their young.

> It is objected to them that they furnish occasion for remissness in the discharge of parental duties, by devolving the care of infancy on teachers, instead of leaving with the mother the full weight and responsibility of her natural relations (Beatty, 1981, p. 29, cited in Cahan, 1989, p. 12) . . . [T]he primacy of the family as the ideal agent of childhood socialization and early learning [went] unchecked. (Cahan, 1989, p. 12)

These earliest interventions in the lives of young children were rooted in the strongly held belief that poverty was a function of poor moral fiber and a spiritual problem, not an economic one. Three views still evident today and influencing child care policy that can be found in this early history are:

1. The vestiges of belief that poverty is a moral issue and not an economic one and that work is a spiritual and moral remedy as well as an economic necessity to be achieved through self-help.
2. Parents must be the primary if not sole provider and determiner of the social, intellectual, and moral development of their children as well as the provider of food, clothing, and shelter.
3. Government has no direct, mandated role in the care and education of very young children and, in fact, can be seen as an intrusive agent.

> Historically, the care and rearing of children was regarded as a private family affair, not as a public responsibility. Americans held as a fundamental tenet the right of parents to raise their children according to their own values and beliefs. (Hayes, Palmer, & Zaslow, 1990, p. 7)

By the end of the nineteenth century, what was evolving in America was a two-tier system (Cahan, 1989) developing along two separate tracks: for the poor, custodial care (child-minding) in all-day nurseries for very young children whose mothers were employed; and for the more affluent, nursery programs operating for a few hours daily designed to help children socialize and have access to early enrichment experiences not available in the home—education for the affluent, minimal care for the poor. Those nurseries that continued to exist were at best custodial, lacking resources to provide adequate care, food, and even milk to the children in their care.

These day nurseries' funding and impetus came from private charitable and religious organizations who continued to be concerned about the welfare of the children of the poor, whose numbers swelled as America's cities teemed with new immigrant arrivals. The settlement houses that came into being before the turn of the century were among the few places in the country where children of the poor could attend both day care and kindergarten programs that were clearly educational in purpose. For the children of immigrants, day nurseries and settlement houses were a primary way of helping children become assimilated Americans by changing their speech and eating habits and by teaching them American social customs.

Support for these programs eroded, however, for a variety of reasons. Jane Addams, one of the great pioneers of the settlement house movement, stated that mothers became "bent under the double burden of earning the money which supports them and [giving] their children the tender care which alone keeps them alive" (Addams, 1910, p. 169, cited in Cahan, 1989, p. 21). Women could not be wage earners, homemakers, and mothers. Their children were declared no better than full orphans while women worked exceedingly long hours for pitifully small wages. "Critics claimed that 'the home crumbles' and the 'physical and moral well-being of the mother and the children is seriously menaced'" (Anonymous, 1914, p. 809, cited in Cahan, 1989, p. 22). Grace Abblot, who became director of the Children's Bureau, held "that day nurseries were not a necessary part of child welfare services and that the nation could well afford to support

mothers at home" (Cahan, 1989, p. 23). Concerns were also raised that the "undeserving poor" as opposed to the "worthy poor" would receive this service for their children and would get used to "the charity habit" (cited by Tank, 1980, p. 125, and quoted in Cahan, 1989, p. 23), fostering greater indolence and encouraging irresponsible behavior.

Approximately 90 years ago, ambivalence about maternal employment, the American work ethic versus social welfare programs that coddle the poor, and the perception of child care outside the home as an instrument of both good and evil, depending on who was making the argument, appeared in much the same way it appears today. There was no clear, developing, conceptual role for government as a means of supporting families and their children, which is not to say that government programs did not exist.

From 1911 to 1915, 29 states passed Mother's Pension Legislation (the precursor to Aid to Dependent Children) that financially supported poor mothers and allowed them to stay at home with their children and be responsible for their very young children's development. Many mothers and children eligible for pensions, however, did not receive them because funding was not provided for all those eligible for the program (a reality still existing today). Some counties endorsed the pension program and others did not. "Blacks in particular faced discrimination—receiving only 3 percent of the total pensions" with some counties barring their participation completely (Leff, 1973, p. 414, cited in Cahan, 1989, p. 27). It was not until 1935, with the enactment of Social Security legislation and the Aid to Dependent Children program, that federal guidelines were established that paved the way for uniformity in eligibility criteria for financial support of poor women with young children.

The number of available day nurseries continued to decline under the onslaught of criticism and the alleged availability of pensions. Once again, mothers who had to work to either supplement their allotment or who were still not eligible for federal subsidies were forced to rely on makeshift child care arrangements using friends, neighbors, and relatives as they do today.

It was the Great Depression that got government into the business of child care. Six million dollars was allocated under the Federal Emergency Education Program which ultimately funded 3,000 child care facilities serving 65,000 needy children ages two to five whose families were "on relief." However, "in any one year, between 44,000 and 72,000 children were enrolled, only a fraction of the 10 million children eligible for the program" (National Advisory Committee, 1935, p. 356, cited in Cahan, 1989, p. 38). The focus of the programs was on children's health, nutrition, and general welfare. Although these programs were designed to help relieve the suffering of the children of the poor, their true purpose was to offer employment to out-of-work teachers, cooks, custodians, nurses, and the like. "The narrow scope [and] uneven quality" (Cahan, 1989, p. 40) reflected the country's conflicted feelings toward its role in providing child care.

When World War II broke out, the nation no longer faced unemployment problems. Instead, with men out of the workforce, women entered in large numbers to take their places. The immediate demand for child care for 1.5 million mothers of dependent children once more brought the federal government into the child care business. By the end of the war, one mother out of eight with dependent children under the age of six was employed in the war effort (Cahan, 1989). Studies that were conducted at this time regarding women's performance in the workplace indicated that a major factor causing poor attendance by women was the lack of constant, reliable, adequate child care—a factor still operating today and a major obstacle to the 1996 implementation of the Welfare to Work legislation.

The Lanham Act was the means by which child care was funded during World War II. Even though the need for child care reached epic proportions, the federal government provided child care assistance for only 13 percent of children who needed it. The difficulty in accessing these funds discouraged states from applying for them. In fact, the president of the United States, Franklin Delano Roosevelt, on the day that he released $400,000 from the emergency war fund to stimulate the growth of centers and to coordinate day care programs said, "I do not believe that further federal funds should be provided for actual operation of child care programs at this time" (Chafe, 1972, pp. 299–300, n. 33, cited in Cahan, 1989, p. 43). Roosevelt's administration clearly saw the funding of child care as a reluctant response to a national emergency, not as a potential adjunct to America's educational system or as an addition to America's developing social welfare system.

The end of the war saw the immediate termination of the Lanham Act, but it was forced to continue for another year because of the public outcry over the federal government's withdrawal of support to child care programs. With the closing of these federally subsidized centers, working mothers were once again forced back into making temporary, often unreliable, makeshift child care arrangements.

Mothers were urged to stay at home and attend to their most important job, that of raising their children to become productive members of American society. In a climate essentially indifferent, if not hostile, to the needs of working mothers, the group care that was available was funded primarily by social welfare agencies as a social welfare program, while those middle-class mothers who worked made private arrangements for their children's care. Public money supporting day care services that was available was to be used as a means of getting the poor off the welfare rolls and into the workplace. So strong was feeling about the use of public money to fund day care that in 1948, Governor Thomas E. Dewey of New York terminated the use of public funds for day care and called all those who disagreed "Communists." Federal education dollars were to be provided for the education of older children. The care and education of very young children was to be the sole responsibility of the family.

Attitudes about the poor had also shifted. Reflecting attitudinal shifts in the greater society, poverty was no longer a function of a moral and spiritual deficiency. Instead, it was seen as a social maladjustment to the greater society, and the poor were seen as needing help in the areas of personal and social adjustment. Although the language had changed, the message had not: The need for child care and other social welfare programs was a glaring indicator of personal inadequacy and social incompetence. Failure to succeed belonged squarely to the individual, not to the greater society.

In the early 1960s, a major shift in governmental policy and politics occurred and was sustained by two presidents committed to the eradication of poverty through the "War on Poverty," to the concept of "The Great Society," and to providing full enfranchisement for America's Black citizens. At the same time, a growing body of knowledge concerning human development that challenged previously held beliefs regarding the immutability of heredity and maturity as the primary determinants of human behavior, moved from the social science arena into the popular culture. This new body of knowledge coming out of the social sciences connected nicely with the optimistic mood of the country.

> Hunt (1961, 1971), for example, surmised that given the right experiences, children's IQs could be raised as much as 70 points. Bloom (1964) popularized the notion of magical periods in development, arguing that these "right" experiences had to be provided early in the child's life to have the maximal impact. (Zigler, 1998, p. 8)

Unlike earlier periods in which psychological and social research remained separate and apart from social policy, in the

1960s there was a growing willingness to include academic research into the design of new programs. Head Start was an example of this. If early experiences could dramatically change a child's capacity to utilize education and since the poor could not offer these positive early experiences to their children, thereby limiting their potential, government intervention in the form of a compensatory education program called Head Start would do the job. As in the day nursery program of the 1900s, early intervention in the early education of the children of the poor was seen as a tool of social engineering.

Launched in the summer of 1965 for children ages three to six, Head Start exists today and still enjoys bipartisan support. "The program's original goal was (and remains) to help poor children enter school as ready to learn as their middle-class peers" (Zigler, 1998, p. 6). Head Start was never designed as a comprehensive child care program for America's children. It is essentially a deficit-oriented, compensatory program available only to the children of the poor for a fixed number of hours each week. It is still serving only a fraction of the children eligible for the program.

Government's role in child care expanded through the 1960s and into the early 1970s fueled by optimism and the belief that government had a major role in changing people's lives for the better. Federal child care standards were developed and subsidies for child care to low-income families were expanded. In 1971, however, when Richard Nixon vetoed the Comprehensive Child Care Act, citing overriding concern regarding the weakening of the family, the opportunity for a comprehensive, cohesive child care plan that could unite the early education program of the nursery school with the full-day child care program of the early day nursery, with standards and guidelines for the care of all of America's children, was defeated. By the 1980s, the role of the federal government had declined, and those primarily concerned about federally subsidized child care as a direct threat to the sovereignty of the family had prevailed. Child care was left to develop as a consumer service to meet the needs of a changing group of mothers who were entering the workforce in unprecedented numbers.

A devolution in the role of the federal government began, and with it came the possibility of uniform standards for child care practices throughout America. While widespread acceptance exists for the need for federal regulations regarding safety standards for airlines, in health care (strict standards exist in order to qualify for Medicaid reimbursement), in food processing, highways, and in other critical areas of American life, no such standards exist today for caring for children at their most vulnerable age.

The Future of Child Care in America

There is no single factor or moment that one can point to as being responsible for the unprecedented change in the role of women in America. Certainly, the advent of the Pill, which allowed women for the first time to reliably and comfortably control conception, was of enormous importance. The political activism that was part of the social revolution of the 1960s fueled the feminist movement of the 1970s, resulting in greater opportunities for better education, professional training, and the movement toward parity for women in the workplace.

Unlike other times in the history of this country, when women entered the workforce because of family misfortune or to help the nation during a national crisis with the understanding that they would return to their homes and children as soon as possible, women are now in the workforce to stay. In earlier times, it was assumed that work would not be a viable source for personal gratification for women. At the close of the twentieth century, most women with young children are working because work is an economic necessity, and for many, there has been a considerable financial and emotional investment in building a professional career.

There is much that is confusing and contradictory within America's economic situation today—a booming economy, but for many people there is a workplace where they work harder for less money, fewer benefits, and poor job security. Whether the answer lies all or in part in America's role in an increasingly global economy, greed inside corporations as evidenced by the huge disparity between the salaries of CEOs and of workers, a weakening in the interpretation and enforcement of America's labor laws, and an ineffective labor movement perceived to be riddled by internal strife and corruption, or the general attitude that what is good for Wall Street is good for the country, there is no governmental or corporate safety net under America's workers. Governmental policy appears to be based on a model of rugged individualism instead of an understanding of the great interdependencies required to survive and thrive in an increasingly complex, technocratic society. This desire to return to a period of less government, such as in the 1940s and 1950s, for example, ignores the fact that government subsidies provided training and education for returning veterans from World War II and subsidized housing put many people in those eras on the road to a middle-class life.

The future of child care is, therefore, complicated by many factors: (1) the political climate of Washington with goals of shrinking the deficit and reducing the role of government and its outright hostility to social welfare programs, (2) perceptions of child care as a program historically for the poor, thereby subject to America's long history of biases and conflictual feelings, (3) intense concerns by the political right and the political left about what will happen to children and families when children are raised outside the home by non–family members, (4) ambivalent feelings about the increasing numbers and successes of women in the workforce and their attendant political and economic power particularly as it affects the status of men, and (5) belief in the responsibility of the individual to solve his own personal problems away from and without the help of the work situation or the government.

These issues are joined by another one. In the early history of this country, care for children developed on two separate tracks: nursery school for middle-class children, which was essentially socialization and education-through-play, and day care, which was primarily a social welfare program to change the children of the poor so they could move into the middle class. Today, for the first time in American history, there is a felt need for a meaningful, positive child care experience for *all* children that cuts across social, racial, and ethnic lines.

However, nothing in America's child care history offers a theoretical conceptual model for what is good child care. The preschool model has been continually reworked to fit the frame of day care. With its emphasis on social and cognitive development, it pays little attention to the basic emotional needs to be met when children are away from their families for 10 to 11 hours each day. Good child care must be responsive, attentive, and nurturing. It must meet the emotional, social, cognitive, and physical needs of each individual child and be organized around protecting the primary relationship of the child and the parent. It must make available to the child in some form what is missing when the child is not with their family. However, the reality of child care today is vastly different from what we know children need in order to grow to be healthy, functioning, productive adults.

In 1994, the prestigious Carnegie Corporation of America sounded the alarm by describing "a quiet crisis" in the lives of America's children in a report called *Starting Points: Meeting the Needs of Our Youngest Children*. This remarkable report painstakingly described the plight of families with young children and documented societal and governmental neglect. It cited the criticality of the first three years of life, discussed the consequences of parents having less time with their young children, and cited the danger to children in a child care system that included "poor-quality care, lack of affordable care, high turnover among providers due to inadequate compensation and working conditions, weak consumer protection and a fragmented system of delivery" (Carnegie Task Force on Meeting the Needs of Young Children, 1994, p. 44).

The long-term implications of the available substandard child care for the infants and toddlers of the 53 percent of American women who returned to the workforce before the end of their baby's first year were detailed. It cited child care so poor as to threaten the intellectual and emotional development of children under the age of three. It also clearly stated that the challenge of supporting children's development when they are in care outside the home no longer could rest solely on the family but needed to be shared with policymakers. Its well-documented, specifically defined areas for action clearly stated that families could no longer be expected to go it alone.

The Cost, Quality, and Child Outcomes study (Cost, Quality, and Child Outcomes Study Team, 1995), conducted in 1993 by four universities in four states and designed to provide the first comprehensive econometric and psychometric analysis of child care and children's outcomes, found that while child care varies from state to state, most child care was mediocre in quality and some sufficiently poor as to interfere with a child's emotional and intellectual growth. Market forces were also seen as constraining the cost of child care and at the same time depressing the quality of care.

While most child care was found to be poor to mediocre across the United States, almost one-half of the infant and toddler programs were reported to be of less than minimal quality.

The level of quality at most U.S. child care centers, especially in infant/toddler rooms, does not meet children's needs for health, safety, warm relationships, and learning. . . . Child care for infants or toddlers is of particular concern. Of the 225 infant or toddler room observations, only 1 in 12 (8%) met the good-quality level, while 2 in 5 (40%) rated less than minimal. (Cost, Quality, and Child Outcomes Study Team, 1995, p. 2)

The centers described exist across America. Regulations governing them are minimal. Their caregivers are poorly trained, if they are trained at all. Little ongoing supervision or ongoing support is available to caregivers. They are woefully underpaid, resulting in reported annual turnover rates as high as 40 percent. Even in the best centers charging premium fees, there is no guarantee that a young child's need for a close, ongoing relationship will be met, because those needs are simply not part of the recognized program design.

The resistance to fully accepting how damaging it is to young children when their emotional needs are not met is supported by parents because they cannot acknowledge that placing children in child care (often without choice) can have long-term detrimental affects on their child's life. Policymakers, bureaucrats, and the general public are for the most part naive, uninformed, and resistant to learning about complex psychological issues.

Public policy in America tends to be short-term in orientation, designed to meet specific goals. In the new Welfare to Work legislation, sufficient new money for child care was neither planned for nor appropriated. What would happen to those children whose mothers would be entering training and/or the workforce was not fully considered.

Nor is government prepared to deal with the unintended consequences of its legislation. Prior to the enactment of the Welfare Reform legislation, a formula existed for states to determine what they would pay for child care for children eligible for subsidies. Simply put, states could pay up to the 75th percentile of market rates surveyed in their area. The 25th percentile, which would be expected to reflect better child care because costs for good child care are high, would, therefore, not be available to the children of the poor. Although current laws no longer contain these restraints, many states still use them and continue to pay well below market rates.

Because resources are so limited, a constant tension exists between providing good quality care to a smaller number of children and providing minimal care for a larger number of children. Only a small percentage of all children eligible for child care subsidies receive them. The most difficult balancing issue is allocating limited resources. Deciding to serve fewer children in ways they need to develop well or providing substandard care for as many children as possible to move a large number of individuals into the workforce is a kind of "Sophie's Choice" of public policy. To put the need for parents to be in the workforce ahead of the child's need for intimate, attentive care is a disaster in progress.

The National Institute of Child Health and Development (NICHD) 1997 study, previously cited, found that children at the highest and lowest income levels were more apt to receive higher quality center-based care (centers where group sizes and child-adult ratios were smaller and caregivers held less authoritarian beliefs about child rearing) than those children in the middle. Children from very low income families were more apt to attend directly subsidized centers that were comparable in quality to centers available to the more affluent. The children of the working poor were more likely to be shut out from quality care.

The NICHD study was designed to learn the effects of early child care experiences on children's development. Thirteen hundred families from 10 locales throughout the country were studied by investigators at the NICHD and 14 universities nationwide. Study investigators asked a number of questions. They examined the patterns of infant care usage during the first 12 months. They looked at what structural features and caregiver characteristics were associated with higher quality infant child care, and they looked at who uses what child care arrangements. They found that when nonmaternal family income is higher, families use child care for fewer hours. When maternal incomes are higher, child care is used for more hours. They also found that families whose children enter child care the earliest had low nonmaternal incomes. Higher nonmaternal incomes were associated with families utilizing higher quality day care.

Using the Strange Situation procedure with babies age 15 months, the study set about to examine three hypotheses:

1. The main effects hypothesis postulated that children in early, extensive, unstable, or poor quality care would have increased likelihood of insecure attachment, independent of conditions at home or in the child.

2. The cumulative risk hypothesis stipulated that large amounts of care or poor quality care or changes in care arrangements over time would promote insecure attachment principally when the child was otherwise at risk, for example, by having a difficult temperament, being a male, or residing in a home where the mother is relatively insensitive.

3. The compensatory hypothesis stipulated that when family or child risks are high then nonmaternal care that is early, extensive, or of high quality would stabilize the child's experience and thereby foster the formation of a more secure infant-mother attachment.

According to the NICHD findings, no evidence was found to support a child care main effects hypothesis. There was some evidence to support the cumulative risk hypothesis. For children whose mothers were insensitive, the incidence of insecure attachment was further elevated when the quality of observed child care was poor, child care was used for more hours, or child care was unstable. Infants who received poor quality of care, were in care more than 10 hours per week, or were in several child care settings in the first 15 months of life were more likely to be insecurely attached when their mothers were low in sensitivity and relatively unresponsive to their needs. Infants who fit into one of these three dual risk categories were more likely to be insecurely attached to their mothers. In addition, boys who spent more than 30 hours per week in child care had a somewhat increased risk for insecure attachment compared with other boys, whereas girls with fewer than 10 hours per week in child care were at a somewhat increased risk for insecurity (NICHD Early Child Care Research Network, 1997).

The NICHD study indicated that 26 percent of the caregivers of infants were moderately to highly insensitive and 19 percent were rated moderately to highly detached. If one accepts the NICHD finding that poor child care poses an even greater risk for insecure attachment for those babies whose attachment is already at risk and couples this finding with those findings of *Cost, Quality, and Child Outcomes in Child Care Centers* (1995), which tells us that most child care in this country is poor to mediocre, especially for infants, then one has a clearer picture of the developmental danger for most of America's infants who are in child care. A limitation of

exclusively using attachment theory is that it does not in any way measure the continuing process of the internalizing of the object.

In *The Study of Children in Family Child Care and Relative Care* (Galinsky, Howes, Kontos, & Shinn, 1994) regulated family child care providers, nonregulated family child care providers, and nonregulated relatives who provide child care were studied. These care situations are the most prevalent for young children in America. Thirteen percent of regulated home-based providers were found to offer less-than-minimal care, while 50 percent of unregulated home providers offered less-than-minimal care, and 69 percent of relatives offered less-than-minimal care. Only one-half of the children in this study were seen to be securely attached to their providers. Only 9 percent of the homes were rated as good quality (growth-enhancing), while 56 percent of the homes were rated as adequate/custodial, and 35 percent of the homes were rated as inadequate (growth-harming). Another finding of this study was that 81 percent of family homes are operating outside the law and are thus entirely unregulated. This means, realistically, that most care for infants is less than minimal.

We have an unprecedented amount of knowledge about what infants need to grow and develop. We know that all development takes place in the context of early relationships—not just social and emotional but cognitive development as well. It is through the loving exchanges—the feeding, the holding, the changing, the soothing—that the baby develops. It is through the loving tie between a constant nurturer and an infant that an infant's self begins to develop. Since the qualities that make us human—the capacity for intimacy, empathy, interest in the environment, a desire for learning, impulse control, and the capacity to bind one's aggression—come out of these early relationships and experiences, it is essential that such relationships be good enough to do the job. Clearly, in most care for infants, they do not.

The self is developing wherever the child may be. When children are spending 10 to 11 hours a day in an environment with adults who are not nurturing and do not make children feel special and cared for, there are serious developmental implications for the child, the family, and the society. Syracuse University (Lally, Mangione, Honig, & Wittmer, 1988) reports that 10 years after their participation in a high-quality early education and family development research program, children had a 6 percent rate of juvenile delinquency compared to a 22 percent rate for children in a control group. Not only was the control group delinquency rate almost four times greater, the offenses were more severe.

Anecdotal evidence from teachers regarding children who spent their early years in poor child care is quite alarming. They describe these children as being different. They are inappropriately aggressive, even hostile, and it is very difficult, if not impossible, to build relationships with them through which they can become part of the learning community in the classroom. They hurt other children, wander aimlessly, and have short attention spans.

In a 1993 *Washington Post* article, Stanley Greenspan, clinical professor of psychi-atry and pediatrics at the George Washington University Medical School depicted "The Kids Who Will Be Killers" the following way:

> They can't care for others because no one has consistently cared for them. Without loving contact in infancy and early childhood, a sense of human connectedness may never materialize and other people can soon become viewed as things to be kicked or destroyed when they stand in the way.

As a nation we are becoming more and more concerned about the growing incidences of extreme violence by younger and younger children that have occurred in the nation's schools, both in rural areas and in urban communities. While the etiology of each of these incidents is complex and intricate and generalizing runs the risk of trivializing, perhaps they can all be best understood through the lens of early experiences—experiences that failed to tie them in a healthy way to their parents or other caregivers.

America is currently acknowledged as the world's only superpower. Our economy is stable and growing, and our democratic practices are being emulated. We are, however, the only industrialized country that does not have a stated child care policy. Moreover, "American children under age 15 are twelve times more likely to die from gunfire than children in all 25 other industrialized nations combined" (Children's Defense Fund, 1998, p. xvii). Every 100 minutes a child is killed by gunfire (Children's Defense Fund). Why have we, alone among nations, failed to ratify the International Convention on the Rights of the Child?

In industrialized European countries, the perception of child care, particularly regarding infants and toddlers, differs dramatically from the United States. In the United States, concern for infant and toddler care is generated almost exclusively by the need of mothers to have child care in order to work. In Europe, there is growing consideration of "offering even the youngest children an experience providing cognitive stimulation and socialization with peers and other adults, whether or not there is a parent at home during the day" (Kamerman & Kahn, 1994, p. 9). In the three- to five-year age group

> . . . just about *all* [italics added] children . . . attend in some countries (France, Belgium, Italy), *almost all* [italics added] in others (Germany, Denmark, Finland, Sweden). These programs are heavily subsidized, operate largely in the public sector (or with extensive public subsidy) and cover at least the normal school day (in the Nordic countries the full work day is covered). (Kamerman & Kahn, pp. 8–9)

Parents pay 5 to 15 percent of the cost of their children's out-of-home care (Kamerman & Kahn, 1991).

> Apart from the explicit policy regarding the 3–5/6 year olds in most of Europe and the almost universal preschool coverage for this age group, two other differences between the U.S. and Europe should be noted. First is the explicit, special concern with child care policy for the under 3's, dating from the mid 1970's; and second is the universal policy of paid and job protected maternity or parental leaves that directly affects the age at which non-parental infant care is needed by a working parent. (Kamerman & Kahn, 1994, p. 9)

In France, as in many European countries, it is assumed that society is best served by providing good care and education for all children. Early childhood programs are not seen as compensatory, as is Head Start in the United States, but a basic right for all citizens. A complex, interwoven publicly supported series of programs in these countries begins with paid and job-protected maternal leave that the French see as the fulfillment of a social obligation to the infant and to the parents for the good of the country and includes family support and child care programs. So deep is France's commitment to its children that even now, when government programs in France are under strict review as France attempts to readjust its economy and its place in the world market, it is not expected that these programs will be challenged.

The United States is the only industrialized country in the world that does not have paid, job-protected maternity leave following the birth of a child (Zigler & Frank, 1987). In other countries where maternity leave is paid for the first four to nine months, depending on the country, the level of compensation varies from 50 to 100 percent of wages, but most countries pay mothers (and even some fathers) 75 percent of their usual wages. The closest the United States comes to this is the Family and Medical Leave Act of 1993 that requires government employers or any employer with more than 50 employees to allow them up to 12 weeks of unpaid leave each year to care for a newborn or an adopted child, family members with health conditions, or to recover from health problems.

In the United States, the largest form that government subsidies take affecting the largest number of families is the income tax credit. This credit, while helpful to parents, does absolutely nothing to change child care and does nothing to change those things that make it the worst in the industrialized world. Very little in the way government supports child care (through The Child Care and Development Block Grant, through Title XX of the Social Security Act, for example, which is now administered almost exclusively by the states) can be used to improve the child care available to low-income families.

The Costs of Care

The working poor and the low- to middle-income working parents are finding it increasingly difficult to pay the full cost for child care even when care is minimal and costs are minimal. Child care is a financial burden for most families. Lower-income families are often immobilized by the cost of even poor care. Child care also greatly impacts the private sector. Most employers depend on employees who depend on child care in order to be able to work. As of the early 1990s, only 6,000 employers nationwide were estimated to offer child care

benefits to their employees out of a total of six million employers.

Recommendations

First: Paid Parental Leave

In almost every serious study of child care in America, there is a recommendation involving the need for paid parental leave. The time for the parent to develop an unconditional loving bond with the infant, become attuned, and thus develop a relationship for life is irreplaceable and unparalleled. Paid parental leave is the cornerstone for public policy committed to healthy development in young children.

Second: Substantial New Public and Private Financial Support for Child Care

Included in the recommendations in *Starting Points* (1994), the Carnegie Corporation calls for substantial new dollars to be permanently channeled into child care programs "permitting them to expand facilities and adopt sliding fee schedules" (Carnegie Task Force on Meeting the Needs of Young Children, p. 59).

Third: The Dependent Care Tax Credit

. . . and the Dependent Care Tax Credit (DCTC) should be refundable for low and moderate income families. The federal government should provide financial incentives to states to adopt standards of quality for child care, to establish timetables for the enactment of these standards, and to monitor progress toward their enforcement. (Carnegie Task Force on Meeting the Needs of Young Children, 1994, p. 107)

Sylvia Ann Hewlett and Cornel West, in their book *The War against Parents* (1998), echo these recommendations in their parents' bill of rights. They call for:

1. Tougher regulation of the child care industry.
2. Government subsidies to underwrite training and much higher salaries for child care workers.
3. The restructuring for federal funding to cut back the dependent care tax credit for affluent families.
4. Increasing the child care block grants to the states. They also include a special set of tax credits and subsidies to target full-time mothers and fathers that would allow and encourage parents to stay home with their children.

Rob Reiner, the film director and entertainer, has undertaken, through his own foundation and through joining with others, to educate the American public about the criticality of the first three years in life. In a speech before the Commonwealth Club of San Francisco (April 7, 1998) recently aired on National Public Radio, he inferred that the American government was no longer a "player" in the lives of America's children. He accused the federal government of retiring to the sidelines and likened its lack of investment in the lives of its youngest citizens to a major corporation refusing to fund research and development (R & D). Without R & D, he continued, the future of most corporations would be severely compromised. So it will be in the lives of America's children.

R & D for America needs to include a new way of organizing child care to protect what is most at risk when children are away from their families 10 to 11 hours a day— their existing relationship with their families and their capacity for relationship. In Relationship Centered Child Care (RC³)®, a program of The Child Care Group, child care is structured around family groups, that is, small, mixed-age groups of children who have their own constant caregiver. Careful attention is paid to the number and ages of the children that are in the care of any one caregiver. For infants and toddlers, there are no more than five children in a group, and only two of those children are under the age of 18 months. Every effort is made to create a family environment. Children stay with the same caregiver for up to three years, until approximately their third birthday, or when they are ready to move into a preschool environment. The separation from the family group and the constant caregiver is carefully planned over a period of time and occurs only when the child is ready. The day-to-day program is designed to meet the individual needs of each child in the group, and in this way, each child and family feels uniquely cared about (Bemporad, 1996).

In RC³ programs, helping the child keep the personal presence of the parents and for the parent, sharing in some way in the child's day are program priorities with the purpose of helping to sustain and protect the most important parent-child relationship. At the same time, knowing that they may spend up to three years with a child allows caregivers to emotionally invest in the children in their care and provides the child with the intimate, nurturing, consistent care from which the healthy self develops. This, along with higher than average child care salaries, benefits, and an ongoing training program designed to help caregivers develop a professional "self," has resulted in much lower than average turnover rates for caregivers. The program also has shown long-term positive outcomes for children in public school performance.

adolescence. The program needs to be firmly rooted in the knowledge areas of human development rather than "child development" to avoid the fragmentation and segmented thinking that is characteristic of the past.

The data now speaks for itself. The time has come and gone for us to be saying "This is what I believe" and "This is what you believe." It is time for policymakers to stop excluding and start including. What America needs, and must have, is a responsible public policy that ensures and commits to the welfare of its youngest citizens and recognizes what is truly at stake and at risk for the future of our country if these commitments are not made.

Conclusion

Part of America's inability to commit to a comprehensive program to care for its youngest children has its roots deep in the past. It is past time for reframing the issues and recognizing the urgency of the new realities facing all of America's children and families. The changes in the latter half of the 1990s alone—monumental advances in technology, major economic shifts, changes in health care—signal tremendously significant shifts affecting the way Americans will live now and in the future.

To respond to these changes as they affect children and their families, a comprehensive system of programs that support families needs to be designed for all of America's children from birth through

References

Bemporad, S. (1996). Relationship-centered child day care. *The Signal: Newsletter of the World Association for Infant Mental Health, 4*(1), 18–20.

Bronfenbrenner, U. (1990). *Discovering what families do. Rebuilding the nest: A new commitment to the American family.* Milwaukee, WI: Family Service of America.

Bureau of the Census. (1993). *We, the American children.* Washington, DC: Author.

Bureau of Labor Statistics. (1998). *Labor force statistics from the current population survey.* [Announcement posted on the World Wide Web]. Washington, DC: Author. Retrieved July 25, 1998, from the World Wide Web: http://146.142.4.24/cgibin/surveymost.

Cahan, E. (1989). *Past caring: A history of*

U.S. preschool care and education for the poor, 1820–1965. New York: Columbia University, National Center for Children in Poverty.

Carnegie Task Force on Meeting the Needs of Young Children. (1994). *Starting points: Meeting the needs of our youngest children* (Abr. Ed.). New York: Carnegie Corporation of New York.

Children's Defense Fund. (1998). *The state of America's children: Yearbook 1998*. Washington, DC: Author.

Cost, Quality, and Child Outcomes Study Team. (1995). *Cost, quality, and child outcomes in child care centers, executive summary* (2nd ed.). Denver, CO: University of Colorado at Denver, Economics Department.

Galinsky, E., Howes, C., Kontos, S., & Shinn, M. (1994). *The study of children in family child care and relative care: Highlights of findings*. New York: Families and Work Institute.

Goldman, K. S., & Lewis, M. (1976) *Child care and public policy: A case study*. Princeton, NJ: Educational Testing Service.

Greenspan, S. I. (1993, July 15). The kids who will be killers. *The Washington Post*, p. C1.

Hayes, C., Palmer, J., & Zaslow. (1990). *Who cares for America's children? Child care policy for the 1990s*. Washington, DC: National Academy Press.

Hewlett, S., & West, C. (1998). *The war against parents: What we can do for America's beleaguered moms and dads*. New York: Houghton Mifflin.

Kamerman, S. B., & Kahn, A. J. (Eds.). (1991). *Child care, parental leave, and the under 3s: Policy innovation in Europe*. New York: Auburn House.

Kamerman, S. B., & Kahn, A. J. (Eds.). (1994). *A welcome for every child: Care, education, and family support for infants and toddlers in Europe*. Arlington, VA: Zero to Three, National Center for Clinical Infant Programs.

Lally, J. R., Mangione, P. L., Honig, A. S., & Wittmer, D. S. (1988). More pride, less delinquency: Findings from the ten-year follow-up study of the Syracuse University Family Development Research Program. In S. Provence, J. Pawl, & E. Fenichel (Eds.), *The zero to three child care anthology 1984–1992* (pp. 95–103). Arlington, VA: Zero to Three, National Center for Clinical Infant Programs.

Mahler, M. S., Pine, F., & Berman, A. (1975). *The psychological birth of the human infant: Symbiosis and individuation*. New York: Basic Books.

NICHD Early Child Care Research Network. (1997). Child care in the first year of life. *Merrill-Palmer Quarterly, 43*, 340–360.

Reiner, R. (1998, April 27). A Crusade for Children. Transcript in *The Commonwealth*, pp. 2–4.

Secrest, P., & Bergman, R. (1986). *Child care Dallas: A history of caring 1981–1986*. Dallas, TX: Child Care Dallas.

Winnicott, D. W. (1965). *The maturational processes and the facilitating environment: Studies in the theory of emotional development*. Madison, CT: International Universities Press.

Zigler, E. F. (1998). By what goals should Head Start be assessed? *Children's services: Social, policy, research, and practice, 1*(1), 5–17.

Zigler, E. F., & Frank, M. (Eds.). (1997). *The parental leave crisis: Toward a national policy*. New Haven, CT: Yale University Press.

2

Parenting Toddlers: Developmental and Clinical Considerations

Alicia F. Lieberman and Arietta Slade

2

Introduction

Raising toddlers looms in the popular imagination as one of the most difficult stages of parenting, comparable only to the challenge of raising adolescents. Indeed, toddlers and adolescents, each in their own way, face a common developmental task: expanding their worldview and the realms of their motor, cognitive, and social activities while preserving and reworking their emotional connections with their parents. The overriding developmental theme in both periods is the struggle to achieve autonomy without alienation. Child rearing at these ages is greatly facilitated by the parents' awareness of the pressures, uncertainties, and inner conflicts as well as the exhilaration the child experiences in negotiating the dangers and pleasures of increasing autonomy. However, raising a toddler can confront parents with considerable emotional upheaval as they inevitably revisit unresolved issues from their own childhood (Fraiberg, 1980). This chapter examines the process of parenting toddlers from four major points of view. First, it provides an overview of the developmental issues of toddlerhood, with particular attention to the psychological reorganization ushered in by the achievement and expansion of locomotion, language, and symbolic capacities and the implications of these skills for affect regulation, the experience of anxiety, and the development of a social conscience. Second, it explores the impact of these developmental changes on the parents' experience and on the contributions that the toddler's unique individual characteristics make to the parent-child relationship and the parenting experience. Third, it discusses the role of the parents' own past and present experiences in shaping their child-rearing attitudes and behaviors toward the toddler. Finally, it examines the processes that underlie clinical disturbances in toddlerhood, presenting two case examples that highlight the intricate interrelationships between ecological factors, family structure, parental personality, and child characteristics in the ontogenesis of psychopathology.

The Toddler Period: Developmental Issues and Conflicts

Toddlerhood is usually defined as the relatively brief period of time that begins at about 12 to 14 months, when the child starts to walk autonomously and use intentional symbolic communication, and ends when locomotion and language are well consolidated, at approximately 36 months. By definition, this period ushers in two developmental milestones that have come to define the human species: the capacity for bipedal locomotion and the capacity for symbolic representation. The sometimes laborious, sometimes quick expansion and refinement of these skills transform the child-parent relationship from one of total dependence to one of increasing negotiation and adjustment to each partner's individual plans and wishes.

Locomotion and Its Meanings

Erik Erikson (1950), in his classic study of childhood and society, pointed out that locomotion permeates our views of who is a worthy member of society, someone who is "an upright person," can "stand on his own two feet," and has the capacity to "go far." The toddler acquires a new status by virtue of his capacity for autonomous movement. Between 13 and 18 months, locomotion is its own justification. The child does not need to go anywhere specific. The child is content with walking for its own sake, an activity quickly followed by the giddy experiences of climbing and running. The exuberant, fearless mood of this age has been characterized as the child's "love affair with the world" (Mahler, Pine, & Bergman, 1975).

Parents often regard this period with mixed feelings of pride and loss. Mothers, in particular, tend to speak of their longing for the cuddly baby who could stay placidly in their arms, an image that stands in sharp contrast to the squirmy toddler who can barely be contained for a moment or two before setting off in yet another bout of exploration. Toddlers, particularly those under 18 months, can be quite unpredictable. They may take off without warning, fully expecting to be followed and retrieved. Their whereabouts cannot be taken for granted, and the constant surveillance and redirection needed to keep them safe, particularly in novel surroundings that are not "childproof," can be wearying indeed for an adult. Many of the struggles of this age stem from the clash between the child's motive of exercising to the fullest the newly acquired locomotor skills and the parental goal of spending the least possible amount of energy keeping the child contained.

Once locomotion is comfortably mastered, the child's attention shifts to the question of what to do with it. The world beckons, and there is much to see and learn. At the same time, the child has now acquired some sobering experiences about the dangers of unfettered exploration, and there is a certain dampening of the initial exuberance.

Sometime between 18 and 24 months the toddler goes through a period of increased demandingness, with heightened distress on separation from the mother

(Marvin, 1977). Mahler and her colleagues (1975) attributed considerable psychological significance to this behavior, which they called "shadowing" because the child seems to incessantly monitor each of the mother's moves. For some mothers, this period raises the worrisome possibility of regression in the child's development, with questions about the child's supposed "dependency" on them. For others, the increased need for their presence brings back cherished moments of physical intimacy that seemed lost at the height of the toddler's absorption in practicing locomotion skills. The sudden alternation between "shadowing" and bouts of darting away can be quite confusing for caregivers, although this pattern can be understood as the toddler's wish to be scooped up in the mother's arms and to be reassured of her protective presence and her love (Mahler et al., 1975).

After approximately 24 months, a more predictable pattern of separation and reunion begins to emerge as language becomes an increasingly reliable tool for communication between parents and child. The negotiation of closeness and distance between the toddler and the parents has been extensively described by Mahler and colleagues (1975), who introduced the images of "refueling," "shadowing," "darting away," and "rapprochement," and by Mary Ainsworth (1969), who used the image of "secure base." While each of these concepts stems from very different theoretical views of the inner life of the toddler, both describe a fundamental pattern of toddler behavior—namely, the child's recurrent transitions from proximity with the mother to forays away from her for the purpose of exploration. When the child has no urgent internal needs (e.g., hunger, fatigue, illness, fear of loss) that must be attended to and when he or she feels confident of the mother's availability, the toddler can move away from her and devote his or her attention to learning about the world. When what he or she encounters gives cause for alarm or when internal needs prevail, the child's attachment motivation holds sway, and he or she returns to the mother for care and comfort (Ainsworth, 1967). The child's initiative in experimenting with physical closeness vis-à-vis the attachment figure has important psychological implications for the child's emerging ability to learn which situations are safe and which situations pose a threat to his or her well-being.

Symbolic Representation and Its Role in Autonomy and Communication

The development of representational intelligence, as it is manifested in the development of language, imaginary play, and other forms of symbolic communication, sets the stage for many of the shifts and complexities inherent in the toddler's struggle to find a balance between closeness and autonomy. The earliest stages of representational intelligence bring with them anxiety and uncertainty, because the child recognizes in a new way that he or she is separate from the mother. At the same time, the child does not yet have the capacities to replace her physical presence with an internal one. However, as language and symbolic communication burgeon over the course of the second year, the anxiety of separateness gives way to the thrill of self-hood and to the pleasures of an enhanced relationship with the parents. Children begin to use their imagination to evoke absent objects and communicate their thinking through signs and symbols that are understood by others. They become capable of deferred imitation, mimicking behavior they observed hours or even days before by retrieving images stored in their long-term memory (Piaget, 1954). They use words and begin to use phrases to communicate their desires and fears.

Language has a paradoxical double role in human relations because while it serves as a bridge between the child's inner experience and that of the parents, it also provides a means for the child to assert his or her own separate reality (Stern, 1985). The acquisition of language allows for the expansion of reciprocity. Parent and child can now describe to each other what they want or need to do, explain the reasons for their actions, allay fears, resolve misunderstandings, and provide predictability by giving advance notice of what is about to happen, including pivotal daily emotional transitions such as separations and reunions. By using words as a bridge between two subjectivities, the parent helps the child to make sense of his or her internal experience (Fonagy & Target, 1997). At the same time, the child learns what is in another's mind when the parents talk to him or her about their own experiences. As a result, toddlers' representational skills—including language, imitation, imagination, and symbolic play—receive a powerful boost when the parent uses words as a vehicle for explaining the world.

While promoting communication and reciprocity, language also offers a powerful means for the child's assertion of independence. Toddlerhood is a time for recognizing that different minds hold different agendas. Spitz (1957) identified the toddler's use of the word *no* as the psychological marker of a profound transformation in the child's sense of self. Although even very young babies can signal rejection and refusal through body movements (arching the back, turning the head away), saying "no" signals the toddler's unambiguous assertion that she or he will not yield to the will of others. Fortunately, the renowned negativism of this age loses much of its mystique when parents can interpret it as the toddler's way of learning about the differences between herself and others and his or her method of finding a place in the world.

Creating a Partnership

From a toddler's perspective, the world would be ideal if the parents never interfered with his or her exploration but were always there when needed. Some experts construe this childhood wish as the optimal mode of child rearing, one that hypothetically should maximize the child's self-confidence by building confidence in their loved ones. This is a rather idealized proposition. In the mundane ways of the world, mothers and fathers constitute mobile secure bases with plans, needs, duties, and wishes of their own. The toddler, as one member of the family, must find his or her place among the other members, sometimes taking precedence, sometimes having to yield to the needs of others. Security cannot be built on the precarious platform of parental efforts to gratify the child's wishes. Rather, security at this age is a byproduct of a candid recognition that, while separateness entails conflict, the parents will be reliably available for trustworthy negotiations when the different agendas clash.

Bowlby (1973) coined the expression "goal-corrected partnership" to describe this process. The toddler's growing skills in symbolic representation enable the child to use his or her observations of the parents' behavior to make inferences and reach conclusions about their motivations and plans for action. This capacity, in turn, allows the child to take action aimed at influencing or changing disliked parental behavior—for example, protesting and clinging to the mother when she puts on her coat before going to work or hiding when the bath is being prepared. The parent, in turn, needs to develop strategies that will maximize the chances for cooperation or at least acceptance on the child's part. A goal-corrected partnership involves the capacity of both partners to understand each other's point of view and agree on a mutually acceptable course of action. Genuine collaboration as well as intractable conflict become possible when toddler and parent come to grips with their different perceptions and individual agendas.

The cognitive egocentrism (Piaget, 1924) of young children presents a major handicap in building a goal-corrected partnership because the child is largely inca-pable of appreciating somebody else's point of view. Toddlers interpret events in terms of how they affect them. As a result, they reach their own idiosyncratic conclusions about cause-effect relations ("mommy left, so she does not love me"), have unrealistic perceptions of the magnitude of their own and their parents' power, and develop unique theories about what is real and what is pretend, what is safe and what is scary, and what is alive and what is inanimate. Because their language is still rudimentary, toddlers cannot always put their perceptions of the world into words, and parents are often unable to see things from their toddler's point of view. In this sense, childhood egocentrism becomes contagious and can lead to prolonged impasses in the parent-toddler relationship. Indeed, home observations of mothers and toddlers indicate that mild to moderate conflicts take place once every three minutes and major conflicts occur at the rate of three per hour (Fawl, 1963; Forehand, King, Peed, & Yoder, 1975; Minton, Kagan, & Levine, 1971; Patterson, 1980).

The toddler's capacity to join in a partnership with the parent is also impeded by the limitations in the capacity for affect regulation. The modulation and containment of affect is a constant struggle during the toddler period, and affect storms are the rule rather than the exception. Often considered the hallmark of the toddler years, temper tantrums are nothing more than collapses in coping ability that occur when the child's feelings of disappointment, anger, and fear are too overwhelming to be contained in words or other symbols. Although much maligned, tantrums are an important ingredient of healthy development. When parents manage to avoid joining in the child's temper tantrum and remain emotionally available but firm in their positions, the child learns that he or she will not be abandoned during difficult moments, that momentary rage will not result in lasting alienation, and that there is calm after the storm (Lieberman, 1993). The child also learns that his or her affects can be contained and do not necessarily derail the adult's competent functioning.

Unfortunately, tantrums can be contagious and dysregulating if they touch on a parent's vulnerable points. When parents have limitations in their capacity for affect regulation, they cannot help their child in the gradual mastering of this skill. In worst case scenarios, parents may consistently interpret a temper tantrum as the child's deliberate efforts at manipulation or control. A chronic power struggle is likely to ensue from this perception.

Anxieties of Toddlerhood

Parents often find the toddler's eloquent expressions of self-assertion so compelling that they fail to empathize appropriately with the anxieties of this age. Because the toddler is always trying to understand that autonomy will not come at too heavy a price, namely the loss of the parents' love or physical proximity, such anxieties are intrinsic to toddlerhood. Thus, it is no accident that the two major anxieties of toddlers consist of separation anxiety and fear of disapproval. Separation anxiety involves the fear of losing the parent and is often seen as early as one year of age. Fear of disapproval, which emerges later in development after the cognitive changes of the second year, involves the fear of losing the parent's love. Like all anxieties, these two often overlap.

Separation anxiety is relatively concrete, in keeping with the young toddler's cognitive limitations. Such anxieties shift and change character as the child's capacity for symbolic communication and sense of time develop. At whatever stage it occurs, separation anxiety involves the child's fear that being physically away from the parent means that the parent will never come back and will be lost for good. Like everything else at this age, time is experienced subjectively, and sadness or longing can seem to last forever even if objectively the parent has only been gone for one hour.

Many cultures have evolved wonderful early games to teach young children that parents come back after an absence: peek-a-boo for the premobile child and hide-and-seek and chasing and retrieval games for older children who can walk, run, and hide on their own. These games are examples of the wonderful power of play to help master anxiety. Their use by parents enriches the parent-child relationship as well as the child's repertoire of coping mechanisms.

Fear of disapproval is less concrete and as a result less amenable to mastery through games. It is the result of two major cognitive acquisitions of the second year of life: the child's ability to appreciate adult standards (for example, clean and dirty, neat and messy, good and bad) and the toddler's increased capacity to imagine and fantasize. Fear of disapproval is a direct consequence of the toddler's wish to live up to social standards (Kagan, 1982) and please the parent. In other words, fear of disapproval is the other side of the toddler's wish to please. This wish to please is the earliest substrate in the formation of a moral conscience and a sense of social responsibility. It is perhaps the parent's single most powerful ally in the socialization process. Appealing to the child's sense of belonging and wish for approval are natural incentives to cooperation.

How do we know whether a toddler is growing well or not? Toddlers who are growing well seek approval but are not obsessed with it. They can tolerate reasonable amounts of frustration, and they can go back and forth flexibly between asserting their will and complying with the will of others. The healthy toddler also feels comfortable with a full range of emotions. A three-year-old was asked by his solicitous mother if he was happy. After thinking for a minute, he replied, "I am happy and sad and angry and bitey and clingy." He refused to be seduced into acknowledging only his happy side (Lieberman, 1993).

This child was able to experience and acknowledge what many adults fear to admit even to themselves: that a human being is neither all good nor all bad, totally happy or absolutely unhappy, only loving or always at war with others, but capable of all these states of mind. Indeed, much of the challenge of raising a toddler stems from the fact that this stage is such a mirror of the struggles that adults constantly wage inside themselves.

Parenting Toddlers: Developmental Challenges and Opportunities

What makes it possible for some parents to find—enough of the time—a comfortable balance between facilitating autonomy and maintaining physical closeness and intimacy? How is it that some parents are able to create a partnership that moves easily between the language of the body and the language of words and physical separateness, whereas others find the toddler period a time of constant challenge, conflict, and loss? What makes it possible for some parents to hold and contain the intensity, ambiguity, and poignancy of this period, when they are often just as rocked and challenged as their children?

For parents, toddlerhood is a time of great emotional complexity, of contradictory desires, wishes, and impulses. Mother and father both are often awash in a range of feelings: loss, anxiety, anger, guilt, joy, and delight (Slade & Aber, 1986). There is loss in the realization of the child's moving away physically and psychologically, their anxiety at the child's forays into arenas outside parental control, and anger at the child's expressions of aggression. There is guilt and sometimes shame at one's own anger and perceived hurts and abandonments. There is joy and delight at the magic of the child's self-discovery—and at his or her increasingly direct expressions of affection and love. For the first time, the child is speaking and thinking autonomously, all the while becoming less dependent on the parents. Something is lost, and something is gained, all at once.

This newly attained separateness and autonomy sets the stage for a redefinition of how parent and child can reestablish a sense of intimacy and connection. The relatively easy and magical intimacy of infancy must give way to a far more complex experience of closeness, a oneness modified by twoness (Stern, 1985). This is not to say that intimacy is less important in toddlerhood than it is in infancy. In fact, because of the fragility of self at this age, the feeling of being met and "held in mind" by the parent is particularly important to the child's developing sense of his or her wholeness and efficacy (Fonagy & Target, 1997; Mahler et al., 1975; Pine, 1985; Winnicott, 1965). However, relative to infancy, intimacy will now necessarily be experienced in different and increasingly more dimensional ways. The child's will, autonomy, aggression, and burgeoning sensuality must be incorporated into the relationship and into the parent's sense of what is knowable and lovable about her child.

Decades ago, Therese Benedek (1959) noted that each phase in a child's life offers parents the opportunity to rework and reintegrate developmental difficulties and failures in their own early experience. In effect, she suggested that parenthood is a developmental process in that the changing demands of a child's development offer parents a second chance to heal wounds and conflicts inherent to their early experience of being parented. By helping their child achieve resolution and organization that they themselves had difficulty achieving, parents heal their own wounds at the same time that they facilitate development for their children.

Although Benedek suggests that each phase of a child's development provides opportunities for parental reorganization and resolution, it seems evident that—because of its particular demands and emotional valence—the toddler period is a time of both great challenge and opportunity for parents. It is at this moment in development that all of the building blocks of the representational and experienced self begin to emerge—language, symbolization, and abstract thought. Thus, the parent's capacity to make the best of this second chance is particularly important.

As described previously, the toddler period confronts parents with a series of exquisite and often acutely difficult dilemmas. The child is moving ahead developmentally, sometimes working hard to manipulate and coerce the parent to do his or her bidding, sometimes working hard to distinguish the self from the parent and to maintain physical and psychological distance, sometimes needing comfort and complete abandon, and sometimes simply overwhelmed by the pain of managing the complexity of it all (Mahler et al., 1975; Sander, 1965). Faced with these everchanging and often vociferously expressed needs and demands, the parent must remain what clinicians and developmentalists have described as "emotionally available," "sensitive," and "attuned" to the child (Ainsworth et al., 1978; Emde, 1991; Mahler et al., 1975; Stern, 1985). This is because the child needs the parent to hold his or her separateness, exploration, and autonomy, and to join in the feeling that the "world is his or her oyster." However, the mother must also limit her child, contain and regulate excessive assertiveness and impulsiveness, and assure the child's safety. She must keep her child from hurting others (including her), from becoming hurt, and from becoming imperious and unrestrained in his or her demands on others. Thus, just as she must emotionally accompany the child in discovering the world, the mother must check and modulate those discoveries. The mother will inevitably evoke the child's sadness and anger and provoke conflict between them, and the child will do the same. What a contradictory, complex, and sometimes seemingly impossible task!

Parents meet this dilemma in a variety of ways and with varying degrees of success. Some find the pain of losing the intimate and easy connection of infancy very painful and subtly thwart developments that will provoke the conflict and anger that invariably accompany autonomy and exploration. Others find the aggression and demandingness of their toddlers intolerable. Some respond by yielding to what rapidly becomes tyrannical behavior and unbridled aggression, effectively transforming healthy exploration and self-assertion into dangerous self-absorption and what Winnicott called "ruthlessness" (Winnicott, 1965). Not only is exploration distorted, but for these children, intimacy is experienced in terms of dominance and submission. Other parents are so relieved by their toddlers' separateness that they miss all signs of their toddlers' need for closeness and physical intimacy. While such parents may well be able to take pleasure in their children's autonomy, they fail to undergird autonomy with the feeling that closeness is intrinsic to healthy separateness.

A number of overlapping and intertwined factors contribute to a parent's success in finding his or her way through this maze. First is the degree to which the parent is able to negotiate the intensity of feelings and old conflicts that are an inevitable part of life with a toddler. For the first time, the parent is being faced with directed aggression (the child means to kick his father where it hurts), overt sensuality and sexuality (the little girl coquettishly displays her genitals while getting dressed for bed), and real loss and separation from the child ("I hate you! Go 'way!"). However a parent has come to terms with his or her own inevitable conflicts regarding anger, sexuality, and loss, these achievements will be evoked, challenged, and replayed during the toddler period. To the degree that the adult can use such awakenings to understand the toddler, the crisis will be an opportunity for growth in both parent and child. To the degree that such awakenings cause the parent to respond rigidly, irrationally, or erratically, the crisis will intensify and pathology might be a likely result.

The child's meaning to the parent is an essential factor in determining how and to what degree the past will be replayed in the current relationship. What place does this child have in the parent's psychological life? How does he or she experience and represent the child in light of these meanings (Slade & Cohen, 1996; Slade, Belsky,

Aber, & Phelps, in press; Zeanah, Benoit, Hirshberg, Barton, & Regan, 1994)? How do these attributions affect the relationship with the child (Lieberman, 1997)? Every parent has a history, but each child comes to take on a particular meaning to the mother and father.

Representations of the child begin to form even prior to conception but become increasingly structured and organized as the pregnancy proceeds. The child has an active and meaningful place in both parents' psychological life before he or she is born. The quality and function of these representations are, of course, multiply determined. They emerge as a function of the real-life and psychological circumstances into which the child is born: the mother-father relationship, child's birth order, and the place the child is expected to fill in the parent's life. The possible permutations are endless: "This is the baby who will save my marriage," "This is the baby who ruined my life," or "This is the baby who saved my life."

These representations are also shaped by the nature and quality of the parent's relationship to his or her own parents. In fascinating ways, the "stories" that comprise adults' recollections of their childhood relationship with their parents will color their experience of the child, beginning shortly after conception (Slade & Cohen, 1996). For instance, a woman who had bridled at her mother's controlling and domineering ways throughout childhood and adolescence imagined her son as a "Little Dictator" when she was pregnant. When he was a toddler, she experienced him as willful and persistent, just as she had been. An-

other mother, still enraged at her own mother's cruelty and rejection, was already angry with her baby before the baby was born. As might be expected, she found the toddler period a time of endless conflict and confrontation.

All parents bring their pasts into their relationship with their toddler. Nevertheless, the extent to which childhood conflicts and repetitions color and distort the parent-toddler relationship has much to do with the degree to which a parent has been able to reflect upon and integrate aspects of his or her own history. Selma Fraiberg long ago made clear the damaging effects of unintegrated, unacknowledged negative affect upon the parent-child relationship. Unresolved conflict, dissociated trauma, unacknowledged grief, and rage are all poisonous when injected into the relationship with the child. This is particularly true when the child is a toddler, just coming into his or her own, finding his or her way, and testing his or her wings (Pine, 1985). This has been documented again and again by two decades' work in parent-infant psychotherapy (Fraiberg, 1980; Lieberman, 1992; Lieberman & Pawl, 1993; Seligman, 1994).

Attachment researchers have also provided evidence for the link between adults' resolution of their own early childhood experience and their quality of parenting. Adults with secure attachment organizations (Main, Kaplan, & Cassidy, 1985)— who have managed to integrate and reflect upon the exigencies of their own early attachment experiences and the feelings, thoughts, and memories intrinsic to these relationships—are much more able to manage the complex feelings evoked by their toddlers than are those parents with insecure attachment organizations (Slade et al., in press; Aber, Belsky, Slade, & Crnic, in press). Secure parents are able to respond more sensitively and supportively to their toddlers' autonomous strivings, and they are likely to represent their relationship with their toddlers in more coherent, joyful, and less angry ways.

In effect, parental attachment security seems to provide a kind of protective factor in the parent's negotiation of the complexities of this period. For instance, the mother described previously—who saw her child as willful and persistent—was herself secure. As a function of her relatively high capacity for reflectiveness and coherence, she experienced his willfulness as a positive characteristic and one with which she could herself identify. She enjoyed his stick-to-itiveness, and she could laugh at her own propensity to get engaged in power struggles, just as she had with her own mother. "We're the Willfuls!" she joked. The second mother, who was insecure and still preoccupied with her own mother's relentless criticisms and cruelty, was having a much more difficult time with her child's willfulness and autonomy. She found herself perpetually on the brink of rage and seemed very invested in emphasizing her daughter's autonomy, perhaps as a means of protecting herself from the rage she felt at their entanglement. She was surprised at the fun and loving moments and seemed to have little sense of how these fit into the overall context of her relationship with her child. The toddler period was for her a fragmenting and fragmented time.

It is important to note that both parents play a pivotal role in the toddler's successful negotiation of this period. Fathers take on new importance with both boys and girls and often function as safer transitional figures in the move away from the complex relationship with the mother. Fathers have much to offer the female child in her developing representation of herself as lovable, assertive, separate, and efficacious. Likewise, they have much to offer the boy, who must balance his assertiveness with the capacity to remain intimate and open to emotion. Often, the tone for this delicate balance is set by the relationship with the father (Benjamin, 1988; Ogden, 1986; Pruett, 1987).

It is equally important not to leave the child's characteristics out of this discussion. Children are born with temperamental characteristics that become an intrinsic part of parental representations and attributions: "You've been a screamer since the day you were born," "You've never seemed to care one way or the other who held you," and so forth. This is particularly true of extremely difficult or slow to warm up children. Temperament is, of course, never purely biological (Sroufe, 1987); nevertheless, the child's inherent characteristics profoundly color the degree to which parents experience themselves as able to care for and understand him or her. Temperamental difficulties can have a particularly deleterious impact upon the parent-child interaction during the toddler period.

Gender also impacts a parent's representation of the child. Gender identity solidifies sometime between the ages of one and three, and children begin to exhibit play that is societally associated with maleness or femaleness. Boys are often fascinated by vehicles of great speed and power, whereas girls often occupy themselves with dolls, cooking, and other domestic activities. For some parents, the phallic aggression of their toddler boys may be quite discomfiting, while for others, it expresses some of their own deepest needs to crash heedlessly through the world. The same may be said of parental responses to the play of girls. Children's violation of gender stereotypes can be threatening as well. Some parents can tolerate their toddlers finding pleasure in play that is typical of the opposite gender, whereas others cannot. At most ages, but particularly during the toddler period, gender issues are very powerful in their "pull" for parents. Often, they set the stage for explicit reenactment of parental conflicts, to the great detriment of the development of representational and affect regulation capacities in the toddler (Coates & Wolfe, 1997). In a myriad of ways, gender becomes a lens through which parental representations of the child are further solidified and defined.

When Parenting Toddlers Goes Awry

Simon: A Child's Hypersensitivity and Maternal Anxiety

The case of Simon illustrates some of the ways that a child's temperamental difficulties, manifested in hypersensitivity and overarousal, can intersect with maternal anxiety and rigidity in a way that severely disrupts development during the toddler period and compromises the movement to autonomy and to more complex, triangulated relationships.

REASON FOR REFERRAL

The family pediatrician referred Simon and his parents for consultation shortly before the child's third birthday. The pediatrician described the mother as "at the end of her rope" in dealing with Simon's behavioral difficulties. Simon was extremely controlling, rigid, and angry, and he was demanding, intrusive, and highly separation anxious. Also—most disturbing to the parents—he would throw a temper tantrum readily, often for as long as an hour or two. The pediatrician had not detected anything overtly troubling about the child clinically. He appeared to be developing normally. He described the parents as "good people," motivated and bright, and as having tried in a variety of ways to solve the problem on their own. None of the "usual" suggestions had helped. In fact, since the birth of Simon's younger brother, Nick, when Simon was 25 months old, things had worsened considerably. Simon gave no sign of resolving the tasks of the toddler period. If anything, he seemed to be digging his heels in deeper and deeper, causing himself, his parents, and his baby brother great pain and torment.

INITIAL ASSESSMENT

The initial assessment lasted for six sessions. The therapist first met with the mother and father twice, then the mother and child twice, the father and child once, and finally the parents together again for a feedback session.

During the first two evaluation sessions, the parents painted a grim picture: This was a child out of control. The parents, especially the mother, were obviously very distressed and overwhelmed. The mother was someone who liked and needed to be in control and who had a relatively difficult time with her own vulnerability and distress. At the time of the evaluation, however, she was fairly fragile and anxious. She tried to maintain tight control of her emotions, but was on the verge of tears much of the time. The father was generally more passive and distant, and although he made it clear that he too struggled with Simon, it was obviously the mother who was both receiving and managing the brunt of Simon's anger and anxiety. The father withdrew when things got difficult and appeared mildly depressed.

Daily life was a constant struggle in the home. Everything seemed to upset Simon. Even the tiniest disruption would send him into long, screaming tantrums, during which he would scream, "I can't stop! I can't stop!" When his mother would try to reason with him, he would scream louder, and when she tried to physically restrain him, he would yell, "Don't touch me! You're not fair! You're mean! You're going to hurt me!" He had no capacity to transition at a reasonable pace from one activity to another, and he could not tolerate change in routines. Playdates were a disaster, and he was utterly unable to manage any large family functions. He would rapidly escalate into a temper tantrum, and the family would have to leave. Both parents came from large families and found it very painful to routinely skip family parties because of Simon's difficulties. The fact that Simon could not develop friendships made the mother feel trapped and powerless to find any space away from him.

Simon was unable to tolerate separation from his mother. She worked one day a week as a bookkeeper, usually on a weekend day. She had choir practice one night per week. He was cared for by his father or maternal grandmother at these times. The grandmother lived a few houses' distance down the block and was an integral part of the family's life. Simon would begin to worry about these regular and stable separations days in advance and would beg his mother not to leave him. Once she had left, he would cry bitterly for much of the time she was away. This was especially true when his father was caring for him. The mother began to question the wisdom of her leaving him at all. As might be expected, Simon was also very jealous of his brother Nick. When the mother was feeding or caring for Nick, Simon would become very demanding and insistent. When Nick was napping, Simon would demand his mother's complete attention. This was a time she liked to use for exercising, but Simon would not tolerate it. His demands, of course, were not restricted to these times. He needed to control his mother all the time and would relentlessly insist that she do his bidding. Any resistance on her part was met with more tantrums.

Simon had a relatively undeveloped relationship with his father and rarely tolerated being left with him. He wanted to be with his mother all the time. His father was a poor substitute at bathtime, bedtime, or waking. He needed her to himself, and he needed her all the time. This is not to say that he did not do well with his father when he was not anxious. He would accept him as a playmate and enjoyed watching television with him or horsing around. But when his anxiety about losing his mother was aroused, he clung to her for his life. Clearly, he had not resolved one of the critical tasks of the latter end of the toddler period: moving out of intense dyadic relationships, usually with the mother, and into more flexible, triangular relationships with both parents.

Importantly, Simon was clearly a hypersensitive child, becoming easily overaroused and agitated when exposed to stimuli that were noxious to him (Greenspan, 1995; Lieberman, 1993; Turecki & Tonner, 1989). In particular, he would react very negatively to any smells, tastes, and sounds that seemed unpleasant to him. He was extremely sensitive, for instance, to the feel and look of his clothes. If he was the least bit bothered by a fabric or by the way his clothes felt on his body, he would take them all off, immediately. He would cry at loud sounds and angrily rejected any foods whose smell or taste he did not like.

The developmental history indicated that such overarousal and hyperreactivity had typified his behavior from his earliest days. He was awake for long periods from the first days after birth and was frequently fussy and cranky. He was soothed only by nursing. His unremitting crying, wakefulness, and irritability did not diminish over the course of his first year. By the time he was one year old, he was having tantrums that would last for at least an hour. He slept poorly throughout his infancy, often waking up numerous times during the night.

Developmental milestones had otherwise been normal. He crawled, walked, and talked on schedule, and in fact seemed quite bright and verbal.

By the time the therapist had completed the first two evaluation sessions with the parents, several things had become clear: (1) Simon was clearly what is often referred to as a "difficult" or "hard to soothe" child, with a long history of overarousal, hyperreactivity, and inability to tolerate a variety of intense stimuli, including shifts in his own affective state, (2) his move into any sort of autonomy had been severely compromised, and (3) he had little capacity for comfortable intimacy with his parents. He had a conflicted and angry relationship with his mother and a very limited and circumscribed relationship with his father. For their part, it was also clear that the parents had little sense of how to either understand or regulate his affective overarousal and hypersensitivity. His behavior unnerved the mother. She felt guilty and imagined that she had created the problem, and she felt that she should be able to control him by setting firm limits and refusing to be dominated by him. Unfortunately, she did not understand that when she responded to his needs in rigid or angry ways or abandoned him in the midst of a tantrum, she was actually making him feel that his dysregulation could not be contained and drove the people he loved away. Neither parent understood how anxious this child was, nor did they have any concrete sense of what set him off. In particular, they did not see that their responses to his behavior often made his anxiety worse.

The therapist began by telling the parents that they certainly were not responsible for Simon's difficulties and that setting limits and refusing to be controlled would be working very well if Simon did not have such significant and inherent regulatory difficulties. Simon's behavior and developmental history clearly fit the pattern of a difficult child, who was indeed from the beginning hard to comfort and soothe and who was so beset by biologically based hyperarousal that he could not internalize and make use of his parents' physical presence and emotional availability. This was a child who could not experience his universe as secure because of the degree to which he was buffeted by affective storms and upheavals, from the earliest days of his life. This had made him especially dependent upon his parents. The therapist described to the parents what it might feel like to be so highly aroused and reactive and made explicit the need to avoid situations that triggered his hyperreactivity until he had better control. Most important, they needed to understand better what it felt like to be him, so that they could anticipate and verbalize for him some of the experiences he was having. This was a child for whom the verbal developments of the toddler period had made little difference. He was not able to use language in an anticipatory way or as a means of communicating his anxiety and worry to his parents until it was too late and he was already upset. The therapist used the visual image of a gauge gone out of whack. Once Simon entered his own personal "red zone," he could not bring himself back, and he needed their containment, regulation, and support to do so. The parents were very relieved to

have their son described to them in a way that made sense. Most important, they were relieved to know that they had not made him difficult. Clinically speaking, of course, there is no question that the mother's relative inflexibility and anger in response to him, coupled with the father's passivity and unavailability, aggravated inborn temperamental qualities. However, to reassure them that they had not created a monster made it possible for them to begin to empathize with and understand him.

Simon and his mother came together for the next two sessions. There were several surprises in these meetings. Simon was a physically small, adorable, perfectly groomed little boy, with a shock of wiry hair. He was extremely wary of the therapist and avoided looking at her or being in any physical proximity to her. If she spoke or tried to engage him, he would move onto his mother's lap and look pleadingly at her. He was obviously intrigued by the toys in the room but was too fearful to take things off the shelves himself. He made his mother get the toys he wanted, and he insisted that she answer the gentle questions the therapist posed to him. He initiated no play and actually needed his mother's active involvement to keep the play going. Although it was quite obvious that he was verbal and capable of symbolic communication, his play was ritualistic and devoid of overt symbolization. The simple fact of his impoverished play made evident the degree to which this child had struggled with autonomous thought and language. To the therapist's surprise, however, he allowed his mother to leave the room briefly during the initial session. Although he did not look at the therapist during his mother's absence and continued to mutely line up soldiers and animals, he did not cry or seek his mother. When she returned, he looked at her briefly and went back to his play, gradually reincluding her in his activity. Also surprising was the fact that he and his mother seemed able to enjoy each other in important ways. Despite the fact that he was obviously both controlling and needy, he clearly enjoyed his mother, and she enjoyed him. They seemed to have fun together.

When the therapist saw Simon with his father, it was evident that there were strengths in this relationship as well and that the dyad was capable of warm, reciprocal play when Simon's anxieties about the therapist and about the room were assuaged. As long as the father would do Simon's bidding, he was comfortable and transiently happy. There was again little symbolic play or self-initiated activity. Simon needed his father to contain and organize his play.

It was then time for the final feedback session. The therapist decided to proceed slowly and refrain from recommending treatment and take the tack of providing developmental guidance. This was a family with obvious strengths, and she hoped that the parents' increased understanding and empathy would allow them to be more sensitive and containing of Simon's anxiety. Hopefully, their understanding would allow them to anticipate his difficulties themselves, verbalize and anticipate anxiety-provoking situations with Simon, and back off of fruitless power struggles, understanding how helpless these made him feel. They had little appreciation of the

need to pick their battles. With a child like Simon, picking battles is terribly important because every battle becomes a war. It was also suggested that the father become much more actively involved in caring for Simon. His tendency was to come home and lie down on the couch at the end of what were truly long and exhausting days, but this meant there was no relief for the mother and no break for the angry, exhausted triad of mother, Simon, and Nick.

In this feedback session, the mother unexpectedly announced that she wanted to start Simon in a two-day-per-week preschool that autumn, now a month away. She felt desperately the need of some break from Simon and hoped this would give her and Nick some time together. The therapist felt that this move was poorly timed and said so to the parents. She was certain that he would not yet be able to tolerate the separation. The mother looked very unhappy with this news. It was evident that the whole situation with Simon made her so anxious and angry that she had to have him away a few hours each week. Despite the fact that her own mother could easily have taken Simon for the equivalent time without facing him with the anxiety of preschool, putting him in school was the only solution she felt would provide her with the respite she needed. But as the therapist was not to understand for some time, the whole issue of asking her mother for help was actually very complicated for the mother. So Simon was to go to school.

THE TREATMENT

The call came six months later from the mother, who reported that the preschool experiment had failed dismally. Simon had at first tolerated school, largely by latching onto another child with whom he became obsessed. When this child was ill or involved in other activities, Simon was inconsolable. Finally, he began to have a great deal of anticipatory anxiety about going to school and would often throw a tantrum on the days school was in session. The mother called several weeks before she finally withdrew him from school, perhaps hoping that the therapist would be able to remedy the problem quickly and keep him in school. A short while later, several weeks after treatment had begun, the mother took him out of school. Interestingly, before she finally pulled him out, the classroom's head teacher called the therapist and voiced her feelings that the mother was too soft on Simon and only needed to learn to set limits and her suspicion that something was really wrong at home, "perhaps abuse." The latter accusation, which seemed totally off the mark, is unfortunately not particularly rare. Even experienced teachers will level such punitive and judgmental accusations at parents when they are faced with difficult children that they themselves cannot control. First, the mother is blamed for not being more clear in her limit setting, and then a far more malevolent charge is leveled. These children make teachers feel as angry and helpless as they do parents.

Infant-parent psychotherapy, modified for Simon's age, was begun (Fraiberg, 1980; Lieberman, 1991). Mother and child would come weekly for dyadic sessions, and the parents would come for their own sessions intermittently. Within a few months' time, it became clear that the mother needed time of her own to sort out the complexity of her feelings toward Simon. For six months, mother and child were seen every week, mother alone every other week, and father with mother intermittently. Eventually, as Simon improved and was able to tolerate (and look forward to) individual sessions, his sessions were increased to twice a week. The mother continued to come every other week on her own.

Simon's treatment continued until he was seven. The story of that work is complex, as is always the case in any lengthy treatment (Slade, in press). We now focus on several key issues relating to the intersection of Simon's difficultness and his mother's anxiety. The early phases of the treatment had three goals. The first was to help the mother understand the nature of Simon's distress and anxiety, so that she might respond more sensitively. One day, for instance, Simon asked for chocolate milk before dinner. She told him that he would have to wait for dinner, nearly an hour away. He began a temper tantrum that lasted through dinner and ruined the evening. The therapist explored with the mother the ways in which Simon had difficulty tolerating delay and tolerating the arousal of a wish. He was in the "red zone" almost immediately. Was this a battle worth having? Would a glass of milk really spoil his dinner? Of course, the answer to both questions was no. With time, the mother became much more flexible in her response to a wide array of Simon's needs and much more able to give in to things that were essentially unimportant. Her becoming less rigid helped Simon feel, likely for the first time, that he did have some control and autonomy.

The second goal was to help build in Simon a feeling that his mother was with him, no matter how angry and upset he became. In effect, the therapist was trying to help Simon feel some fundamental sense of security in the face of his affective storms. She worked on this concretely with the mother, helping her to understand how critical it was for her to remain with Simon when he threw a temper tantrum. This was a child who needed concrete reassurance of his mother's love and availability even when he was angry. This would make the "red zone" of his hyperreactivity less lonely and vulnerable. In dyadic sessions as well, the therapist would voice Simon's need to be reassured of his mother's availability and made a game of the idea that—like one of his limbs—Mom was there for good. She was not going anywhere.

Finally, Simon was encouraged, session after session, to exercise his autonomous capacities during the sessions. Slowly, as his relationship with the therapist developed and his feeling of safety in functioning at a distance from his mother grew, he began to play symbolically, move away from his mother, and bring the therapist into his inner world. One day he turned to his mother and said jauntily, "Now, it's time for you to go, Buster!"

Simon began to look more and more like a healthy toddler, although he was now nearly four years old. He could function apart from his mother, tolerate separation, and use language to express his needs. His relationship with his mother was becoming

more satisfying and comfortable. His temper tantrums slowly began to diminish in length and intensity. The affect storms of the terrible twos were calming, two years behind schedule.

Critical to Simon's eventual success in treatment was the mother's developing understanding of how her relationship with her own mother had complicated her capacity to respond to Simon in a containing and nurturing way. Her mother was a cool, remote, no-nonsense kind of person who had little tolerance for emotional upset or distress. Although her mother was very helpful to her with respect to child care, she helped out as it suited her and would become irritable and controlling when she had to care for the children at inopportune times. She would go away for weeks at a time and bridle at being asked to call the children. She clearly did not understand how much she meant to them. She kept her boundaries firm and clear and was unmoved by the distress of her daughter or her grandsons.

It took the mother some time to recognize how painful this was for her and realize how limited her mother's support really was. As she worked to untangle her relationship with Simon and grapple with the massive separation anxiety she felt as he became more autonomous, her mother became more intolerant and dismissive. "Get on with your life!" was her mother's message. The mother began to realize how much her mother's dismissiveness had set the stage for her difficulties with Simon. Just as her mother had been unable to respond to her separation anxiety and distress as a child, so had she been unable to soothe Simon. Realizing that her mother could not and would not tolerate or respond to her anxiety and distress, she realized that she had buried her own needs and anxieties as she had moved through her childhood, developing a tough, rigid veneer of independence and rebelliousness. When Simon was born, this veneer was broached with unfortunate consequences for both of them.

The mother was slowly able to reconstruct how her own facade of toughness had crumbled at Simon's birth. She was terrified of anything happening to him. She did not trust the hospital nurses with him, and she was content only when he was in her arms. His fitfulness and irritability of course worsened her anxiety, and she redoubled her efforts to control herself and control him. Having a baby made her feel anxiety for the first time in a long time. Having a difficult baby made her more anxious than she could manage. So began their dance: he escalating and cycling into his "red zone" and she rigidly responding to his neediness without understanding its source or dynamics. She was no more able to manage his distress than she was able to manage her own. Had he made her less anxious, she might well have been more containing and sensitive. Had he been an easier baby, her anxiety might have led to healthy changes in her functioning. But as it was, the combination of her anxiety and his hypersensitivity set the stage for a powerful and destructive pattern.

As the treatment progressed, the mother became far more sensitive to Simon's needs and understanding of his hypersensitivity. She became a comforting and present "secure base" (Lieberman, 1993). Van den Boom (1994) has recently provided evidence suggesting that just a short amount of instruction makes it much more possible for women to mother difficult or hypersensitive children. When maternal anxiety is high, however, limiting the capacity to recognize and contain the child's distress, the mother must at the same time come to understand the nature and dynamics of her own anxiety in response to the child. In this treatment, the mother's appreciation of how hard it sometimes was to be Simon came only after she was able to acknowledge and make meaning of her own anxiety. This allowed her to become a more responsive and compassionate caregiver.

Jose: Negative Parental Attributions and Child Psychopathology

The case of Jose and his parents illustrates how the parental distorted perceptions of a normal toddler's behavior can have profoundly negative repercussions on the child's mental health (Lieberman, 1997). This case can be understood from at least four different perspectives. First, it provides an unusually clear example of the power of the parents' unresolved psychological conflicts in setting the stage for the unconscious repetition, with the child, of interpersonal problems that originated in the parents' past (Fraiberg, 1980). Second, a family systems perspective suggests that Jose fulfilled the role of marital scapegoat for the disappointments and rage that the parents felt toward each other. Third, the role of the parents' circumstances—including cultural uprooting, loss of social status, and severe financial hardship—should not be overlooked as a set of stressors that contributed significantly to their problems with their child. Finally, Jose's very severe behavioral problems can also be understood as the result of his compliance with the parental pressure to conform to their negative attributions (Lieberman, 1997). From this perspective, Jose appears to be a toddler whose behavior was shaped by his parents' view of him as dangerous, unruly, and out of control. This view represented a distorted perception, through the lens of the parents' terrifying past, of normal toddler negativism. As Jose learned to understand himself and his behavior through the parents' messages of who he was, he internalized these attributions and turned into the overwhelming child they believed him to be. In this process, he became an active contributor to his own difficulties because his behavior confirmed, reinforced, and perpetuated the parents' negative perceptions as well as their resulting rejection and punitiveness.

REASON FOR REFERRAL

Jose was referred by his pediatrician, who described himself as becoming "frantic" while providing the child with medical care. In his words, Jose was a "monster on the loose, impossible to control." He reported that during a recent routine pediatric visit Jose climbed on his desk, threw the contents of the drawers on the floor, bit the telephone cord, and eluded the adults as they tried to "capture him" and calm him down. The doctor described the parents as a warm and loving middle-class couple in their mid-twenties who had immigrated from Colombia three years earlier and were eager to get help for their son. Jose was their only child. They had told the doctor that Jose bit and hit them so often that they were now resorting to hitting and biting him back. The pediatrician was entertaining a diagnosis of hyperactivity and was about to prescribe Ritalin, but he wanted a mental health evaluation before going through with this plan.

INITIAL ASSESSMENT

The assessment consisted of six weekly sessions: Two one-hour home visits with Jose and his parents, one session with both parents, one individual session with each of the parents, one session where the Bayley Scales of Infant Development were administered to Jose, and one feedback session.

During the first home visit, the parents—an attractive, articulate, and clearly very intelligent couple—greeted the therapist effusively. The mother exclaimed, "At last we are getting some help!" as she told the therapist how glad she was for the visit, and her husband nodded in assent. They briefly introduced the therapist to Jose, who watched the adults intently with a subdued facial expression. Almost immediately, the mother launched into a detailed description of her daily battles with her son. She said that Jose did as he pleased. He threw food around, urinated and defecated on the floor, refused to stay in his bed for a nap, and broke her most precious things, mementos of her home country. "Nothing I do makes any difference," she said. "He is the leader of the band." Her husband sat quietly next to her, listening. He occasion-

47

ally said that Jose was difficult only with his mother and that he had no trouble at all with the child when the two of them were alone. The mother ignored those remarks.

As his mother spoke, Jose listened quietly while watching her. After about 10 minutes, he sprang into action and in quick succession tried to open the window of the family's third-floor apartment, noisily banged his head on the window glass, broke off leaves from his mother's plants, and threw a half-eaten sandwich on the floor. During the entire visit he did not approach his mother for play or positive physical contact, although he occasionally cuddled up to his father. Several times he hit his mother and father for no apparent reason, and twice he approached and hit the therapist. Sometimes the parents responded with half-hearted efforts at stopping him but gave up quickly when Jose protested or eluded them. Other times they threatened to spank him, told him that a witch would come to take him away, or said they would call the police. These more extreme measures had the effect of quieting Jose for a few minutes, but he soon engaged again in other behaviors that exasperated his parents.

The timing of Jose's behavior was as striking as its content. He seemed intensely attuned to his mother, and his behavior often served as an illustration of her verbal descriptions. In effect, Jose seemed compelled to perform the role of "monster" in which he heard himself cast. This impression was reinforced when he stopped in the middle of a forbidden action to look at the therapist and then smiled sheepishly when she met and held his gaze. The therapist commented that Jose was showing her what his parents were talking about, that he wanted to make sure she understood. Later in the visit she said that everybody seemed to be having a hard time, and looking at Jose, she added pointedly, "You too, Jose. You are having a very hard time. I will try to help." The child responded by bringing a toy and sitting quietly next to the therapist to play. This response suggested that Jose had a good command of receptive language, that he was aware of the family difficulties and of his involvement in them, and that his seemingly uncontrollable behavior subsided when he encountered an empathic response. No less than his parents, Jose seemed to be looking for help.

During the second home visit, more self-endangering behaviors emerged. Jose bit not only his parents but also himself, hard enough to leave marks. His parents reported that he was accident prone, got hurt often, was intensely scared of monsters, witches, and the dark, cried and clung frantically to his parents when they prepared to go out, had difficulty going to sleep, and woke up crying during the night. In contrast with this disorganized functioning, Jose performed very well on the Bayley Scales, attaining a score that placed him three months above age level. He concentrated well and cooperated with the therapist, working quietly and effectively until he solved the task at hand. He responded to praise with a wide smile. His expressive and receptive language was advanced for his age.

During the session with both parents alone, a torrent of feeling emerged when the therapist asked them what it had been like to become parents. It had been a disaster, they said. When they found out about the pregnancy, they were new in this country, spoke little English, and had no friends or family nearby. In addition, they were trying to start a restaurant and working long hours, exhausted, discouraged, and broke.

The pregnancy was difficult. There was a danger of miscarriage and the mother was told to have bed rest. But she was the only cook at the restaurant, and her bed rest would have spelled financial collapse. Childbirth was described as a life-or-death situation. Although they were told that the mother might die, the parents could not understand the medical reasons for this possibility. They reported that doctors and nurses yelled at them when they did not understand instructions that were given in English. Forceps were required, and the baby had head lacerations that later became infected.

Jose's early months were no less trying. The parents reported that Jose slept well and ate well, and they did not remember difficulties related to his temperament or his care. However, the external circumstances of the family were very difficult. One month after Jose's birth, the restaurant had to close, and all the parents' savings were lost. When Jose was two months old, the mother began cleaning houses in spite of an infected episiotomy that had not yet healed, while the father worked as a bartender during the evenings and took care of Jose during the day. These circumstances were in stark contrast to their middle-class upbringing and their expectations of success in this country. They also hardly saw each other because of their respective schedules.

The circumstances were clearly overwhelming, but an additional factor soon became evident. In recounting these events, the parents seemed locked in their respective painful experiences and unaware of the other's. As the session progressed, they began to hurl bitter recriminations at each other, and their voices soon rose until they were yelling at each other. The mother attributed their restaurant's collapse to her husband's laziness and incompetence and contrasted her current situation with her life in Colombia, where she had worked as a legal secretary and studied photography and ceramics. Looking angrily at her husband, she told him loudly that she felt degraded. He replied that she expected him to be a superman, that she only noticed her own hardships and took for granted his current back-breaking schedule as a waiter at two local restaurants after having been a successful chef in Colombia. "You can only bitch," he yelled. "Nothing Jose does pleases you, and nothing I do pleases you."

When the therapist asked if this kind of exchange happened in front of Jose, both parents agreed that it happened daily and that Jose responded variously by standing between them and crying or by hitting them and himself. The father added quietly, "Jose is the one that is paying for our fights." After a silence, the mother said, "I don't want Jose to be the victim of what is happening to us." This openness to the damaging effect their fights had on Jose was a hopeful prognostic indicator of the parents' capacity for insight and their motivation to engage in therapeutic work on behalf of their son. But this respite was short-lived. When the father suggested to his wife that she should work less, she replied sharply that he did not earn enough for that choice. Then very quickly this beautiful and stylish woman started cursing her husband and her fate. "You are good for nothing," she screamed. "My mother told me so. I should have stayed in Colombia. I only came here so that my child would not be a bastard." It then emerged that the father had been married before, and in the eyes of his very Catholic family, he was still married to his first wife in spite of his divorce. The couple had come to the United States to escape being branded as sinners by her family. When the mother called her family in Colombia to tell them she was pregnant, her mother replied, "Get an abortion. It is a sin, but it's better than giving birth to a bastard." Jose had been branded before he was born.

The individual sessions with each parent confirmed the initial impressions that Jose's difficulties were related more to the harsh and acrimonious family atmosphere and the punitive parenting he received than to constitutional factors. The mother spent the bulk of her individual session describing her terrifying memories of her mother while growing up. The vividness and immediacy of these distant memories was striking, as were the parallels with the mother's perceptions of her son. Her mother often repeated to her, "The day of your birth will be the cause of my death." She cursed the day her daughter was born and wished she had killed her at birth. She forbade her to associate with other children and beat her with a broom or a chair if she saw her walking home from school with other children. "You should only love your family," she screamed. "Everyone else is filth." Her mother forced her to eat hated foods and used force-feeding if the child threw up. The physical punishments were so frequent, unpredictable, and severe that she tried to kill herself at age 12 by attempting to throw herself from their fourteenth-floor apartment. This attempt came to a stop when she accidentally broke a lamp and could not open the window, but thoughts of killing herself persisted throughout her adolescence until she met her husband at age 19. (The window episode was chillingly reminiscent of Jose's unsuccessful efforts to open the window during the first assessment visit.) The mother spoke of her father with some affection, but she also complained that he had never protected her from her mother. When she appealed to him, he only responded, "She wants what is best for you."

In his individual session, Jose's father was also quite candid about his childhood experiences. He saw himself as the "black sheep" of the family and described his mother as "mean" and his father as "unavailable." He explained that he had essentially grown up in the streets, coming home as late as he could from an early age. At the same time, the father denied any feelings of pain, anger, or regret, saying that he was a forgiving person and that his parents had done the best they could. He was able to describe his behavior toward Jose without any semblance of understanding its psychological implications. For example, he said laughingly that he liked to tease his wife by asking Jose to pinch her breasts and buttocks, something that led her to paroxysms of rage. Complaining that Jose's nightmares made him a frequent visitor to the marital bed, he reported matter-of-factly that he sometimes insisted on having sex in spite of the child's presence. If Jose was awake, the father told him to "look away" and hit him if the child did not obey. Such examples indicated that the father used denial and isolation of affect as pervasive defense mechanisms to cope with his deep-seated anger and fear and that he could be as unfeeling and frightening as his wife in his treatment of Jose.

DIAGNOSTIC PICTURE

Jose did not fit the diagnosis of hyperactivity originally suggested by his pediatrician. He had no difficulty restraining his motor activity when he was not under acute stress. He was able to concentrate and stay on task for several minutes at a time during the developmental assessment when he played with puzzles, looked at books, or assembled block structures at home and in the playroom. Restlessness and disorganization were only observable when he was clearly made anxious by his parents' behavior or by a situation where he felt danger, as during the pediatric visit that led to the referral.

Diagnostically, Jose fit the profile of Attachment Disorder with Recklessness and Self-Endangerment (Lieberman & Zeanah, 1995) and the category of Anxiety Disorder of the *DC: Zero to Three Classification Manual* (Zero to Three, 1994). The harsh, unpredictable, and often abusive treatment he received from his parents and the angry fights that he witnessed between the parents emerged as the primary etiological

factors for his condition. Jose's plight illustrates the process of intergenerational transmission of psychopathology through disorders of attachment. The childhood experiences of both his mother and his father had given both parents few if any opportunities for feeling valued and protected. Their capacity to value and protect each other as well as their child had in turn been seriously thwarted, leading to marital strife and to serious symptomatology in their child. Both suffered from rather rigid personality disorders, although their capacity to acknowledge suffering and seek help was prognostically hopeful.

RECOMMENDATIONS FOR TREATMENT

Facing the multiple areas of difficulty presented by a case like this, a therapist wishes that it were realistic to recommend infant-parent psychotherapy to address the relational problems between parents and child, individual psychotherapy for each of the adults as well as for the child, and couples therapy to address the marital problems. In the absence of unlimited financial and time resources, a more circumscribed treatment plan must be developed in the hope that the progress made in one area of functioning will generalize to other areas as well.

The urgent need to focus on Jose's emotional distress and help the parents become more nurturing and less psychologically abusive of their son prompted the recommendation for infant-parent psychotherapy (Fraiberg, 1980) as the preferred mode of treatment. However, it must be stressed that this form of treatment, initially developed for the first year of life, needs substantial modification when extended to toddlers (Lieberman, 1991). By the time a toddler is referred for treatment, the psychological problems tend to be so intense and pervasive that the parents often believe that all the difficulties reside in the child, and they resist an examination of how their own conflicts may be expressed in their parenting. Often, the negative parental perception of the child is reinforced by the support they receive from pediatricians, baby-sitters, and child care providers, who grow exasperated by the trials and tribulations of dealing with a disturbed child. In addition, the toddler may have internalized the negative parental attributions to such an extent that the behavioral problems may persist for a time even after the parents succeed in improving their parenting behavior.

These factors call for the therapist to be alert to the child's contribution to the family's interpersonal problems no matter what its origins might be, accept the compelling reality of the child's contribution, and offer a combination of direct intervention with the child, developmental guidance to the parents, and psychodynamic and relationship-based interpretations as necessary to address the parents' individual or marital conflicts. Flexibility of format is a must in these situations, and it reflects the therapist's flexibility in moving from one area of difficulty to another without losing sight of the ultimate focus of treatment, which is to restore and reinforce the mental health of the child. This means that although the basic format involves joint sessions with the parent(s) and the child, it is also possible and often desir-

able to introduce well-thought-out modifications involving focused child-therapist interventions as well as individual and marital sessions with the parents to clarify how these conflicts affect the child and chart an appropriate course of therapeutic action.

Conclusion

The almost simultaneous achievement of autonomous locomotion and symbolic representation opens new horizons for toddlers, who can now make their own decisions about where to be and when to say "no." A major emotional task of this period is to expand and consolidate this emerging autonomy without relinquishing the feelings of security provided by closeness with the parents. The child's balancing of exploration and attachment motivations is mirrored by the parents' developmental task of balancing two complementary sets of caregiving behaviors: protective behaviors that provide security and nurturance and "letting go" behaviors that stimulate self-reliance.

Although complementary, the child's and the parents' developmental agendas are quite different. The toddler's goal is to explore, learn, and individuate. The parents' role is to protect, socialize, and educate. Given these different functions, discrepancies of opinion and struggles to prevail are inevitable. The toddler's perception of what is safe and what is dangerous is likely to differ dramatically from the parents'; likewise parents' perception of what is forbidden and what is permissible.

Bowlby (1973) discussed the painstaking development of skills in appraising the environment for cues to danger and to safety and the equally painstaking evolution of a goal-corrected partnership where each partner in the parent-child dyad learns when and how to compromise and rearrange his or her individual plans for the sake of the relationship or to accommodate the more urgent priorities of the other. This process is both facilitated and hampered by the toddler's increasing capacity to symbolize, which helps him or her to imagine outcomes and anticipate consequences. Rage, fear, shame, self-consciousness, and other emotions are often triggered by the toddler's sometimes accurate, sometimes quite faulty understanding and predictive capabilities. In the often tumultuous process of forming a partnership, the ordinary parent learns to empathize with the toddler's emotional swings and may relax certain rules when possible and appropriate. The toddler, in turn, gradually internalizes the parents' emotional support and standards of behavior, incorporating them as stable components of his or her sense of self.

Clinical distortions in this process occur when the parent and the child, for many different reasons that differ from family to family, are locked into a rigid stance where empathic communication breaks down and neither partner can understand or cooperate with the emotional or developmental agenda of the other. Toddler-parent psychotherapy presents a powerful avenue for moving beyond psychological and interactional impasses that derail the child's developmental course. At the same time, the very characteristics of toddlers and parents that contribute to the problem tend to present dilemmas in joint parent-child psychotherapy. Toddlers' emerging individuality is expressed in the therapy sessions through insistence on the adults' attention, efforts to develop a separate and exclusive relationship with the therapist, and intolerance for adult exchanges that leave him or her out. A major therapeutic dilemma confronting the therapist is how to be available to each partner in ways that do not marginalize, anger, or alienate the other to the point that no productive therapeutic work becomes possible.

Another clinical dilemma is that toddlers can understand statements by the parents that may be damaging to them. When a parent launches into a diatribe against the child or against a spouse, the child may be overwhelmed by fears that are too powerful and primitive to contain.

Both of these clinical dilemmas have a constructive aspect. When competitive struggles occur between parent and child during the therapeutic session, it is likely that they are an accurate reflection of what goes on in everyday life. They give an opportunity for the therapist to put into words how difficult it is to find a way where everybody feels heard and understood and to work out solutions that accommodate the needs of the child and the parent. Similarly, if the parent engages in accusatory diatribes or other frightening outbursts during the session, it is likely that similar communications are witnessed by the child outside of the therapist's presence. In such situations, the therapist must often decide, very fast, what material is appropriate to pursue, how to convey this to parent and child, and how to contain the terrifying emotions that the parent and child may be expressing.

The clinical cases presented previously, although different in etiology, illustrate how treatment of toddlers and parents needs to involve simultaneous attention to the child's difficulties, the parents' perception of those difficulties, and the parents' own psychological struggles.

This need for flexibility in focus of attention and simultaneous empathy to the plight of the different players in the family drama calls for self-discipline and maturity on the part of the therapist. In the treatment of toddlers and parents, the therapist is faced with the need to move from a dyadic (patient-therapist) to a triadic format that includes child, parent, and therapist. When both parents participate in the treatment, the challenge increases, but its essence remains unchanged. Nobody can be the sole recipient of the therapist's total attention and empathic concern, because by being attuned completely with one participant, the therapist by definition loses track of what the others are feeling. This therapeutic challenge derives its emotional power from its developmental origins. Just as toddlers need to learn that they are not always and exclusively the center of their parents' lives, each partner in the parent-toddler pair needs not only to share with each other the therapist's concern and attention, but also sometimes to temporarily relinquish this attention and concern for the sake of the partner. To guide the toddler-parent dyad successfully through this developmental pathway, the therapist needs to have achieved an internal state where the childhood fantasy of perfection is traded for "good enough." Such a therapist can tolerate comfortably and without a collapse in professional self-esteem the impossibility of being totally attuned to each member of the family all the time.

References

Aber, J. L., Belsky, J., Slade, A., & Crnic, K. (1998). Stability and change in maternal representations of their relationship with their toddlers. *Developmental Psychology.*

Ainsworth, M. D. S. (1967). *Infancy in Uganda: Infant care and the growth of attachment.* Baltimore, MD: The Johns Hopkins University Press.

Ainsworth, M. D. S., Blehar, M. C., Waters, E., & Wall, S. (1978). *Patterns of attachment: A psychological study of the Strange Situation.* Hillsdale, NJ: Erlbaum.

Benedek, T. (1959). Parenthood as a developmental stage. *Journal of the American Psychoanalytic Association, 65,* 389–417.

Benjamin, J. (1988). *The bonds of love.* New York: Pantheon.

Coates, S., & Wolfe, S. (1997). Gender identity disorders of childhood. In J. Noshpitz (Ed.), *The handbook of child and adolescent psychiatry* (pp. 452–473). New York: Wiley.

Emde, R. (1991). Positive emotions for psychoanalytic theory: Surprises from infancy research and new directions. *Journal of the American Psychoanalytic Association, 39,* 5–44.

Erikson, E. (1950). *Childhood and society.* New York: Norton.

Fawl, C. L. (1963). Disturbances experienced by children in their natural habitat. In R. Baker (Ed.), *The stream of behavior.* New York: Appleton-Century-Crofts.

Fraiberg, S. (1980). *Clinical studies in infant mental health.* New York: Basic Books.

Fonagy, P., Steele, M., Steele, H., Leigh, T., Kennedy, R., Mattoon, G., & Target, M. (1995). Attachment, the reflective self, and borderline states: The predictive specificity of the Adult Attachment Interview and pathological emotional development. In S. Goldberg, R. Muir, & J. Kerr (Eds.), *Attachment theory: Social, developmental and clinical perspectives* (pp. 233–279). Hillsdale, NJ: Analytic Press.

Fonagy, P., & Target, M. (1996). Playing with reality: I. Theory of mind and the normal development of psychic reality. *International Journal of Psychoanalysis, 77,* 217–233.

Forehand, R., King, H. E., Peed, S., & Yoder, P. (1975). Mother-child interactions: Comparison of a noncompliant clinic group and a nonclinic group. *Behavior Research and Therapy, 13,* 79–84.

Greenspan, S. (1995). *The challenging child: Understanding, raising, and enjoying the five "difficult" types of children.* Reading, MA: Addison-Wesley.

Lieberman, A. F. (1991). Infant-parent psychotherapy with toddlers. *Development and Psychopathology, 4,* 559–574.

Lieberman, A. F. (1993). *The emotional life of the toddler.* New York: Free Press.

Lieberman, A. F. (1997). Toddlers' internalization of maternal attributions as a factor in quality of attachment. In L. Atkinson & K. Zucker (Eds.), *Attachment and psychopathology* (pp. 277–291). New York: Guilford.

Lieberman, A. F., & Pawl, J. H. (1993). Infant-parent psychotherapy. In C. H. Zeanah (Ed.), *Handbook of infant mental health* (pp. 427–441). New York: Guilford.

Mahler, M., Pine, F., & Bergman, A. (1975). *The psychological birth of the human infant.* New York: Basic Books.

Main, M., Kaplan, N., & Cassidy, J. (1985). Security in infancy, childhood and adulthood: A move to the level of representation. In I. Bretherton & E. Waters (Eds.), Growing points of attachment theory and research *Monographs of the Society for Research in Child Development, 50,* 66–104.

Marvin, R. S. (1977). An ethological-cognitive model for the attenuation of mother-child attachment behavior. In T. Alloway, L. Kramer, & P. Pliner (Eds.), *Advances in the study of communication and affect: Vol. 3. Attachment behavior* (pp. 25–60). New York: Plenum.

Minton, C., Kagan, J., & Levine, J. (1971). Maternal control and obedience in the two-year-old. *Child Development, 42,* 1873–1894.

Ogden, T. (1986). *The primitive edge of experience.* New York: Aronson.

Patterson, G. R. (1980). Mothers: The unacknowledged victims. *Monographs of the Society for Research in Child Development, 45*(5).

Piaget, J. (1924). *The language and thought of the child.* London: Routledge & Kegan Paul.

Pine, F. (1985). *Developmental theory and clinical process.* New Haven: Yale University Press.

Pruett, K. (1987). *The nurturing father.* New York: Warner Books.

Sander, L. (1962). Issues in early mother-child interaction. *Journal of the American Academy of Child Psychiatry, 1,* 141–166.

Seligman, S. (1994). Applying psychoanalysis in an unusual context: Adapting infant-parent psychotherapy to a changing population. *Psychoanalytic Study of the Child, 49,* 481–501.

Slade, A. (in press). Representation, symbolization and affect regulation in the concomitant treatment of a mother and child: Attachment theory and child psychotherapy. *Psychoanalytic Inquiry.*

Slade, A., & Aber, J. L. (1986, April). *The internal experience of parenting toddlers: Toward individual and developmental differences.* Paper presented at the International Conference of Infant Studies, Los Angeles, CA.

Slade, A., & Aber, J. L. (1992). Attachments, drives and development: Conflicts and convergences in theory. In J. Barron, M. Eagle, & D. Wolitzsky (Eds.), *Interface of psychoanalysis and psychology* (pp. 154–186). Washington, DC: APA Publications.

Slade, A., Belsky, J., Aber, J. L., & Phelps, J. L. (1996). Maternal representations of their relationship with their toddlers: Links to adult attachment and observed mothering. *Developmental Psychology, 35,* 611–619.

Slade, A., & Cohen, L. J. (1996). Processes of parenting and the remembrance of things past. *Infant Mental Health Journal, 17,* 217–239.

Sroufe, L. A. (1985). Attachment classification from the perspective of infant-caregiver relationships and infant temperament. *Child Development, 56,* 1–14.

Stern, D. N. (1985). *The interpersonal world of the infant.* New York: Basic Books.

Turecki, S., & Tonner, L. (1989). *The difficult child: A guide for parents* (Rev. ed.). New York: Bantam.

van den Boom, D. (1994). The influence of temperament and mothering on attachment and explorations: An experimental manipulation of sensitive responsiveness. *Child Development, 65,* 1457–1477.

Winnicott, D. W. (1965). *Maturational processes and the facilitating environment.* New York: International Universities Press.

Zeanah, C. H., Benoit, D., Hirschberg, L., Barton, M., & Regan, C. (1995). Mothers' representations of their infants are concordant with infant attachment classifications. *Developmental Issues in Psychiatry and Psychology, 1,* 1–14.

Zero to Three: National Center for Clinical Infant Programs. (1994). *Zero to Three: Diagnostic Classification of Mental Health and Developmental Disorders of Infancy and Early Childhood.* Arlington, VA: Author.

3

The Emotional Lives of African American Parents in Their Interpretations of Emotions of Infants

Marva L. Lewis

3

Introduction

African American parents in the United States face a compelling set of psychosocial realities as they attempt to rear their infants and children. The emotional domains associated with these realities have received little systematic attention by infant mental health researchers. Over the past several decades, many studies focused attention on the maternal behaviors of low-income African American mothers because of their disproportionate representation in such sociological risk factors as poverty, single parenthood, and adolescent maternal status (Bradley, Elardo, Rosenthal, & Friend, 1979; Brown, Bakeman, Snyder, Fredrickson, Moran, & Hepter, 1975; Burchinal, Follmer, & Bryant, 1996;

This study was funded by grants from the Early Childhood Transitions Network of the John D. and Catherine T. MacArthur Foundation, the University of Colorado Dean Small Grant Award, University of Colorado, Boulder, and the Social Science Research Council, Award for Research on the Urban Underclass, New York. The author extends appreciation for the generous support and guidance in the development of this chapter to Robert N. Emde, O. J. Harvey, JoAnn Robinson, Perry Butterfield, Joy D. Osofsky, and Hiram E. Fitzgerald.

McLoyd, 1990). Poverty and single-parent status have been associated with:

- Diminished expression of affection and less responsiveness to the socioemotional needs explicitly expressed by the child (McLoyd, 1990; Crittenden & Bonvillian, 1984).
- Psychological distress in the form of anxiety, depression, and health problems (Goodman & Brumley, 1990; Taylor, Roberts, & Jacobson, 1997).
- Observations that low-income Black mothers hit and scold their children more frequently (Brown et al., 1975; McLoyd, 1988).
- Recently separated mothers, in comparison to married low-income Black mothers, had significantly higher scores of rejecting attitudes toward their children (Lewis, 1986).
- Family disruption and work problems were associated with lower maternal acceptance (Taylor et al., 1997).

Attachment researchers have neglected the identification of sociocultural antecedents to caregiver-child attachment relationships within minority populations in the United States (Harwood, 1995; Jackson, 1993; Randolph, 1989). Sociocultural factors include sociological factors such as racial group membership and socioeconomic status as well as cultural factors such as parental beliefs about childhood, emotional display rules, culturally defined goals for socialization, and the structure of the caregiving environment (Skinner, 1985; Super & Harkness, 1997; Thoits, 1989; Valsiner, 1988).

Minority Status and the Emotional Lives of African American Parents

The history and experiences associated with minority status within a dominant White society are underexplored sources of influence on the emotions associated with the role of parent in African American communities (Taylor et al., 1997). At all socioeconomic levels, the experience of African American families as members of a minority group within the United States is one characterized by emotionally charged experiences of discrimination, prejudice, and individual and institutional racism (Coner-Edwards & Spurlock, 1988; Hines & Boyd-Franklin, 1996; Sparks, 1998; Tatum, 1997). Black parents must rear their children to be bicultural, that is, able to function in both the dominant group and within the African American cultural group (Peters, 1997; Slaughter-Defoe, 1995; Spencer & Markstrom-Adams, 1990).

The need for more vigilance on the part of single mothers rearing several children alone in neighborhoods with chronic high crime has also been reported as a correlate of mental distress (Lewis, 1994, 1996; Randolph, Koblinsky, & Roberts, 1998; Taylor et al., 1997). Low-income African American mothers have been reported more likely to use fear-inductive, power-assertive methods to control children (McLoyd, 1990), as well as more autonomy-promoting methods than other ethnic groups (Bartz & LeVine, 1978). There is also a cultural emphasis on obedience and preference for utilization of corporal punishment methods by low-income African

American parents (Hale-Benson, 1986; Lassiter, 1987; Wright, 1982).

The sociocultural influences on the emotional relationship developing between African American parents and their young children and the process of racial identity formation among ethnic minority children has received little empirical attention (Green, 1990; Spencer & Markstrom-Adams, 1990). Further, there are few methodologies identified to understand this phenomenon. Racial socialization is a process whereby parents consciously and unconsciously prepare their children to negotiate racial barriers in the larger society (Green, 1990; Peters, 1985; Thornton, 1997). The process of racial socialization may implicitly convey emotionally charged cultural developmental scripts reflecting values for independence and interdependence on the group and family (Branch & Newcombe, 1986; Greenfield, 1994).

Racial Socialization of Children and the Emotional Demands for Black Parents

Black mothers live in a racially stratified society where Blacks are at the bottom both socially and economically (Green, 1990). Black infants and children are prime candidates for a myriad of psychosocial risk indicators such as infant mortality, youth homicide, and urban violence (Collins & Hawkes, 1997; Edelman, 1997). The psychological consequences of the emotionally intense experiences of the everyday hassles of racism and discrimination may be internalized racism or oppression or simple rage, anger, or depression (Coners-Edwards & Spurlock, 1988; Fannon, 1963). The internalized oppression may also be a source of variability in the beliefs, attitudes, and behavior of African American parents. Parents are bombarded with negative images of Blacks by the media. Green (1990) argues that in order for Black parents to rear emotionally healthy children in a racially discriminatory society, they must be vigilant for those negative images. Parental child-rearing strategies and techniques used to accomplish goals of biculturality and racial socialization also have concurrent emotional dimensions (Lewis, 1993). The emotional dimension includes the messages of acceptance or rejection the parent communicates tied to racial features of the child. The parents' techniques may reflect their internal working models of relationships and their childhood experiences related to racial socialization.

Childhood experiences of racial acceptance and rejection and their relation to the parent's current perception of children, parenting behaviors, and attitudes is an important area for study. Within the family, issues of skin color and other racial features and characteristics may be tied to important affective qualities of the relationships between mothers and children (Boyd-Franklin, 1989; Neal & Wilson, 1989). Further, messages of conditional acceptance or rejection may be communicated by remarks about racial features of the child, such as skin color and hair texture. The messages that primary caregivers communicate to their children about the child's physical features associated with race are an important yet unexplored domain of unconditional acceptance (Lewis, 1993). If a child has been teased, denigrated, or constantly criticized by a significant attachment figure or peers about race-related features, they may then feel some degree of stigmatization, shame, and rejection (Lewis, Turnage, Taylor, & Diaz, 1999).

Though beyond the scope of this study to assess personality as a whole, the dimension of affective style is one important aspect of parenting behavior that is examined. Specific early childhood experiences may form the emotional foundation for the framework used by parents to interpret emotions in children. First, a discussion is presented that summarizes what is currently known about early childhood experiences and affective aspects of parental behaviors. A conceptual model of early childhood experiences and parental affective frameworks is then proposed. A premise of this model is that it is the intensity of affects from children's early experiences with their parents that provides the link and core theme for later parental affective frameworks. These intense emotions may be later revived when the child, as an adult in the role of parent, is performing childrearing behaviors similar to the practices they were subjected to when the intense emotion was first experienced.

The major focus in this chapter is to explore how African American parents' current perceptions of children's emotions may be shaped by early patterns of emotional responses to experiences with their own parents within a sociocultural context. The conceptual model of influences is then used as the basis to explore the affective styles of African American parents.

Early Childhood Experiences and Affective Aspects of Parenting

There are several theoretical areas that suggest ways that early parent-child experiences may shape affective aspects of adult personality and create characteristic emotional styles. From the area of social psychology, Harvey, Hunt, and Schroder (1961) propose that ongoing interactions between parent and child lead to the formation of different belief systems or worldviews that shape an individual's cognitive and affective orientation to the world. Rohner (1986) argues that, around the world and across cultures, parental acceptance and rejection (without positive counteracting experiences) have consistent effects on their child's expectations and worldview.

Object relation theorists propose that the quality of early parenting influences the formation of the internal object representations that govern later relational behavior (Fishler, Sperling, & Carr, 1990). These internal representations and their accompanying feelings provide the blueprint for all future relations. Early parent-child interactions and childhood experiences are accompanied by emotionally intense responses and create a characteristic cognitive and emotional style (Bowlby, 1969; Harvey et al., 1961; Rohner, 1975). The emotional residue from a mother's[1] early experiences with her parent may be manifested in the relationship with her own child (Fraiberg, Adelson, & Shapiro, 1975) and specifically to her perceptions of emotions in children. Zahn-Waxler and Wagner (1993) summarize the importance of studying the relationship between the mother's early experiences and her perception of emotions in children.

One major source of influence undoubtedly includes the parents' histories of affective experiences with their caregivers. This history of experience, in interaction with temperament, presumably results in particular emotional styles or traits that become elements of personality organization. These more enduring patterns, in turn, are likely to influence how the emotions of others are perceived. If these perceptions contain significant distortions, there may be maladaptive consequences for parent-child interaction. (p. 1)

How a mother interprets the emotional communications of her child will influence how sensitively she responds to her child's needs (Ainsworth, Blehar, Waters, & Wall, 1978). Sensitive and immediate maternal responsiveness to infant cues was found to foster more secure attachments in middle-class samples of White infants (Bretherton & Waters, 1985). To react sensitively, the mother must have the ability to see things from the baby's point of view, perceive the infant's signals or needs, interpret them correctly, select an appropriate response, and implement it effectively (Bretherton, 1987). If a mother's perceptions of her child's needs are distorted or biased, then her behavioral responses may also be distorted, mechanical, misdirected, or not related to her child's behavior. Therefore, understanding the factors that influence a mother's perceptions of her child's emotions may be critical to planning parent education programs or interventions de-

signed to increase a mother's sensitivity by changing her perceptions of her child. In addition, understanding how these early experiences influence parental behavior and responses to children may lead to the design of more effective intervention and prevention programs for child maltreatment.

Few studies have specifically investigated how mothers' early emotional experiences later influence their interpretations of emotions in children (Lewis, 1993). In one study, distinctive differences and distorted perceptions of infants' emotions were predicted by the mother's early experiences of child abuse (Butterfield, 1993). In comparison to a control group of nonabused mothers, mothers with histories of child maltreatment used a very restricted range of categories of emotions for infants. In addition, abused mothers showed more extremes in their choices and used predominantly sad emotions to describe infants' feelings.

Early attachment relationships present intense emotional involvement for the child related to survival (Bowlby, 1969). Thus, different levels of intensity of the adult's recollection of aspects of the attachment-related parental behaviors during the important developmental stage of identity formation and consolidation (ages 6 to 11 years old) may affect how the adult interprets emotions in children. It follows that just as attachment behavior emerges in times of intense arousal, so too do the emotions associated with those behaviors. The affective dimension of a parent's personality may be characterized by early survival-related primary emotions. Accessing these primary emotions associated with early attachment relationships may provide information that will help to understand how a parent's current affective world may be organized.

Individuals are susceptible to a number of biases in remembering or reconstructing their past relationships (McCrae & Costa, 1988). What a person actually recalls or "forgets" often constitutes the most salient affects associated with the relationship (Pottharst, 1990). Mayman (1968, p. 304, cited in Fishler et al., 1990) suggests that early memories

> . . . are not autobiographical truths, nor even "memories" in the strictest sense of the term, but largely retrospective inventions developed to express psychological truths rather than objective truths about a person's life. . . .

It is hypothesized that a person's adult character structure is organized around object-relational themes that intrude projectively into the structure and content of his or her early memories just as they occur repetitively in his or her relations with significant persons in his or her life. In part, these biases may be the focal point of individual variations in parents' interpretations of emotions in children.

Certain core cognitions and cognitive-affective sequences learned originally in particular affective states, such as emotional responses to abusive parental behaviors or traumatic separations from an important attachment figure, may become evident when those states are revived (Bowlby, 1973; Harvey et al., 1961). These emotional states may be kinetically revived when the adult performs child-rearing behaviors similar to the ones when intense emotion was experienced as a child. For example, disciplining a child may evoke old emotions and influence the adult's cognitions and perceptions of the child. Recollections of these "hot cognitions" may lead to specific patterns of emotional labeling. How these specific revived emotional states may influence a parent's perception of emotions in children is important to consider.

A Model of Early Childhood Emotions and Parental Affective Frameworks

A *parental affective framework* is defined as the characteristic affect (that is, all the emotions, feelings, and moods that accompany a cognition) that an adult, in the role of parent, uses to interpret and respond to the behaviors and emotional displays of a child. There are at least three affective domains of early childhood experiences that are critical to the development of these frameworks: (1) the qualities of parental warmth, coldness, acceptance, or rejection experienced by the child (Rohner, 1986), (2) the child's emotional responses to the methods of control used by his or her parents to achieve compliance (Harvey et al., 1961), and (3) individual experiences such as depression and a history of separation and loss from primary attachment figures (Bowlby, 1973). Sociocultural influences such as poverty, stress, and cultural-emotional display rules (Thoits, 1989) provide additional contemporary influences

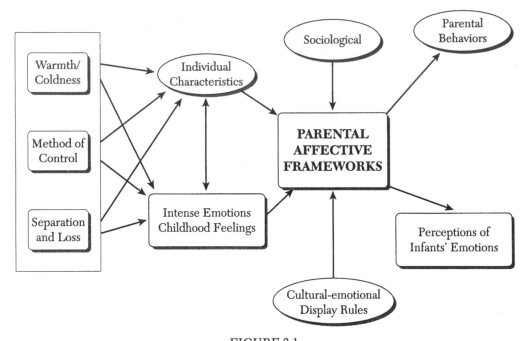

FIGURE 3.1
A theoretical model of factors influencing parental perceptions
of infants' and children's emotions.

on parental affective frameworks. Figure 3.1 illustrates this model of early emotionally charged childhood experiences. Mediated by the temperament and unique characteristics of the child, these three domains provide the template for the formation of parental affective frameworks.

This model provides a conceptual basis for understanding how childhood emotional experiences may lead to individual parental affective frameworks in which interpretations of emotions in children are based.

The First Domain of Parental Affect Frameworks: The Warmth Dimension

Parental acceptance and rejection form the warmth dimension of parenting (Roh-

ner, 1986). Rohner argues that two dimensions consistently emerge in studies of children's perceptions of parenting practices: parental control (ranging from strict to permissive) and acceptance and rejection (warmth). The warmth factor is the strongest predictor of a myriad of developmental outcomes for children.

Warm parents are those who show their love or affection toward children physically or verbally, but not excessively and within standards defined by their culture or community (Rohner, 1986). Rejecting parents are defined as those who dislike, disapprove of, or resent their children. Rejection is seen in parental behavior as hostility and aggression or parental indifference and neglect. Behaviors defined as warm have been consistently identified across many cultural groups (Rohner, 1975). In a cross-cultural study examining maternal behavior in six cultures around the world, mothers observed to be warm were characterized by high general warmth and low general hostility (Minturn & Lambert, 1964). Control of the children was achieved through praise rather than through punishment and threat of punishment. Maternal warmth did not include routine caretaking.

Parental warmth results in a child feeling loved and accepted (Rohner, 1975). Conversely, parental rejection leads to a child feeling unloved and rejected. Thus, Rohner's theory lends support to the proposal that the emotions associated with early parent-child interactions may serve as a basis for the general affective style of the individual. But it is not simply the qualities of warmth and acceptance that contribute to the formation of affective frameworks. It is also the emotional response of the child to the methods of control used by their primary attachment figures.

The Second Domain: Method of Parental Control

Parental control is defined as all the psychological and physical techniques used to coerce, discipline, or punish children to achieve compliance to the parent's unique values, beliefs, and child-rearing goals. Methods of parental control provide the child with protection in the form of guidelines, culturally defined rules and standards for behavior, predictability, and a sense of competency that, in turn, contributes to a general feeling of security or insecurity.

Most adults can recall the discipline, punishment, or consequences they received from their parents and can describe their emotional responses during those experiences. Clinical interviews with adults describing the types of discipline they received as a child typically elicit emotional responses such as "I felt so angry when I got spanked," "I hated when my mom would pull her crying routine if I had done something wrong," and "I was very frightened whenever my father yelled at me for not following directions." Whether they were spanked, lectured, ignored, blamed, or given other negative consequences as a child, the emotional reactions they experienced were likely to be intense and long remembered into adulthood.

Five methods of parental control were identified by Harvey et al. (1961) and are named for the psychological states they tend to induce. These methods lead to the formation of the child's expectation and belief system or worldview. Each method induces one or a combination of at least five superordinate psychological states of *fear, denigration, shame, guilt,* and *autonomy.* The defining characteristic of the first four methods is that control of a child is achieved by inflicting physical or psychological pain. Control is achieved in the last method, autonomy, by the creation of choice, exploration, and empirical testing.

The affective states that evolve from these methods of control are neither the direct nor often the intentional goal of parental behavior. Parents generally aim to achieve short-term compliance of the child to parental demands. What the child also may learn and internalize are the *emotions* the parent displays with their method of control. For example, a fearful African American mother's goal may be to protect her children from what she perceives as a world hostile to Black children by the use of power-assertive and physically coercive discipline tactics (McLoyd, 1990). The children may develop secure attachment relationships based on a strong belief that their mother had positive intent to protect. Yet, they may concurrently have a high degree of fear and anxiety as part of their affective repertoire stemming from these early control methods. Based on extensive studies with adults, Harvey et al. (1961) describe the parental behaviors for each method of control and the resulting belief system or worldview that evolves in the child. Intense emotions are associated with each of these belief systems and their antecedent methods of control.

The Third Domain: Separation and Loss

Separations from primary attachment figures during childhood and unresolved experiences of separation and loss may reciprocally influence the parent-child attachment relationship (Cohn, Cowan, Cowan, & Pearson, 1992; Main & Hess, 1990). Main, Kaplan, & Cassidy (1990) suggest that traumatic loss of parents or other attachment figures and abuse by attachment figures are considered likely to overwhelm the developing attachment behavioral system.

Bowlby (1973) and others identified a universal sequence of children's emotional reactions to separation from an attachment figure, consisting of protest, anger, depression, sadness and mourning, and eventually detachment and defensive avoidance of the feelings associated with the loss of the attachment figure. These intense emotions may substantially contribute to the development of an ongoing emotional style in the adult.

Individual Factors and Parental Affective Frameworks

The formation of the affective domains of the parenting role is suggested from an understanding of the subjective nature of emotions. Emde (1993, p. 9) notes that emotions must not be considered reactive, intermittent processes but argues that at a psychological level, emotions are organized and anchored in the individual's unique experience. "Each individual actively pulls together or freshly 'constructs' the meaning of each emotion using particular memories and expectations."

Another factor influencing sensitivity to infant cues and how mothers interpret emotions in children, though not necessarily part of early experiences, is the mother's current level of depression (Crittenden & Bonvillian, 1984; Goodman & Brumley, 1990). Studies have clearly established that a mother's current level of depression interferes with her interactions with her infant and children (Belle et al., 1982) and her perceptions of emotions (Goodman & Brumley, 1990). In one study, depressed mothers' perceptions of infant emotions reflected the emotions associated with their depression, such as sadness, anxiety, and lack of pleasure (Zahn-Waxler & Wagner, 1993). This group also viewed the infants as more fearful and less joyous than nondepressed mothers.

How mothers interpret emotions in children may reflect more contemporary issues (for example, current level of stress, social support, or marital relationships), but early experiences may provide the emotional template and framework.

Sociocultural Influences on Parental Affective Frameworks

Sociocultural factors may serve as important determinants for the interpretation of emotions in young children by parents. Less is known about sociocultural factors that may contribute to group and individual differences in how parents interpret emotions in children (Thoits, 1989). Sociocultural factors include sociological factors (for example, socioeconomic status and other demographics) and the cultural origins of child-rearing practices. These practices hinge on parental beliefs about children and related cultural values.

The cultural context includes the child-rearing practices that socialize affect (Garcia Coll & Meyer, 1993). Super and Harkness (1986, p. 557) note, "The responses of parents and other caretakers to children's emotional displays also are directed by ideas, often implicit, about the development of the self in the context of the particular culture."

Beliefs about spoiling and their relation to parenting behaviors of responsiveness to infant cries, holding, and displays of affect are an underexplored area of research in child development (Pascoe & Solomon,

1994; Smyke, 1996). Overconcern about spoiling has been found to be associated with parental attitudes of neglect and abuse in the few studies that have been conducted. In a study of 68 low-income African American mothers, Smyke (1996) found significant differences in developmental expectations of children based on the degree of concern about the long-term impact of spoiling five-month-old infants. In comparison to the mothers who had fewer concerns about spoiling, the mothers with more concerns about spoiling scored higher on measures of inappropriate developmental expectations and lower on parental empathy. A new pattern of beliefs about spoiling was also suggested from the findings in this study. Some mothers anecdotally reported that spoiling was good. They thought one could and should spoil an infant less than five months of age although they still cautioned that "too much" spoiling would be bad for the child.

The findings of these studies suggest that a number of cultural, social, and individual factors, including certain early experiences and current level of depression, may influence how mothers interpret emotions in children.

Parental affective frameworks begin with the earliest emotions associated with experiences of warmth or coldness and acceptance or rejection by a primary attachment figure (Rohner, 1986). This framework is further solidified throughout early childhood by the emotions evoked by physical or psychological methods of control and experiences of separation or loss of a primary attachment figure. Contemporary sociocultural and individual factors such as cultural beliefs, poverty, and depression also contribute to the formation of a parent's characteristic style of interpreting emotions in children.

These domains and their distinctive cultural and socioeconomic determinants compose the model of early childhood experiences. The emotions that may be associated with these domains may be critical to understanding the formation and development of enduring parental affective frameworks used by African American parents to interpret the emotions of children. Methods of control used by parents to achieve compliance in children may carry with them intense emotions that will define the child's personality and emotional style in very concrete ways.

Psychological strain stemming from neighborhood violence and poverty, coupled with cultural values for obedience in children, may encourage the parent to adopt specific disciplinary strategies. The strategies require less effort; they include, for example, physical punishment, commanding without explanation, and reliance on authority rather than reasoning, explaining, or negotiation (McLoyd, 1990).

A Study of Early Experiences of Parents and Perceptions of Emotions in Infants

The foundation for this study is the premise that intense affects are associated with the model of two domains of early parent-child interactions: warmth and acceptance or coldness and rejection, the method of

parental control used to achieve compliance in the child. The emotions associated with these affective domains of early childhood experiences may be distinctive and may vary according to dimensional aspects of emotions. The two dimensional qualities of emotions are a hedonic dimension, ranging from pleasure to nonpleasure, and an arousal (or activation) dimension going from low arousal to high arousal (Emde, Osofsky, & Butterfield, 1993). The dimensional aspects of parental affective frameworks may be more closely associated with early childhood emotions and experiences than a more straightforward categorical view. In addition, there may be a number of similar categories of emotions used by parents with sharply contrasting early experiences. For example, a person who experienced the early loss of a parent may have a tendency to use a high number of sad emotions. But people who were severely abused by their parent may also use a high number of sad emotions (Butterfield, 1993). What may differ are the dimensional qualities associated with the sad emotion words. One set of sad emotion words may reflect higher levels of arousal (for example, disappointed versus miserable). These experiences may also differentially influence the hedonic tone (pleasurable, unpleasurable) dimension of the emotions associated with the framework.

Background of Study

This study was designed to examine the associations of recollections of maternal behaviors and specific behavioral aspects of the early parent-child relationship with the perceptions of emotions of children by a sample of African American mothers. The research design included a projective technique that assessed internal representations of feelings and emotions related to children and self-report questionnaires on current affective states of depression (Radloff, 1977) and the recalled maternal behaviors and discipline techniques and childhood feelings of security, acceptance, and rejection.

A convenience sample of 102 low- to middle-income African American mothers was recruited from the greater metropolitan area of a large, urban midwestern city in the United States. Names of potential participants were also obtained from several agencies serving low-income families as well as at a popular three-day Black Arts festival held in the city. All mothers approached agreed to participate in the study "The Feelings of Black Children."

All of the participants in the study were mothers, with a mean age of 31 years and an average of two children. There was a normal distribution of socioeconomic status (computed by summing the number of years of education and the amount of income reported by the mother). The majority of the sample (80 percent) had received a high school education or more, and 60 percent were employed. Thirty-six percent of the sample were married or living together; 33 percent were divorced, separated, or widowed; and 30 percent were never married.

The IFEEL measure and self-report questionnaires assessed the dependent variables, perceptions of children's emotions and levels of current depression. *The Infant's Facial Expressions of Emotions from Pictures* (IFEEL; Emde et al., 1986) was used for participants to record their perceptions of children's emotions. The IFEEL is a projective method that measures a mother's interpretation rather than accuracy of perception of emotions and does not predict actual behaviors. The IFEEL consists of a set of 30 color pictures of infant boys and girls portraying a variety of emotions. Twenty-five of the pictures are of Caucasian children, and five of the pictures are of an African American child. Figure 3.2 shows several of the pictures from the IFEEL. Based on a computer-scoring program created by the authors of the IFEEL, a reference sample of mothers' responses to the pictures (Figure 3.2) were assigned to 12 discrete categories of emotions. (See Applebaum et al., 1993, for full discussion of psychometric properties of the IFEEL.) These categories of emotions are surprise, interest, joy, content, passive, sad, caution/shy, distress, guilt/shame, fear, and anger. Scores for the levels of arousal and hedonic tone (that is, positive, pleasurable qualities) of each emotion word within the 12 categories were based on a rating by the reference sample (100 Caucasian, middle-class mothers of infants) used in the development of the measure (Emde et al., 1986).

The free response method of categorizing emotions of the set of IFEEL pictures was used. The mothers viewed the pictures, one by one, and were given the following instructions: "This book contains some pictures of babies' facial expressions. Please tell us in one word, if possible, the strongest and clearest feeling that each baby is expressing. There are no right or

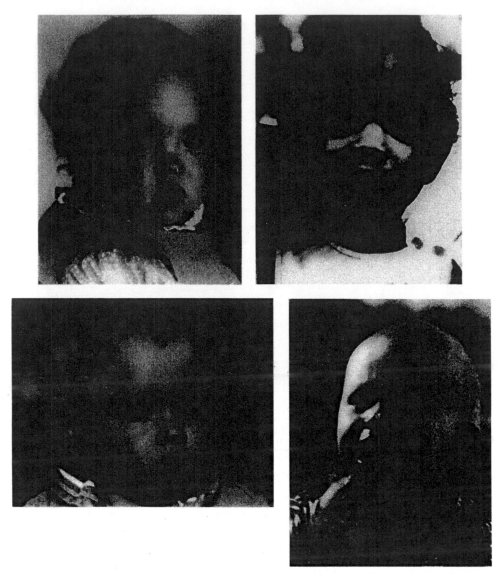

FIGURE 3.2
Sample of pictures from IFEEL measure.

wrong answers. Please answer what first comes to your mind." A computer program categorized the responses into 12 categories of emotions (Applebaum et al., 1993) and assigned a score of hedonic tone and level of arousal for each category.

A self-report questionnaire that con-ceptually reflects the model of early childhood experiences (Figure 3.1), was administered. The *Parent-Child Relationship Questionnaire* assesses an adult's recollection of her mother's specific behaviors, discipline techniques, and her affective responses to those behaviors during her childhood, defined as ages 6 to 12 years old. (see Lewis, 1993, for a complete description of the development of this measure.) The PPQ is composed of three subscales. Part A measures the recalled maternal behaviors of warmth or coldness and acceptance or rejection. Examples of items from Part A are "told me she wished that I'd never been born" and "ridiculed and made fun of me," which assesses the domain of rejection. Other items such as "hugged and kissed me" and "spoke to me in a warm and friendly voice," assesses the domain of maternal warmth.

Part B measures the discipline techniques used by the respondent's mother. Examples of items from Part B, which assessed the physical, psychological techniques used to control and discipline the respondent as a child, are "When I was disobedient or did something she disapproved of my mother spanked me with a switch," "did not allow me to talk on the telephone," "threatened to hit or spank me without doing it," and "physically abused me."

Part C measures the specific emotions the respondent recalled feeling as a child in response to each behavior. Part C assessed childhood emotions in response to maternal behaviors. All items were prefaced with the stem, "As a child I felt." Examples of responses in this section are "my mother could do anything," "my mother wanted to get the things for me she felt I needed," "loved," and "like a burden to my mother."

The respondent rated each item for frequency of occurrence on a Likert scale of 1 = *never* to 5 = *always*. All items were prefaced with the stem, "When I was about 6 to 12 years old my mother. . . ."

The Childhood Experiences of Racial Acceptance/Rejection Scale (CERARS; Lewis, 1993) consists of 14 items that assess recalled maternal statements about race-related aspects of the child's physical features that may have resulted in feelings of acceptance, rejection, or shame. It also assesses the perception of the mother as a model for handling racial conflicts and ethnic pride. Examples of items from this scale began with the stem, "When I was about 6 to 12 years old my mother" and included items such as "treated my light-skinned brothers or sisters differently than me," "teased me about my large lips or nose," and "taught me to be proud of my racial heritage."

See Lewis (1993) for a more complete description of other variables assessed in this questionnaire.

The measures were administered to the mothers in their homes, places of employment, or the at home of a friend. Prior to administration of the PPQ, the respondent was asked to first think of the name of the elementary school they attended, their favorite teacher, their most hated teacher, the place they lived when ages 6 to 12, and where they slept. They were also asked to recall their nickname during that period. This procedure was designed to stimulate the affective environment they experienced during those developmental years.

Findings from the Study

This study was concerned with hypotheses about the correlation between a model of early childhood experiences and outcome measures of perceived and current emotions. The first questions concerned the correlation between African American mothers' recall of how they were parented and disciplined with the childhood feelings produced by these styles and techniques. Large and significant correlations were found in support of the hypothesis that specific childhood feelings would be associated with different maternal styles. The second set of hypotheses examined the correlation between childhood feelings and the interpretations of emotions of infants depicted in photographs from the IFEEL measure. Indirect support was found for these hypotheses. It was found that patterns of significant correlations between childhood feelings and the perceptions of children's emotions varied based on the respondent's recollection of her mother's behavioral style. Similarly, the recalled childhood feelings did not have a straightforward correspondence to the dimensional qualities (hedonic tone and arousal) of perceived emotions but also varied according to the level of maternal styles.

The final set of questions tested the hypothesis that the same model of early childhood experiences that predicted the interpretations of emotions in children would also predict current levels of depression and anxiety. Strong support was found for this hypothesis. The statistical analyses and results for each of these predictions follows.

Factors from Parenting Practices Questionnaire

To determine the maternal styles, discipline techniques, and childhood feelings recalled by the respondents, factor analyses were completed on each of three sections that com-

prised the Parenting Practices Questionnaire. (see Lewis, 1993, for a more detailed description of this analysis.) Each individual was scored on each factor, and these scores were used in the analyses. Cronbach's Alphas, computed for each scale composed of items for each factor, ranged from .66 to .92.

The maternal style factors were: *warmth, autonomy,* and teaching *social-racial skills.* Two of these factors, warmth and autonomy, were consistent with parental styles described in the literature, and the third factor, social-racial skills, based on items unique to the present questionnaire, may reflect what may be the cultural values of this sample of African American women. The warmth factor included positively loaded items that reflected a warm style and negatively loaded items that reflected a cold and rejecting maternal style. The items reflecting a warm maternal style dealt with physical demonstration of affection ("my mother hugged and kissed me"), unconditional acceptance ("my mother appeared to understand my problems and worries"), humor ("my mother teased and joked with me"), and nurturance or care ("my mother comforted me whenever I was hurt or sick"). Items that reflected a cold maternal style included emotional unavailability ("was preoccupied with her own problems"), clear rejection ("told me she wished that I'd never been born"), intentionally negative or hurtful behaviors ("ridiculed and made fun of me"), and inconsistency ("was inconsistent in enforcing the rules").

The second maternal style factor included items encouraging autonomy as well as negatively loaded items encouraging dependency. The autonomy style included items such as "encouraged me to think for myself." The dependency end of the continuum included items such as "tried to make me dependent on her." This style also included items that reflected an autocratic maternal style that included behaviors such as "forbade me to argue or disagree with her."

The styles labeled teaching social-racial skills included such maternal behaviors as "stressed the importance of education," "taught me to listen to others' points of view, even when they were very different from my own," and "taught me how to deal with prejudice." This factor also included items reflecting racial ambivalence that dealt with attitudes and behaviors about physical racial features, for example, "said she wished I was a different skin color" or "teased me about my large hips/buttocks."

These three factors are strongly and positively correlated with each other but were used as separate factors for subsequent analysis as they measured qualitatively different aspects of maternal behaviors of interest in this study. The correlations among all the predictor variables are discussed in detail in Lewis (1993).

MATERNAL DISCIPLINE FACTORS

Three methods of psychological and physical discipline were identified and labeled *belittlement, restriction,* and *corporal punishment.* Belittlement included items denoting denigration of the person ("criticized me personally when punishing me") and the induction of guilt and shame ("tried to make me mind her by making me feel guilty" and "shamed me in front of my playmates when I misbehaved"). Physical and emotional abuse were also part of this factor as well as noncontingent hitting (for example, "hit me, even when I didn't do anything wrong") and threats of expulsion (for example, "threatened to call the police or other authorities to come and take me away"). This factor accounted for 32 percent of the variance, the most of the three factors. Restriction included items such as "did not allow me to talk on the telephone" and "gave me restrictions or grounded me." Corporal punishment was composed of physical discipline methods of spanking.

These three factors were highly independent, the highest interfactor correlation being .29 between belittlement and restriction. Belittlement and corporal punishment were not significantly correlated ($r = -.18$), nor was there a significant correlation between corporal punishment and restriction.

CHILDHOOD FEELINGS FACTORS

A second-order factor analysis of the original 16 childhood feeling items yielded three factors labeled *security, guilt-shame,* and *succorance.* Security accounted for 42 percent of the variance. Items in this factor included feelings of simple security, feeling loved, predictability ("I could count on my mother to get the things she felt I needed"), importance ("I was important in my mother's eyes"), zestful curiosity, confidence, and a sense of self-agency ("I loved to try new things"). These factors reflected emotions of low to intense arousal but positive hedonic tone. Insecurity was composed of feelings labeled disengagement, indifference, hate, anger, and feeling alone. These items reflected intense emotional arousal and intense negative hedonic tone ("I felt defiant of my mother" and "tense and fearful around my mother").

Guilt-shame accounted for 12 percent of the variance. The items included in this factor were feelings of the sacrifice made by the mother to raise the child, feelings of guilt ("if I disobeyed I had let my mother down"), shame ("I felt like hiding because I was so ashamed when I broke the rules"), and what has been labeled respect ("my mother was widely respected by other adults").

Succorance, defined in the American Heritage Dictionary as "relief" or "provision of assistance or help in time of distress," accounted for 9 percent of the variance. The items that composed this factor included feeling "a great need to take care of my mother" and "responsible for my mother's safety," as well as items of indulgence and symbiosis; for example, "spoiled rotten by my mother," "like I could get away with anything," and "I might lose my mother's love when I misbehaved."

These three factors were highly independent with no significant correlations between any of them. The next section addresses the associations between the three sets of early experiences and perceptions of emotions of children depicted in the IFEEL measure.

Correlations of Maternal Styles, Discipline Techniques, and Childhood Feelings with Perception of IFEEL Emotions

Maternal style variables (warmth, autonomy, and social-racial skills), discipline techniques (belittlement, restriction, corporal punishment), and childhood feelings (security, guilt-shame, and succorance) were correlated with the responses to the IFEEL measure. Three continuous dependent variables were derived from the IFEEL measure: (1) the number of times each of the individual emotion categories was selected, (2) the mean hedonic tone (or positive qualities) of the words for the category, and (3) the mean arousal associated with the words for the category.

An examination of the frequency distributions of each emotion category revealed that two of the IFEEL categories, guilt/shame and disgust/dislike, were used by less than 1 percent of the respondents. These two categories were dropped from the analyses, leaving 10 categories of perceived emotions with their associated hedonic tone and levels of arousal. The retained categories are surprise, interest, joy, content, passive, sad, caution/shy, anger, distress, and fear.

In other studies using the IFEEL, the socioeconomic status and age of the respondent have been reported as significantly correlated with some of the emotion categories (Butterfield, 1993; Zahn-Waxler & Wagner, 1993). These two variables are not the primary focus of this study. Therefore, what is reported are partial correlation coefficients controlling for the respondent's age and SES.

Partial correlations were computed between the nine childhood experiences variables and the sets of three IFEEL variables (mean number of times each emotion category was used, mean hedonic tone, and mean score for arousal) for the entire sample. Modest significant correlations were found. The patterns of correlations suggest that the women's perceptions of their mothers' general parenting styles, the discipline they experienced, and their childhood feelings of security were differentially correlated with the types of emotions they saw in the pictures of infants.

To address the hypothesis that the patterns of associations between the predictor and dependent measures would differ based on the maternal style of the respondent reported, the sample was divided (by median split) into groups according to maternal style. This split resulted in six groups: high warmth versus low warmth, high in fostering autonomy versus low in fostering autonomy, and high in teaching social-racial skills and low in teaching social-racial skills. This grouping was done because the items representing the high and low end of each maternal style variable, though strongly and negatively correlated with each other, were composed of qualitatively different items, indicating that the scales were not bipolar. For example, items with a positive factor loading for the warmth factor included behaviors such as hugs and kisses that were absent from the low end of the warmth factor. Low warmth included items such as "said she wished I had never been born," which was absent in the high warmth end of the scale.

The partial correlations between the childhood feelings variables (security, guilt-shame, and succorance) with the dependent IFEEL variables for each of the high and low maternal style groups were computed. By dividing the sample into groups based on maternal style, the corre-

lation coefficients were much stronger and distinctive patterns of correlations emerged. These correlations are presented in Tables 3.1 through 3.3.

FREQUENCY OF CATEGORIES

Overall, the highest number of significant correlations between childhood feelings and the selection of various categories of emotions in the groups occurred when the mothers were recalled as low in warmth (or cold) and for those who were recalled as encouraging dependency (or low in encouraging autonomy). These same childhood experiences were associated with higher levels of depression. Maternal styles fostering dependency were also associated with higher levels of depression but not anxiety. This style was also highly correlated with the belittlement method of control. So, respondents whose mothers encouraged dependency and who felt belittled and insecure reported higher levels of depression. These patterns of correlations suggest childhood feelings of powerlessness and lack of self-agency or control.

These associations suggest that childhood feelings of insecurity may be associated with a later parental affective framework that is more restricted and concrete cognitive style where children are perceived with a limited range of emotions. This group of respondents chose fewer interest words and more anger and passive words. There may be a wide variety of dimensional qualities associated with these emotion words. As noted earlier, this combination of categories of emotion words suggests an aroused but passive affective state. These findings suggest that one way

TABLE 3.1

Partial Correlations between Childhood Feelings and Frequency of Categories
of IFEEL Based on Perception of Maternal Style

Childhood Feelings	Maternal Style					
	Warmth		*Autonomy*		*Social-racial skills*	
	High	Low	High	Low	High	Low
Secure	—	Surprise −.24°	Interest .31°	Anger −.27°	Content .24°	—
	Passive −.32°	—	Passive −.30°	—	—	Sad −.27°
	—	Anger −.26°	—	Anger −.25°	—	—
Guilt-Shame	—	Interest .24°	—	Interest −.27°	—	—
	—	Passive −.45°	—	Content .24°	—	—
	—	—	—	Passive −.27°	—	—
Succorance	Distress −.25°	Distress .23°	Joy .25°	Shy −.28°	Distress −.28	Distress .33°
	—	Anger −.26°	—	Anger −.26°	—	—

Note: ° = p ≤ .05; °° = p. ≤ .001

children might affectively respond to their parents' guilt-induction method of control is with ambivalence between obligation and rebellion.

THE AROUSAL DIMENSION

This pattern of perceptions of emotions in the IFEEL suggests such wide variability in dimensional aspects that no specific pattern emerged. This would make intuitive sense in that depression may be associated with lower levels of arousal and anxiety may be associated with higher levels of arousal,

effectively canceling each other out. It would also make intuitive sense that both these affects would not be particularly associated with positive qualities of any emotions for respondents who felt depressed, anxious, and grew up with mothers who were cold and rejecting.

In contrast, childhood feelings of guilt-shame increased the arousal in some categories and decreased the arousal in other categories based on different maternal styles. These patterns were most pronounced in less-than-adequate maternal

TABLE 3.2

Partial Correlations between Childhood Feelings and Hedonic Tone
of IFEEL Based on Perception of Maternal Style

Childhood Feelings	Maternal Style					
	Warmth		*Autonomy*		*Social-Racial skills*	
	High	Low	High	Low	High	Low
Secure	Anger .36°	—	Distress −.26°	—	Interest .29°	Anger .28°
	Shy .37°	—	—	—	Passive .46°	Fear .47°
Guilt-Shame	—	Joy .26°	—	Distress .34°	—	Joy .24°
	—	Distress .30°	—	—	—	Passive .31°
	—	—	—	—	—	Distress .41°°
Succorance	Surprise −.31°	Suprise .38°	Passive .38°	Passive .39°	Passive .50°	Passive .33°
	Passive .47°	Joy .32°	—	Anger .34°	Anger .42°°	Distress .26°
	—	Passive .38°	—	Fear .35°	—	—
	—	—	—	Distress .25°	—	—

Note: ° = p ≤ .05; °° = p. ≤ .001

styles. It is noteworthy that guilt-shame was the only childhood emotion associated with higher levels of arousal in the anger words used in two maternal style groups, that is, those mothers perceived as warm and those perceived as low in teaching social-racial skills. Childhood feelings of guilt-shame seemed to intensify the emotions selected for children in these two groups, suggesting a parental affective framework that includes more intense emotions. So, childhood feelings of guilt and shame may be associated with a parental affective framework that includes a wide lexicon of emotion words to describe the feelings of children.

HEDONIC TONE

Childhood feelings of security were predicted to be related to the overall positive qualities of words used to describe children in the IFEEL. This was only true for a

TABLE 3.3

Partial Correlations between Childhood Feelings and Arousal of IFEEL Emotions
Based on Perception of Maternal Style

| Childhood Feelings | Maternal Style | | | | | |
| | Warmth | | Autonomy | | Social-racial skills | |
	High	Low	High	Low	High	Low
Secure	Anger −.38°	—	Passive −.38°	Passive −.34°	Interest .25°	Anger −.32°
	Distress .43°	—	Distress .33°	—	—	—
Guilt-Shame	Anger .34°	—	—	Content .29°	—	Anger .28°
	Distress −.29°	—	—	Passive −.34°	—	—
	—	—	Distress .45°°	—	—	—
Succorance	Sad −.30°	Interest −.26°	Interest −.39°	—	—	Interest −.28°
	—	Distress −.29°	Content −.34°°	—	Sad −.33°	Distress −.29°
	—	—	Sad −.40°°	—	—	—

Note: ° = p ≤ .05; °° = p. ≤ .001

few emotion categories. Instead, feelings of succorance toward the mother, regardless of her perceived inadequacies, were correlated with an increased overall positive hedonic tone for many of the emotions used to describe children. This relationship was most pronounced in the low warmth and low autonomy and low social-racial groups. Thus, for respondents whose mothers were lowest in the maternal qualities generally viewed as desirable, their childhood feelings of succorance were associated with the use of words to describe children that had more positive qualities.

This childhood emotion seemed to have a compensatory effect for less-than-adequate maternal styles. The desire in these respondents to provide for their mothers or the feelings of gratitude they felt despite mothers reported as cold and rejecting enabled them to see more positive qualities in the perceptions of emotions of children. In addition, feelings of succorance generally decreased the arousal associated with a number of different emotions in all the maternal style groups. It was as if feelings of succorance had a type of dampening or lowering effect on the arousal associated with the emotion words selected to describe children. Whether this childhood feeling, defined in this study as feelings of interdependence, responsibility to the mother, is associated with other personality traits or individual characteristics like maturity, remains to be studied.

The other noteworthy significant correlations of early experiences are with the use of the category of emotions of joy and distress. In other studies using the IFEEL measure, the higher frequency of use of the joy/distress category was associated with childhood experiences of child abuse and current affects of depression (Butterfield, 1993).

The use of the category of joy emotions was positively correlated to childhood feelings of succorance in the group that perceived their mothers as high in encouraging autonomy. The dimensional qualities of this category of emotions were positively correlated to childhood feelings in two different maternal style groups. The hedonic tone of joy was positively correlated to both feelings of guilt-shame and succorance in the group who perceived their mothers as low in warmth (cold) and was positively correlated to feelings of guilt-shame in the group perceiving their mothers as low in teaching social-racial skills.

More distress was perceived in children by respondents who felt succorance for mothers who were perceived as cold and low in teaching social-racial skills. So, as feelings of succorance increased for mothers who were perceived as cold or low in teaching social skills, there was also an increase in the number of distress emotions selected for infants. As maternal warmth

and teaching of social-racial skills increased and the respondents felt succorance, the distress emotions chosen for children decreased. A different pattern of relationships emerged for the dimensional qualities of the distress category.

The arousal associated with distress emotions increased with the respondents who felt secure and were reared by mothers who were warm and encouraging of autonomy. In these same maternal style groups, the childhood feeling of guilt-shame was associated with a decrease in the arousal of distress words. So, though both groups of respondents reporting these childhood feelings used distress words to describe the emotions of children, one group's words were associated with higher levels of arousal and a different pattern of hedonic tone. Respondents feeling guilt-shame chose words that reflected less arousal and more positive hedonic tone for the distress words.

Summary and Conclusion

A model of early childhood experiences as a way to understand individual differences in the perceptions of emotions of children by African American mothers was presented. The final model based on these data resulted in three correlated maternal styles, discipline techniques, and childhood feelings and highlighted what could be cultural values of this sample. The primary hypothesis based on this model was that the childhood feelings associated with these experiences would be similar to emotions used to describe the feelings of children. Thus, the results of these data, though not always in the direction predicted, provide support for the viability of this model. The straight linear relationships that were predicted between these early experiences and perceived emotions were not evident. These results suggest a more complex association between the early affective experiences and later interpretation of emotions in children.

These early childhood experiences seem to be associated with more stable elements of personality and support the thesis that they contribute to the formation of a parent's characteristic style of responding to the emotional displays of children. The findings of this study supported Harvey and colleagues (1961) proposal that parent-child interactions lead to the formation of specific affective states. For example, in this sample the use of belittlement as a discipline technique was clearly correlated with childhood feelings of insecurity and current affective states in the adult of higher levels of depression and trait-like anxiety. These results replicate other findings through the strong correlations between early methods of parental control and current states of depression in adults (Harvey et al., 1961). However, there was no correlation between belittlement and the other two childhood feelings labeled guilt-shame and succorance. These feelings most likely evolved from a different maternal style, one that taught social skills and racial pride.

The results from these data also support the central premise of Rohner's (1984) theory that maternal warmth and acceptance contribute to feelings of childhood security and other positive affective outcomes and maternal coldness and rejection contribute to feelings of insecurity. Findings from cross-cultural studies guided by Rohner's (1986) theory suggest that the *cultural context* defines the perceptions of maternal behaviors classified as warm or cold and subsequently feelings of security. Based on the findings of this study, this thesis also appears to be true intraculturally, that is, when African American culture is viewed as a subculture within United States society.

CATEGORIES AND DIMENSIONAL ASPECTS OF EMOTIONS

Childhood feelings of security or insecurity did not simply lead to the selection of more positive or negative emotion words. Also, feelings of insecurity did not simply lead to the choice of more negative, higher arousal words to describe children. Instead, these correlations depended on the level of maternal style. Patterns of significant correlations between childhood feelings and emotion words used to describe children's feelings varied based on the respondent's *perception* of her mother's behavioral style. Similarly, the dimensional qualities of recalled childhood feelings did not have a straightforward correspondence to the dimensional qualities of perceived emotions but also varied according to the level of maternal styles. At different levels of each maternal style, different patterns of correlations emerged between each of the three childhood feelings with perceived emotions of children depicted in the IFEEL measure.

The variety of significant but differing patterns of correlation between childhood feelings and projected emotions for each group suggest that perception of maternal style may be an important mediator variable between childhood feelings and interpretations of emotions of infants. The variation in patterns of significant correlations based on the dimensional aspects of the emotions selected suggest that these too may be important factors for a clearer understanding of these complex relationships.

Cold and rejecting maternal styles were associated with childhood feelings of insecurity in some respondents and feelings of succorance in others. Early experiences of maternal rejection may also have been associated with the formation of psychological defenses that then mediate the interpretation of the emotions of children. Childhood feelings of security and succorance reported by respondents of cold and rejecting mothers may have also been due to other early experiences. Less-than-adequate maternal behavioral styles may have been compensated by other positive childhood experiences such as support from other adults or extended family members, strong attachment relationships with the father, older siblings, or other caregivers, or simply the resilience and temperament of the child. These childhood feelings and experiences with less adequate mothers may increase the ability of the adult, when in the role of parent, to be empathic with children. In addition, these experiences may contribute to the formation of parental affective frameworks that reflect an ability to see a wide variety of emotions for children that have more positive qualities and lower levels of arousal associated with them. Evidence for this spec-

ulation is suggested by the results where there was a consistent pattern of positive correlations between childhood feelings of succorance and the hedonic tone of the words used to describe children by respondents who recalled their mothers as cold and rejecting.

RECOMMENDATIONS FOR
FUTURE STUDIES

A number of methodological issues in this study must be taken into account when interpreting the findings from this study. The critical dependent measure depicted a majority of pictures of White infants and was standardized on a middle-class White sample. The sample in this study was all Black. The choice was made to use the measure with no modifications on a pragmatic basis. Development and piloting of IFEEL measures with pictures of all-Black children was prohibitive due to limited resources. This issue has the most implications for the interpretations of the results based on the dimensional aspects of the dependent measure. The ratings of dimensional qualities of individual emotion words for level of arousal and hedonic tone may vary with speakers of Black English and variations of standard English (Smitherman, 1985). The distinctive patterns of results suggest that this concern was not a major problem. Even so, the use of a same-race measure may elicit even more clearly the patterns of associations between childhood affective states and the creation of parental affective frameworks used to interpret emotions by African American mothers.

The next step will be to replicate these

patterns of associations using this model in samples of Black parents from diverse regions of the country and parents from other ethnic groups. These studies will provide a test for the generalizability of the model. These results also suggest further studies are needed to extend findings from the perceptions of emotions in pictures of children to actual parenting behavior. Also needed are studies using longitudinal or cross-sectional designs that test specific hypotheses about maternal sensitivity, discipline methods, and interpretations of emotions by mothers and then examine the socioemotional outcomes as their infants develop.

These results suggest that the model of childhood experiences, maternal warmth or coldness and methods of control, may provide a way to sort out individual differences in the way African American mothers interpret the emotional cues of their children. Other childhood experiences may also act as a mediator between the childhood feelings resulting from a particular method of control and the later parental affective framework used to interpret emotions in children. The different patterns of correlations based on maternal style suggest the presence of other psychological processes and states underlying the choice and dimensional qualities of emotions used to describe children in the IFEEL measure. These other psychological processes, such as defensive denial or overidentification with an abusive or rejecting parent, may also have their origins in the same maternal styles but now serve as a filter in the associations between childhood feelings and the perceptions of emotions of children.

The original goal of this study was not to identify group differences based on culture; however, the distinctive aspects of maternal behaviors and childhood feelings found in this study suggest that there is an underlying cultural element. Future studies comparing African American samples to other ethnic groups matched for socioeconomic status and using multimodal and multivariate measures would offer support to a cultural element.

More research is necessary using models that first identify and incorporate the overarching cultural belief systems held by African American parents as a group at all income levels. Studies are needed that explore individual differences of both the parent and the child's developmental outcomes in normative samples of African American families. Each of these culturally bound child-rearing practices, cultural norms and values, and issues facing Black families needs systematic investigation with a focus on the impact on the emotional response of the child.

Note

1. The term "parent" in African American communities includes a broad range of primary caregivers. In this discussion, reference will be primarily made to the mother in order to be consistent with the literature referenced.

References

Ainsworth, M. D., Blehar, M. C., Waters, E., & Wall, S. (1978). *Patterns of attachment:*

A psychological study of the Strange Situation. Hillsdale, NJ: Erlbaum.

Applebaum, M. E., Butterfield, P. M., & Culp, R. (1993). Operating characteristics and psychometric properties of the IFEEL pictures. In R. N. Emde, J. D. Osofsky, & P. M. Butterfield (Eds.), *The IFEEL pictures: A new instrument for interpreting emotions* (pp. 97–130). Madison, CT: International Universities Press.

Bartz, K., & Levine, E. (1978). Child rearing by Black parents: A description and comparison to Anglo and Chicano parents. *Journal of Marriage and the Family, 40,* 709–719.

Belle, D., Longfellow, C., & Makosky, V. P. (1982). Stress, depression and the mother-child relationship: Report of a field study. *Journal of Sociology of the Family, 12,* 251–263.

Bowlby, J. (1969). *Attachment and loss: Vol. 1. Attachment.* New York: Basic Books.

Bowlby, J. (1973). *Attachment and loss: Vol. 2. Separation.* New York: Basic Books.

Boyd-Franklin, N. (1989). *Black families in therapy: A multisystems approach.* New York: Guilford.

Bradley, R. H., Elardo, R., Rosenthal, D., & Friend, J. H. (1979). A comparative study of the home environments of infants from single-parent and two-parent Black families. *Acta paedologica, 1*(1), 33–47.

Branch, C. W., & Newcombe, N. (1986). Racial attitude development among young Black children as a function of parental attitudes: A longitudinal and cross-sectional study. *Child Development 57,* 712–721.

Bretherton, I. (1987). New perspectives on attachment relations: Security, communication and internal working models. In J. D. Osofsky (Ed.), *Handbook of infant development* (pp. 1061–1100). New York: Wiley.

Bretherton, I., & Waters, E. (1985). Growing points of attachment theory and research. *Monographs of the Society for Research in Child Development, 50*(1–2, Serial No. 209).

Brown, J., Bakeman, R., Snyder, P., Fredrickson, W., Moran, S., & Hepler, R. (1975). Interactions of black inner-city mothers with their newborn infants. *Child Development, 46,* 677–686.

Burchinal, M. R., Follmer, A., & Bryant, D. M. (1996). The relationship of maternal social support and family structure with maternal responsiveness and child outcomes among African American families. *Developmental Psychology, 32,* 1073–1083.

Butterfield, P. (1993). Responses to IFEEL pictures in mothers at risk for child maltreatment. In R. N. Emde, J. D. Osofsky, & P. M. Butterfield (Eds.), *The IFEEL pictures: A new instrument for interpreting emotions* (pp. 161–174). Madison, CT: International Universities Press.

Cohn, D. A., Cowan, P. A., Cowan, C. P., & Pearson, J. (1992). Mothers' and fathers' working models of childhood attachment relationships, parenting styles, and child behavior. *Development and Psychopathology, 4,* 417–431.

Collins, J. W., & Hawkes, E. K. (1997). Racial differences in post-neonatal mortality in Chicago: What risk factors explain the Black infant's disadvantage? *Ethnicity and Health, 2,* 117–125.

Coner-Edwards, A., & Spurlock, J. (Eds.). (1988). *Black families in crisis: The middle class.* New York: Brunner/Mazel.

Crittenden, P. M., & Bonvillian, J. D. (1984). The relationship between maternal risk status and maternal sensitivity. *American Journal of Orthopsychiatry, 54,* 250–261.

Edelman, M. W. (1997). An advocacy agenda for Black families and children. In H. F. McAdoo (Ed.), *Black families* (3rd ed.; pp. 167–182). Thousand Oaks, CA: Sage.

Emde, R. N. (1993). A framework for viewing emotions. In R. N. Emde, J. D. Osofsky, & P. M. Butterfield (Eds.), *The IFEEL pictures: A new instrument for interpreting emotions* (pp. 3–26). Madison, CT: International Universities Press.

Emde, R. N. (1989). The infant's relationship experiences: Developmental and affective aspects. In R. N. Emde & A. J. Sameroff (Eds.), *Relationship disturbances in early childhood* (pp. 33–51). New York: Basic Books.

Emde, R. N., Osofsky, J. D., & Butterfield, P. M. (1986). *The IFEEL pictures: A new instrument for interpreting emotions.* Denver: Regents of the University of Colorado.

Fannon, F. (1963). *The wretched of the earth.* New York: Grove Weidenfeld.

Fishler, P. H., Sperling, M. B., & Carr, A. C. (1990). Assessment of adult relatedness: A review of empirical findings from object relations and attachment theories. *Journal of Personality Assessment, 55,* 499–520.

Fraiberg, S., Adelson, E., & Shapiro, V. (1975). Ghosts in the nursery: A psychoanalytic approach to the problems of impaired infant-mother relationships. *Journal of the American Academy of Child Psychiatry, 14,* 387–421.

Garcia Coll, C. T., & Meyer, E. C. (1993). The sociocultural context of infant development. In C. H. Zeanah (Ed.), *Handbook of infant mental health* (pp. 56–70). New York: Guilford.

Goodman, S. H., & Brumley, H. E. (1990). Schizophrenic and depressed mothers: Relational deficits in parenting. *Developmental Psychology, 26,* 31–39.

Green, B. A. (1990). What has gone before: The legacy of racism and sexism in the lives of Black mothers and daughters. In L. S. Brown & M. P. Root (Eds.), *Diversity and complexity in feminist therapy* (pp. 207–230). New York: Harrington Park Press.

Greenfield, P. M. (1994). Independence and interdependence as developmental scripts: Implications for theory, research, and practice. In P. M. Greenfield & R. R. Cocking (Eds.), *Cross-cultural roots of minority child development* (pp. 1–37). Hillsdale, NJ: Erlbaum.

Hale-Benson, J. (1986). *Black children: Their roots, culture, and learning styles.* Baltimore, MD: The Johns Hopkins Press.

Harvey, O. J., Hunt, D. E., & Schroder, H. M. (1961). *Conceptual systems and personality organization.* New York: Wiley.

Harwood, R. L. (1995). *Culture and attachment: Perceptions of the child in context.* New York: Guilford.

Hines, P. M., & Boyd-Franklin, N. (1996). African American families. In M. McGoldrick, J. Giordano, & J. K. Pearce (Eds.), *Ethnicity and family therapy* (2nd ed.; pp. 66–83). New York: Guilford.

Jackson, J. (1993). Multiple caregiving among African Americans and infant attachment: The need for an emic approach. *Human Development, 36,* 87–102.

Lassiter, R. F. (1987). Child-rearing in Black families: Child-abusing discipline. In R. L. Hampton (Ed.), *Violence in the Black family: Correlates and consequences* (pp. 39–54). Lexington, MA: Lexington Books.

Lewis, M. L. (1986). Risk factors for child maltreatment and perceptions of acceptance and rejection of children by African American mothers. Unpublished manuscript, University of Colorado, Boulder.

Lewis, M. L. (1993). Factors influencing the interpretation of emotions in infants by African-American mothers. Unpublished doctoral dissertation, University of Colorado, Boulder.

Lewis, M. L. (1994, December). *Parental beliefs, attitudes and protective behaviors in a context of violence.* Paper presented at the ninth annual conference of the National Center for Clinical Infant Programs, Zero to Three Institute, Dallas, TX.

Lewis, M. L. (1996, April). *Remembering mama: African American mother-child relationships, a model for community parenting.* Plenary address, Michigan Association of Infant Mental Health, Ann Arbor, MI.

Lewis, M. L., Turnage, B. Taylor, S., & Diaz, L. (1999, April). *Ethnicity predicts parenting styles in African American mothers.* A poster presented at the biennial meeting of the Society for Research in Child Development, Albuquerque, New Mexico.

Main, M., Kaplan, N., & Cassidy, J. (1990). Parents' unresolved traumatic experiences are related to infant disorganized attachment status: Is frightened and/or frightening parental behavior the linking mechanism? In M. T. Greenberg, D. Cicchetti, & E. M. Cummings (Eds.), *Attachment in the preschool years* (pp. 161–181). Chicago: University of Chicago Press.

McCrae, R. R., & Costa, P. T. (1988). Recalled parent-child relations and adult personality. *Journal of Personality, 56,* 417–433.

McLoyd, V. C. (1988, June). Determinants of the mental health of Black and White children experiencing economic deprivation. Paper presented at a study group meeting on poverty and children, University of Kansas, Lawrence.

McLoyd, V. C. (1990). The impact of economic hardship on Black families and children: Psychological distress, parenting, and socioemotional development. *Child Development, 61,* 311–346.

Minturn, L., & Lambert, H. (1964). *Mothers of six cultures: Antecedents to childrearing.* New York: Wiley.

Neal, A. M., & Wilson, M. L. (1989). The role of skin color and features in the Black community: Implications for Black women and therapy. *Clinical Psychology Review, 9,* 323–333.

Pascoe, J. M., & Solomon, R. (1994). Prenatal correlates of indigent mothers' attitudes about spoiling their young infants: A longitudinal study. *Developmental and Behavioral Pediatrics, 15*(5), 367–369.

Peters, M. F. (1985). Racial socialization of young, Black children. In H. P. McAdoo & J. McAdoo (Eds.), *Black children: Social, educational and parental environments* (pp. 159–173). Newbury Park, CA: Sage.

Peters, M. F. (1997). Parenting in Black families with young children: A historical perspective. In H. F. McAdoo (Ed.), *Black families* (3rd ed.; pp. 214–233). Thousand Oaks, CA: Sage.

Pottharst, K. (Ed.). (1990). *Research exploration in adult attachment.* New York: Peter Lang.

Radloff, L. S. (1977). The CES-D Scale: A self-report depression scale for research in the general population. *Applied Psychological Measurement, 3,* 385–401.

Randolph, S. M. (1989). Infant attachment in Black American families: An interim report. In J. L. McAdoo (Ed.), *The twelfth conference on empirical research in Black Psychology.* Washington, DC: National Institute of Mental Health.

Randolph, S. M., Koblinsky, S. A., & Roberts, D. D. (1998). Studying the role of family and school in the development of African American preschoolers in violent neighborhoods. *Journal of Negro Education, 65,* 282–294.

Rohner, R. P. (1975). *They love me, they love me not: A worldwide study of the effects of parental acceptance and rejection.* New Haven, CT: HRAF Press.

Rohner, R. P. (1986). *The warmth dimension.* Newbury Park, CA: Sage.

Skinner, E. A. (1985). Determinants of mother sensitive and contingent-responsive behavior: The role of child rearing beliefs and socioeconomic status. In I. E. Sigel (Ed.), *Parental belief systems: The psychological consequences for children.* Hillsdale, NJ: Erlbaum.

Slaughter-Defoe, D. T. (1995). Revisiting the concept of socialization: Caregiving and teaching in the 90s: A personal perspective. *American Psychologist, 50,* 276–286.

Smitherman, G. (1986). *Talkin' and testifyin': The language of Black America.* Detroit, MI: Wayne State University Press.

Smyke, A. (1996). *Fear of spoiling in at risk African American mothers.* Unpublished manuscript, University of New Orleans.

Sparks, E. (1998). Against all odds: Resistance and resilience in African American welfare mothers. In C. Garcia Coll & J. L. Surrey (Eds.), *Mothering against the odds: Diverse voices of contemporary mothers* (pp. 215–237). New York: Guilford.

Spencer, M. B., & Markstrom-Adams, C. M. (1990). Identity processes among racial and ethnic minority children in America. *Child Development, 61,* 433–441.

Super, C. M., & Harkness, S. (1986). The developmental niche: A conceptualization at the interface of child and culture. *International Journal of Behavioral Development, 9,* 545–569.

Super, C. M., & Harkness, S. (1997). The cultural structuring of child development. In J. W. Berry, P. R. Dasen, & T. S. Saraswathi (Eds.), *Cross-cultural psychology, basic processes and human development: Vol. 2* (pp. 1–40). Needham Heights, MA: Allyn & Bacon.

Tatum, B. D. (1997). Out there stranded? Black families in White communities. In H. P. McAdoo (Ed.), *Black families* (3rd ed.; pp. 214–233). Thousand Oaks, CA: Sage.

Taylor, R. D., Roberts, D., & Jacobson, L. (1997). Stressful life events, psychological well-being, and parenting in African American mothers. *Journal of Family Psychology, 4,* 436–446.

Thoits, P. A. (1989). The sociology of emotions. *Annual Review of Sociology, 15,* 317–342.

Thornton, M. C. (1997). Strategies of racial socialization among Black parents. In R. J. Taylor, J. S. Jackson, & L. M. Chatters (Eds.), *Family life in Black America* (pp. 201–215). Thousand Oaks: Sage.

Valsiner, J. (Ed.). (1988). *Child development within culturally structured environments: Parent cognition and adult-child interaction.* Norwood, NJ: Ablex.

Wright, K. (1982). Sociocultural factors in child abuse. In B. A. Bass, G. E. Wyatt, & G. J. Powell (Eds.), *The Afro-American family: Assessment, treatment, and research issues* (pp. 237–262). New York: Grune & Stratton.

Zahn-Waxler, C., & Wagner, E. (1993). Caregivers' interpretation of infant emotions: A comparison of depressed and well mothers. In R. N. Emde, J. D. Osofsky, & P. M. Butterfield (Eds.), *The IFEEL pictures: A new instrument for interpreting emotions* (pp. 3–26). Madison, CT: International Universities Press.

4

Why Poverty Matters for Young Children: Implications for Policy

Jeanne Brooks-Gunn, Tama Leventhal,
and Greg J. Duncan

4
——

Introduction

The economic well-being of families with children has declined over the last 25 years. Since the early 1980s the child poverty rate has been about 20 percent, and children now constitute the largest segment of the poor population of the United States (U.S. Census Bureau, 1999). The poverty rate for families with young children (birth to age five) is slightly higher at approximately 25 percent (National Center for Children in Poverty, 1997). Family poverty is indicated when a family's income fails to meet a federally established threshold (e.g., $12,802 for a family of three in 1997). Living at or below the poverty threshold indicates that a family lacks basic financial resources and consequently, children may lack access to adequate food, housing, and health care (Center for the Future of Children, 1997; Haveman & Wolfe, 1994). This situation clearly has consequences for children's health and well-being.

The prevalence of poverty among families with young children has profound implications for researchers, policymakers, and practitioners concerned with young children's mental health. This chapter, divided into four sections, addresses the growing need for these individuals to understand the role of poverty in young children's lives. First, a more broad-based review of recent studies examining the effect of poverty on children's physical, cognitive,

The authors would like to thank the NICHD Research Network on Child and Family Well-Being for their support. We are also grateful to the National Institute of Mental Health and Administration for Children, Youth, and Families Head Start Mental Health Research Consortium. We would also like to acknowledge the Robert Wood Johnson Foundation and the Pew Charitable Trusts.

and socioemotional development is provided. Second, we consider issues of whether being poor in the early years is possibly more detrimental for children's well-being than being poor later in childhood. This section includes an examination of how important the depth of poverty, the persistence of poverty, and the occurrence of risk factors are in the first years of life; we focus, in keeping with this volume, on the first through the third years of life (although, in some cases, we consider children up to age five, as studies often examine these effects at ages three to five). Third, the potential pathways through which poverty may influence young children's social and emotional health are discussed. We have chosen to review the home environment, child care, parenting behavior, parental mental health, neighborhoods, health care, exposure to violence, and separations from the primary caregiver. Finally, given the extent of the literature, we examine the implications of the findings for public policy; first implications for early childhood programs are considered, and then the potential consequences of recent welfare reform for future generations of poor children are reviewed.

Poverty: Definitions, Trends, and Children's Development

Measuring Poverty

In the United States, income poverty is determined by official poverty thresholds that take household size into account and that are adjusted each year for changes in the cost of living based on the Consumer Price Index. The official poverty threshold was first established in 1959. The poverty threshold, as it was originally defined, was based on expected food expenditures for families of different household sizes, and these values were then multiplied by three because in 1959 food expenditures constituted approximately one-third of all household expenses (Orshansky, 1965). For example, in 1993 the poverty threshold for a family of three was just under $12,000 and in 1996 it was just over $12,500. Families whose incomes are above the poverty threshold for any given year are considered not poor, whereas those whose incomes fall at or below the poverty line are considered poor. For research purposes, income-to-needs ratios are often calculated to adjust income for household size (need) while taking into account the current poverty thresholds. For our hypothetical family of three in 1996, a ratio of 1 is defined as living at the poverty threshold ($12,500); a ratio of 0.5 is defined as living at half the poverty threshold ($6,250); a ratio of 2 is defined as living at twice the poverty threshold ($25,000); and a ratio of 3 or above is defined as living at three times the poverty threshold or above ($37,500 or greater). Brooks-Gunn and colleagues have used the income-to-needs ratio to examine differential depths of poverty (Duncan & Brooks-Gunn, 1997; Duncan et al., 1994). For instance, an income-to-needs ratio of less than 0.5 was defined as deep poverty, between 0.5 and 1.0 as poor, and 1.0 to 1.5 as near poor. These more nuanced categories reflect the fact that policies are more likely to move families in deep poverty to the poverty threshold rather than above the poverty threshold, and likewise, families at the poverty threshold are likely to move to near poverty rather than twice the poverty threshold. Another approach has been to explore the effects of the duration or persistence of poverty on development (Corcoran, Gordon, Laren, & Solon, 1992; Duncan & Brooks-Gunn, 1997; Duncan et al., 1994). In this instance, the number of years spent in poverty is considered as well as whether family poverty is persistent or transient over time or, in other words, long- or short-term.

The poverty threshold in the United States is absolute (i.e., based on an absolute level of resources or need), indicating that a family's poverty status is not affected by the income of other families. Canada and most of the western European nations, on the other hand, employ relative poverty thresholds (i.e., relative to the resources of the average family). These thresholds are typically defined in terms of about half of the median or mean income of all households (Smeeding & Torrey, 1988). Consequently, the absolute dollar amount of the poverty thresholds for these countries changes as the median or mean income of households changes, indicating that the income of other families can alter a family's status despite potential stability in income over time (adjusted for cost of living).

Some researchers and policymakers argue that an absolute poverty threshold, such as that of the United States, underestimates the number of poor families, while others believe that it overestimates the poverty rate. Hernandez (1993, 1997) used a relative measure of poverty (half the median income) and demonstrated that employing such a measure would increase the number of poor children in 1993 from one in five to one in three. Still others have tracked the decreases in the number of poor children when income transfers occur (Plotnick, 1997; see Table 4.1). As illustrated in Table 4.1, existing government income support and tax policies reduce childhood poverty. The first row displays child poverty rates while considering only earned income (pretransfer), and the second row shows the child poverty rate after considering all cash transfer benefits in family incomes (official poverty thresholds). The fourth row lists the child poverty rate after accounting for food, housing, and medical benefits as well as tax credits and net of paid taxes. Also noteworthy is historical changes; in 1979 government antipoverty programs lifted 40.3 percent of children out of poverty, and after severe cuts during the early 1980s these programs lifted only 25.3 percent of children out of poverty. By the 1990s, the reduction of children in poverty from antipoverty programs began to rise with increased expansion of the Earned Income Tax Credit (EITC) during this time (see Plotnick, 1997, for additional details). Mayer (1997a), on the other hand, has argued that the current poverty measure may overestimate poverty. According to Mayer (1997a), while income may have declined, real wealth has increased due to improvements in families' material living conditions over time. Consequently, she suggests using measures of material wealth, such as housing conditions, medical care, consumer

TABLE 4.1

Impact of Government Cash, Food, Housing, Health Care Benefit Programs,
and Taxes on Child Poverty, 1979 to 1995

	1979	1985	1990	1995
Pretransfer child poverty rate	20.1%	23.7%	23.5%	24.2%
Post–cash transfer child poverty rate	16.4%	21.5%	20.6%	20.8%
Percentage reduction in child poverty rate due to cash transfers	18.4%	9.3%	12.3%	14.0%
Posttransfer, posttax child poverty rate	11.4%	16.8%	15.8%	14.2%
Percentage reduction in child poverty rate due to all transfers and taxes	40.3%	25.3%	29.8%	38.0%

Source: For 1979, 1985, and 1990, U.S. Bureau of the Census, Measuring the effect of benefits and taxes on income and poverty: 1979 to 1991. *Current Population Reports,* P-60, No. 182RD. Washington, DC: U.S. Government Printing Office, 1992, pp. 98, 109, 111. For 1995, U.S. Bureau of the Census, Poverty in the United States: 1995. *Current Population Reports,* P-60, no. 194. Washington, DC: U.S. Government Printing Office, 1996, pp. 24, 25. Pretransfer income is measured as all cash income from private sources, excluding capital gains. Post–cash transfer income is pretransfer income plus all cash government transfers. Posttransfer, posttax income is post–cash transfer income minus Social Security taxes and federal and state income taxes, plus Earned Income Tax Credits, food stamp benefits, and the estimated value of Medicare, Medicaid, school lunch, and housing benefits. Reprinted with permission from: Plotnick, R. D. (1997). Child poverty can be reduced. *Futures of Children,* 7(2), p. 81.

durables, and telephone service, in addition to income measures.

Recently, the National Research Council (NRC) of the National Academy of Sciences undertook a scientific review of the official U.S. measure of poverty as mandated by Congress under the Family Support Act of 1988. The findings of this panel are presented in a volume edited by Citro and Michael (1995; see Betson & Michael, 1997, for a review) and reflect the criticisms noted thus far. The major critiques of the current poverty measure include its failure to take into account in-kind benefits (such as food

stamps, Medicaid, and housing subsidies) that have increased since the 1960s. Another omission is the government's failure to deduct paid taxes from a family's overall available resources, an expense which has increased for low-income families over time. Nor does the official measure take into account the EITC as available income. A further criticism of the current measure is its inability to distinguish between differential family needs, such as child care or transportation. Another problem identified is the general increase in health care costs. Finally, critics argue that this measure fails to recognize geographical and regional differences in the cost of living.

Measures of socioeconomic status (SES; e.g., occupational status, class and prestige, years of formal education, labor market earnings, household income, wealth, and average neighborhood income or a composite index of these attributes) are often used as an alternative to income measures. Research on family SES indicates that the various components of SES are conceptually and empirically distinct (Duncan & Petersen, 1997; Entwisle & Astone, 1994; Hauser, 1994; Haveman & Wolfe, 1994; Hill & Duncan, 1987; Sewell & Hauser, 1975). Recently, scholars have argued for differentiating between the various components of SES in order to identify the unique contribution of each, especially income (Duncan & Brooks-Gunn, 1997). Together, this research suggests that income does have a unique contribution to child and adolescent well-being; however, income effects are usually reduced when parents' educational and occupational status and other family circumstances are taken into account (e.g., Hauser & Sweeny, 1997). These distinctions are particularly important for drawing policy implications. For example, if a policy seeks to improve young children's emotional health, would raising families' overall incomes be more effective than attempting to alter parents' educations? There are different policy levers depending on which component of SES is the focus. If a policy attempts to address familial income, the EITC is one approach. In fact, research indicates that the EITC has been effective at moving nearly one million children out of poverty and de-creasing the depth of poverty (Plotnick, 1997; Primus, 1997; see Table 4.1). Another approach to altering the financial resources of low income would be to raise the minimum wage. On the contrary, policies targeting parents' educations would invest in education and job training. According to estimates by Heckman, Lochner, and Taber (1998), reducing the growing trend toward wage inequality between college graduates (high-skilled workers) and individuals with the equivalent of a high school education or less (low-skilled workers) would require transforming approximately 5 percent of the low-skilled workforce (or 5.4 million people) to the equivalent of college graduates. Among the lowest skilled workers, an additional concern is that some training programs have substituted GED training for high school graduation, and the economic returns of a GED in the labor market are lower than that of a high school diploma (Cameron & Heckman, in press).

Historical Trends in Childhood Poverty

While the rates of childhood poverty (one in four of all young children) are quite shocking, these figures are even more alarming when viewed in conjunction with poverty rates for other segments of the population. Table 4.2 presents poverty rates for children (younger than 18), adults (18 to 64 years), and senior citizens (65 years and older) over the past 40 years. As can be seen in Table 4.2, a shift in the distribution of poverty has occurred since 1959 (the first year poverty rates were available). The poverty rate for the elderly,

TABLE 4.2

Trends in Poverty Rates from 1959 to 1997 by Age (Percentage Poor)

Year	Under 18 Years Old	18 to 64 Years Old	65 Years and Older
1959	27	17	35
1967	17	10	30
1977	18	8	14
1987	20	11	11
1997	20	11	11

Source: U.S. Census Bureau, March 1999 Current Population Survey

who in 1959 comprised the largest poor segment of the population, has markedly declined over the past several decades, to the point where it has converged with the rate of adults age 18 to 64 (the segment of the population most capable of supporting themselves). The rate of childhood poverty was also quite high in 1959 (27 percent), but declined over the subsequent two decades and began to rise again in the 1980s. The childhood poverty rate in 1997 was roughly double that for adults and the elderly (20 percent versus 11 percent). These figures capture only the number of children poor at a single point in time, and the vast majority of these children move in and out of poverty while a smaller subset of children remains consistently poor over time. For example, in a nationally representative study that has tracked families over time, about 6 percent of European American children were poor at least five years, while 40 percent of African American children were poor for this length of time (Duncan, Brooks-Gunn, & Klebanov, 1994). Moreover, poor families were more likely than nonpoor families to reside in low-income neighborhoods, especially African American families with children

(Brooks-Gunn, Duncan, Klebanov, & Sealand, 1993; Duncan et al., 1994).

Causes of Increases in Child Poverty Rates

The changing face of poverty can be traced to demographic shifts in family composition and labor force participation, growing wage inequality, and changes in government spending. Specifically, the drop in poverty among the elderly over the past 30 years can primarily be explained by expanded Social Security benefits for the elderly (Hernandez, 1993, 1997).

The rise in childhood poverty, on the other hand, can be explained by multiple factors. First, the increase in the number of single-parent families due to divorce as well as children born to unmarried mothers has contributed to the high rate. The rate of marital disruptions has increased over the last 25 years to the extent that a majority of children will experience some type of family disruption during their youth (Chase-Lansdale & Hetherington, 1990; Cherlin, 1992; Hofferth, 1995; McLanahan & Sandefur, 1994). Families headed by a divorced or never-married mother are more likely to be poor than two-parent married families because family income declines, on average, almost 50 percent for female-headed households following marital dissolution (Duncan & Hoffman, 1985). One in three children in the United States was born to unmarried couples by the mid-1990s (Ventura, 1995). Nonmarital childbearing is most prevalent among adolescent mothers, but rates are also high among mothers in their early 20s. Single-parent families with children are likely to be poor because they are dependent on a single wage earner, and because such parents are likely to be young and have low levels of education or employment experience (Furstenberg, Brooks-Gunn, & Morgan, 1997; Hernandez, 1993; McLanahan & Sandefur, 1994).

Another major factor accounting for the rise of children living in poverty is growing wage inequality. Research tracking labor market and poverty trends revealed that despite economic expansion during the mid-1980s and a resultant reduction in unemployment, the poverty rate was not affected (Blank, 1993). Also accounting for the falling inflation-adjusted earnings of low-skilled workers was the exodus of manufacturing jobs abroad and to the suburbs during the late 1980s, which led to a significant decrease of semiskilled jobs and subsequent unemployment and declining wages among low-skilled workers who were primarily concentrated in urban areas (Wilson, 1991, 1997). For example, the inflation-adjusted earnings for men age 25 to 34 with a high school education or less are significantly lower today than in 1973

(Ellwood & Kane, 1998). In addition, the decreasing value of cash assistance from government transfer programs, such as Aid to Families with Dependent Children (AFDC), did not help the plight of low-income children and their families.

Poverty and Child Well-Being

In this section, we provide a broad overview of the effects of poverty on children's and youths' development. Findings are presented for five age groups—prenatal to two years, early childhood (age three to six), late childhood (age 7 to 10), early adolescence (age 11 to 15), and late adolescence (age 16 to 19). Each of these age groups encompasses at least one major transition in a child's life, such as school entrance or exit, biological maturation, role shifts, and potential cognitive alterations. The developmental challenges faced during each period are relatively universal and require new modes of adaptation to biological, psychological, or social changes (Graber & Brooks-Gunn, 1996). Somewhat different indicators of child and adolescent well-being are associated with each epoch. We present data from all five age groups, even though the focus of this chapter is the first years of life, in order to see whether income matters more in the earlier than later years of childhood and adolescence. The domains of well-being considered are:

- *Physical health.* For very young children, low birthweight, premature delivery, perinatal complications, infant death, and lead exposure are assessed. For children and youth of all ages, overall health, chronic asthma, days hospitalized, height, and weight are measured.

- *School readiness and achievement.* For children and young adolescents, IQ tests and general language and verbal ability tests are used. Among both younger and older children, learning problems are also assessed. For older children and young adolescents, tests also measure performance in a specific domain, such as reading and mathematics. Other indicators for older children and young adolescents are grade point average, poor attendance, grade repetition, and suspension or expulsion from school. For older adolescents, educational attainment is evaluated with respect to total years of schooling completed, high school completion, college attendance, and earnings.

- *Behavior, social, and emotional problems.* Behavior and emotional problems, including depression, anxiety, and aggression as well as delinquency and conduct problems, are assessed for both children and youth. These measures can be either observed or child-, parent-, or peer-reported, and may entail reports of one or more of a list of behavioral or emotional problems. Another social outcome measured for both young and older adolescents is early entry into parenthood.

This evaluation draws heavily from two recent efforts to examine the influence of poverty on child well-being. The first study is a comprehensive review of the findings on poverty and children's cognitive, physical, and emotional development undertaken by Brooks-Gunn and Duncan (1997). This analysis gives a snapshot of the effects of poverty by examining child indicators for poor and nonpoor children drawn from large, nationally representative cross-sectional surveys (see Table 4.3 for a summary of the findings). In essence, the findings reported provide a risk assessment of the effects of poverty on children and youth at a given point in time. The second effort focuses on the dynamics of poverty and is part of a joint initiative to conduct replication analyses across multiple data sets with income data measured over the life course to explore the role of the timing, duration, and depth of poverty on a diverse set of developmental outcomes. These findings are reported in a volume, *Consequences of Growing Up Poor*, and provide a first look at the long-term effects of poverty on children and adolescents (Duncan & Brooks-Gunn, 1997). For the replication analyses, the following criteria are used to determine the magnitude of income effects on child well-being. An effect is considered large if it amounted to at least one-third of a standard deviation and a majority of the coefficients were significant at the .05 level or below. An effect is considered small to moderate if the effect sizes were not consistently large (i.e., less than one-third of a standard deviation), and most of the coefficients were significant at the .05 level. "No effect" was characterized by few if any significant coefficients across the models.

The primary data sets used across these two efforts were: (1) the *Panel Study of Income Dynamics* (PSID), an ongoing, rep-

TABLE 4.3
Selected Population-Based Indicators of Well-Being for Poor and Nonpoor Children in the United States

Indicator	Pecentage of Poor Children (unless noted)	Percentage of Nonpoor Children (unless noted)	Ratio of Poor to Nonpoor Children
Physical Health Outcomes (for children between 0 and 17 years unless noted)			
Reported to be in excellent health[a]	37.4	55.2	0.7
Reported to be in fair to poor health[a]	11.7	6.5	1.8
Experienced an accident, poisoning, or injury in the past year that required medical attention[a]	11.8	14.7	0.8
Chronic asthma[a]	4.4	4.3	1.0
Low birthweight (less than 2,500 grams)[b]	1.0	0.6	1.7
Lead poisoning (blood lead levels 10/dl or greater[c]	16.3	4.7	3.5
Infant mortality[b]	1.4 deaths per 100 live births	0.8 death per 100 live births	1.7
Deaths during childhood (0 to 14 years)[d]	1.2	0.8	1.5
Stunting (being in the fifth percentile for height for age) for 2 to 17 years[e]	10.0	5.0	2.0
Number of days spent in bed in past year[a]	5.3 days	3.8 days	1.4
Number of short-stay hospital episodes in past year per 1,000 children[a]	81.3 stays	41.2 stays	2.0
Cognitive Outcomes			
Development delay (includes both limited and long-term developmental deficits) (0 to 17 years)[a]	5.0	3.8	1.3
Learning disability (defined as having exceptional difficulty in learning to read, write, and do arithmetic) (3 to 17 years)[a]	8.3	6.1	1.4
School Achievement Outcomes (5 to 17 years)			
Grade repetition (reported to have ever repeated a grade)[a]	28.8	14.1	2.0
Ever expelled or suspended[a]	11.9	6.1	2.0
High school dropout (percentage of 16- to 24-year-olds who were not in school or did not finish high school in 1994[f]	21.0	9.6	2.2

TABLE 4.3

Continued

Indicator	Pecentage of Poor Children (unless noted)	Percentage of Nonpoor Children (unless noted)	Ratio of Poor to Nonpoor Children
Emotional / Behavioral Outcomes (3 to 17 years)			
Parent reports child has ever had an emotional or behavioral problem that lasted three months or more[g]	16.4	12.7	1.3
Parent reports child ever being treated for an emotional problem or behavioral problem [a]	2.5	4.5	0.6
Parent reports child has experienced one or more of a list of typical child behavioral problems in the last three months (5 to 17 years)[h]	57.4	57.3	1.0
Other			
Female teens who had an out-of-wedlock birth[i]	11.0	3.6	3.1
Economically inactive at age 24 (not employed or in school)[j]	15.9	8.3	1.9
Experienced hunger (food insufficiency) at least once in past year[k]	15.9	1.6	9.9
Reported cases of child abuse and neglect[l]	5.4	0.8	6.8
Violent crimes (experienced by poor families and nonpoor families)[m]	5.4	2.6	2.1
Afraid to go out (percentage of family heads in poor and non-poor families who report they are afraid to go out in their neighborhood)[n]	19.5	8.7	2.2

Note: This list of child outcomes reflects findings from large, nationally representative surveys that collect data on child outcomes and family income. While most data come from the 1988 National Health Interview Survey Child Health Supplement, data from other nationally representative surveys are included. The rates presented are from simple cross-tabulations. In most cases, the data do not reflect factors that might be important to child outcomes other than poverty status at the time of data collection. The ratios reflect rounding.

[a]Data from the 1988 National Health Interview Survey Child Health Supplement (NHIS-CHS), a nationwide household interview survey. Children's health status was reported by the adult household member who knew the most about the sample child's health, usually the child's mother. Figures calculated from Dawson, D. A., *Family structure and children's health: United States, 1988*, Vital Health and Statistics Series 10, no. 178, Hyattsville, MD: U.S. Department of Health and Human Services, Public Health Service, June 1991; and Cairo, M. J., Zill, N., and Bloom, B., *Health of our nation's children*, Vital Health and Statistics, Series 10, no. 191, Hyattsville, MD: U.S. Department of Health and Human Services, Public Health Service, December 1994.

TABLE 4.3

Continued

[b]Data from the National Maternal and Infant Health Survey, collected in 1989 and 1990, with 1988 as the reference period. Percentages were calculated from the number of low birthweight births per 1,000 live births as reported in Federman, M., Garner, T., Short, K., et al., What does it mean to be poor in America? *Monthly Labor Review* (May 1996) *119*, 5:10.

[c]Data from NHANES III, 1988-1991. Poor children who lived in families with incomes less than 130% of the poverty threshold are classified as poor. All other children are classified as nonpoor.

[d]Percentages include only Black and White youths. Percentages calculated from Table 7 in Rogot, E., *A mortality study of 1.3 million persons by demographic, social, and economic factors: 1979-1985 Follow-up.* Rockville, MD: National Institutes of Health, July 1992.

[e]Data from NHANES II, 1976-1980.

[f]National Center for Educational Statistics. Dropout rates in the United States: 1994. Table 7, Status dropout rate, ages 16-24, by income and race ethnicity: October 1994. Available online at: *http://www.ed.gov/NCES/pubs/r9410t07.html.*

[g]Data from the NHIS-CHS. The question was meant to identify children with common psychological disorders such as attention deficit disorder or depression, as well as more severe problems such as autism.

[h]Data from the NHIS-CHS. Parents responded "sometimes true," "often true," or "not true" to a list of 32 statements typical of children's behaviors. Each statement corresponded to one of six individual behavior problems—antisocial behavior, anxiety, peer conflict/social withdrawal, dependency, hyperactivity, and headstrong behavior. Statements included behaviors such as cheating or lying, being disobedient in the home, being secretive, and demanding a lot of attention. For more complete descriptions, see Section P-11 of the NHIS-CHS questionnaire.

[i]Data from the Panel Study of Income Dynamics (PSID). Based on 1,705 children ages 0 to 6 in 1968; outcomes measured at ages 21 to 27. Haveman, R., and Wolfe, B. New York: Russell Sage Foundation, 1994, p. 108, Table 4.10c.

[j]Data from the PSID. Based on 1,705 children ages 0 to 6 in 1968; outcomes measured at ages 21 to 27. In *Succeeding generations: On the effects of investments in children.* Haveman, R., and Wolfe, B. New York: Russell Sage Foundation, 1994, p. 108, Table 4.10d. Economically inactive is defined as not being a full-time student, working 1,000 hours or more per year; attending school part time and working 500 hours; a mother of an infant or mother of two or more children less than five years old; a part-time student and the mother of a child less than five years old.

[k]Data from NHANES III, 1988-1991. Figures reflect food insufficiency, the term used in government hunger-related survey questions. For a more in-depth discussion, see Lewit, E. M., and Kerrebrock, N. Child indicators: Childhood hunger. *The Future of Children* (Spring 1997) 7, 1:128–137.

[l]Data from Study of National Incidence and Prevalence of Child Abuse and Neglect: 1988. In *Wasting America's future.* Children's Defense Fund. Boston: Beacon Press, 1994, pp. 5–29, 87, Tables 5–6. Poor families are those with annual incomes below $15,000.

[m]Data from the National Crime Victimization Interview Survey. Results are for households or persons living in households. Data were collected between January 1992 and June 1993 with 1992 as the reference period. Percentages are calculated from number of violent crimes per 1,000 people per year. Reported in Federman, M., Garner, T., Short, K., et al., What does it mean to be poor in America? *Monthly Labor Review* (May 1996) *119*, 5:9.

[n]Data from the Survey of Income and Program Participation. Participation data collection and reference periods are September through December 1992. Reported in Federman, M., Garner, T., Short, K., et al., What does it mean to be poor in America? *Monthly Labor Review* (May 1996) *119*, 5:9.

Reprinted with permission from: Brooks-Gunn, J., & Duncan, G. J. (1997). The effects of poverty on children. *Futures of Children, 7*(2), 58–59.

resentative longitudinal survey of U.S. households initiated in 1968 and conducted annually (Duncan & Hill, 1989; Hill, 1992); (2) the *National Longitudinal Survey of Youth* (NLSY) an ongoing, representative longitudinal survey of U.S. households initiated in 1979 and conducted biannually (Baker & Mott, 1989); (3) *Children of the NLSY*, a follow-up of children born to women in the original NLSY cohort initiated in 1986 and also conducted biannually (Chase-Lansdale, Mott, Brooks-Gunn, & Phillips, 1991); (4) the *National Survey of Families and Households* (NSFH), a national probability sample of adults in the United States and a randomly selected child (Sweet, Bumpass, & Call, 1988); (5) the *National Health and Nutrition Examination Survey* (NHANES), a nationwide survey of children's and youths' health that included a physical examination; (6) *National Health Interview Survey Child Health Supplement* (NHIS-CHS), a national household survey using an adult who knew the most about a randomly selected child's health; and (7) the *Infant Health and Development Program* (IHDP), a multisite intervention program for low-birthweight premature infants (Infant Health and Development Program, 1990; Brooks-Gunn, McCarton et al., 1994; Gross et al., 1997; see Brooks-Gunn, Brown, Duncan, & Moore, 1995, for a review of the national data sets).

PHYSICAL HEALTH

The threat to poor children's health begins before they are born. Poor children are almost two times more likely than nonpoor children to be born low birthweight (less than 2,500 grams); and other risks to their health include lead poisoning and experiences of hunger (Brooks-Gunn & Duncan, 1997; see Table 4.2). Additional health indicators on which poor children and youth are likely to fare less well than their nonpoor peers are child mortality, number of hospital days, and stunting (small for height; Brooks-Gunn & Duncan, 1997). Children and youth from poor families also display more health problems than children from affluent families (Newacheck, Hughes, & Stoddard, 1996; Newacheck, Stoddard, & McManus, 1993). When experiences with poverty are tracked over time, living in poverty during childhood has been found to be associated with subsequent stunting (Korenman & Miller, 1997).

SCHOOL READINESS AND ACHIEVEMENT

Poor children and youth of all ages are more likely to display deficits in cognition and achievement than nonpoor children. According to findings from national surveys reported in Table 4.2, poor children aged 3 to 17 are approximately one and a half times more likely to display learning disabilities, and elementary- and high school-aged children are about twice as likely as nonpoor children to repeat a grade and be expelled or suspended from school (Brooks-Gunn & Duncan, 1997). By late adolescence, poor youth are also twice as likely as their nonpoor peers to drop out of high school. From these figures, it is clear that poor children are at a disadvantage in terms of their academic trajectories compared to nonpoor children; however, from these studies we know little about the long-term effects of poverty on school readiness and achievement outcomes.

Perhaps the most extensive studies of young and late childhood have been conducted by Brooks-Gunn and colleagues, who have used two data sets, the IHDP and Children of the NLSY, to examine the effects of poverty on children's cognitive and school achievement (Brooks-Gunn & Duncan, 1997; Brooks-Gunn, Klebanov, & Duncan, 1996; Duncan et al., 1994; Liaw & Brooks-Gunn, 1994; Smith, Brooks-Gunn, & Klebanov, 1997). Most recently, Smith and colleagues (1997) employed parallel analyses across these two studies as part of the replication analyses undertaken in Duncan and Brooks-Gunn (1997). Their findings were strikingly consistent across the IHDP and the Children of the NLSY. Overall, income had large and consistent effects on children's cognition, verbal ability, and achievement from ages two to five, with a large effect defined as one-third of a standard deviation or greater. Since standardized intelligence, verbal, and achievement tests have a mean of 100 and a standard deviation of about 15, this means that a hypothetical child whose family income was at the poverty threshold (1) would have an IQ score five to six points lower than a child whose family income was twice the poverty threshold, after holding constant family and child background characteristics. The depth of poverty also mattered with children who were very poor (income-to-needs ratio less than 0.5), scoring particularly low on the measures of cognitive and school achievement (see Figure 4.1). For example, young children (three to four years of age) who lived in deep poverty (income/needs of 0.5 or less) had verbal scores, measured via the PPVT-R, that were

on average nine points lower than low-income children (income/needs between 1.5 and 2). In this study, the number of years a child lived in poverty was also associated with that child's school readiness. Children who were persistently poor during the first five years of their life (lived in poverty all years) scored six to nine points lower than children who were never poor during this time, and children who were transiently poor (poor at least one year) scored approximately four to five points lower than children who were never poor.

Studies of young adolescents have focused on indicators of school performance, such as grade placement and grade point average, and overall, only small to modest effects have been reported in these studies. For example, Pagani, Boulerice, and Tremblay (1997) examined the association between income and 6- to 12-year-old children's grade placement using data from a national school-based study in Canada. The researchers found that persistent poverty was especially harmful: Children who were always poor were more than two times as likely not to be in the age-appropriate class compared with their peers who were never poor. Several other studies have reported small positive associations between family income-to-needs ratio and young adolescents' self- and parent-reported grade point average (Conger, Conger, & Elder, 1997; Hanson, McLanahan, & Thomson 1997).

Among studies of late adolescence, indicators of completed schooling have been the primary focus. In general, across the various data sets in the replication analyses undertaken in *Consequences of Growing Up Poor,* small to moderate income effects

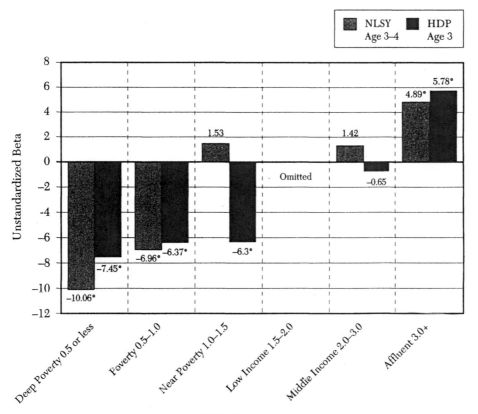

FIGURE 4.1

Peabody Picture Vocabulary Test-Revised (PPVT-R) Scores for Children Ages Three and Four: Depth of Poverty. Regression controls for child's race, birthweight, and sex; mother's education; and family structure. Regression for IHDP also controls for site and treatment group. For NLSY (1986), $N = 734$, and for IHDP, $N = 718$. $°p < .05$. Source: Smith, J. R., Brooks-Gunn, J., & Klebanov, P. K. (1997). The consequences of living in poverty for young children's cognitive and verbal ability and early school achievement. In G. J. Duncan & J. Brooks-Gunn (Eds.), *Consequences of Growing Up Poor* (pp. 154–155). New York: Russell Sage Foundation.

were reported (Duncan & Brooks-Gunn, 1997). A 10% increase in the family income-to-needs ratio was associated with approximately a 0.2 percent to 2.0 percent increase in the number of school years completed (see also Haveman & Wolfe, 1994). Several additional studies also report income effects on achievement in the late adult years, especially for the number of years spent in poverty (Hauser & Sweeny, 1997; Corcoran & Adams, 1997; Corcoran et al., 1992).

BEHAVIOR AND EMOTIONAL PROBLEMS
As with the other outcomes under consideration, the risks to poor children's social and emotional health are high. Specifically, poor children are twice as likely to be the victim of a violent crime as nonpoor children, and these children are also two

times as likely to live in an unsafe neighborhood (as reported by their parents) than their peers (see Table 4.2). Among poor female adolescents, the rate of teenage out-of-wedlock parenthood is three times greater than that of their nonpoor peers (Brooks-Gunn & Duncan, 1997). This snapshot suggests that poor children face challenges to their emotional and social well-being.

In longitudinal studies, behavior problems are the most common indicator of children's mental health (Achenbach, Edelbrock, & Howell, 1987; Richman & Graham, 1971). This literature is based on maternal reports of children's behavior problems, including aggression, tantrums, anxiety, depression, social withdrawal, and the like. Overall, much more modest income effects are found for children's mental health compared to the rather large effects reported for achievement-related outcomes. Family income is linked to the prevalence of young children's behavior problems, but the effects are small to moderate (Duncan et al., 1994; Smith et al., 1997). Among children three years of age in the IHDP, children living in deep poverty (income/needs 0.5 or less) had internalizing behavior problems scores (depressive/anxious symptoms) that were approximately two points higher than low-income children (income/needs 1.5 to 2; Klebanov, personal communication). By age five, the negative effects of deep poverty and poverty (compared to low income) appear to increase (see Figure 4.2). Specifically, for children in the IHDP, deep poverty was associated with total behavior problems scores that were nine points higher than low-income children, and internalizing and externalizing

(aggressive/acting out symptoms) behavior problems scores that were, on average, 5.5 points higher than low-income children. The negative effects of poverty were about half the size of those reported for deep poverty. Deep poverty was also associated with increased behavior problems scores among five- to six- and seven- to eight-year-old children in the NLSY (Smith et al., 1999). In addition, experiences with poverty during early childhood have been found to be associated with high levels of depression that persist into late childhood (McLeod & Shanahan, in press). In addition, children who were continuously poor from early to late childhood displayed higher levels of antisocial behavior in late childhood than their peers who were never poor. Among school-age children, teacher reports of behavior problems also are associated with family income (Klebanov, Brooks-Gunn, & McCormick, 1994). In the replication analyses, small to moderate income effects were reported for adolescent anxiety and hyperactivity (Pagani et al., 1997). Unfortunately, the findings on poverty and children's mental health are limited by the lack of good detailed measures on children's emotional well-being.

A majority of the research on the influence of poverty on children has focused on achievement-related outcomes with much less on mental and physical health. The research presented in this section on the direct effects of poverty on children's development suggests that poverty has detrimental short- and long-term influences on children's health and well-being. In the following section, we turn to whether the timing of poverty matters for children's development.

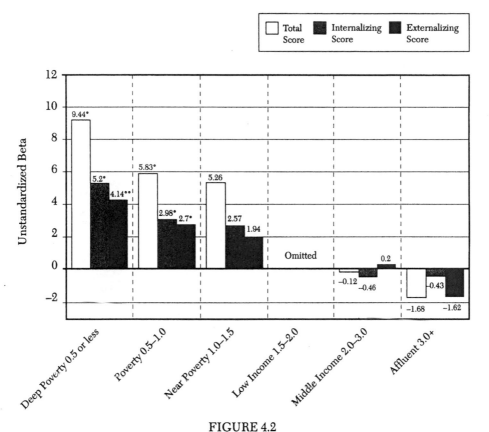

FIGURE 4.2

Behavior Problem Scores for IHDP Children at Age Five: Depth of Poverty. Regression controls for child's race, birthweight, and sex; mother's education; family structure; site; and treatment group. $^*p < .05$ and $^{**}p < .01$.

Does Early Income Matter?

In this section, we consider the question of whether income in early childhood matters more than income in the later childhood years and adolescence. We draw upon research on children's cognition and achievement to address this question. In our examination of the importance of timing of poverty, we also review more closely issues of the depth and duration of family poverty as well as the presence of risk factors.

Studies reviewed in the previous section on poverty and cognitive test scores in the first 18 months of life, generally, did not find significant effects (Klebanov, Brooks-Gunn, McCarton, & McCormick, 1998; Korenman & Miller, 1997; Smith et al., 1997). This situation does not necessarily imply that early poverty does not influence young children's development. To the contrary, we suspect that this occurs because infant IQ tests focus on social and motor skills that are quite different than the verbal and analytic abilities tapped by IQ tests

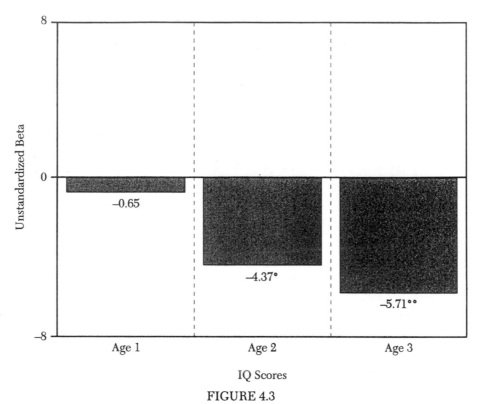

IQ Scores

FIGURE 4.3

IQ Scores at Ages One, Two, and Three for IHDP Children: Effect of Family Poverty.
Regression controls for race, sex, family poverty, family risks, neighborhood poverty, and site.
Follow-up only group: $N = 347$.

for older populations (Brooks-Gunn, Liaw, & Klebanov, 1992; Lewis, 1983; McCall, 1983). In a recent study, we examined the association between family poverty, environment, and biological risk factors on children's achievement during the first three years of life (Klebanov et al., 1993). Findings from this study are presented in Figures 4.3 to 4.5. It is clear that by age two, poverty has rather large negative effects on children's cognitive test scores that persist at age three (see Figure 4.3). By age two, poor children had IQ scores that were 4.4 points lower than nonpoor children after controlling for child, maternal, and family characteristics. At one year of age, on the other hand, the presence of familial risk factors comprised of social, economic, family structural, and maternal characteristics are associated with compromised child development (see Figure 4.4; see also Liaw & Brooks-Gunn, 1994). Children who experienced a low number of risk factors (zero to one) had cognitive test scores that were, on average, 5.7 points higher than their peers who experienced a moderate number of risks (two to three) after taking into account family and neighborhood poverty. Finally, as illustrated in Figure 4.5, we see that biological risk factors, in this

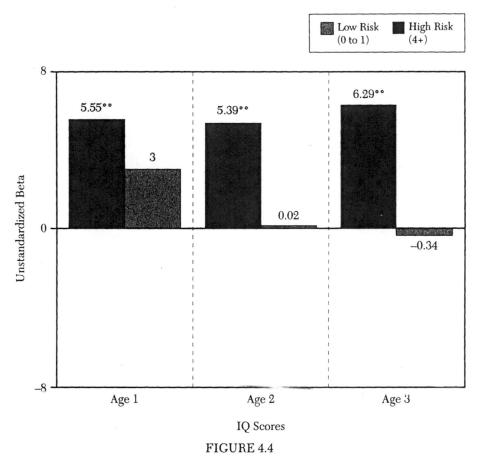

FIGURE 4.4

IQ Scores at Ages One, Two, and Three for IHDP Children: Effect of Low Family Risk (0 to 1) and High Family Risk (4+). Regression controls for race, sex, family poverty, family risks, neighborhood poverty, and site. Comparison group is Middle Risk (2 to 3). Follow-up only group: N = 347.

case being born at a very low birthweight (1,500 grams or less) or in poor neonatal health (lowest 25 percent according to standardized neonatal index), have a large negative effect on children's cognition at age one; however, as the influence of environmental circumstances, such as poverty, increases with children's age, the impact of biology is reduced (Klebanov et al., 1998).

The effects of childhood poverty persist into late adolescence. Although the findings among older adolescents' educational achievement reviewed in the previous section presented a rather consistent portrait of the negative effects of poverty on educational attainment, the timing of poverty appears to be especially important in determining the magnitude of the effect, with family poverty during young childhood particularly detrimental to long-term achievement. Accordingly, Duncan and colleagues (1998) examined the association between timing of poverty and late adolescents' (age 16 to 25) high school

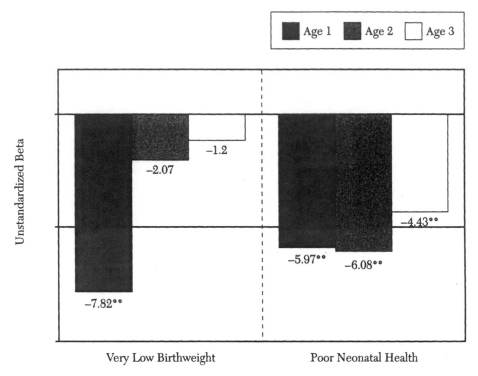

FIGURE 4.5

IQ Scores at Ages One, Two, and Three for IHDP Children: Effect of Very Low Birthweight (1,500 grams or less) and Poor Neonatal Health (92 or less; 25th Percentile). Regression controls for race, sex, family poverty, family risks, neighborhood poverty, and site. Comparison of VLBW to Heavier LBW (1,501–1,500 grams). Comparison of Poor Neonatal Health to Better Neonatal Health. Follow-up only group; $N = 347$.

completion and total years of schooling completed in the PSID. They found that poverty during early and late childhood and early adolescence was negatively associated with educational achievement, but that poverty during early childhood was the most important determinant of completed schooling. When a more conservative sibling-analyses (fixed effects) approach was employed to control for possible selection bias, only poverty during early childhood

was associated with completed schooling. Also using data from the PSID, Haveman and Wolfe (1994) examined the influence of timing of poverty for three periods— ages 6 to 8, ages 9 to 11, and ages 12 to 15— and found that only experiences with family poverty during ages 9 to 11 were negatively associated with years of schooling completed; however, family poverty during early childhood was not examined. In a subsequent study also based on the PSID,

Haveman, Wolfe, and Wilson (1997) investigated whether various indicators of the family income-to-needs ratio, assessed when the youth were ages 6 to 15, were associated with high school graduation when the youth were in their twenties. Longer durations of poverty had especially detrimental effects on youths' chances of graduating high school.

Several other studies focusing more on young adulthood also report that family poverty during childhood and adolescence is associated with young adult achievement, including years of schooling completed and early labor market experiences. For example, among a birth cohort in Detroit, income was assessed from young childhood to the point at which the youth reached age 23, and average family income (income-to-needs ratio) was positively associated with years of schooling completed, and persistent poverty was negatively associated with completed schooling (Axinn, Duncan, & Thornton, 1997). When Axinn and colleagues (1997) investigated the role of the timing of poverty, findings indicated that poverty during early childhood was especially detrimental to educational attainment. However, when additional measures of wealth, such as home equity and number of cars, were taken into account, the effects of income were reduced. Another study based on the NLSY found that average family income-to-needs, measured during late adolescence, was positively associated with achievement test scores, completed schooling, and labor market experiences in young adulthood; however, the effect sizes were generally small (less than one-third of a standard deviation) and overall, the duration of poverty was not a significant factor (Peters & Mullis, 1997). Finally, Teachman, Paasch, Day, and Carver (1997) used data from the National Longitudinal Surveys of Young Men and Women to explore the effects of experiences of family poverty during late adolescence (age 14/15 to 17/18) and found that an average family income-to-needs ratio was not associated with high school completion, college attendance, or years of schooling completed at age 25. However, the researchers did find a nonlinear income effect suggesting that deep poverty and affluence were more strongly associated with high school graduation than the middle income ranges.

The timing of poverty appears to be especially important in determining the magnitude of the effect, with experiences of poverty during young childhood particularly harmful to children's development over time. These findings are consistent with a growing body of evidence on the importance of children's experiences in the first few years of life for healthy development (Carnegie Corporation, 1994). Early experiences have even been linked to brain development (Greenough, Black, & Wallace, 1987; Shatz, 1992). It appears that early economic deprivation leads to impaired child functioning, which sets the stage for continued problems into young adulthood. While there are few studies examining the timing of poverty on children's mental health, it is likely that the findings on children's cognition and achievement extend to children's emotional well-being.

Poverty and Pathways of Influence

Thus far, we have reviewed the direct effects of poverty on children's well-being, and the findings present a coherent portrait of the deleterious influence of poverty, especially during young childhood. To further our understanding of the influence of income on children's health and well-being, it is necessary to consider the processes through which income may alter these outcomes. In addressing the mechanisms through which poverty may alter child outcomes, we focus on young children's mental health, the theme of this volume. However, when necessary we draw upon other relevant research. Several potential pathways of influence have been hypothesized to intervene between the effects of income and children's emotional well-being, including the home environment, child care, parenting behavior, parental mental health, neighborhoods, health care, exposure to violence, and separations from the primary caregiver (see Brooks-Gunn & Duncan, 1997, for a review). Each of these possible mechanisms is reviewed.

Home Environment

A primary pathway through which income may affect child well-being is the quality of a child's home environment. The quality of the home environment includes: the emotional warmth conveyed by parents during interactions with their children; opportunities for learning, such as the presence of reading and learning materials and the use of developmentally appropriate activities; and the physical environment, such as the safety of play areas and the lighting and decor. Children from poor families are likely to have lower quality home environments in terms of the emotional, cognitive, and physical stimulation available than children from more affluent families (Brooks-Gunn, McCormick, Klebanov, & McCarton, 1998). Among a sample of five-year-old children, there is evidence that the quality of the home learning environment partially mediated the effect of family income on children's reported externalizing (acting out) behavior problems (Duncan et al., 1994). Several studies also suggest that differences in the home learning environment may account for as much as 50 percent of the income effect on young children's cognition and school readiness outcomes (Brooks-Gunn et al., 1998; Duncan et al., 1994; Smith et al., 1997).

Child Care

Among young children, child care is a salient context that may act as a mediator of income effects on young children's outcomes. During early childhood, high-quality child care and early intervention programs have been shown to have long-term positive effects on poor children's socioemotional outcomes, such as behavior problems, persistence and enthusiasm for learning, and even young adult crime and delinquency (Lee, Brooks-Gunn, & Schnur, 1988; Lee, Brooks-Gunn, Schnur, & Liaw, 1990; McKey, Condelli, Granson, Barrett, McConkey, & Plantz, 1985; Yoshikawa, 1994). Low-quality child-care, on the other hand, is associated with high adult-to-child ratios, which may lead to reduced supervision and monitoring of children's behavior and increased tolerance of aggressive behavior (Hayes, Palmer, & Zaslow, 1990). High-quality childcare and early childhood programs also increase the school readiness of children and continue to enhance the verbal ability and reasoning skills of poor and middle-income children throughout childhood (Burchinal et al., 1997; Campbell & Ramey, 1994; Infant Health and Development Program, 1990; McKey et al., 1985; Reynolds, 1994; Zigler, 1987). In addition, these programs may alter parenting outcomes, including mental health, coping skills, knowledge about child rearing, and maternal-child interactions (Benasich, Brooks-Gunn, & Clewell, 1992; Brooks-Gunn, Berlin, & Fuligni, in press; Klebanov, Lee, Brooks-Gunn, & McCormick, in press).

Parenting Behavior

The work of researchers, such as Conger and McLoyd, suggests that economic hard-ship resulting from income loss, unemployment, job instability, and economic insecurity rather than low income per se is associated with child well-being. According to the Family Stress Model, economic hardship is associated with parental stress and depression, which in turn is associated with more inconsistent, unsupportive, harsh, and punitive parenting behavior; these lower quality parent/child interactions lead to emotional and school problems among children (Conger et al., 1994; McLoyd et al., 1994). This research has primarily focused on adolescents, but recent work by our group has extended these findings to young children at ages three and five. Among children in the Infant Health and Development Program, we have examined the premise that the effect of income on young children's behavior problems and IQ scores is mediated by maternal emotional health and parenting (Linver, Brooks-Gunn, & Kohen, 1999; see Figure 4.6). Parenting was assessed via

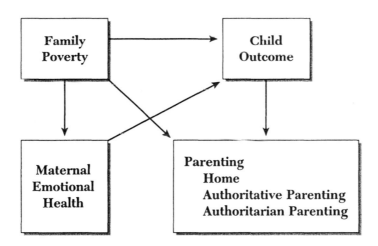

FIGURE 4.6
Theoretical model of family poverty effects on parental mental health
and behavior and subsequent child outcomes.

semistructured observations of the quality of the home environment when the children were three years old (HOME scale; Caldwell & Bradley, 1984) and via videotaped observations of parent-child interactions when the children were 30 months of age. During the observation, the mother and child engaged in an eight-minute free play with developmentally appropriate toys (Spiker, Ferguson, & Brooks-Gunn, 1993, 1997). The interactions were coded for authoritative and authoritarian parenting along five-point scales (Chase-Lansdale, Brooks-Gunn, & Zamsky, 1994; Hetherington & Clingempeel, 1988; Kohen, 1997). Authoritative parents tend to be warm, employ firm control, use reason when giving instructions, and allow children to make independent decisions; while authoritarian parents tend to be less warm, stress firm limits and control, permit little verbal give and take, and maintain a punitive orientation with an emphasis on children's obedience (Baumrind, 1966; Maccoby & Martin, 1983). In general, authoritative parenting is viewed as optimal for children's emotional well-being. Consistent with the adolescent research, findings among young children indicate that the effect of income is largely mediated through maternal mental health and parent-child interactions. Specifically, family income indirectly affected the child outcomes through parenting.

Parental Mental Health

While parental mental health is considered under the Family Stress Model, it is also likely that the parent's emotional well-being is a path through which income may alter children's development (rather than operating indirectly through parenting behavior). A number of studies have documented the negative consequences of living in poverty on adult and maternal depression and mental health (Adler, 1994; Adler, Boyce, Chesney, Folkman, & Syrne, 1993; Brody & Flor, 1997; Elder, Eccles, Ardelt, & Lord, 1995; Kessler, 1997). Other research has demonstrated links between maternal emotional health and child behavior problems (Links, 1983; Velez, Johnson, & Cohen, 1989). In addition, low family income is associated with reduced levels of social support available to mothers (Klebanov, Brooks-Gunn, & Duncan, 1994; McLoyd, 1990). There is also some evidence that income may have an indirect effect on preschool children's behavior problems and IQ scores vis-à-vis maternal-reported depression and coping skills (Duncan et al., 1994).

As discussed under Family Stress Models, additional studies also suggest that maternal mental health is associated with parenting behavior, which in turn is linked to child well-being. Specifically, studies with young children have found that maternal depression is associated with lower quality parent-child relationships (Lyons-Ruth, Alpern, & Repacholi, 1993). Maternal depression is also associated with less optimal parenting practices within the home, including the provision of learning experiences (Brooks-Gunn, Klebanov, & Liaw, 1995). As illustrated in Figure 4.6, the association between parent-child interactions is not direct, but may be mediated by maternal mental health (Linver et al., 1999).

Neighborhoods

The neighborhoods in which poor families with young children live is another possible pathway through which family income effects may be transmitted to children. Low-income families are economically constrained in their choice of neighborhood residence, and consequently, low-income families may live in very poor neighborhoods marked by crime, unemployment, and lack of adult supervision of children and youth. Such neighborhoods are also likely to have few resources to draw upon for their children's development, such as libraries, family resource centers, museums, and literacy programs for families. Most studies examining the neighborhoods in which children live have found that neighborhood conditions influence children's well-being above and beyond family income (rather than indirectly). Low SES neighbors appear to have an adverse effect on young children's mental health, possibly more so for externalizing behaviors than internalizing behaviors. The presence of more affluent neighbors, on the other hand, appears to be more salient for young children's school readiness outcomes (see Leventhal & Brooks-Gunn, 1999, for a review).

Neighborhood residence is also associated with parenting practices (e.g., provision of learning experience, maternal warmth, and physical environment) over and above family income (Klebanov, Brooks-Gunn, Chase-Lansdale, & Gordon, 1997; Klebanov et al., 1994). A study based on the IHDP and Children of the NLSY found that the benefit of affluent neighbors for children's cognitive and achievement outcomes was accounted for largely by the quality of the learning environment inside the home (Klebanov et al., 1997, 1998). Living in a poor neighborhood, on the other hand, has been found to be associated with low-quality physical home environments, low maternal warmth, and harsh and controlling parenting (Klebanov et al., 1994; Lamborn et al., 1996).

Health Care

Access to health care is another mechanism through which the effects of income on young children's health may be mediated. Despite poorer health, children from economically disadvantaged families are less likely than their nonpoor peers to receive health care services (Newacheck, Hughes, & Stoddard, 1996; Newacheck, Stoddard, & McManus, 1993). A recent study of biologically vulnerable children examined discrepancies in health care among poor, middle-income, and affluent families, and found that children from poorer families were more likely to be hospitalized and have more emergency room visits than were children from higher income families, and poor children had fewer doctor visits than middle-income families (Brooks-Gunn, McCormick, Klebanov, & McCarton, 1998). This latter finding is especially noteworthy because primary care physicians are a frequent source of referral for mental health services.

Exposure to Violence

The next possible pathway is exposure to violence both inside and outside the home. While possibly related to parenting behavior, children's exposure to violence in the home, whether as a witness or as a victim, may mediate income effects on young children's health. The prevalence of violence within the home is associated with family income (Children's Defense Fund, 1994). At the neighborhood level, poor neighborhoods are more likely than affluent neighborhoods to be characterized by crime and violence (Sampson, Raudenbush, & Earls, 1997). Most studies have found that a majority of school-age children surveyed report having been exposed to violence in the community by either witnessing an event, knowing a victim, or being a victim in events such as robbery, beating, stabbing, shooting, or murder (Campbell & Schwarz, 1996; Martinez & Richters, 1993). This situation appears to hold true for children in low-income urban areas as well as children in middle-income suburban areas; however, children in urban areas report experiencing higher levels of community violence (Campbell & Schwarz, 1996). Exposure to violence, in turn, is associated with symptoms of sleep disorders, depression, and Posttraumatic Stress Disorder (Campbell & Schwarz, 1996; Duncan, 1996; Martinez & Richters, 1993). Several researchers are beginning to explore how the intersection of violence in the home and the community influences children's mental health (Earls, personal communication; see Kindlon, Wright, Raudenbush, & Earls, 1996, and Selner-O'Hagan, Kindlon, Buka, Raudenbush, & Earls, 1998, for methodological work under way).

Separations from Primary Caregiver

The final mechanism through which poverty may operate on young children's emotional health is separations from the primary caregiver. A separation from the primary caregiver may entail a separation for some given length of time or may involve an actual change in primary caregivers. Poor parents may face more stresses that place them at risk for separations from their children (Furstenberg et al., 1987). Several classic studies of institutionally reared children find that a separation from the primary caregiver is associated with emotional and behavioral problems into adulthood (Bowlby, 1969, 1973; Tizard & Hodges, 1978). Other research documents that maternal hospital admissions (i.e., short-term separation from a primary caregiver) are associated with emotional disturbances among young children (Rutter, 1981). A majority of these studies, however, have not included measures of family income. Our own recent work exploring separations from a primary caregiver among children drawn from a large multisite study (noninstitutional sample) found that separations during very early childhood were especially detrimental to children's cognition and achievement in the short and long term after accounting for differences in family income; socioemotional outcomes were not examined (Leventhal, 1999).

There is an emerging body of literature on the potential pathways through which income effects may be transmitted to young children. Given the relatively modest direct effects of income on young children's mental health, it is likely that poverty influences young children's mental health indirectly. The evidence suggests that parents (behavior and health) and the home environment may be the primary means through which income effects alter young children's emotional well-being. However, further research in the area of pathways of influence is clearly needed.

Poverty and Children's Mental Health: Policy Implications

Based on the research on poverty and child development presented thus far, we know that deep and persistent poverty during early childhood is especially harmful to child well-being. Experiences with poverty may have direct as well as indirect effects on young children, with indirect effects transmitted through several mechanisms, most notably parents and the home environment. In light of these findings, we consider the policy implications. First, we review how such findings inform early childhood educational programs. Next, we consider recent welfare reform and the potential consequences for child and family well-being.

Early Childhood Programs

Government investments in low-income families with children fall into two categories, in-kind transfer programs and cash programs (Brooks-Gunn & Duncan, 1997; Currie, 1997; Devaney et al., 1997). This section addresses in-kind programs, such as health care, parenting education, literacy programs, family support, and preschool education. Clearly, parents play a vital role in all of these programs in terms of

their ability to access services for children, their engagement or involvement in programs with their children, and monitoring their children's participation. Usually, the mother rather than the father is responsible for most of these activities.

Early childhood programs are perhaps the most widespread approach to enhancing the well-being of poor children. Early childhood programs have as their primary goal enhancing young children's school readiness. School readiness, however, is thought to encompass physical, emotional, social, cognitive, and linguistic domains of child competence (Love, Brooks-Gunn, & Aber, 1994; Shonkoff & Meisels, in press). In addition, readiness is now defined in terms of the parent, family, school staff, and the child. That is, readiness is no longer thought to reside solely in the child. This change in perspective has vast implications for how early childhood programs serve children and families as well as how they interact with other community institutions serving young children (i.e., mental health and health care; Leventhal, Brooks-Gunn, McCormick, & McCarton, in press). However, at the present, early childhood education programs, while sometimes providing referrals to other services, have not become well-integrated with the schools or other community institutions (Leventhal, Brooks-Gunn, & Kamerman, 1997).

Early childhood programs are typically administered in a home-based or center-based setting or a combination of both. These programs also provide services directly to parents (and the home environment), parents and children, or children. Services targeting parents include counseling, informal support networks, parenting education and instruction and job training; services targeting children include education (home- or center-based) and health care (Barrett, 1995; Brooks-Gunn, 1995; Olds, Henderson, & Kitzman, 1994). A recent example of such a program is Early Head Start, which provides home visiting and center-based preschool to low-income (and disabled) children during the first three years of life. Like Head Start, which serves older preschool children, Early Head Start has multiple goals—enhancing child well-being in the broadest sense (i.e., not just focusing on cognitive and linguistic child outcomes), strengthening the relationship between the parent and child, providing links to community services, and building parenting skills.

Given the links between poverty, parents, and young children's health and well-being presented in the previous section, we here consider parents as a target of early childhood programs. The inclusion of parents in these programs is often based on the implicit (rather than explicit) premise that programs will have direct effects on parents and that programs will influence children indirectly through impacts on their parents. Such mediated effects on children via parental well-being are viewed as critical to sustaining program impacts on children's development (Smith, 1995). In other words, during the early years of children's lives, parents are viewed as "engines of change" on their children's behalf (Brooks-Gunn, Berlin, & Fuglini, in press). In targeting parents, several outcomes are of interest: (1) parent employment and education; (2) parent mental and physical well-being; (3) observed parent-child interactions and relations; (4) use of child-related services; (5) parenting attitudes, knowledge, and the quality of the home environment; and (6) child maltreatment (Brooks-Gunn et al., in press). We focus here on maternal mental health, parenting behaviors, and provision of learning and literacy experiences in the home as potential pathways through which early interventions for poor families may influence child well-being.

At some level, most early childhood programs view parents as engines of change; however, indirect programs' effects on children vis-à-vis parents have not been widely investigated. Several studies based on the Infant Health and Development Program provide some evidence for parents as mediators of early childhood intervention. The first study is based in part on Models of Family Stress, presented in the previous section (Conger et al., 1994; McLoyd, 1990). Specifically, economic hardship is hypothesized to influence children indirectly via parental mental health and subsequent parent-child interactions (see Figure 4.6). In terms of early intervention, Linver and colleagues (1998) adapted this model to examine whether intervention effects on children were mediated through maternal mental health (depressive symptoms) and parenting behavior. The treatment group received home visits for the first three years of life and center-based early childhood education for the second two years. Home visits included Learning Games, a curriculum comprised of parent-child activities designed to enhance children's emotional, social, cognitive, fine and gross motor, and verbal abilities. The curriculum facilitated parent-child interactions around fun and developmentally appropriate activities. Maternal depressive symptoms were assessed by the Center for Epidemiological Studies Depression Inventory (CES-D) at the one- and two-year assessment points. Parenting was observed in a free-play session between the mother and child at the hospital clinic during the child's 30-month assessment. Authoritative and authoritarian dimensions were coded from a videotape (Smith, Brooks-Gunn, Kohen, & McCarton, 1999). Findings indicate that the intervention influenced maternal depressive symptoms, which in turn were associated with parenting behavior and subsequent child cognitive test scores when the children were three years of age (controlling for maternal, child, and family background characteristics). In addition, parenting behavior was enhanced by participation in the intervention program (i.e., more authoritative and less authoritarian behavior). Similar findings were reported when behavior problems were the outcome, rather than child test scores.

Another study based on the IHDP has focused on the role of early childhood programs (particularly those offering support and problem solving) to alter maternal mental health and resultant child functioning (Klebanov, Lee, Brooks-Gunn, & McCormick, in press). Accordingly, links between maternal depressive symptoms, coping skills, and stressful life events were first investigated, and then associations with young children's IQ scores. Participation in the intervention was associated with

maternal mental health; this effect was moderated by the number of stressful life events experienced. Emotional well-being was enhanced by the intervention for mothers who had experienced a high number of stressful life events. Children in the intervention who had mothers with high levels of depressive scores and a high number of life events had higher cognitive test scores and fewer depressive/anxious symptoms than did follow-children with mothers who had similar levels of depressive symptoms and life events. Together, these initial studies suggest that parents may be a pathway through which early child programs influence children.

Finally, among families who participated in Abecedarian and Project Care (early intervention programs that have followed children over an extended period of time), Burchinal and colleagues (1997) did not find any mediated effects of home visiting or center-based care on child outcomes via parenting attitudes or the home environment. The parenting measures, however, were not based on observational data, which might be more sensitive to intervention effects (Berlin et al., 1995; Chase-Lansdale et al., 1994).

Welfare Reform

The passing of the Personal Responsibility and Work Opportunity Reconciliation in 1996 ushered in a new era of welfare reform. Aid to Families with Dependent Children (AFDC), the federal entitlement program for low-income families, was replaced with Temporary Assistance to Needy Families (TANF), in which states receive block grants (pegged to state welfare expenditures in 1995) to administer welfare services. Under TANF, individuals are limited to 60 months of cash assistance (whether consecutive or not), but cash assistance is contingent upon participation in work or job-related activities after 24 months, and failure to comply with the work requirement results in sanctions. States have the discretion to implement shorter time limits on total receipt and to change the onset of work requirements, and in fact, over half of all states have opted to do so. States are also allowed to exempt up to 20 percent of their welfare caseloads from the lifetime limits due to hardship. Preliminary evidence from a few states suggests that about 20 to 25 percent of mothers are hitting their limits without having a job (Bloom, 1999). In addition, the 1996 welfare legislation made significant changes affecting child care, the Food Stamp Program, Supplemental Security Income for children, benefits for legal immigrants, and the Child Support Enforcement program. Prior to the passage of this legislation, 35 states had received federal waivers under the Family Support Act of 1988 and were already experimenting with welfare reform and other programs (Chase-Lansdale & Brooks-Gunn, 1995).

For poor families with young children, welfare reform has profound implications. Specifically, under TANF, mothers with young children are now expected to work. Under AFDC and the Family Support Act, mothers with preschool-age children (under six years of age) were exempt from the work requirement (even though states were allowed to require mothers with younger children to work). Welfare assistance for poor families, including those with young children, is now intended to provide only short-term assistance. The rationale behind the shift from welfare as an entitlement to welfare as short-term assistance was that many long-term welfare recipients tended to enter the welfare rolls when they were young and their children were young (Bane & Ellwood, 1994; Duncan & Rodgers, 1988). Long-term welfare recipients represent a high proportion of the welfare rolls. Finally, prior welfare-to-work programs typically focused on education, literacy, job training, and job search skills to prepare mothers for the workforce, but recent changes put much less emphasis on education and training than actual employment (aside from teenage mothers who are now required to complete high school).

Thus far, the new state-designed welfare programs appear to be effective, at least as measured by declining caseloads. Since 1994, caseloads have fallen by approximately 25 percent and up to 80 percent in some counties in Wisconsin. However, it is not clear what accounts for these startlingly large declines, as they started prior to the passage of the 1996 welfare bill. At the same time, it is not known how many families will reach the time limits, since only a handful of families have reached their time limits. By the year 2005, it is estimated that about half of all families receiving welfare in each state will reach their five-year benefit cutoff (Duncan, Harris, & Boisjoly, 1997). This estimate includes approximately two million families and four million children, which is about twice as many families as can be exempt from the cutoff under the law. Although some of these families will make successful transitions into the workforce, it is a point of concern that many may not do so. Estimates of the characteristics of recipients most likely to reach their five-year limit—two-thirds lack a high school education; more than half lack work experience; two-thirds were age 21 or younger when they first received benefits; and a majority have low levels of cognitive skills—are similar to the characteristics of long-term welfare recipients (Bane & Ellwood, 1994; Duncan & Brooks-Gunn, 1997). If no additional children are born during the five-year period of receipt, families reaching their time limit are not likely to have very young children.

While time limits are likely to affect the income available to low-income families, with perhaps the most vulnerable families falling into deeper poverty, other provisions of the welfare reform legislation are likely to influence the amount of income available to families with young children. Specifically, a number of states have adopted "family caps" that prevent additional benefits being given to women who have additional children while receiving public assistance. Consequently, the per capita income of families who bear any additional children will be cut at a time when children, especially the newborn, may be most sensitive to the effects of income. Potentially more problematic for families with young children are sanctions for noncompliant behavior and categorical restrictions on eligibility that result in a loss of all cash assistance. Some families who lose benefits as result of sanctioning for not complying with program rules (or reaching time limits) will replace lost cash assistance with income from work or other sources, but possibly as many as half of all families will not. A common reason that parents are sanctioned with a resultant cut or termination of benefits is for failing to meet work requirements. Mothers with young children often have difficulty meeting such requirements because of constraints such as available child care. The result will be that these families and their young children fall deeper into poverty, a situation that may have consequences for their well-being. Moreover, mothers with very young children are the least able to support their families through paid employment. In addition, there are state-specific provisions, such as denial of cash benefits to children born to teenage unmarried mothers, that will significantly alter the income for a subset of families with young children.

The effects of welfare reform on young children's development is also likely to be mediated by parents (Brooks-Gunn, Smith, Berlin, & Lee, in press). Based on the Family Stress Model, if mothers face financial strain as a result of sanctioning or time limits, it may impact their emotional health and, in turn, parenting and subsequent child well-being. Research based on the Newark Young Family Study, a subset of families from the Teenage Parent Demonstration (a welfare demonstration program for first-time, AFDC-eligible teenage mothers) has examined this premise. Findings suggest that increased economic self-sufficiency is linked to positive child outcomes and less harsh parenting (Aber, Brooks-Gunn, & Maynard, 1995;

see Brooks-Gunn, Smith et al., in press, for a more detailed review of these findings). Similar findings have been reported among families with different patterns of welfare and nonwelfare receipt in the IHDP (Smith, Brooks-Gunn, Kohen, & McCarton, 1999).

Given the importance of income during the early years of a child's life, some policy recommendations are as follows. First, states should consider exempting families with infants and toddlers from time limits, sanctions, and categorical restrictions. A few states already exempt mothers with infants from some provisions of welfare reform. A further recommendation is that states could mandate part-time work for mothers with young children under three years of age.

Second, states may also consider implementing EITC benefits (which include incentives for paid work) to augment the federal EITC benefits. A number of states have already done so. Third, if the ultimate goal of welfare reform is to promote the health and well-being of children, it is imperative that policies reach beyond cash assistance and consider in-kind benefits, discussed earlier, such as early childhood programs, health care, food and nutrition, and housing. Many of these services are available through existing programs, including Head Start; Medicaid; Food Stamps; Women, Infants, and Children (WIC); and public housing. These services directly affect the health of young children (Currie, 1997; Devaney et al., 1997).

We have highlighted the importance of avoiding economic deprivation during the early years of a child's life. Early educational programs that incorporate parents are one means of mitigating the direct and indirect effects of poverty on young children. Recent welfare reform threatens to be particularly harmful to families with young children: States need to recognize the importance of supporting families during a child's earliest years as a critical step toward promoting healthy development.

Conclusion

This chapter addressed the growing need for researchers, policymakers, and practitioners to understand the role of poverty in young children's lives. Poverty has negative consequences for children's development across different domains of well-being, including mental health. We have tried to draw attention to the particularly dire consequences of experiencing poverty during the earliest years of life (as opposed to later in childhood or adolescence). Deep poverty and persistent poverty are especially harmful to children's health and well-being. Of concern is that the effects of early experiences with poverty appear to persist into adulthood. While the research on poverty and children's mental health is limited, there is compelling evidence on links between poverty and children's cognition and achievement. In all likelihood, these findings extend to emotional well-being. This position is supported in part by a growing body of research on environmental deprivation and early brain development. Additional research indicates that for a subset of young children who display early signs of behavior problems, emotional and social problems persist into adulthood (McCord, 1990).

Poverty may affect children's health and well-being directly as well as indirectly. The processes through which poverty may alter children's mental health occur at the familial (parenting, parental mental health, home environment, and separation from primary caregiver) and community (neighborhood, child care, and health care) levels or both (exposure to violence). During very early childhood, it is likely that poverty has more indirect effects on children's emotional well-being. In terms of children's mental health, parental mental health and behavior are probably the primary pathways through which the effects of poverty are transmitted to children. Accordingly, many early childhood programs incorporate parents into programs because they are viewed as engines of change. Initial studies examining this premise find that early intervention programs can enhance the well-being of young children by providing support and assistance to parents.

At the other extreme are recent changes in welfare legislation that disproportionately harm families with young children. Policymakers need to recognize the importance of a child's early years as well as parents' roles in supporting their children's healthy development. It is quite clear that some families with young children will see their incomes fall well below the poverty line at a time when income matters most. Further, financial strain caused by lost income is likely to affect parents' mental health and behavior and, in turn, children's

emotional well-being. In the long term, our children will pay the price unless policies are amended to foster the well-being of families with young children. Increasing links between early childhood programs and state welfare programs is likely to facilitate meeting the needs of both parents and children.

References

Aber, J. L., Brooks-Gunn, J., & Maynard, R. (1995). Effects of welfare reform on teenage parents and their children. *The Future of Children: Critical Issues for Children and Youth, 5*(2), 53–71.

Achenbach, T. M., Edelbrock, C. S., & Howell, C. T. (1987). Empirically based assessment of the behavioral/emotional problems of 2- and 3-year-old children. *Journal of Abnormal Child Psychology, 15,* 629–650.

Adler, N. E., Boyce, T., Chesney, M. A., Cohen, S., Folkman, S., Kahn, R. L., & Syme, S. L. (1994). Socioeconomic status and health: The challenge of the gradient. *American Psychologist, 49,* 15–24.

Adler, N. E., Boyce, T., Chesney, M. A., Folkman, S., & Syrne, L. (1993). Socioeconomic inequalities in health: No easy solution. *Journal of the American Medical Association, 269,* 3140–3145.

Axinn, W., Duncan, G. J., & Thornton, A. (1997). The effects of parents' income, wealth, and attitudes on children's completed schooling and self-esteem. In G. J. Duncan & J. Brooks-Gunn (Eds.), *Consequences of growing up poor* (pp. 518–540). New York: Russell Sage Foundation.

Baker, P. C., & Mott, F. L. (1989). *NLSY child handbook 1989: A guide and resource document for the National Longitudinal Survey of Youth 1986 Child Data.* Columbus, OH: Center for Human Resources Research, Ohio State University.

Bane, M., & Ellwood, D. (1994). *Welfare realities.* Cambridge: Harvard University Press.

Baumrind, D. (1966). Effects of authoritative control on child behavior. *Child Development, 37,* 887–907.

Berlin, L. J., Brooks-Gunn, J., Spiker, D., & Zaslow, M. J. (1995). Examining observational measures of emotional support and cognitive stimulation in Black and White mothers of preschoolers. *Journal of Family Issues, 16*(5), 664–686.

Betson, D. M., & Michael, R. T. (1997). Why so many children are poor. *The Future of Children, 7*(2), 25–39.

Blank, R. (1993). Why were poverty rates so high in the 1980s? In D. B. Papadimitriou & E. N. Wolff (Eds.), *Poverty and prosperity in the USA in the late twentieth century.* London: Macmillan.

Bowlby, J. (1969). *Attachment and loss: I. Attachment.* London: Hogarth Press.

Bowlby, J. (1973). *Attachment and loss: II. Separation, anxiety and anger.* London: Hogarth Press.

Brody, G. H., & Flor, D. L. (1997). Maternal psychological functioning, family processes, and child adjustment in rural, single-parent, African American families. *Developmental Psychology, 33,* 1000–1011.

Brooks-Gunn, J. (1995). Children and families in communities: Risk and intervention in the Bronfenbrenner tradition. In P. Moen, G. H. Elder, & K. Lusher (Eds.), *Examining lives in context: Perspective on the ecology of human development.* (pp. 467–519). Washington, DC: American Psychological Association Press.

Brooks-Gunn, J., Berlin, L. J., & Fuligni, A. S. (in press). Early childhood intervention programs: What about the family? In J. P. Shonkoff & S. M. Meisels (Eds.), *Handbook of early childhood intervention* (2nd ed.). New York: Cambridge University Press.

Brooks-Gunn, J., Brown, B., Duncan, G., & Moore, K. A. (1995). Child development in the context of family and community resources: An agenda for national data collection. In National Research Council Institute of Medicine, *Integrating federal statistics on children: Report of a workshop* (pp. 27–97). Washington, DC: National Academy Press.

Brooks-Gunn, J., & Duncan, G. J. (1997). The effects of poverty on children. *The Futures of Children, 7*(2), 55–71.

Brooks-Gunn, J., Duncan, G. J., Klebanov, P. K., & Sealand, N. (1993). Do neighborhoods influence child and adolescent development? *American Journal of Sociology, 99*(2), 353–395.

Brooks-Gunn, J., Klebanov, P. K., & Duncan, G. J. (1996). Ethnic differences in children's intelligence test scores: Role of economic deprivation, home environment, and maternal characteristics. *Child Development, 67,* 396–408.

Brooks-Gunn, J., Klebanov, P. K., & Liaw, F. (1995). The learning, physical, and emotional environment of the home in the context of poverty: The Infant Health and Development Program. *Children and Youth Services Review, 17*(1/2), 251–276.

Brooks-Gunn, J., McCarton, C., et al. (1994). Early intervention in low birth-weight, premature infants: Results through age 5 years from the Infant Health and Development Program. *Journal of the American Medical Association, 272*(16), 1257–1262.

Brooks-Gunn, J., McCormick, M. C., Klebanov, P. K., & McCarton, C. (1998). Young children's health care use: Effects of family and neighborhood poverty. *Journal of Pediatrics, 132,* 971–975.

Brooks-Gunn, J., Liaw, F., & Klebanov, P. K. (1992). Effects of early intervention on low birth weight preterm infants: What aspects of cognitive functioning are enhanced? *Journal of Pediatrics, 120,* 350–359.

Brooks-Gunn, J., Smith, J., Berlin, L. & Lee, K. (in press). Familywork: Welfare changes, parenting and young children. In G. K. Brookins (Ed.), *Exits from poverty.* New York: Cambridge University Press.

Burchinal, M. R., Campbell, F. A., Bryant, D. M., Wasik, B. H., & Ramey, C. T. (1997). Early intervention and mediating processes in cognitive performance of children of low-income African American families. *Child Development, 68*(5), 935–954.

Caldwell, B. M., & Bradley, R. H. (1984). *Home observation for measurement of the environment.* Little Rock, AR: University of Arkansas Press.

Cameron, S., & Heckman, J. J. (in press). Should college attendance be further subsidized to reduce rising wage inequality? Does family income foster ability or is it an important cash constraint limiting college attendance? In M. Kosters (Ed.), *Financing college tuition: Government policies, social priorities.* Washington, DC: AEI Press.

Campbell, C., & Schwarz, D. F. (1996). Prevalence of impact and exposure to interpersonal violence among suburban and urban middle school students. *Pediatrics, 98*(3), 396–402.

Campbell, F. A., & Ramey, C. T. (1994). Effects of early intervention on intellectual and academic achievement: A follow-up study of children from low-income families. *Child Development, 65,* 684–698.

Carnegie Corporation (1994). *Starting points: Meeting the needs of our youngest children.* New York: Author.

Chase-Lansdale, P. L., Brooks-Gunn, J., & Zamsky, E. S. (1994). Young African-American multigenerational families in poverty: Quality of mothering and grandmothering. *Child Development, 65*(2), 373–393.

Center for the Future of Children. (1997). *The Future of Children.* Special issue on Children and Poverty, 7(2), Summer/Fall.

Chase-Lansdale, P. L., & Brooks-Gunn, J. (Eds.). (1995). *Escape from poverty: What makes a difference for children?* New York: Cambridge University Press.

Chase-Lansdale, P. L., & Hetherington, E. M. (1990). The impact of divorce on life-span development: Short and long term effects. In P. Baltes, D. Featherman, & R. M. Lerner (Eds.), *Life-span development and behavior* (Vol. 10; pp. 105–150). Hillsdale, NJ: Erlbaum.

Chase-Lansdale, P. L., Mott, F. L., Brooks-Gunn, J., & Phillips, D. (1991). Children of the NLSY: A unique research opportunity. *Developmental Psychology, 27*(6), 918–931.

Cherlin, A. J. (1992). *Marriage, divorce, remarriage.* Revised and enlarged edition. Cambridge, MA: Harvard University Press.

Children's Defense Fund. (1994). *Wasting America's future.* Boston: Beacon.

Citro, C. F., & Michael, R. T. (Eds.). (1995). *Measuring poverty: A new approach.* Washington, DC: National Academy Press.

Conger, R. D., Conger, K. J., & Elder, G. H., Jr. (1997). Family economic hardship and adolescent adjustment: Mediating and moderating processes. In G. J. Duncan & J. Brooks-Gunn (Eds.), *Consequences of growing up poor* (pp. 288–310). New York: Russell Sage Foundation.

Conger, R. D., Conger, K. J., Elder, G. H., Jr., Lorenz, F. O., Simons, R. L., & Whitbeck, L. B. (1992). A family process model of economic hardship and adjustment of early adolescent boys. *Child Development, 63*(2), 526–541.

Conger, R. D., Conger, K. J., Elder, G. H., Jr., Lorenz, F. O., Simons, R. L., & Whitbeck, L. B. (1993). Family economic stress and adjustment of early adolescent girls. *Developmental Psychology, 29*(2), 206–219.

Conger, R. D., Ge, X., Elder, G. H., Jr., Lorenz, F. O., & Simons, R. L. (1994). Economic stress, coercive family process, and developmental problems of adolescents. *Child Development, 65*(2), 541–561.

Corcoran, M., & Adams, T. (1997). Race, sex, and the intergenerational transmission of poverty. In G. J. Duncan & J. Brooks-Gunn (Eds.), *Consequences of growing up poor* (pp. 461–517). New York: Russell Sage Foundation.

Corcoran, M., Gordon, R., Laren, D., & Solon, G. (1992). The association between men's economic status and their family and community of origin. *Journal of Human Resources, 27*(4), 575–601.

Currie, J. M. (1997). Choosing among alternative programs for poor children. *The Future of Children, 7*(2), 113–131.

Devaney, B. L., Ellwood, M. R., & Love, J. M. (1997). Programs that mitigate the effects of poverty on children. *The Future of Children, 7*(2), 88–112.

Duncan, D. F. (1996). Growing up under the gun: Children and adolescents coping with violent neighborhoods. *The Journal of Primary Prevention, 16*(4), 343–356.

Duncan, G. J., & Brooks-Gunn, J. (Eds.). (1997). *Consequences of growing up poor.* New York: Russell Sage Foundation.

Duncan, G. J., Brooks-Gunn, J., & Klebanov, P. K. (1994). Economic deprivation and early-childhood development. *Child Development, 65*(2), 296–318.

Duncan, G. J., Harris, K., & Boisjoly, J. (1997). *Time limits and welfare reform: New estimates of the number and characteristics of affected families.* Evanston, IL: Joint Center for Poverty Research, Northwestern University.

Duncan, G. J., & Hill, D. (1989). Assessing the quality of household panel survey data: The case of PSID. *Journal of Business and Economic Statistics, 7*(4), 441–451.

Duncan, G. J., & Hoffman, S. F. (1985). A reconsideration of the economic consequences of marital disruption. *Demography, 22*, 485–498.

Duncan, G. J., & Petersen, E. (1997). *The long and short of asking questions about income, wealth and labor supply on surveys.* Northwestern University: Unpublished manuscript.

Duncan, G. J., & Rodgers, W. L. (1988). Longitudinal aspects of childhood poverty. *Journal of Marriage and Family, 50*(4), 1007–10021.

Duncan, G. J., Yeung, W. J., Brooks-Gunn, J., & Smith, J. R. (1998). How much does childhood poverty affect the life chances of children? *American Sociological Review, 63*, 406–423.

Elder, G. H., Eccles, J. S., Ardelt, M., & Lord, S. (1995). Inner-city parents under economic pressure: Perspectives on the strategies of parenting. *Journal of Marriage and the Family, 57*, 771–784.

Ellwood, D. T., & Kane, T. J. (1998, October). *Who is getting a college education: Family background and the growing gaps in enrollment.* Paper presented at the conference "Investing in Children" sponsored by the Ford Foundation. New York: October 15–17, 1998.

Entwisle, D. R., & Astone, N. M. (1994). Some practical guidelines for measuring youth's race/ethnicity and socioeconomic status. *Child Development, 65,* 1521–1540.

Furstenberg, F. F., Jr., Brooks-Gunn, J., & Morgan, S. P. (1987). *Adolescent mothers in later life.* New York: Cambridge University Press.

Graber, J. A., & Brooks-Gunn, J. (1996). Transitions and turning points: Navigating the passage from childhood through adolescence. *Developmental Psychology, 32*(4), 768–776.

Greenough, W. T., Black, J. E., & Wallace, C. S. (1987). Experience and brain development. *Child Development, 58,* 539–559.

Gross, R. T., Spiker, D., & Haynes, C. W. (Eds.). (1997). *The Infant Health and Development Program for low birth weight premature infants.* Stanford, CA: Stanford University Press.

Hanson, T. L., McLanahan, S., & Thomson, E. (1997). Economic resources, parental practices, and children's well-being. In G. J. Duncan & J. Brooks-Gunn (Eds.), *Consequences of growing up poor* (pp. 190–238). New York: Russell Sage Foundation.

Hauser, R. M. (1994). Measuring socioeconomic status in studies of child development. *Child Development, 65,* 1541–1545.

Hauser, R. M., & Sweeney, M. M. (1997). Does poverty in adolescence affect the life chances of high school graduates? In G. J. Duncan & J. Brooks-Gunn (Eds.), *Conse-*

quences of growing up poor (pp. 541–595). New York: Russell Sage Foundation.

Haveman, R., & Wolfe, B. (1994). *Succeeding generations: On the effects of investments in children.* New York: Russell Sage Foundation.

Haveman, R., Wolfe, B., & Wilson, K. (1997). Childhood poverty and adolescent schooling and fertility outcomes: Reduced-form and structural estimates. In G. J. Duncan & J. Brooks-Gunn (Eds.), *Consequences of growing up poor* (pp. 419–460). New York: Russell Sage Foundation.

Heckman, J., Lochner, L., & Taber, C. (1998). Explaining rising wage inequality: Explorations with a dynamic general equilibrium model of earnings with heterogeneous agent. *Review of Economic Dynamics.*

Hernandez, D. J. (1993). *America's children: Resources from family, government, and the economy.* New York: Russell Sage Foundation.

Hernandez, D. J. (1997). Poverty trends. In G. J. Duncan & J. Brooks-Gunn (Eds.), *Consequences of growing up poor* (pp. 18–34). New York: Russell Sage Foundation.

Hetherington, E. M., & Clingempeel, G. (1988). *Longitudinal study of adjustment to remarriage: Family interaction global coding manual* (Unpublished manuscript). University of Virginia, Charlottesville.

Hill, M. (1992). The Panel Study of Income Dynamics. *The Sage series guides to major social science data bases* (Vol. 2). Newbury Park, CA: Sage.

Hill, M., & Duncan, G. J. (1987). Parental income and the socioeconomic attainment of children. *Social Science Research, 16,* 39–73.

Hofferth, S. L. (1985). Updating children's life course. *Journal of Marriage and the Family*, 93–115.

The Infant Health and Development Program. (1990). Enhancing the outcomes of low birthweight, premature infants: A multisite randomized trial. *Journal of the American Medical Association, 263*(22), 3035–3042.

Kessler, R. C. (1997). The effects of stressful life events on depression. *Annual Review of Psychology, 48*, 191–214.

Kindlon, D. J., Wright, B. D., Raudenbush, S. W., & Earls, F. (1996). The measurement of children's exposure to violence: A Rasch analysis. *International Journal of Methods in Psychiatric Research, 6*, 187–194.

Klebanov, P. K., Brooks-Gunn, J., Chase-Lansdale, P. L., & Gordon, R. (1997). Are neighborhood effects on young children mediated by features of the home environment? In J. Brooks-Gunn, G. J. Duncan, & J. L. Aber (Eds.), *Neighborhood poverty: Context and consequences for children (Volume 1)* (pp. 119–145). New York: Russell Sage Foundation.

Klebanov, P. K., Brooks-Gunn, J., & Duncan, G. J. (1994). Does neighborhood and family poverty affect mothers' parenting, mental health, and social support? *Journal of Marriage and the Family, 56*(2), 441–455.

Klebanov, P. K., Brooks-Gunn, J., McCarton, C., & McCormick, M. C. (1998). The contribution of neighborhood and family income to developmental test scores over the first three years of life. *Child Development, 69*(5), 1420–1436.

Klebanov, P. K., Brooks-Gunn, J., & McCormick, M. C. (1994). School achievement and failure in very low birth weight children. *Journal of Developmental and Behavioral Pediatrics, 15*(4), 248–256.

Klebanov, P. K., Lee, K., Brooks-Gunn, J., &

McCormick, M. C. (in press). Maternal copying strategies: Early interventions and low birth weight child development. *Developmental Psychology.*

Kohen, D. E. (1997). *Parenting behaviors: Associated characteristics and child outcomes.* Unpublished doctoral dissertation, Teachers College, Columbia University, New York.

Korenman, S., & Miller, J. E. (1997). Effects of long-term poverty on physical health of children in the National Longitudinal Survey of Youth. In G. J. Duncan & J. Brooks-Gunn (Eds.), *Consequences of growing up poor* (pp. 70–99). New York: Russell Sage Foundation.

Lamborn, S. D., Dornbusch, S. M., & Steinberg, L. (1996). Ethnicity and community context as moderators of the relations between family decision making and adolescent adjustment. *Child Development, 67,* 283–301.

Lee, V., Brooks-Gunn, J., & Schnur, E. (1988). Does Head Start "close the gap"?: A comparison of children attending Head Start, no preschool, and other preschool programs. *Developmental Psychology, 24*(2), 210–222.

Lee, V., Brooks-Gunn, J., Schnur, E., & Liaw, T. (1990). Are Head Start effects sustained? A longitudinal comparison of disadvantaged children attending Head Start, no preschool, and other preschool programs. *Child Development, 61,* 495–507.

Leventhal, T. (1999). Poverty and turbulence: Familial and neighborhood influences on children's achievement. Unpublished doctoral dissertation, Teachers College, Columbia University, New York.

Leventhal, T., & Brooks-Gunn, J. (1999). *The neighborhoods they live in: The effects of neighborhood residence upon child and adolescent outcomes.* Manuscript submitted for publication.

Leventhal, T., Brooks-Gunn, J., & Kamerman, S. (1997). Communities as place, face, and space: Provision of services to poor, urban children and their families. In J. Brooks-Gunn, G. J. Duncan, & J. L. Aber (Eds.), *Neighborhood poverty: Policy implications in studying neighborhoods (Volume 2)* (pp. 182–205). New York: Russell Sage Foundation.

Leventhal, T., Brooks-Gunn, J., McCormick, M. C., & McCarton, C. M. (in press). Patterns of service use in preschool children: Correlates, consequences, and the role of early intervention. *Child Development.*

Lewis, M. (Ed.). (1983). *Origins of intelligence: Infancy and early childhood* (2d ed.). New York: Plenum.

Liaw, F., & Brooks-Gunn, J. (1994). Cumulative familial risks and low birth weight children's cognitive and behavioral development. *Journal of Clinical Child Psychology, 23*(4), 360–372.

Links, P. S. (1983). Community surveys of the prevalence of childhood psychiatric disorders: A review. *Child Development, 54,* 531–548.

Linver, M. R., Brooks-Gunn, J., & Kohen, D. (1998). *Effects of poverty and of intervention group on young children's cognitive and socioemotional development.* Manuscript submitted for publication.

Linver, M. R., Brooks-Gunn, J., & Kohen, D. (1999). *Parenting behavior and emotional health as mediators of family poverty effects upon young children's development.* Manuscript submitted for publication.

Love, J. M., Aber, L., & Brooks-Gunn, J. (1994). *Strategies for assessing community progress toward achieving the first national educational goal.* Princeton, NJ: Mathematica Policy Research, Inc.

Lyons-Ruth, K., Alpern, L., & Repacholi, B. (1993). Disorganized infant attachment classification and maternal psychological problems as predictors of hostile-aggressive behavior in the preschool classroom. *Child Development, 64,* 572–585.

Maccoby, E. E., & Martin, J. A. (1983). Socialization in the context of the family: Parent-child interaction. In E. M. Hetherington (Ed.), *Handbook of child psychology* (4th ed., Vol. 4: Socialization, personality and social development, pp. 1–101). New York: Wiley.

Martinez, J. E., & Richters, P. (1993). The NIMH Community Violence Project: II. Children's distress symptoms associated with violence exposure. *Psychiatry, 56,* 22–35.

Mayer, S. E. (1997). Trends in the economic well-being and life chances of America's children. In G. J. Duncan & J. Brooks-Gunn (Eds.), *Consequences of growing up poor* (pp. 49–69). New York: Russell Sage Foundation.

McCall, R. B. (1983). A conceptual approach to early mental development. In M. Lewis (Ed.), *Origins of intelligence: Infancy and early childhood* (2nd ed.; pp. 107–133). New York: Plenum.

McKey, R. H., Condelli, L., Granson, H., Barrett, B., McConkey, C., & Plantz, M. (1985). *The impact of Head Start on children, families and communities.* Final report of Head Start Evaluation, Synthesis and Utilization.

McLanahan, S., & Sandefur, G. (1994). *Growing up with a single parent: What hurts and what helps.* Cambridge: Harvard University Press.

McLeod, J., & Shanahan, M. J. (in press). Trajectories of poverty and children's mental health. *Journal of Health and Social Behavior.*

McLoyd, V. C. (1990). The impact of economic hardship on Black families and development. *Child Development, 61,* 311–346.

McLoyd, V. C., Jayaratne-Epstein, T., Ceballo, R., & Borquez, J. (1994). Unemployment and work interruption among African American single mothers: Effects on parenting and adolescent socioemotional functioning. *Child Development,* 65(2), 562–589.

National Center for Children in Poverty. (1997). *Young Children in Poverty Fact Sheet.* New York: Retrieved April 7, 1998 from the World Wide Web: http://cpmc-net.columbia.edu/dept/nccp/ycpf.html.

Newacheck, P. W., Hughes, D. C., & Stoddard, J. J. (1996). Children's access to primary care: Differences by race, income, and insurance status. *Pediatrics,* 97(1), 26–32.

Newacheck, P. W., Stoddard, J. J., & McManus, M. (1993). Enthnocultural variations in the prevalence and impact of childhood chronic conditions. *Pediatrics,* 91(5), 1031–1038.

Olds, D., Henderson, C. R., & Kitzman, H. (1994). Does prenatal and infancy nurse home visitation have enduring effects on qualities of parental caregiving and child health at 25 to 50 months of life? *Pediatrics,* 93(1), 89–98.

Orshansky, M. (1965). Counting the poor: Another look at the poverty profile. *Social Security Bulletin, 26* (July), 3–29.

Pagani, L., Boulerice, B., & Tremblay, R. E. (1997). The influence of poverty on children's classroom placement and behavior problems. In G. J. Duncan & J. Brooks-Gunn (Eds.), *Consequences of growing up poor* (pp. 311–339). New York: Russell Sage Foundation.

Peters, H. E., & Mullis, N. C. (1997). The role of family income and sources of income in adolescent achievement. In G. J. Duncan & J. Brooks-Gunn (Eds.), *Consequences of growing up poor* (pp. 340–381). New York: Russell Sage Foundation.

Plotnick, R. D. (1997). Child poverty can be reduced. *The Futures of Children,* 7(2), 72–87.

Primus, W. E. (1997, March). *Supports for working poor families: A recent history of federal policy.* Paper presented at the Well-Being of Children in Working Poor Families Conference sponsored by the Foundation for Child Development. March 19, 1997.

Reynolds, A. J. (1994). Effects of a preschool plus follow-on intervention for children at risk. *Developmental Psychology, 30*(6), 787–804.

Richman, N., & Graham, P. J. (1971). A behavioural screening questionnaire for use with three-year-old children: Preliminary findings. *Journal of Child Psychology and Psychiatry, 12,* 5–33.

Rutter, M. (1981). Stress, coping and development: Some issues and some questions. *Journal of Child Psychology and Psychiatry, 4,* 323–356.

Sampson, R. J., Raudenbush, S. W., & Earls, F. (1997). Neighborhoods and violent crime: A multilevel study of collective efficacy. *Science, 277,* 918–924.

Selner-O'Hagan, M. B., Kindlon, D. J., Buka, S. L., Raudenbush, S. W., & Earls, F. J. (1998). Assessing exposure to violence in urban youth. *Journal of Child Psychology and Psychiatry and Allied Disciplines, 39*(2), 215–224.

Sewell, W., & Hauser, R. (1975). *Education, occupation, and earnings: Achievement in early career.* New York: Academic Press.

Shatz, C. J. (1992, September). The developing brain. *Scientific American,* 61–67.

Shonkoff, J. P., & Meisels, S. J. (Eds.). (in

press). *Handbook on early childhood intervention.* (2nd ed.). New York: Cambridge University Press.

Smeeding, T. M., & Torrey, B. B. (1988). Poor children in rich countries. *Science, 11*(242), 873–877.

Smith, J. R., Bastiani, A., & Brooks-Gunn, J. (1998). Poverty and mental health. In H. Friedman (Ed.), *Encyclopedia of Mental Health, Vol. 3* (pp. 219–228). San Diego, CA: Academic.

Smith, J. R., Brooks-Gunn, J., & Klebanov, P. K. (1997). The consequences of living in poverty for young children's cognitive and verbal ability and early school achievement. In G. J. Duncan & J. Brooks-Gunn (Eds.), *Consequences of growing up poor* (pp. 132–189). New York: Russell Sage Foundation.

Smith, J. R., Brooks-Gunn, J., Kohen, D., & McCarton, C. M. (1999). *Transitions on and off welfare: Implications for parenting and children's cognitive development.* Manuscript submitted for publication.

Smith, S. (1995). Two-generation programs: A new intervention strategy and directions for future research. In P. L. Chase-Lansdale & J. Brooks-Gunn (Eds.), *Escape from poverty: What makes a difference for poor children* (pp. 299–314). New York: Cambridge University Press.

Spiker, D., Ferguson, J., & Brooks-Gunn, J. (1993). Enhancing maternal interactive behavior and child social competence in low birth weight, premature infants. *Child Development, 64*(3), 754–768.

Spiker, D., Ferguson, J., & Brooks-Gunn, J. (1997). Mother-child interactions. In R. T. Gross, D. Spiker, & C. W. Haynes (Eds.), *Helping low birth weight, premature babies: The Infant Health and Development Program* (pp. 257–275). Stanford, CA: Stanford University Press.

Sweet, J. A., Bumpass, L., & Call, V. (1988). *The design and content of the National Survey of Families and Households.* NSFH Working Paper I. Madison, WI: University of Wisconsin, Center for Demography and Ecology.

Tizard, B., & Hodges, J. (1978). The effects of early institutional rearing on the development of eight-year-old children. *Journal of Child Psychology and Psychiatry, 19,* 971–975.

Teachman, J. D., Paasch, K. M., Day, R. D., & Carver, K. P. (1997). Poverty during adolescence and subsequent educational attainment. In G. J. Duncan & J. Brooks-Gunn (Eds.), *Consequences of growing up poor* (pp. 382–418). New York: Russell Sage Foundation.

Velez, C. N., Johnson, J., & Cohen, P. (1989). A longitudinal analysis of selected risk factors for childhood psychopathology. *Journal of the American Academy of Child and Adolescent Psychiatry, 28,* 861–864.

Ventura, S. J. (1995). Births to unmarried mothers: United States 1980–1992 (NCHS Series 21, No. 53). United States Department of Health and Human Services, Washington, DC: U.S. Government Printing Office.

Yoshikawa, H. (1994). Prevention as cumulative protection: Effects of early family support and education on chronic delinquency and its risks. *Psychological Bulletin, 115*(1), 28–54.

Wilson, W. J. (1991). Studying inner-city social dislocations: The challenge of public agenda research. *American Sociological Review, 56*(1), 1–14.

Wilson, W. J. (1997). *When work disappears.* New York: Knopf.

Zigler, E. F. (1987). The effectiveness of Head Start: Another look. *Educational Psychologist, 13,* 71–77.

5

Understanding Parenting: Contributions of Attachment Theory and Research

Lisa J. Berlin and Jude Cassidy

5

Introduction

Parenting is widely perceived as one of humans' most important and most demanding undertakings. Parenting is not only a challenging task but also a controversial subject. Freud identified parenting as an "impossible profession" (cited in Bornstein, 1995). Moreover, as Bornstein (1995) noted in the recently published *Handbook of Parenting,* "despite the fact that most people become parents and everyone who ever lived has had parents, parenting remains a mystifying subject about which almost everyone has opinions but about which few people agree" (p. xiii). In the past three decades, attachment theory and research have made a substantial contribution to the field of human development, especially with respect to understanding the infant-parent relationship and its influence on subsequent socioemotional functioning (Ainsworth, Blehar, Waters, & Wall, 1978; Bowlby, 1969/1982, 1973, 1980; Cassidy & Shaver, 1999; Thompson, in press; see Belsky & Cassidy, 1994, for a review). Attachment theory and research offer compelling evidence not only about the influence of the infant-parent relationship but also about the contribution of the parent—and of parenting—to individual differences in the quality of this relationship. Attachment theorists and researchers, in fact, emphasize the influence of parenting on the development of the infant-parent attachment. Viewed in the larger scheme of nature and nurture arguments, that is, attachment theory and research emphasize nurture and have contributed importantly to the understanding of parenting.

In this chapter, the contributions of attachment theory and research to understanding parenting are considered. The chapter begins with a brief overview of Bowlby's attachment theory, focusing on its predictions about parenting. Next, attachment research on the associations between parenting behavior and individual differences in infant-parent attachment is considered. Finally, attachment-related influences on parenting are discussed. Throughout this review, we aim to examine the extent to which attachment research supports the claims of the theory. We also aim to identify pressing questions and to suggest next steps for advancing the understanding of parenting.

A Brief Overview of Attachment Theory and Its Predictions about Parenting

The Attachment Behavioral System

According to attachment theory, the infant-parent attachment relationship is an evolutionarily adaptive relationship whose principal function is the protection of the child. Bowlby argued that all people are genetically predisposed to form enduring and preferential relationships with principal caregivers because, in humans' earliest environments, such relationships were evolutionarily advantageous. Beginning in early infancy, instinctive behaviors such as crying and reaching for help draw caregivers' ministrations. By the middle of the first year, infants begin to direct these behaviors toward specific people. By the end of the first year, the infant's attachment behavioral system is fully developed.

Bowlby (1969/1982) maintained that the attachment behavioral system is one of several species-specific control systems that have evolved to facilitate protection, survival, and ultimately, reproductive fitness. According to Bowlby, behavioral systems are goal-corrected systems, which operate to keep the individual in a stable, equilibrious state. Each system's output varies depending on the degree to which the system is activated. The degree of activation of the attachment system is thought to depend on the condition of the child, the condition and location of the parent, and the state of the environment. The corresponding output of the attachment behavioral system consists of discrete attachment behaviors, behaviors which have the predictable outcome of increasing proximity to attachment figures. The greater the activation of the attachment system, the more likely the deployment of attachment behaviors.

Bowlby argued that the attachment behavioral system functions in tandem with other behavioral systems, including the exploratory system, sociability system, and fear/wariness system. Ainsworth (1963; Ainsworth, Bell, & Stayton, 1971) argued further that the attachment and exploratory systems have a special relation to one another in that they are complementary yet mutually inhibiting. Specifically, the physical or psychological availability of the attachment figure is thought to facilitate exploration by providing the child a "secure base from which to explore" (Ainsworth, 1963). At the same time, there exists an attachment-exploration balance (Ainsworth et al., 1971). The activation of the attachment system reduces the activation of the exploratory system, and the activation of the exploratory system reduces the activation of the attachment system.

Internal Working Models

Bowlby was concerned not only with all human infants' attachment systems but also with differences between individuals. At the heart of Bowlby's thinking about individual differences is the notion of internal working models. Specifically, Bowlby argued that individuals draw on their earliest experiences to create cognitive maps or internal working models (also called representational models; 1969/1982, 1973) to facilitate the goal-corrected functioning of each behavioral system. The term *working model* is intended to stress the potentially flexible and dynamic nature of these cognitive representations. Whereas working models are forged in particular environments, they are most efficient if they can guide behavior across different environments. Working models include information not only about the environment but also about the individual's capabilities within the environment. They guide people's expectations, attention, interpretations, and memories. These processes, in turn, guide behavior. With continual use, internal working models become "overlearned" (Bowlby, 1980, p. 55), and they come to operate automatically and unconsciously. Over time, individuals are more likely to define their experiences using existing working models than to modify their representations to accommodate new, possibly inconsistent information. Thus, internal working models can be viewed as operating in a self-fulfilling manner.

Internal working models, however, are not considered to be immutable. As environments and individuals change and develop, working models are likely to require updating. Major changes in the environment and/or in the person require the reformulation of internal working models. Such factors as traumas, losses, and new attachments may well alter internal working models.

In discussing the development of internal working models of the attachment behavioral system, Bowlby (1973) emphasized parents' contributions. Specifically, Bowlby asserted that repeated daily transactions between the infant and the parent—especially those in which the parent is interpreting and responding to the infant's signals—lead the infant to develop expectations about the parent's caregiving. These expectations, in turn, are gradually organized into internal working models of the caregiver and of the self in relation to this caregiver. Sensitive caregiving potentiates the development of an internal working model of the caregiver as trustworthy and helpful and of the self as deserving of the caregiver's sensitive treatment. Conversely, insensitive caregiving leads to working models of the caregiver as unavailable and untrustworthy and of the self as unworthy of the caregiver's benevolent treatment.

Conditional Behavioral Strategies

A consideration of Main's (1990) concept of conditional behavioral strategies reveals even more specific predictions about the associations between caregiving behaviors and the quality of the infant-parent attachment. Main asserted that in addition to their adaptive propensity to form attachments, infants are equipped with biologically based abilities to tailor the output of the attachment behavioral system to particular caregiving contexts. These tailoring abilities, which function to garner as much parental protection as possible, are attachment strategies. Attachment strategies can also be viewed as unconscious plans, guided by internal working models of relationships, which in turn guide cognition and behavior. In sensitive caregiving environments, attachment strategies allow for a relatively direct relation between the activation of the attachment system and its output. For example, in a sensitive environment, a frightened baby will cry for her parent. In insensitive caregiving environments, strategies dictate that the output of

the attachment system be manipulated and tailored to the particular demands of the caregiver.

Main (1990) proposed two general types of insensitive caregiving environments: one in which the caregiver exaggerates the importance of independence and one in which the caregiver exaggerates the importance of dependence. When the caregiver exaggerates the importance of independence, the output of the attachment system will be minimized. Thus, a frightened baby will suppress fear and not cry for her parent or will cry as little as possible. When the caregiver exaggerates the importance of dependence, the output of the attachment system will be maximized. Thus, if a baby is afraid or anticipates becoming afraid, she will exaggerate her fear and cry as much and as loudly as possible. In each of these cases, the baby's attachment strategies allow her to obtain as much parental protection as possible in her particular caregiving context.

In summary, attachment theory emphasizes the adaptive nature of the infant-parent relationship. Both the proclivity to form attachments and the flexibility to organize attachment behaviors in response to particular caregiving environments are understood to be biologically based and adaptive features of the attachment behavioral system. According to attachment theory, it is caregivers' (parents') responses to the infant's signals that play the largest role in shaping the infant's working models of attachment and attachment-based strategies and, in turn, guide subsequent behavior and development.

Associations between Parenting Behavior and Individual Differences in the Infant-Parent Attachment

Beginning with Ainsworth's pioneering Baltimore study (Ainsworth et al., 1978), a large number of investigations have addressed the associations between parenting behavior and individual differences in the infant-parent attachment. This body of work indicates considerable correspondence between specific patterns of parenting behavior and the quality of the infant-parent attachment. A review of this work also highlights unanswered questions for future attachment theory and research pertaining to the role of parenting in the development of the infant-parent attachment.

Individual Differences in Infant-Parent Attachment

Ainsworth's development of the laboratory Strange Situation procedure galvanized the systematic identification and investigation of individual differences in infant-parent attachment (Ainsworth & Wittig, 1969; Ainsworth et al., 1978). This 20-minute assessment involves a 12- to 20-month-old infant, her parent, and an unfamiliar female "stranger" in seven increasingly stressful episodes. There are two brief infant-parent separations when the infant remains in a laboratory playroom with a selection of age-appropriate toys. Based largely upon the infant's response to the parent in the two reunion episodes, the Strange Situation's accompanying classifi-

cation system distinguishes three main patterns of infant-parent attachment: secure (Group B), insecure-avoidant (Group A), and insecure-ambivalent (Group C).

Approximately 65 percent of infants in most nonpathological samples are classified secure (Ainsworth et al., 1978; Campos, Barrett, Lamb, Goldsmith, & Stenberg, 1983; see also van IJzendoorn & Kroonenberg, 1988, for evidence of generally similar cross-national distributions). During the separations, secure infants generally reduce their exploration of the toys and may become distressed. During the reunions, these infants actively seek interaction, proximity to, and/or contact with their parent. Comforted by their parent's return, secure infants then return to play. In their ability to seek and receive comfort from their parent and then resume exploration, secure infants are thought to use their parent as a secure base from which to explore.

Approximately 20 percent of infants in most nonpathological samples are classified insecure-avoidant (Ainsworth et al., 1978; Campos et al., 1983; see also van IJzendoorn & Kroonenberg, 1988). Infants classified as avoidant are unlikely to cry during the separations. During the reunions, these infants actively avoid interaction with the parent and may appear to ignore their parent completely.

Approximately 15 percent of infants in most nonpathological samples are classified insecure-ambivalent (Ainsworth et al., 1978; Campos et al., 1983; see also van IJzendoorn & Kroonenberg, 1988). Infants classified as insecure-ambivalent are highly likely to express distress during the separations. During the reunions, however, these infants appear to derive little comfort from their parent's return. These infants demonstrate ambivalence about interacting with the parent that is frequently accompanied by angry, resistant behavior. In their inability to be soothed by their parent, ambivalent infants appear less able than secure infants to use their parent as a secure base from which to explore.

More recently, a fourth group, insecure-disorganized (Group D), has been identified (Main & Solomon, 1986, 1990). Disorganized, disoriented, and frightened reunion behaviors characterize the infants in this group. When a coder classifies an infant as disorganized, the coder also identifies which of the three principal patterns (secure, insecure-avoidant, or insecure-ambivalent) appears to coexist with or underlie the infant's disorganization. Subsequently, infants who are classified disorganized are also assigned a best-fitting, "forced" classification (of secure, insecure-avoidant, or insecure-ambivalent). When all four classifications are used, the proportion of insecure-disorganized infants in the sample varies with the extent of social and/or psychological risk (i.e., poverty, child maltreatment, parental psychopathology; see Lyons-Ruth, 1999, and van IJzendoorn, 1999, for reviews). For example, one study of child maltreatment found 82 percent of the maltreated infants to be insecure-disorganized compared to 18 percent of the (nonmaltreated) control group (Carlson, Cicchetti, Barnett, & Braunwald, 1989), a proportion that is typical of low-risk samples. A recent meta-analysis focusing on the insecure-

disorganized group suggests that this classification may be more closely associated with the insecure-ambivalent pattern than any other. Across over 1,200 cases, 14 percent of the insecure-disorganized infants received forced classifications of secure, 34 percent received forced classifications of insecure-avoidant, and 46 percent received forced classifications of insecure-ambivalent (van IJzendoorn et al., 1999; see Ainsworth & Eichberg, 1991, for further discussion of the association between the insecure-ambivalent and disorganized classifications).

Evidence of the Strange Situation's predictive validity has come from a large body of research that has demonstrated associations between the quality of infant-parent (usually infant-mother) attachment and the child's subsequent socioemotional functioning (see Belsky & Cassidy, 1994, and Thompson, 1999, for reviews). In brief, children classified as secure in infancy generally appear more socially competent than children who were classified as insecure.

The Attachment Q-Sort (AQS; Waters & Deane, 1985; see Waters, Vaughn, Posada, & Kondo-Ikemura, 1995) is another, more recently developed measure of individual differences in infant-parent attachment security. Designed to tap key features of the infant attachment, exploratory, and fear behavioral systems, the Q-Sort involves the infant's parent or a trained observer sorting 90 cards (items) into a fixed distribution. The resulting distribution is compared to (correlated with) a predetermined sort of a prototypically secure infant, which then yields a continuous measure of attachment security. Although both mother- and observer-sorted AQS scores have been found to relate to theoretically predictable aspects of children's subsequent development (e.g., Park & Waters, 1989; Teti & Ablard, 1988), some recent findings suggest that Q-sort data, especially that generated by parents, should be interpreted with caution. In addition to being correlated with socially desirable responses (Belsky & Rovine, 1990) mothers' sorts also yield less evidence of discriminant and convergent validity than observers' sorts (van IJzendoorn, Vereijken, & Riksen-Walraven, in press).

Ainsworth's Baltimore Study

Ainsworth's Baltimore study of 23 white, middle-class dyads included extensive narrative records of four-hour naturalistic home observations made every three weeks during the infants' first year. These data yielded painstakingly detailed information of a magnitude that has yet to be replicated. They also set the stage for the ensuing 20 years of investigation of the associations between parenting behavior and infant-parent attachments.

In synthesizing these narrative records, Ainsworth and her colleagues paid careful attention to mothers' responses to their infants' cues along the full spectrum of the attachment-exploratory balance, examining mothers' responsivity not only to their infants' attachment behaviors but also to their infants' bids for autonomous action and exploration (Ainsworth et al., 1978). Specifically, Ainsworth and her coworkers examined discrete maternal behaviors as

well as more global characterizations. Discrete behaviors included mothers' responsiveness to infants' crying and mothers' behavior relevant to separation and reunion, close bodily contact with their infants, face-to-face interaction, infant obedience, and feeding.

There were also four global scales that reflected these discrete behaviors: (1) "sensitivity-insensitivity to the baby's signals and communications," defined as the extent to which the mother took the infant's perspective, accurately perceived the infant's cues, and promptly and appropriately responded to these signals, or did not take action, if that was appropriate; (2) "acceptance-rejection," defined as the mother's feelings about her infant and her ability to balance the positive and negative emotions that parenting evokes; (3) "cooperation-interference," defined as the mother's controlling and intrusive behaviors; and (4) "accessibility-ignoring," defined as the mother's emotional availability to her infant. These global characterizations can be condensed further into two broad interrelated dimensions: The first, as embodied by the acceptance scale, centers on the mother's feelings about being a mother and the second, as embodied by the sensitivity, cooperation, and accessibility scales, refers to the mother's ability to read and respond to the infant's cues and to follow the infant's "agenda." The low ends of the cooperation and accessibility scales (interference and ignoring, respectively) can be viewed as tapping different types of *in*sensitivity.

Ainsworth and her colleagues went on to uncover a range of associations between the Baltimore mothers' behavior toward their infants across the first year of life and the three principal patterns of infant-mother attachment observed in the Strange Situation at 12 months. Analyses of both first- and fourth-quarter parenting behaviors indicated mothers of secure infants to be significantly more likely than mothers of avoidant infants as well as mothers of ambivalent infants to behave sensitively and to serve as a secure base to their infants. For example, during the first three months, mothers of infants classified as securely attached at 12 months were significantly more likely than mothers of infants classified as insecure to hold their infants carefully and tenderly and to time their interactions according to the infant's signals and significantly less likely to be unresponsive to their infants' crying and to handle their infants in a routine manner. Global characterizations of maternal behavior in the fourth quarter of the infant's life were especially revealing. Specifically, mothers of secure infants were significantly more sensitive, accepting, cooperative, and accessible to their babies than mothers of avoidant or ambivalent infants.

In reflecting on these findings, Ainsworth emphasized maternal sensitivity as both a pervasive aspect of caregiving behavior and a key influence on the quality of infant-mother attachment. Ainsworth wrote, "The most important aspect of maternal behavior commonly associated with the security-anxiety dimension of infant attachment is manifested in different specific ways in different situations, but in each it emerges as sensitive responsiveness to infant signals and communications" (Ainsworth et al., 1978, p. 152). Ainsworth emphasized maternal sensitivity not only to infants' attachment signals but also to infants' bids for autonomous exploration. She noted, "Among a child's behavioral cues are those indicating that he enjoys the adventures of exploring, he dislikes being interrupted when absorbed in autonomous activity, and he is gratified when he masters a new skill or problem on his own. A parent cannot be truly sensitive to a child's cues if she ignores these" (Ainsworth, 1984, p. 568).

The majority of Ainsworth's analyses on the associations between parenting behavior and infant attachment quality were devoted to differences between securely and insecurely attached infants. Ainsworth's small sample size prohibited rigorous comparison of the two insecure groups (six avoidant infants and four ambivalent infants). Some initial information on the caregiving behaviors of mothers of avoidant and ambivalent infants did, however, emerge. This information centers on the nature of these mothers' insensitivity. In particular, mothers of avoidant infants appeared rejecting and controlling. In the first quarter, mothers of avoidant infants received significantly higher scores on the scale for aversion to physical contact than mothers of ambivalent infants on this scale. Mothers of avoidant infants were also more significantly more likely than mothers of secure infants to be lacking in emotional expression and to behave rigidly and/or compulsively. In the fourth quarter, mothers of avoidant infants were significantly more likely than mothers of secure infants to pick up their babies in an abrupt and interfering manner and to use physical interventions to elicit infant obedience.

Different behaviors characterized mothers of ambivalent infants. These mothers appeared inconsistent and inept. In the fourth quarter, these mothers took significantly longer than mothers of secure infants to respond to their infants' cries. They also demonstrated significantly less skill in handling their infants and significantly less affection when picking up their babies than mothers of secure infants (see Cassidy & Berlin, 1994). Unlike mothers of avoidant infants, however, these mothers were not perceived as averse to close physical contact, "affording some comforting experience when in close bodily contact, albeit inconsistently" (Ainsworth, 1984, p. 582). Mothers of ambivalent infants also appeared to interfere with their infants' initial exploratory forays. These mothers were significantly more likely than mothers of secure infants to be "occupied with routines," while holding their infants, frequently holding their infants to feed them, and tending to "resist any effort the baby made to feed himself" (Ainsworth et al., 1978, p. 146).

In summary, Ainsworth's Baltimore study yielded not only the now classic Strange Situation procedure for assessing individual differences in infant-parent attachment but also the first data on the associations between parenting behavior and patterns of attachment. Mothers of infants later classified as secure were characterized as warm, sensitive, and clearly attuned to their infants' signals, especially in comparison to the mothers of infants later classified as insecure. Mothers of insecure-

avoidant and insecure-ambivalent infants were both characterized as less sensitive than mothers of secure infants, with their insensitivities seeming to take different forms. Mothers of avoidant infants appeared harsh and controlling, whereas mothers of ambivalent infants appeared inconsistent and inept.

Parenting Behavior and Individual Differences in the Infant-Parent Attachment: Finer Distinctions

Since the Baltimore study, there have been over 70 longitudinal and cross-sectional investigations addressing the associations between infant-parent (usually infant-mother) interactions observed both in the home and in the laboratory and the quality of the infant-parent attachment assessed with the Strange Situation or the Attachment Q-Sort (see Belsky & Cassidy, 1994, and Belsky, 1999, for reviews). These inquiries have been conducted in several countries, including the United States, Germany, Great Britain, the Netherlands, Japan, Israel, and Canada, and have included both middle- and low-income families. This body of research has yielded data that both parallel and extend Ainsworth's original findings. Specifically, the data have continually revealed associations between parental sensitivity in relation to both attachment and exploration and infant-parent attachment quality (although see Seifer, Schiller, Sameroff, Resnick, & Riordan, 1996, and Schneider-Rosen & Rothbaum, 1993, for nonsignificant findings). Finer distinctions, moreover, among the behaviors of parents of secure, insecure-avoidant, insecure-ambivalent, and inse-cure-disorganized infants have emerged. These data suggest particular internal working models of attachment and attach-ment-based strategies for each of the four attachment groups.

PARENTING BEHAVIOR ASSOCIATED WITH

THE SECURE PATTERN OF ATTACHMENT

Inquiries into the associations between parenting behavior and infant-parent at-tachment have confirmed and extended Ainsworth's initial characterization of par-ents of securely attached infants. Specifi-cally, studies have consistently linked parental sensitivity—and/or various as-pects of parental sensitivity—to a secure infant-parent attachment. For example, in the first replication of the Baltimore study, conducted in Northern Germany at two and six (but not ten) months, mothers of se-cure infants received significantly higher scores on a composite measure of sensitiv-ity than mothers of insecure-avoidant and insecure-ambivalent infants (Grossmann, Grossmann, Spangler, Suess, & Unzner, 1985; see also Miyake, Chen, & Campos, 1985, and Nakagawa, Lamb, & Miyake, 1992, for partially convergent findings from studies conducted in Japan). More recently, a multisite study of infant child care including over 1,100 infants found maternal "sensitivity in the home" at six and fifteen months to distinguish secure and insecure infants. Moreover, mothers of securely attached infants received higher scores than mothers of insecure-avoidant infants on both "sensitivity in the home" and "sensitivity in play" (NICHD Early Child Care Research Network, 1997; see

also Isabella, 1993, and Pederson & Moran, 1996). Another investigation found "dyadic distress management," a measure of mothers' responsiveness to their infants' fussing and crying, to distinguish secure and insecurely attached infants (Del Car-men, Pederson, Huffman, & Bryan, 1993; see also Crockenberg, 1981). Still another inquiry yielded positive correlations be-tween mothers' and fathers' "positive in-teraction" and "physical affection" and in-fants' attachment security scored on a con-tinuous scale (Cox, Owen, Henderson, & Margand, 1992; see also Bates, Maslin, & Frankel, 1985). Consistent findings have emerged from a study using (observer) Q-sort techniques to assess not only attach-ment but also maternal sensitivity, defined as involving "an openness to signals in the context of the need to attend to other com-peting events" (Pederson et al., 1990, p. 1976), a definition bound to resonate with many parents. Pederson and his colleagues discerned a significant correlation of .52 between maternal sensitivity and infant at-tachment security (see also Moran, Peder-son, Pettit, & Krupka, 1992, and Vereij-ken, Riksen-Walraven, & Kondo-Ikemura, 1997). Consistent findings have also emerged from the Minnesota Mother-Child Project of low-income mothers and their infants. For example, in both feeding and play sessions at six months, mothers of infants later classified secure were rated as more sensitive than mothers of insecure-avoidant and insecure-ambivalent infants (Egeland & Farber, 1984; see also Susman-Stillman, Kalkoske, Egeland, & Wald-man, 1996). Studies addressing clinical is-sues such as maternal depression (Teti,

Gelfand, Messinger, & Isabella, 1995) and mothers' prenatal alcohol consumption (O'Connor, Sigman, & Kasari, 1992) have also linked maternal sensitivity to infant attachment security.

Further insight into the practices of parents of secure infants comes from considering the extent of these parents' involvement with their infants. Specifically, Belsky has argued that in their *contingent* responsiveness to their infants' signals, parents of secure infants should show neither uniformly high nor uniformly low levels of involvement with their infants but rather intermediate levels of involvement, relative to the parents of insecure-avoidant and insecure-ambivalent infants (Belsky, Rovine, & Taylor, 1984). Invoking Aristotle's golden mean, Belsky emphasized, "it would be inappropriate to conclude that more maternal involvement and interaction with the infant is synonymous with sensitive care. Indeed . . . too much involvement and interaction can be as insensitive as too little involvement, given its potential for overstimulating the infant. . . . " (Belsky et al., 1984, p. 719). Belsky and his colleagues uncovered a significant linear trend in which, at nine months, mothers of secure infants received intermediate scores on an aggregate rating of involvement with their infants. There were similar, albeit nonsignificant trends at one and three months (Belsky et al., 1984; see also Isabella & Belsky, 1991, and Isabella, Belsky, & von Eye, 1989).

As discussed earlier with respect to the attachment-exploration balance and the parent's provision of a secure base from which the infant can explore, sensitive caregiving is expected to maximize the infant's opportunities to explore his environment and to contribute to the infant's emerging sense of himself as an independent person. Bowlby (1973) associated a "stable and self-reliant personality" (p. 322) with "not only . . . unfailing parental support when called upon but also . . . steady yet timely encouragement towards increasing autonomy. . . . " (pp. 322–323). Thus, the sensitive caregiving found to characterize mothers of secure infants should be viewed as contributing not only to the infant's emotional security but also to his or her developing autonomy. Moreover, the studies associating parenting behavior and infant-parent attachment characterize parents of secure infants as more sensitive not only to their infants' attachment behaviors but also to their infants' bids for autonomy than parents of insecure infants. For example, in Miyake et al.'s (1985) investigation, at 7½ months, mothers of secure infants were significantly less likely than mothers of insecure-ambivalent infants to intrude by "interrupting the baby's ongoing activity without a bid from the baby" (p. 292). Additionally, in Egeland and Farber's (1984) investigation, in the six-month feeding session, mothers of secure infants were rated as significantly more cooperative (i.e., less intrusive) than mothers of insecure-avoidant and insecure-ambivalent infants. In the six-month play session, mothers of secure infants were rated as significantly more cooperative than mothers of insecure-avoidant infants. Finally, in a 1985 laboratory-based study, although there were no contemporaneous associations between maternal behavior and infant-mother attachment quality, both stability of attachment from 12 to 20 months and change (between 12 and 20 months) from an insecure to a secure infant-mother attachment were associated with greater maternal sensitivity as well as greater maternal "support for [the infant's] autonomy" (Frodi, Grolnick, & Bridges, 1985).

Thus, the studies of the associations between parenting behavior and infant-parent attachment portray mothers of secure infants as warm, sensitive, moderately involved with their babies, and supportive of their infant's initial striving toward autonomy. These parenting behaviors can be viewed as communicating the message that the infant's signals will be acknowledged and that the infant's needs will be fulfilled. Barring mitigating circumstances (e.g., a trauma), this type of parenting behavior is expected to result in the infant developing internal working models of her parent as available and supportive and of herself as deserving of sensitive and supportive care. These internal working models, in turn, inform the infant's conditional behavioral strategy, which in this case is thought to involve a direct relation between the activation of the attachment system and its output. Attachment figures are sought in times of stress, and opportunities for exploration are optimized. This strategy stands in stark contrast to that of insecure infants, which is discussed next.

PARENTING BEHAVIOR ASSOCIATED WITH THE INSECURE-AVOIDANT PATTERN OF ATTACHMENT

Ainsworth's Baltimore study tentatively portrayed mothers of insecure-avoidant infants as rejecting and controlling. Since then, theory and research pertaining to parenting behavior and attachment have both supported and extended this portrait (see Cassidy & Kobak, 1988, and Main, 1981, for reviews; see also Main, 1990). Drawing on the work of Ainsworth and her colleagues, two studies have examined maternal rejection vis-à-vis mothers' physical contact with their infants. Belsky et al. (1984) found no differences between mothers of avoidant and secure infants in the frequency of mothers' "holding outside of the context of feeding." Egeland and Farber (1984), however, found mothers of insecure-avoidant infants to exhibit significantly lower rates of "nonfunctional handling" than mothers of secure and insecure-ambivalent infants. Whereas more data on mothers' handling of their infants is required, some additional hints into the possibly rejecting behaviors of mothers of avoidant infants have come from two studies focusing on mothers' responses to their infants' affective expressions. In the first, mothers of avoidant infants were more likely than mothers of secure infants to ignore their babies' emotional signals. Additionally, these mothers participated in their infants' play until the infants expressed negative affect, at which point these mothers withdrew (Escher-Graub & Grossmann, 1983). Connections between the insecure-avoidant pattern and mothers' tendencies to downplay their infants' negative affect have also been suggested by an investigation wherein infants and their mothers participated in face-to-face interactions several times during the infants' first year (Malatesta, Culver, Tesman, &

Shepard, 1989). Mothers' surprise in response to their infants' angry expressions—which can be viewed as an intimation that the infant's anger is inappropriate—was associated with infants' suppressed anger in the Strange Situation, an expression that was most characteristic of avoidant infants.

Research has also characterized mothers of avoidant infants as both controlling and overstimulating. For example, in Egeland and Farber's (1984) study, in the six-month feeding session, mothers of insecure-avoidant infants were rated as significantly less cooperative (i.e., more intrusive) than mothers of secure and insecure-ambivalent infants. In the six-month play session, mothers of insecure-avoidant infants were rated as significantly less cooperative than mothers of secure infants. In Belsky et al.'s (1984) study, the linear trend analyses portrayed mothers of avoidant infants as the most attentive, vocal, and stimulating (see also Lewis & Feiring, 1989). Two follow-up inquiries with additional cohorts illuminated the extent to which these types of behaviors were noncontingent and insensitive. Mothers of avoidant infants were revealed to vocalize to their infants, "almost without regard to what the baby was doing but rarely in response to the baby's own vocalizations" (Isabella et al., 1989; see also Isabella & Belsky, 1991). Several laboratory investigations are also relevant. In one, mothers of avoidant infants scored significantly higher than mothers of secure and insecure-ambivalent infants on intrusiveness (Smith & Pederson, 1988). In another, mothers of avoidant infants were rated as significantly

more controlling than mothers of secure infants (Vondra, Shaw, & Kevinedes, 1995). Finally, in Malatesta et al.'s (1989) inquiry, infants who had experienced "extremely high rates" (p. 76) of maternal contingent facial responding were significantly more likely to be classified avoidant at 22 months.

Taken together, these studies portray mothers of insecure-avoidant infants as distancing and perhaps also rejecting, in response to their infants' attachment signals as well as controlling and overly stimulating of their babies. These parenting behaviors can be viewed as communicating the message that the infant's attachment signals are illegitimate and will not be acknowledged, that the infant's own agenda cannot be executed, and that dyadic harmony can be achieved by the infant's withdrawal. These parenting behaviors, moreover, are expected to result in the infant developing internal working models of her parent as consistently unavailable and of herself as unworthy of sensitive and supportive care. These internal working models, in turn, inform a strategy whereby both the activation and output of the attachment behavioral system are minimized (Main, 1990). This strategy precludes the deployment of attachment behaviors that the infant anticipates will be met with further repudiation and, in so doing, allows the infant to maintain as much contact with her parent as possible. This strategy involves not only minimization of attachment but also exaggeration of the importance of independence. Emphasizing independent exploration helps the infant minimize attachment as well as circumvent the parents' excessively controlling behaviors.

It is important to note that although insecure-avoidant infants may explore more than secure infants, this exploration in the absence of a secure base is likely to result in costs to the individual. For example, one team of researches measured infants' heart rates during the Strange Situation and adrenocortisol levels 15 and 30 minutes after the Strange Situation (Spangler & Grossmann, 1993). Despite the typical diverse behaviors among the different attachment groups, heart rate assessments did not distinguish the insecure-avoidant group from the secure group (the one infant in this study classified insecure-ambivalent was omitted from analyses). Specifically, although the avoidant infants were less likely to become upset and more likely to explore than the secure infants, their heart rates indicated that they were as aroused as their clearly upset, securely classified counterparts. The cost of greater exploring for these avoidant infants, thus, appears to have been suppressed arousal and/or emotion. Suppression of emotion, moreover, has been linked to health problems in both adults and children (see, e.g., Pennebaker & Beall, 1986).

PARENTING BEHAVIOR ASSOCIATED WITH THE INSECURE-AMBIVALENT PATTERN

Ainsworth's Baltimore study suggested that the mothers of the insecure-ambivalent infants were inconsistent and inept. Since then, theory and research pertaining to parenting behavior and attachment have both supported and refined this view (see Cassidy & Berlin, 1994, for an extensive review of the insecure-ambivalent pattern; see also Main, 1990). Specifically, studies have suggested that mothers of insecure-ambivalent infants are inconsistently and/or insufficiently responsive to their infants' attachment signals yet, at the same time, interfering with their infants' efforts at exploration. In Belsky et al.'s (1984) study, the linear trend analyses portrayed mothers of ambivalent infants as the least attentive, vocal, and stimulating; in the second cohort, dyads containing insecure-ambivalent infants were observed to exhibit "relatively few" (p. 18) mutual and reciprocal exchanges (Isabella et al., 1989; see also Isabella & Belsky, 1991). Crockenberg (1981) found a significant positive correlation between mothers' latency to respond to their infants' crying and these infants' resistant behavior in the Strange Situation, a behavior most characteristic of infants classified insecure-ambivalent (see also Egeland & Farber, 1984, and Lewis & Feiring, 1989). Laboratory data tell a similar story. One investigation indicated that, compared to both other groups of mothers at six months, mothers of infants later classified ambivalent initiated the fewest number of interactions with their infants (Kiser, Bates, Maslin, & Bayles, 1986). In Smith and Pederson's (1988) investigation, compared to both other groups of mothers, mothers of ambivalent infants received significantly more "insufficient" ratings and significantly fewer "appropriate" ratings (see also Vondra et al., 1995).

Curiously, although mothers of insecure-ambivalent infants appear less responsive than other mothers to their infants' attachment signals, these mothers have also been characterized as interfering with their infants' bids for autonomy. As discussed earlier, Ainsworth described mothers of ambivalent infants as interfering with their babies' efforts to feed themselves. A similar pattern emerged from Isabella and Belsky's (1991) investigation. Mothers of insecure-ambivalent infants were described as attempting to initiate interaction when their infants were "otherwise involved or seemingly unwilling to interact" (Isabella & Belsky, 1991, p. 975). Finally, in Miyake et al.'s (1985) investigation, at 7½ months, mothers of ambivalent infants were significantly more likely than mothers of secure infants to interfere by "interrupting the baby's ongoing activity without a bid from the baby" (p. 292). Like the mothers of avoidant infants, thus, the mothers of ambivalent infants behave intrusively. But whereas the mothers of avoidant infants appear consistently controlling and overstimulating, the intrusiveness of the mothers of ambivalent infants takes a subtler form. These mothers appear to interfere selectively, in response to their infants' bids for exploration.

These studies portray mothers of insecure-ambivalent infants as both underresponsive to their infants' attachment signals and interfering with their infants' developing autonomy. Taken together, these parenting behaviors can be viewed as communicating the message that the infant should remain engaged with the parent: The infant's attachment signals must be amplified to be heard, and the infant's interest in exploring will not be recognized. This type of parenting behavior is expected to result in the infant developing internal working models of her parent as both unreliable and interfering and of herself as a person who will receive only intermittent care and whose attempts to explore autonomously will not succeed. These internal working models, in turn, inform a strategy whereby both the activation and output of the attachment behavioral system are maximized (Main, 1990). Amplifying attachment signals serves to draw the attention of the caregiver who otherwise may or may not be available and allows the infant to maintain as much contact with her parent as possible. The insecure-ambivalent strategy involves not only emphasizing attachment but also de-emphasizing exploration. Diminished exploration keeps the infant's attention focused on the parent and prevents the infant from developing skills that will increase her independence and individuation.

PARENTING BEHAVIOR ASSOCIATED WITH INSECURE-DISORGANIZED ATTACHMENT

As we discussed earlier, there is a direct, positive correlation between family risk and insecure-disorganized attachment. Risk factors associated with the insecure-disorganized category include poverty and/or low socioeconomic status, documented child maltreatment, maternal psychopathology, and maternal prenatal alcohol consumption. There is also some evidence of an association between the severity of family risk and disorganized infants' forced classifications, with more severe and/or chronic problems going hand in hand with forced classifications of insecure (see Lyons-Ruth & Jacobvitz, 1999, and Lyons-Ruth et al., 1991). Thus, parental risk can contribute not only to infants' developing a disorganized attachment but also to the pattern of attachment underlying the infant's disorganization.

Information about the particular parenting behaviors that underlie the association between parental risk status and a disorganized infant-parent attachment is just becoming available (see Lyons-Ruth & Jacobvitz, 1999, and van IJzendoorn et al., in press, for reviews). Main and Hesse (1990) argued that the infant's disorganization results from being frightened by the parent. They suggested further that a parent may frighten her infant via direct assaults, as in the case of a maltreating parent, or by being frightened herself, as in the case of a clinically depressed, anxious, or traumatized parent. Frightening and frightened behaviors are speculated to include unusual vocal patterns, speech content, and movements, such as looming at the infant or expressing extreme timidity in handling the infant (Main & Hesse, 1990). Preliminary evidence of associations between these types of behaviors and the insecure-disorganized pattern has come from two recent studies. In one study, home observations of mothers' frightening behaviors toward their 10- to 11-month-old infants discriminated disorganized infants from nondisorganized infants at 14 to 15 months. Mothers of disorganized infants received higher scores for frightening behaviors than mothers of nondisorganized infants (Schuengel, Bakermans-Kranenburg, & van IJzendoorn, in press). In a second investigation, frightening or frightened maternal behaviors not only discrim-

inated disorganized from nondisorganized infants but also appeared to be part of a larger pattern of "disrupted affective communication" (Lyons-Ruth, Bronfman, & Parsons, in press).

The practices of parents of insecure-disorganized infants forecast bleak consequences with respect to these infants' internal working models and attachment strategies. In particular, these parenting behaviors are expected to result in the infant developing internal working models of her parent as a source of disorganization and/or hostility and of herself as a target of aggression and/or source of fear. As Main and Hesse (1990) have so poignantly noted, the disorganized infant is faced with an "irresolvable paradox wherein the haven of safety is at once the source of the alarm" (p. 180). This conflict, in turn, leaves the infant unable to create a coherent strategy with which to guarantee even a measure of parental protection. The disorganized infant, in fact, has been characterized by his *lack* of a coherent strategy (Main & Solomon, 1986).

SUMMARY

Since the Baltimore study, the many investigations addressing the associations between infant-parent interaction and the quality of the infant-parent attachment have both parallelled and extended Ainsworth and her colleagues' findings of the associations between maternal sensitivity in relation to both attachment and exploration and infant-mother attachment. This body of research has not only illustrated the sensitivity of the parents (principally mothers) of secure infants but also delineated the *in*sensitivities of the parents (mothers) of insecure infants. The parenting behaviors associated with each pattern of attachment, moreover, have direct implications for the infants' developing working models and attachment-based strategies, especially vis-à-vis the attachment-exploration balance. The sensitive behaviors of parents of secure infants allow the infants to develop a strategy of using the parent as a secure base. The parents of insecure-avoidant infants appear harsh and controlling, resulting in their infants developing a strategy of minimizing attachment. Independent exploration is emphasized, although this exploration may be compromised and/or exact costs to truly healthy functioning. The parents of insecure-ambivalent infants appear both underresponsive and interfering, resulting in their infants developing a strategy of maximizing attachment. Independent exploration is minimized, and barring changes to the infant-parent relationship, the child's increasingly limited autonomy is likely to contribute to an increasing overdependence on the parent. Both the insecure-avoidant and insecure-ambivalent patterns, thus, reflect disruptions to the attachment-exploration balance: The avoidant pattern is imbalanced in the direction of exploration, and the ambivalent pattern is imbalanced in the direction of attachment. Both the avoidant and ambivalent patterns, however, allow the infant to maintain a measure of proximity to the parent and presumably to gain at least basic protection from the parent in the face of danger. Within the insecure-disorganized pattern, the infant cannot find a way to maintain proximity to the parent. Rather, the infant is left in a state of fear and confusion in which he can move neither toward nor away from the parent.

Parenting Behavior and Individual Differences in the Infant-Parent Attachment: Additional Perspectives

Whereas the studies of infant-parent interaction and infant-parent attachment have been enormously valuable in delineating the parenting behaviors associated with each of the four attachment patterns, it is also helpful to gain additional perspectives on—and perhaps even a broader view of—this body of research. In this section three additional perspectives are considered. One perspective comes from a recent meta-analysis of the "parenting antecedents" of infant-parent attachment. A second perspective comes from considering intervention studies of infant-parent attachment. Finally, fathering and the infant-father attachment is discussed. Examination of these three additional perspectives reveals additional evidence of an association between parental sensitivity and infant-parent attachment quality.

A META-ANALYSIS OF THE PARENTING ANTECEDENTS OF INFANT-PARENT ATTACHMENT

The meta-analysis of the association between parenting behavior and infant-parent attachment drew on data from 66 studies and included over 4,000 infant-mother pairs (De Wolff & van IJzendoorn, 1997). Each study included at least one assessment of the mother's behavior toward her infant and of infant-mother attachment quality. In light of concerns about the validity of mother-sorted attachment Q-sets, studies based on these data were excluded.

Based on their examination of the relevant studies, De Wolff and van IJzendoorn (1997) created nine categories of maternal behavior to examine in relation to infant-parent attachment: (1) *sensitivity* and (2) *cooperation,* defined according to Ainsworth, et al. (1978); (3) *contiguity of response,* defined as the frequency of the mother's response to the infant's signals; (4) *synchrony,* defined as reciprocal and mutually rewarding interaction; (5) *mutuality,* defined as harmonious and mutually satisfying exchanges; (6) *support,* defined as the extent to which the mother is attentive and supportive; (7) *positive attitude,* defined as a balance of positive and negative emotions; (8) *stimulation,* defined as any maternal action directed toward the infant; and (9) *physical conctact,* including all constructs referring to quantity and quality of physical contact. Infant-parent attachment was examined along the secure-insecure dichotomy. After some collapsing across both maternal and attachment variables (e.g., in cases in which there were multiple assessments), each of the nine sets of maternal behavior was examined in relation to infant-parent attachment. Controls were built into the analysis to assess such factors as quality of the studies and the extent to which findings might be attributable to published versus unpublished data. The authors also examined key features of the studies' samples and designs such as the socioeconomic status of the participants,

the extent to which the participants were in any way special (e.g., having mental or physical disabilities), the age of the child at each assessment, the type of attachment assessment, and the location of the assessment of maternal behavior. Of particular concern was the association between maternal sensitivity and infant-mother attachment.

The meta-analysis revealed significant associations between maternal behavior and infant-mother attachment for each of the nine sets of caregiving behavior. Effect sizes ranged from .09 for physical contact to .32 for mutuality. The mean effect size was .18. The effect size for the association between maternal sensitivity and infant-mother attachment was .22, considered to indicate a "moderately strong" association (De Wolff & van IJzendoorn, 1997). When examining only the 30 studies that used Ainsworth's original sensitivity scale, the effect size was .24. Applying a binomial effect size display (BESD) approach to this effect yields another view of the data. Specifically, the BESD describes an effect size in terms of the improvement rate that is attributable to the predictor variable. For the 30 studies using Ainsworth's sensitivity scale, the BESD indicates that infants with more sensitive mothers improve their chances of becoming securely attached from 38 to 62 percent. Infants whose mothers are less sensitive decrease their chances of becoming securely attached from 62 to 38 percent.

There was also some indication, for some of the caregiving behaviors, that aspects of the studies' samples and designs moderated the association between caregiving and attachment quality. For example, for sensitivity, the older the child at the time of both (maternal and attachment) assessments, the stronger the effect. The effect size also increased as the time interval between these assessments decreased. Of particular interest is the finding that for the studies that used Ainsworth's scale to assess sensitivity, participants' socioeconomic status moderated the association between sensitivity and infant-mother attachment. The effect was significantly stronger in middle-class samples ($r = .27$) than lower-class samples ($r = .15$). Thus, maternal sensitivity appeared to have less of an influence on infant-mother attachment among infant-mother dyads of lower socioeconomic status than among infant-mother dyads of higher socioeconomic status. Additionally, for the domains of cooperation and positive attitude, participants' membership in a special group (i.e., being mentally or physically disabled) decreased the association between caregiving and attachment quality. There were no effects of the type of attachment assessment used, although most (86 percent) of the studies included used the standard Strange Situation procedure.

In summary, De Wolff and van IJzendoorn's meta-analysis indicates consistent, albeit low to moderate, associations between several aspects of mothers' caregiving and infant-mother attachment. Although the authors interpret their findings as indicating that "sensitivity cannot be considered to be the exclusive and most important factor in the development of attachment" (p. 585), we offer a somewhat different interpretation. First, we differ on

the operationalization of sensitivity. De Wolff and van IJzendoorn distinguished maternal sensitivity from "other" aspects of caregiving such as cooperation, emotional support, and quality of physical contact. They interpreted associations between these types of behaviors and infant-parent attachment as detracting from the association between sensitivity and attachment. We view behaviors such as cooperation, emotional support, and quality of physical contact as *aspects* of maternal sensitivity/insensitivity (see also van den Boom, 1997). Therefore, we view associations between these behaviors and infant-mother attachment as buttressing the association between sensitivity and attachment. Secondly, De Wolff and van IJzendoorn did not test the differences between the effect sizes for the various parenting behaviors examined and cannot claim that other maternal behaviors are more strongly related to attachment than is sensitivity. Thus, we view the findings as emphasizing the contribution of sensitivity to the development of the infant-mother attachment. Although we agree that sensitivity is not the exclusive factor in the development of attachment, we suggest that it is premature to conclude that sensitivity is not the most important factor in the development of the infant-parent attachment.

INTERVENTION STUDIES OF INFANT-PARENT ATTACHMENT

Further evidence of an association between parenting behavior and infant-parent attachment has come from experimental intervention studies aiming to enhance maternal sensitivity and/or infant-mother attachment (e.g., Jacobson & Frye, 1990; van den Boom, 1994, 1995). Data from these studies on the associations between experimentally manipulated sensitivity and infant-parent attachment are especially valuable because they are less susceptible than nonexperimental findings to "third variable" explanations for the associations between maternal sensitivity and infant-parent attachment (the explanation, for example, that an infant's easy temperament accounts for both sensitive parental behavior and a secure infant-parent attachment). Particularly informative data have emerged from a Dutch study of low-income mothers and their temperamentally irritable infants (van den Boom, 1994). In this study, home visitors targeted maternal sensitivity by coaching mothers to recognize and respond to their infants' cues. Intervention group mothers were subsequently found to be significantly more sensitive and significantly more likely to have securely attached infants than control group mothers. A follow-up study indicated that these differences persisted into the children's preschool years (van den Boom, 1995). The findings from this sample of irritable infants are particularly compelling because they directly rebut the most frequently offered alternative explanation for the association between parental sensitivity and infant-parent attachment, that an infant's easy temperament accounts for both sensitive parenting and a secure infant-parent attachment.

In addition to van den Boom's compelling findings, it is also important to consider the results of a recent meta-analysis of 12 attachment-based intervention studies including almost 900 infant-mother pairs (van IJzendoorn, Juffer, & Duyvesteyn, 1995). This meta-analysis (which included van den Boom's 1994 data) indicated a significant medium to strong effect ($d = .58$) of these interventions on maternal sensitivity. The meta-analysis also revealed a weak ($d = .17$) although significant effect of these interventions on infant-mother attachment examined along the secure-insecure dichotomy. Taken together, these effects indicate that although intervening in maternal sensitivity can affect the infant-parent attachment, increasing sensitivity does not necessarily lead to a secure infant-parent attachment. These meta-analyses, thus, illuminate the importance of understanding the *limits* of the association between sensitivity and attachment and/or the constraints of the existing assessments of sensitivity and attachment quality.

FATHERING AND
INFANT-FATHER ATTACHMENT

So far, our discussion of the associations between parenting and infant-parent attachment has been based almost exclusively on studies of mothers and their infants. Compared to the studies of mothers' parenting, there are both fewer and less consistent studies of fathering. Although fathers typically are less likely than mothers to be their children's principal caretakers, fathers generally do serve as an attachment figure to their child as well as to their child's mother (Bowlby, 1958; see also Parke, 1995). Understanding fathering and the infant's bond to his or her father, thus, are important tasks, especially as mothers' labors become increasingly divided between child rearing and work outside of the home.

Some insight into fathering and the infant-father attachment has come from a recent meta-analysis of the association between parenting behavior and infant-father attachment (van IJzendoorn & De Wolff, 1997). This meta-analysis drew on data from eight studies and included 545 infant-father pairs. The meta-analysis revealed significant associations between paternal behavior and infant-father attachment, with estimated correlations between .13 and .20. At the same time, the association between fathering and infant-father attachment was found to be significantly weaker than the association between mothering and infant-mother attachment. As in the case of mothers, fathers' sensitive parenting predicted the quality of their infants' attachments. Yet the meta-analysis also suggests that factors other than sensitivity may shape the infant-father attachment and perhaps interact differently than in the infant-mother attachment. Preliminary support for this perspective has come from Cox et al.'s (1992) inquiry (discussed earlier) in which both mothers' and fathers' interactive behaviors were associated with infants' attachment security. Fathers' self-reported attitudes about the infant and about parenting added significantly to the prediction of infant-father attachment whereas, mothers' same self-reports did not.

Clearly, considerably more data on fathering and on the infant-father attachment are required. As these data accumulate, it will be especially interesting to ex-amine the interactions among fathering, mothering, and the development of the infant's attachments. For example, fathering may influence mothering in a number of ways. The mother may model the father's parenting behavior and/or the mother may (consciously or unconsciously) act to challenge or compensate for the father's parenting behavior. The father's behavior toward the infant may also influence the ways in which the infant behaves toward the mother which, in turn, influences the mother's parenting behavior. Fathers' parenting behaviors, thus, may influence the quality of the infant-mother attachment. Similarly, mothers' parenting behaviors may influence the quality of the infant-father attachment. These dynamics may well be magnified in families in which an infant's parents behave quite differently (e.g., in cases in which one parent's behavior is principally sensitive and the other parent's behavior is principally insensitive).

SUMMARY

Beginning with Ainsworth's pioneering Baltimore study (Ainsworth et al., 1978) wherein individual differences in infant-parent attachment were first identified, many inquiries have addressed the associations between parenting behavior and the quality of the infant-parent attachment. This research has offered increasingly specific information on the links between parenting behaviors and the four categories of infant-parent attachment. Van IJzendoorn's meta-analytic work has not only provided evidence of the association between parenting behavior—especially sensitivity/insensitivity—and attachment but also illustrated the parameters of this association. In particular, whereas the meta-analysis of parenting and attachment indicates robust evidence of a moderate association between maternal sensitivity and infant-mother attachment, by definition, the moderate association suggests that there is still considerable variance in infant-parent attachment that remains unexplained. Moreover, the evidence of such factors as socioeconomic status and special group membership (i.e., being mentally or physically disabled) moderating the association between sensitivity and attachment suggests that the influence of maternal sensitivity on infant-mother attachment may not be equally important for everyone (see also Belsky, 1997). Finally, fathering and the infant-father attachment are issues ripe for further inquiry. The quality of the infant-father attachment may even help explain variation in the association between maternal sensitivity and infant-mother attachment. We propose further that greater insight into the associations between parenting behavior and infant-parent attachment—indeed, greater insight into parenting on the whole—can come from considering attachment-related influences on parenting behavior, to which we now turn.

Attachment-Related Influences on Parenting Behavior

In the previous section of this chapter, the ways in which parenting behavior may influence infant-parent attachment were discussed. This section considers factors that influence parenting behavior. As several of the other chapters in this volume illustrate (see, e.g., Barnard & Kelley; Brooks-Gunn & McHale; Solomon & George), there are, of course, numerous factors that influence parenting. We focus on two sets of factors highlighted by attachment theory and research as key influences on parenting behavior: (1) the parent's "state of mind with respect to attachment" and (2) the parent's attachments. As will be discussed, whereas both sets of factors have been shown to contribute importantly to parenting behavior, the most insight may be gained by considering the ways in which these factors interact.

Attachment-Related Influences on Parenting Behavior: The Parent's State of Mind with Respect to Attachment

The development of the Adult Attachment Interview (AAI; George, Kaplan, & Main, 1985) initiated the systematic identification and investigation of individual differences in an adult's "state of mind with respect to attachment" (George et al., 1985). The Adult Attachment Interview is a one-hour, semistructured interview in which adults are asked to discuss early childhood experiences and the influences of these experiences on adult personality. Initially, the interviewee is asked to describe her early relationship with her parents, both generally and with specific memories to illustrate and support the generalities. Subsequent questions probe the subject's memories of emotional upset, physical injury and illness, and separations and losses.

Although the AAI draws heavily on recollections of early attachment experiences, subsequent experiences—especially attachment relationships—are also expected to influence the individual's current state of mind. It is the ways in which the interviewee discusses her experiences that figure most importantly in the individual's classification into one of three groups that parallel the three principal infant attachment patterns: secure/autonomous, dismissing, or preoccupied. Each interviewee is also assigned scores on continuous scales measuring "probable experiences" with early attachment figures (e.g., loving, pressure to achieve, rejection) and "current state of mind" (e.g., coherent, idealizing, angry; see Bakermans-Kranenburg & van IJzendoorn, 1993, for evidence of reliability and validity).

As with the infant attachment classifications, adult attachment classifications are thought to reflect particular internal working models and conditional behavioral strategies (Main, 1990). Whereas infants' strategies operate to optimize protection from the parent, adults' strategies are thought to operate to preserve a particular state of mind (i.e., to preserve mental organization) with respect to attachment. Adults classified as secure appear to value attachment relationships and view them as influential. These adults are also notably objective about both negative and positive attachment relationships and experiences. The strategy of a secure adult, thus, is thought to involve a valuing of and openness about attachment. Individuals classi-

fied as dismissing devalue attachments and dismiss their influence. As with avoidant infants, the strategy of the dismissing adult is thought to involve minimizing both the activation and output of the attachment system. Adults classified as preoccupied appear overwhelmed by past attachment experiences. Their interviews are frequently long and confusing and may be characterized by abrupt vacillations between positive and negative evaluations. As with ambivalent infants, the strategy of the preoccupied adult is thought to involve maximizing the activation and output of the attachment system. It is these strategies that are expected to influence parenting behavior.

The adult's attachment-based strategies are expected to influence parenting behavior by contributing to the parent's attention to and interpretations of her infant's signals (Main, 1990). A secure parent is expected to be open to the full range of the infant's signals and respond in a way that establishes herself as a secure base from which her infant can explore. The strategies of insecure parents, however, dictate selective responsiveness to and/or misinterpretation of their infants' cues. The dismissing parent is expected to misinterpret and/or reject her infant's attachment behaviors. In so doing, the dismissing parent prevents the activation of painful memories of her own experiences of rejection (see Cassidy & Kobak, 1988). By definition, the preoccupied parent's self-involvement prevents her from responding sensitively to her infant's bids for both attachment and exploration. This particular pattern of insensitivity, moreover, serves not only to preserve the preoccupied adult's fixation on her own attachment needs but also to escalate her infant's attachment behaviors (i.e., to maximize his or her focus on her; see also Cassidy & Berlin, 1994). Thus, parents' strategies are hypothesized to prescribe as well as to perpetuate both their parenting and their infants' attachment behaviors.

A burgeoning body of research has, in fact, illustrated striking associations between adults' attachment classifications and their parenting behavior (e.g., Cowan, Cohn, Cowan, & Pearson, 1996; Crowell & Feldman, 1991; Haft & Slade, 1989; see Hesse, 1999, for a review). Moreover, the data from the studies of adult attachment and parenting have recently been subjected to a meta-analysis examining approximately 400 dyads (van IJzendoorn, 1995). This meta-analysis indicated a strong association (combined effect $[d]$ = .72) between adult attachment and parental responsiveness for both mothers and fathers.

Perhaps the most informative findings have emerged from a study illustrating not only the influence of adults' state of mind with respect to attachment on parenting behavior but also the importance of examining adult attachment in interaction with other attachment-related influences (Cohn, Cowan, Cowan, & Pearson, 1992). Specifically, this study included assessments of both fathers' and mothers' adult attachment classifications and parenting behaviors. Both parents' attachment classifications were found to go hand in hand with observations of more supportive parenting behaviors. The influence of the mother's state of mind with respect to attachment on her parenting behavior, however, also varied as a function of her husband's attachment security: Insecure women married to secure men received significantly higher parenting scores than insecure women married to insecure men.

Attachment-Related Influences on Parenting: The Parents' Attachments

Parents' attachments are proposed to contribute importantly to their own security and their ability to serve as a secure base (e.g., Belsky, 1984, 1996, 1999; Bowlby, 1953). Parents' attachments to their own parents and to their spouses are expected to be especially influential.

PARENTS' ATTACHMENTS TO THEIR PARENTS

Arguably the single most important set of attachments to influence parenting are those that parents have to their own parents. Understanding the influence of the parent's attachments to her parents on her parenting behavior, however, has been limited by the absence of prospective longitudinal studies. Some insight can be gained from studies using the AAI scales to illustrate links between parents' early relationships with their parents and their infants' attachments to them. For example, one study revealed a strong correlation between a mother's (AAI coder-rated) experience of rejection by her own mother and her infant's avoidance of her during the Strange Situation (Main & Goldwyn, 1984). In another study, mothers of secure infants were judged during pregnancy to have had more loving mothers than mothers of avoidant infants: Notably, there were no differences associated with judgments of the parenting of these mothers' fathers (Fonagy, Steele, & Steele, 1991). Whereas neither of these studies included measures of parenting behavior per se, the existing research on the association between parenting behavior and infant-parent attachment (reviewed earlier) suggests that at least part of the variance in these infants' attachments was explained by their mothers' behavior toward them.

Perhaps the most intriguing information about the influence of parents' attachments to their parents on parenting has come from two recent studies examining the parents' early experiences with their parents in interaction with parents' current state of mind with respect to attachment. Both investigations focused on cases in which early experiences and current state of mind were discordant, and both demonstrated a greater influence on parenting of current state of mind than of the parent's early experiences of *being* parented, per se. In the first study, the researchers examined the parenting behavior of two subgroups of adults classified according to the AAI as secure. One "continuously secure" subgroup was coded as having supportive early attachments, and one "earned secure" subgroup was coded as having unsupportive early attachments (Pearson, Cohn, Cowan, & Cowan, 1994). Although the earned and continuously secure parents had different early attachment experiences, observational assessments of parenting indicated no differences in the ways that these parents behaved toward their preschool-age

children. Additionally, the earned secure parents were observed to be warmer and provide more structure for their preschoolers than insecure parents.

Parallel findings emerged from another investigation of earned and continuous security in which mothers' positive parenting of toddlers was observed under varying degrees of daily parenting stress (Phelps, Belsky, & Crnic, 1998). Earned and continuously secure mothers demonstrated equally positive parenting. Moreover, under high (but not low) stress, both groups of secure mothers were more positive with their toddlers than mothers classified insecure. Thus, as Pearson et al.'s (1994) data also indicate, these findings illustrate that the quality of early attachments does not necessarily forecast later parenting and that the influence of adults' current attachment status can outweigh the influence of adults' early attachment experiences.

In addition to examining the influence of parents' *early* relationships with their parents on parenting, researchers have investigated the influence of parents' *contemporaneous* relationships with their parents. Several studies have provided preliminary evidence of concurrent links between supportive mother-grandmother relationships and a greater likelihood of a secure infant-mother attachment (Frodi et al., 1984; Levitt, Weber, & Clark, 1986; Spieker & Bensley, 1994). What is missing from these studies for our purposes, of course, are data on the extent to which the mother-grandmother relationship influenced the mother's parenting behavior. At the least, though, these studies suggest that

160

it would be fruitful for researchers to examine the influence of the parent's current bonds to her parents on her parenting behavior. Another contemporaneous attachment thought to influence parenting behavior, to which we now turn, is the parent's attachment to his or her spouse.

PARENTS' ATTACHMENTS
TO THEIR SPOUSES

In his earliest writings, Bowlby (1953) discussed marital harmony as a key influence on parenting behavior: "By providing love and companionship [the husband] support[s] the mother emotionally and help[s] her maintain that harmonious contented mood in the atmosphere of which the infant thrives" (p. 13). Marital quality, thus, is expected to contribute importantly to the parent's own security and abilities to serve as a secure base (e.g., Belsky, 1984, 1996, 1999; Bowlby, 1953). Numerous studies have, in fact, revealed associations between marital quality and both mothers' and fathers' parenting behavior (e.g., Cox, Owen, Lewis, & Henderson, 1989; Cowan et al., 1996; Goldberg & Easterbrooks, 1984; Kerig, Cowan, & Cowan, 1993; see Wilson & Gottman, 1995, for a review). Looking across these studies, there is a hint that marital quality may have a stronger influence on fathering than on mothering (Belsky, 1990).

Especially provocative findings on the associations between marital quality and parenting come from a recent inquiry illustrating the importance of examining marital quality in interaction with adults' state of mind with respect to attachment. In this study, the effects of marital quality on infant-parent attachment were moderated by mothers' current working models of attachment. Mothers' self-reported marital quality correlated positively with children's security but only for mothers classified insecure according to the AAI (Das Eiden, Teti, & Corns, 1995). These findings are limited by both their lack of data on parenting per se and by their reliance on mother-sorted Q-set attachment data. Nonetheless, as Cohn et al.'s (1992) study also indicates, this study illustrates not only that it is critical to consider the interactions among attachment-related influences on parenting but also that mothers may be differentially susceptible to attachment-related influences on parenting. Specifically, for secure mothers, it may be that current state of mind drives marital quality and sensitive parenting, whereas for insecure mothers, current state of mind with respect to attachment is more malleable and open to the influence of the current marriage.

SUMMARY

The studies of the attachment-related influences on parenting portray a complex web. Parents' states of mind with respect to attachment influence parenting, as do early and later attachments. Understanding (1) the relations among early attachments, later attachments, and adult state of mind and (2) the relative influences of these three factors on parenting is an important task for attachment theorists and researchers. The interactions among these influences, moreover, can be different for different people.

Conclusion

This chapter discussed the contributions of attachment theory and research to understanding parenting. Beginning with Ainsworth's Baltimore study, the existing research has revealed extensive support for the notion that parents' responses to their infant's signals play a key role in shaping the infant's working models of attachment and attachment-based strategies. These existing investigations have emphasized the contribution of parental sensitivity to the development of the infant-parent attachment. Studies have linked parents' sensitivity in relation to both attachment and exploration to infant-parent attachment security and have also delineated the *in*sensitivities of the parents of insecure infants. The research to date has also illuminated pressing questions and next steps for attachment theorists and researchers studying parenting.

One pressing question concerns the magnitude of the association between parental sensitivity and infant-parent attachment, which has generally been shown to be moderate. Even as we interpret the research as emphasizing the contribution of parental sensitivity to the development of the infant-parent attachment, we acknowledge that there is considerable variance in infant-parent attachment that parental sensitivity does not explain, at least according to current methodologies. It may be that the existing measures of both attachment and sensitivity are simply not precise enough to capture the full extent of the association between sensitivity and at-

tachment. Additionally, as De Wolff and van IJzendoorn's (1997) meta-analytic findings imply, the influence of parental sensitivity on infant-parent attachment may not be equally powerful for everyone (see also Belsky, 1997; Cowan, 1997). It is important that researchers explore the factors that may moderate the association between sensitivity and attachment. De Wolff and van IJzendoorn's (1997) findings suggested that maternal sensitivity had less of an influence on infant-mother attachment among infant-mother dyads of lower socioeconomic status than among infant-mother dyads of higher socioeconomic status. This implication of lower socioeconomic status reducing the *importance* of maternal sensitivity is especially interesting to consider in conjunction with both theory and research linking lower socioeconomic status to reduced parental sensitivity per se and/or to reduced rates of secure infant-parent attachments (see, e.g., McLoyd, 1990; NICHD Early Child Care Research Network, 1997). To the extent that social class and ethnicity overlap, however, these considerations also bring us, again, to stressing the need for researchers to examine the validity of existing measures, especially vis-à-vis the extent to which the significance of particular parenting behaviors may vary by race, ethnicity, and acculturation (see Berlin, Brooks-Gunn, Spiker, & Zaslow, 1995; Chao, 1994; Knight, Tein, Shell, & Roosa, 1992; McGuire & Earls, 1993). Another factor that may moderate the association between parental sensitivity and infant-parent attachment is the sensitivity of the other parent. Fathering, in particular, is considerably less well understood than mothering and deserves further study both in its own right (although see the recent report of the Federal Interagency Forum on Child and Family Statistics, 1998, for recent progress in this area) and in the service of advancing the understanding of the interaction between fathering and mothering.

A second pressing question revealed by attachment theory and research on parenting concerns the interactions among attachment-related influences on parenting. Moreover, researchers addressing this question must bear in mind that in the same way that the influence of parental sensitivity on infant-parent attachment can be different for different people, the interactions among attachment-related influences on parenting are also likely to vary across individuals.

These pressing—if complex—questions only just begin to reflect the complexity of the "impossible profession" of parenting, a subject that merits further rigorous inquiry. To the extent that future studies can address these questions, they will advance the understanding of parenting on the whole.

References

Ainsworth, M. D. S. (1963). The development of infant-mother interaction among the Ganda. In B. M. Foss (Ed.), *Determinants of infant behavior: Vol. 2.* London: Methuen.

Ainsworth, M. D. S. (1984). Attachment. In N. S. Endler & J. M. Hunt (Eds.), *Person-*

ality and the behavioral disorders: Vol. 1 (pp. 559–602). New York: Wiley.

Ainsworth, M. D. S., Bell, S. M., & Stayton, D. J. (1971). Individual differences in Strange Situation behavior of one-year-olds. In H. R. Schaffer (Ed.), *The origins of human social relations* (pp. 17–57). London: Academic.

Ainsworth, M. D. S., Blehar, M. C., Waters, E., & Wall, S. (1978). *Patterns of attachment.* Hillsdale, NJ: Erlbaum.

Ainsworth, M. D. S., & Eichberg, C. G. (1991). Effects on infant-mother attachment of mother's unresolved loss of an attachment figure or other traumatic experience. In P. Marris, J. Stevenson-Hinde, & C. Parkes (Eds.), *Attachment across the life cycle.* New York: Routledge.

Ainsworth, M. D. S., & Wittig, B. (1969). Attachment and exploratory behavior of one-year-olds in a strange situation. In B. M. Foss (Ed.), *Determinants of infant behavior: Vol. 4* (pp. 111–136). London: Methuen.

Bakermans-Kranenburg, M. J., & van IJzendoorn, M. H. (1993). A psychometric study of the Adult Attachment Interview: Stability and discriminant validity. *Developmental Psychology, 29,* 870–880.

Bates, J., Maslin, C. A., & Frankel, K. A. (1985). Attachment security, mother-child interaction, and temperament as predictors of behavior-problem ratings at age three years. In I. Bretherton & E. Waters (Eds.), Growing points of attachment theory and research (pp. 167–193). *Monographs of the Society for Research in Child Development, 50*(1–2, Serial No. 209).

Belsky, J. (1984). The determinants of parenting: A process model. *Child Development, 55,* 83–96.

Belsky, J. (1990). Parental and nonparental care and children's socioemotional development: A decade in review. *Journal of Marriage and the Family, 52*, 885–903.

Belsky, J. (1996). Parent, infant, and social-contextual antecedents of father-son attachment security. *Child Development, 32*, 905–913.

Belsky, J. (1997). Theory testing, effect-size evaluation and differential susceptibility to rearing influence: The case of mothering and attachment. *Child Development, 64*, 598–600.

Belsky, J. (1999). Interactional and contextual determinants of attachment security. In J. Cassidy & P. R. Shaver (Eds.), *Handbook of attachment theory and research* (pp. 249–264). New York: Guilford.

Belsky, J., & Cassidy, J. (1994). Attachment: Theory and evidence. In M. Rutter & D. Hay (Eds.), *Development through life: A handbook for clinicians* (pp. 373–402). London: Blackwell.

Belsky, J., & Isabella, R. A. (1988). Maternal, infant, and social-contextual determinants of attachment security. In J. Belsky & T. Nezworski (Eds.), *Clinical implications of attachment* (pp. 41–94). Hillsdale, NJ: Erlbaum.

Belsky, J., Rosenberger, K., & Crnic, K. (1995). The origins of attachment security: "Classical" and contextual determinants. In S. Goldberg, R. Muir, & J. Kerr (Eds.), *Attachment theory: Social, developmental, and clinical perspectives* (pp. 153–184). Hillsdale, NJ: Analytic Press.

Belsky, J., & Rovine, M. R. (1990). Q-sort security and first-year nonmaternal care. In K. McCartney (Ed.), *New directions in child development: No. 49. Child care and maternal employment* (pp. 7–22). San Francisco: Jossey-Bass.

Belsky, J., Rovine, M., & Taylor, D. G. (1984). The Pennsylvania Infant and Family De-velopment Project, III: The origins of individual differences in infant-mother attachment: Maternal and infant contributions. *Child Development, 55*, 718–728.

Berlin, L. J., Brooks-Gunn, J., Spiker, D., & Zaslow, M. J. (1995). Examining observational measures of emotional support and cognitive stimulation in Black and White mothers of preschoolers. *Journal of Family Issues, 16*, 664–686.

Berlin, L. J., & Cassidy, J. (1999). Relations among relationships: Contributions of attachment theory and research. In J. Cassidy & P. R. Shaver (Eds.), *Handbook of attachment theory and research* (pp. 688–712). New York: Guilford.

Bornstein, M. H. (1995). Preface. In M. H. Bornstein (Ed.), *Handbook of parenting: Vol. 1. Children and parenting* (pp. xiii–xv). Mahwah, NJ: Erlbaum.

Bowlby, J. (1953). *Child care and the growth of love.* Baltimore, MD: Penguin Books.

Bowlby, J. (1958). The nature of the child's tie to his mother. *International Journal of Psychoanalysis, 39*, 350–373.

Bowlby, J. (1969/1982). *Attachment and loss: Vol. 1. Attachment.* New York: Basic Books.

Bowlby, J. (1973). *Attachment and loss: Vol. 2. Separation.* New York: Basic Books.

Bowlby, J. (1979). *The making and breaking of affectional bonds.* New York: Methuen.

Bowlby, J. (1980). *Attachment and loss: Vol. 3. Loss.* New York: Basic Books.

Campos, J. J., Barrett, K., Lamb, M. E., Goldsmith, H., & Stenberg, C. R. (1983). Socioemotional development. In M. M. Haith & J. J. Campos (Eds.), *Handbook of child psychology: Vol. 2. Infancy and developmental psychobiology* (pp. 783–915). New York: Wiley.

Carlson, V., Cicchetti, D., Barnett, D., & Braunwald, K. (1989). Disorganized/disoriented attachment relationships in maltreated infants. *Developmental Psychology, 25,* 525–531.

Cassidy, J., & Berlin, L. J. (1994). The insecure-ambivalent pattern of attachment: Theory and research. *Child Development, 65,* 971–991.

Cassidy, J., & Kobak, R. R. (1988). Avoidance and its relation to other defensive processes. In J. Belsky & T. Nezworski (Eds.), *Clinical implications of attachment* (pp. 300–323). Hillsdale, NJ: Erlbaum.

Cassidy, J., & Shaver, P. R. (Eds.). (1999). *Handbook of attachment theory and research.* New York: Guilford.

Chao, R. K. (1994). Beyond parental control and authoritarian parenting style: Understanding Chinese parenting through the cultural notion of training. *Child Development, 65,* 1111–1119.

Cohn, D. A., Cowan, P. A., Cowan, C. P., & Pearson, J. (1992). Mothers' and fathers' working models of childhood attachment relationships, parenting styles, and child behavior. *Development and Psychopathology, 4,* 417–431.

Cowan, P. A. (1997). Beyond meta-analysis: A plea for a family systems view of attachment. *Child Development, 68,* 601–603.

Cowan, P. A., Cohn, D. A., Cowan, C. P., & Pearson, J. L. (1996). Parents' attachment histories and children's externalizing and internalizing behaviors: Exploring family systems models of linkages. *Journal of Consulting and Clinical Psychology, 64,* 53–63.

Cox, M. J., Owen, M. T., Henderson, V. K., & Margand, N. A. (1992). Prediction of infant-father and infant-mother attachment. *Developmental Psychology, 28,* 474–483.

Crockenberg, S. (1981). Infant irritability, mother responsiveness, and social support influences on the security of infant-mother attachment. *Child Development, 52,* 857–865.

Crowell, J. A., & Feldman, S. S. (1991). Mothers' working models of attachment relationships and mother and child behavior during separation and reunion. *Developmental Psychology, 27,* 597–605.

Das Eiden, R., Teti, D. M., & Corns, K. M. (1995). Maternal working models of attachment, marital adjustment, and the parent-child relationship. *Child Development, 66,* 1504–1518.

De Wolff, M. S., & van IJzendoorn, M. H. (1997). Sensitivity and attachment: A meta-analysis on parental antecedents of infant attachment. *Child Development, 68,* 571–591.

Del Carmen, R., Pedersen, F., Huffman, L. C., & Bryan, Y. E. (1993). Dyadic distress management predicts subsequent security of attachment. *Infant Behavior and Development, 16,* 131–147.

Durrett, M., Otaki, M., & Richards, P. (1984). Attachment and the mother's perception of support from the father. *International Journal of Behavioral Development, 7,* 167–176.

Egeland, B., & Farber, E. (1984). Infant-mother attachment: Factors related to its development and changes over time. *Child Development, 55,* 753–771.

Escher-Graeub, D., & Grossmann, K. E. (1983). *Attachment security in the second year of life: The Regensburg cross-sectional study* (Research Report). University of Regensburg, Germany.

Federal Interagency Forum on Child and Family Statistics. (1998). *Nurturing fatherhood: Improving data and research on male fertility, family formation, and fatherhood* (Research Report). Washington, DC: Author.

Fonagy, P., Steele, H., & Steele, M. (1991). Maternal representations of attachment during pregnancy predict the organization of infant-mother attachment at one year of age. *Child Development, 62,* 891–905.

Frodi, A., Grolnick, W., & Bridges, L. (1985). Maternal correlates of stability and change in infant-mother attachment. *Infant Mental Health Journal, 6,* 60–67.

Frodi, A., Keller, B., Foye, H., Liptak, G., Bridges, L., Grolnick, W., Berko, J., Mc-Anarney, E., & Lawrence, R. (1984). Determinants of attachment and mastery motivation in infants born to adolescent mothers. *Infant Mental Health Journal, 5,* 15–23.

George, C., Kaplan, N., & Main, M. (1985). *An adult attachment interview.* Unpublished manuscript.

Goldberg, W. A., & Easterbrooks, M. A. (1984). Role of marital quality in toddler development. *Developmental Psychology, 20,* 504–514.

Grossmann, K., Grossmann, K. E., Spangler, G., Suess, G., & Unzner, L. (1985). Maternal sensitivity and newborns' orientation responses as related to quality of attachment in northern Germany. In I. Bretherton & E. Waters (Eds.), Growing points of attachment theory and research (pp. 233–256). *Monographs of the Society for Research in Child Development, 50*(1–2, Serial No. 209).

Haft, W. L., & Slade, A. (1989). Affect attunement and maternal attachment: A pilot study. *Infant Mental Health Journal, 10,* 157–172.

Hesse, E. (1999). The Adult Attachment Interview: Historical and current perspectives. In J. Cassidy & P. R. Shaver (Eds.), *Handbook of attachment theory and research* (pp. 395–433). New York: Guilford.

Isabella, R. A. (1993). Origins of attachment: Maternal interactive behavior across the first year. *Child Development, 64,* 605–621.

Isabella, R. A. (1994). Origins of maternal role satisfaction and its influences upon maternal interactive behavior and infant-mother attachment. *Infant Behavior and Development, 17,* 381–387.

Isabella, R. A., & Belsky, J. (1985). Marital change during the transition to parenthood and security of infant-parent attachment. *Journal of Family Issues, 6,* 505–522.

Isabella, R. A., & Belsky, J. (1991). Interactional synchrony and the origins of infant-mother attachment: A replication study. *Child Development, 62,* 373–384.

Isabella, R. A., Belsky, J., & von Eye, A. (1989). Origins of infant-mother attachment: An examination of interactional synchrony during the infant's first year. *Developmental Psychology, 25,* 12–21.

Jacobson, J. L., & Frye, K. F. (1991). Effect of maternal social support on attachment: Experimental evidence. *Child Development, 62,* 572–582.

Kerig, P. K., Cowan, P. A., & Cowan, C. P. (1993). Marital quality and gender differences in parent-child interaction. *Developmental Psychology, 29,* 931–939.

Kiser, L., Bates, J., Maslin, C., & Bayles, K. (1986). Mother-infant play at six months as a predictor of attachment security at thirteen months. *Journal of the American Academy of Child and Adolescent Psychiatry, 25,* 168–175.

Knight, G. P., Tein, J. Y., Shell, R., & Roosa, M. (1992). The cross-ethnic equivalence of parenting and family interaction measures among Hispanic and Anglo-American families. *Child Development, 63,* 1392–1403.

Levitt, M. J., Weber, R. A., & Clark, M. C. (1986). Social network relationships as sources of maternal support and well-being. *Developmental Psychology, 22,* 310–316.

Lewis, M., & Feiring, C. (1989). Infant, mother, and mother-infant behavior and subsequent attachment. *Child Development, 60,* 831–837.

Lyons-Ruth, K., Bronfman, E., & Parsons, E. (in press). Maternal frightened, frightening, or atypical behavior and disorganized infant attachment patterns. In J. Vondra & D. Barnett (Eds.), Atypical patterns of infant attachment: Theory, Research, and Current Directions. *Monographs of the Society for Research in Child Development.*

Lyons-Ruth, K., Connell, D. B., Grunebaum, H., & Botein, S. (1990). Infants at social risk: Maternal depression and family support services as mediators of infant development and security of attachment. *Child Development, 61,* 85–98.

Lyons-Ruth, K., & Jacobvitz, D. (1999). Attachment disorganization: Unresolved loss, relational violence, and lapses in behavioral and attentional strategies. In J. Cassidy & P. R. Shaver (Eds.), *Handbook of attachment theory and research* (pp. 520–554). New York: Guilford.

Main, M. (1981). Avoidance in the service of attachment: A working paper. In K. Immelman, G. Barlow, M. Main, & L. Petrinovich (Eds.), *The Bielefeld interdisciplinary project* (pp. 651–693). New York: Cambridge University Press.

Main, M. (1990). Cross-cultural studies of attachment organization: Recent studies, changing methodologies, and the concept of conditional strategies. *Human Development, 33,* 48–61.

Main, M., & Goldwyn, R. (1984). Predicting rejection of her infant from mothers' representations of her own experience: Implications for the abused-abusing intergenerational cycle. *Child Abuse and Neglect, 8,* 203–217.

Main, M., & Hesse, E. (1990). Parents' unresolved traumatic experiences are related to infant disorganized attachment status: Is frightened and/or frightening parental behavior the linking mechanism? In M. T. Greenberg, D. Cicchetti, & M. Cummings (Eds.), *Attachment in the preschool years* (pp. 161–182). Chicago: University of Chicago Press.

Main, M., & Solomon, J. (1986). Discovery of a new, insecure-disorganized/disoriented attachment pattern. In T. B. Brazelton & M. Yogman (Eds.), *Affective development in infancy* (pp. 95–124). Norwood, NJ: Ablex.

Main, M., & Solomon, J. (1990). Procedures for identifying infants as disorganized/disoriented during the Ainsworth Strange Situation. In M. T. Greenberg, D. Cicchetti, & M. Cummings (Eds.), *Attachment in the preschool years* (pp. 161–182). Chicago: University of Chicago Press.

Malatesta, C., Culver, C., Tesman, J., & Shepherd, B. (1989). The development of emotion expression during the first two years of life. *Monographs of the Society for Research in Child Development, 54*(1–2, Serial No. 219).

McGuire, J., & Earls, F. (1993). Exploring the reliability of measures of family relations, parental attitudes, and parent-child relations in a disadvantaged minority population. *Journal of Marriage and the Family, 55,* 1042–1046.

McLoyd, V. C. (1990). The impact of economic hardship on Black families and development. *Child Development, 61,* 311–346.

Miyake, K., Chen, S., & Campos, J. J. (1985). Infant temperament, mother's mode of interaction, and attachment in Japan: An interim report. In I. Bretherton & E. Waters (Eds.), Growing points of attachment theory and research (pp. 276–297). *Monographs of the Society for Research in Child Development, 50*(1–2, Serial No. 209).

Moran, G., Pederson, D. R., Pettit, P., & Krupka, A. (1992). Maternal sensitivity and infant-mother attachment in a developmentally delayed sample. *Infant Behavior and Development, 15*, 427–442.

Nakagawa, M., Lamb, M. E., & Miyake, K. (1992). Antecedents and correlates of the Strange Situation behavior of Japanese infants. *Journal of Cross-Cultural Psychology, 23*, 300–310.

NICHD Early Child Care Research Network. (1997). The effects of infant child care on infant-mother attachment security: Results of the NICHD study of early child care. *Child Development, 68*, 860–869.

O'Connor, M. J., Sigman, M., & Kasari, C. (1992). Attachment behaviors of infants exposed prenatally to alcohol: Mediating effects of infant affect and mother-infant interaction. *Development and Psychopathology, 4*, 243–256.

Park, K., & Waters, E. (1989). Security of attachment and preschool friendships. *Child Development, 60*, 1076–1081.

Parke, R. D. (1995). Fathers and families. In M. Bornstein (Ed.), *Handbook of parenting: Vol. 3. Status and social conditions of parenting* (pp. 27–63). Mahwah, NJ: Erlbaum.

Pearson, J., Cohn, D. A., Cowan, P. A., & Cowan, C. P. (1994). Earned- and continuous-security in adult attachment: Relation to depressive symptomology and parenting style. *Development and Psychopathology, 6*, 359–373.

Pederson, D. R., & Moran, G. (1996). Expressions of the attachment relationship outside of the Strange Situation. *Child Development, 67*, 915–927.

Pederson, D. R., Moran, G., Sitko, C., Campbell, K., Ghesquire, K., & Acton, H. (1990). Maternal sensitivity and the security of infant-mother attachment: A Q-Sort Study. *Child Development, 61*, 1974–1983.

Pennebaker, J., & Beall, S. (1986). Confronting a traumatic event: Toward an understanding of inhibition and disease. *Journal of Abnormal Psychology, 95*, 274–281.

Phelps, J. L., Belsky, J., & Crnic, K. (1998). Earned-security, daily stress, and parenting: A comparison of five alternative models. *Development and Psychopathology, 10*, 21–38.

Schenider-Rosen, K., & Rothbaum, F. (1993). Quality of parental caregiving and security of attachment. *Developmental Psychology, 29*, 358–367.

Schuengel, C., Bakermans-Kranenburg, M. J., & van IJzendoorn, M. H. (in press). Attachment and loss: Frightening maternal behavior linking unresolved loss and disorganized infant attachment. *Journal of Consulting and Clinical Psychology*.

Seifer, R., Schiller, M., Sameroff, A., Resnick, S., & Riordan, K. (1996). Attachment, maternal sensitivity, and infant temperament during the first year. *Developmental Psychology, 32*, 12–25.

Smith, P. B., & Pederson, D. R. (1988). Maternal sensitivity and patterns of infant-mother attachment. *Child Development, 59*, 1097–1101.

Spangler, G., & Grossmann, K. E. (1993). Biobehavioral organization in securely and insecurely attached infants. *Child Development, 64*, 1439–1450.

Spieker, S. J., & Bensley, L. (1994). Roles of living arrangements and grandmother social support in adolescent mothering and infant attachment. *Developmental Psychology, 30,* 102–111.

Steele, H., Steele, M., & Fonagy, P. (1996). Associations among attachment classifications of mothers, fathers, and their infants. *Child Development, 67,* 541–555.

Susman-Stillman, A., Kalkoske, M., Egeland, B., & Waldman, I. (1996). Infant temperament and maternal sensitivity as predictors of attachment security. *Infant Behavior and Development, 19,* 33–47.

Teti, D. M., & Ablard, K. (1989). Security of attachment and infant-sibling relationships. *Child Development, 60,* 1519–1528.

Teti, D. M., Gelfand, D. M., Messinger, D. S., & Isabella, R. (1995). Maternal depression and the quality of early attachment: An examination of infants, preschoolers, and their mothers. *Developmental Psychology, 31,* 364–376.

Thompson, R. A. (1999). Early attachment and later development. In J. Cassidy & P. R. Shaver (Eds.), *Handbook of attachment theory and research* (pp. 265–286). New York: Guilford.

van den Boom, D. (1994). The influence of temperament and mothering on attachment and exploration: An experimental manipulation of sensitive responsiveness among lower-class mothers with irritable infants. *Child Development, 65,* 1457–1477.

van den Boom, D. (1995). Do first-year intervention effects endure? Follow-up during toddlerhood of a sample of Dutch irritable infants. *Child Development, 66,* 1798–1816.

van den Boom, D. C. (1997). Sensitivity and attachment: Next steps for developmentalists. *Child Development, 64,* 592–594.

van IJzendoorn, M. H. (1995). Adult attachment representations, parental responsiveness, and infant attachment: A meta-analysis on the predictive validity of the Adult Attachment Interview. *Psychological Bulletin, 117,* 387–403.

van IJzendoorn, M. H., & De Wolff (1997). In search of the absent father—Meta-analysis of infant-father attachment: A rejoinder to our discussants. *Child Development, 68,* 604–609.

van IJzendoorn, M. H., Juffer, F., & Duyvesteyn, M. G. C. (1995). Breaking the intergenerational cycle of insecure attachment: A review of the effects of attachment-based interventions on maternal sensitivity and infant security. *Journal of Child Psychology and Psychiatry, 36,* 225–248.

van IJzendoorn, M. H., & Kroonenberg, P. M. (1988). Cross-cultural patterns of attachment: A meta-analysis of the Strange Situation. *Child Development, 59,* 147–156.

van IJzendoorn, M. H., Vereijken, C., & Riksen-Walraven, M. (in press). Is the Attachment Q-sort a valid measure of attachment security in young children? In B. E. Vaughn & E. Waters (Eds.), *Patterns of secure-base behavior: Q-sort perspectives on attachment and caregiving.* Mahwah, NJ: Erlbaum.

Vereijken, C., Riksen-Walraven, M., & Kondo-Ikemura, K. (1997). Maternal sensitivity and infant attachment security in Japan: A longitudinal study. *International Journal of Behavioral Development, 21,* 35–49.

Vondra, J. I., Shaw, D. S., & Kevenides, M. C. (1995). Predicting infant attachment classification from multiple, contemporaneous measures of maternal care. *Infant Behavior and Development, 18,* 415–425.

Waters, E., & Deane, K. E. (1985). Defining and assessing individual differences in attachment relationships: Q-methodology and the organization of behavior in infancy and early childhood. In I. Bretherton & E. Waters (Eds.), Growing points of attachment theory and research (pp. 41–65). *Monographs of the Society for Research in Child Development, 50*(1–2, Serial No. 209).

Waters, E., Vaughn, B. E., Posada, G., & Kondo-Ikemura, K. (Eds.). (1995). Caregiving, cultural, and cognitive perspectives on secure-base behavior and working models: New growing points of attachment theory and research. *Monographs of the Society for Research in Child Development, 60*(2–3, Serial No. 244).

Wilson, B. J., & Gottman, J. M. (1995). Marital interaction and parenting. In M. H. Bornstein (Ed.), *Handbook of parenting: Vol. 4. Applied issues in parenting* (pp. 33–55). Mahwah, NJ: Erlbaum.

6

The Story of Mothers
Who Are Difficult to Engage
in Prevention Programs

*Susan J. Spieker, Joanne Solchany, Margaret McKenna,
Michelle DeKlyen, and Kathryn E. Barnard*

6

Introduction

Over 30 years of attention to the adverse consequences of poverty for children has resulted in a vast array of programs for low-income families. These have very different goals, services, and outcomes and have been ably summarized elsewhere (Delvaney, Elwood, & Love, 1997; Gomby, Larner, Stevenson, Lewit, & Behrman, 1995; Gomby, Larson, Lewit, & Behrman, 1993). Some programs focus primarily on improving outcomes for the adult single parent, usually the mother. These programs include education, job training, and welfare-to-work programs. Little is known about how these programs benefit chil-dren, although the theory is that the benefits of maternal education and employment do trickle down to children (St. Pierre, Layzer, & Barnes, 1995). Other programs have the express purpose of improving outcomes for children. These programs are of two types, those that focus primarily on direct services to the child and others that help parents to learn ways to promote children's development. In general, child-focused programs have addressed the needs of preschool-age children with center-based programs of varying intensity. Head Start is the best known example of a part-day, part-year center-based program, and the Carolina Abecedarian Project (Campbell & Ramey, 1994) typifies full-day, year-round, educational child care.

Family-based programs have focused more on families with children birth to three, using a home-visiting model. Project CARE (Wasik, Ramey, Bryant, & Sparling, 1990) is an example of this model. However, there have always been experimental programs that did not fit this generalization, for example, those that provided center-based education beginning in infancy and others that provided home-visiting services to families with preschoolers.

In response to the limited success of such single-focus approaches, as well as to an understanding of the multigenerational, multidimensional aspects of poverty, the latest wave of programs has combined these approaches. Known as two-generational programs, they target three key service areas: a developmentally appropriate early childhood program, parenting education, and adult education, literacy, or job training. In addition, a case-management approach connects families to existing services, provides crisis intervention, and generally urges families to participate and take advantage of the opportunities offered by the program. An example of the two-generational approach is the Comprehensive Child Development Program (CCDP). A national evaluation of CCDP revealed no differences five years after the program began between program and control families in areas of economic self-sufficiency, parenting skills, or the cognitive or social-emotional development of participating children or the birth or health outcomes of subsequently born children. Why did this program have no effects? The answer may reside in data that

show that although the CCDP was comprehensive, it was not particularly intensive.

We know that intensity is important for child development programs (Ramey & Ramey, 1992), but we know less about the role of intensity in the effectiveness of the parenting and adult education components of two-generational programs. However, if we assume intensity matters for all three components, the resulting multifocus, high-intensity program would be a very expensive program indeed (St. Pierre et al., 1995). Furthermore, programs of this intensity require a high level of commitment and participation from staff and families alike. A program may be theoretically comprehensive and appropriately intensive, but if the participants drop out, miss appointments, or otherwise do not receive the level of services intended for them, then the program is unlikely to be effective in meeting its goals. A sizable number of participants do drop out of these programs or receive minimal intervention. For example, in CCDP, 20 percent of families dropped out in the first year, and 40 percent dropped out by 2.5 years (St. Pierre et al., 1995). Dropping out is only one way in which participants limit their engagement in a program. This paper describes and seeks to understand participants who did not engage in Early Head Start, a two-generational program that first enrolled families in 1996.

Early Head Start (EHS) is a recently mounted program for families and children from the prenatal period through age three. Early Head Start emerged from the work of the Carnegie Task Force on

Meeting the Needs of Very Young Children (1994) and a paper requested by the Clinton transition team (Zigler & Styfco, 1993) and was designed by the Advisory Committee on Services for Families with Infants and Toddlers (1994). Early Head Start is built on four cornerstones: child development, parent development, staff development, and community development. Programs are required to address all cornerstones but may vary in how they do so. Early Head Start services are guided by national quality standards adapted to the needs of young children (Zigler & Styfco, 1998). A national research and evaluation component is included in the design, whereby university-based local research partners team up with EHS programs.

As local research partners connected with an Early Head Start program that provides comprehensive child development and family support services to low-income families with infants and toddlers, we have become interested in understanding families who are difficult to engage in such a program. In our previous association with a CCDP, it seemed that at least one-third of the families engaged readily and made real gains during the course of the program, one-third engaged with some difficulty and required a great deal of staff effort to maintain that engagement in order for some gains to occur, and nearly one-third were extremely difficult to engage at all. Staff members reported that considerable effort (many months of "being there" and available to the parent) went into establishing relationships with these parents before more extensive involvement in the inter-vention could occur. Frequently, these relationships were never established at all. Many resources were expended on the difficult-to-engage families without the intended benefits accruing.

This chapter describes characteristics of difficult-to-engage families from multiple perspectives. First, we report on the Adult Attachment Interview (AAI; George, Kaplan, & Main, 1985, 1996), an interview that specifically requires the mother to evaluate the quality of childhood experiences with attachment figures and report on specific memories in this regard. We discuss the actual classifications assigned the AAIs of these difficult-to-engage women, to add the perspective of attachment theory to our understanding of the phenomenon and as a first step in tailoring interventions to address their needs and the needs of all families eligible for EHS or similar services. Second, we present common themes in the life experiences of these women as reported in their own words during the AAI interviews. Third, we consider the perspective of the home visitors who identified the difficult-to-engage mothers from among all the mothers in their caseloads. How did the home visitors characterize the phenomenon? Fourth, we describe in some detail the nature of the activities in which the women were asked to engage during their participation in this particular Early Head Start program. It may be that the nature of these activities were especially challenging for the women we identified as difficult to engage. Finally, we discuss our findings and present new directions for prevention efforts and inter-vention research.

State of Mind with Regard to Attachment: The AAI

The research described is part of a larger project designed to investigate the role of the mother's early attachment relationships and current state of mind with respect to attachment in EHS program implementation and subsequent mother and child outcomes. In particular, we focus on child-mother attachment security, child language development, and child-staff and mother-staff relationship processes. We expected to observe in some Early Head Start families the same difficult-to-engage profile that we had seen in our prior work. Identifying what roles, if any, that early attachment relationships and current state of mind with respect to attachment might have in program engagement and related process and outcome issues could be a significant contribution to the success of Early Head Start and the field of early intervention.

Eligible participants included low-income, pregnant women or low-income women with a child under six months. These were randomly assigned at recruitment to the EHS program (n = 90) or a community comparison group (n = 89). Thirty-five subjects (16 program) dropped out from the study without providing baseline data. The 154 remaining mothers (program and control) participated in an initial data collection visit, which consisted of the AAI (George et al., 1985) and several questionnaires, including a measure of depressive symptoms (CES-D, Radloff, 1977), verbal intelligence (WAIS Vocabulary sub-

scale, Weschler, 1981), and reading ability (Woodcock-Johnson Achievement Scales, Word Attack subtest, Woodcock & Mather, 1989).

Approximately one year after the program started serving families, home visitors were asked to identify families who had been difficult to engage during home visits or who had missed home visits or were "hard to reach." The criteria for selection of these families were not rigid and did not depend on the service delivery plan; that is, selection was not dependent on the visits that were completed or those that had been missed. The home visitors initially identified the families based on the home visitors' perceptions that the families diverged from the other families. The points of departure that led to identification as hard-to-reach families were the extent to which they were unenthusiastic or nonverbal during home visits, missed home visits or failed to reschedule, reluctantly followed through or failed to follow through on suggestions for parent-child interaction, and did not respond to other opportunities or repeated offers to engage in the program. Characteristics of the identified difficult-to-engage families on the AAI and other measures were then compared to other research participants.

The AAI is a structured, hour-long, semiclinical interview that queries the subject about early experiences with caregivers. Early in the interview, the subject is asked to list five adjectives that describe the relationship with each parent and then to describe specific memories that illustrate each adjective. There are questions about how the parents dealt with the subject's distress and sickness as a young child and whether the subject had been maltreated or experienced the loss of an important person. The intent of these questions is to "surprise the unconscious" of the subject and direct attention to attachment-related events from childhood. The speaker must produce and reflect upon memories related to attachment, some of which may be highly charged with emotion, while at the same time maintaining a coherent discourse with the interviewer. The audiotaped interviews are transcribed verbatim, and the transcripts are coded by individuals who have received extensive training in the analysis of discourse. The rating system is quite complex. The major focus for this report is the five-category classification system of an adult's current "state of mind with respect to attachment" (George et al., 1985, 1996). These can be understood as varying across two dimensions—coherence and organization.

Coherent discourse occurs when the subject is able to both access and evaluate memories in response to specific questions and remain consistent and plausible as a discourse partner. Transcripts are classified as secure-freely autonomous (F) when they are internally consistent and reasonably clear, relevant, and succinct. Individuals with troubled childhoods, as well as those from loving families, may all be classified as secure, because it is the coherence of the discourse and not the content of the early experience reported that determines classification.

It is thus possible that two individuals might both have suffered extreme abuse, but only one whose current state of mind is

preoccupied, unresolved, or dismissing with respect to these past events would be considered insecure. If the other individual was clear about the events in her past, neither denying nor being overwhelmed or disorganized by them, and expressed an ability to move on with her life, judging subsequent relationships objectively and perhaps expressing some understanding of, compassion, or even forgiveness for the perpetrator, the interview would be considered coherent, leading to a classification of free/autonomous. However, within this sample, early trauma was generally associated with either unresolved or dismissing classifications. High levels of coherence did not occur in the wake of clear trauma.

Interviews that are low in coherence receive an insecure classification. There are two types of organized strategies that are low in coherence. Interviews are classified as insecure-dismissing (D) when the discourse appears to minimize attachment-related experiences. This can be done in a variety of ways. The subject may be unable to recall specific memories and as a result, would be unable to support highly idealized presentations of the parents with believable memories, or the subject may acknowledge a difficult childhood but insist that she was unaffected or made stronger by it. The questions are answered in a superficial way, and the coherence of the discourse is undermined by numerous internal contradictions in the interview.

For example, one mother described the relationship with her own mother as "happy, loving, caring," but when asked for specific memories to illustrate those descriptions, she could not recount any, replying, "It's hard to think now, about those things now. . . . Dunno, she—I mean she got us things when we needed things an'—ya know I mean I don't know, she just. . . ." Later, after describing how her father swatted her when she stomped her feet and slammed the door, she added, "I think if it wasn't for, for that then, you know, I'd probably turned out, you know, wouldn't be as good as I am."

As an example of the internal contradictions expressed within some transcripts, one mother said of her own mother that, "I could just tell her anything," yet later noted that when she was raped at age seven she told no one. Insisting that before she was eight years old (a perceived turning point in her life), her relationship with her mother was "great . . . wonderful, close," she also relates that in that period her mother sometimes dropped her off with relatives, failing to tell anyone that she would not return for a few days. Care of this youngster was apparently problematic enough that her mother's own mother arranged for child protective services to investigate when the subject was four years old.

Other subjects normalize their abnormal experiences. For instance, after describing a very difficult childhood marked by her mother's erratic behavior, favoritism to her brother, and demands that she do most of the housework and child care in the home, one participant was asked why she thought her parents behaved as they did. "That's what parents do," she replied.

Interviews are classified as insecure-preoccupied (E) when the discourse reveals a preoccupation with attachment figures and attachment experiences. The strategy is one of maximizing attention to attachment and to the self and is manifest in confusing run-on sentences and angry or passive preoccupation with presenting the subject's point of view and attempts to draw the interviewer to be on the side of the subject. The transcript lacks coherence because the subject has difficulty sticking to the question at hand. The interviewer has trouble discerning the end of an answer so that the next question can be asked. The subject is violating expectations that a discourse partner be clear, relevant, and succinct.

One participant, describing her mother's complaints, exemplified this tendency to lose track of the interview context. In her preoccupation with her own frustration in the relationship she addressed the (absent) parent directly: "She didn't feel that we loved her, 'cause we never asked her to hug us or this or that but—we were kids we shouldn't—ask—you—to do something for us, you should do it. Wh—we were the kids, you were the adult, an'—I didn't ask to be born, I mean. . . ." Later, while talking about her father and current pressures to improve her relationship with him, the same mother explained, "I guess I feel there's certain things that—happens in your life that—you can't—take back and you can't make up for an' you should have been there for me then."

Another preoccupied mother, when asked about her feelings in response to a miscarriage, started to describe her initial reaction, then noted that her sister-in-law was there, next indicated that her ex-husband and his sister got into a fight but later reconciled, and ended by noting that her own relationship with the sister-in-law was destroyed (for unclear reasons) after her divorce and how painful it has been to lose touch with her young niece.

The secure, dismissing, and preoccupied classifications are considered to be organized attachment strategies. Interviews classified in the unresolved-disorganized (U) category show indications of disorganization and disorientation during times in the interview when the subject is asked about loss or trauma, such as the loss of a parent or experiences of physical or sexual abuse. Although the interview as a whole may be primarily secure, dismissing, or preoccupied, specific lapses in monitoring, reasoning, and discourse in relation to the traumatic event result in the U classification (Ul for unresolved with respect to loss or Ut for unresolved with respect to trauma). For example, in the case of loss there may be indications that the subject believes a deceased loved one is still alive, confusion about the time or place of death, or use of eulogistic speech. Main (1995) speculates that these lapses in monitoring may represent interference from normally dissociated memory systems. There may be indications of state shifts or instances when it seems that the subject has entered a peculiar, compartmentalized state of mind regarding the traumatic experience, perhaps as a result of intrusions from frightening, dissociated memories of the event.

The mental disorganization of one mother became apparent when she was asked about her abusive relationship with her father and twice stated that she wanted to kill him. A few moments later she corrected herself and told the interviewer that it was her uncle (who had also been abusive) she wanted to kill, not her father. A more organized individual might have clearly described both perpetrators and her anger at them but should have integrated her knowledge of these events and resolved her responses in such a way that she could move on with her life. She would be unlikely to slip in this way, apparently becoming confused (or unwilling to be honest) about the object of her powerful feelings.

When describing a traumatic experience with her stepfather, one mother who otherwise exhibited normal grammar and speech patterns began to speak as though the event were happening in the present tense and reverted to language a frightened young child might use: "I was very scared. I'm like I am here alone this man is gonna kill me. I'm not trust this man I'm not like this man." Similarly, another mother also slipped into the present tense and perhaps expressed confusion in the identity of who was feeling what emotion when describing physical punishment meted out by her parents: "They go off a little bit every now an' then . . . they get upset with their—their, you know, punishing us."

Another subject seemed to compartmentalize her rape experiences, separating them from the rest of her existence "I would just submit and go to a—different place—and just let it happen" and when "somebody started forcing themselves on me—I'd just go to my little place." Later in the interview, "I put it away for that time being" and "I got away with—after that situation just pretending it didn't happen."

The unresolved classification reflects a breakdown in organization associated with particular traumatic events, in what is otherwise an organized F, D, or E transcript. A small number of transcripts have been more recently assigned to the cannot classify (CC) category because they do not meet criteria for placement in any of the three organized categories (Hesse, 1996). Some CC transcripts contain strong indicators of contrasting states of mind (e.g., dismissing and preoccupied). Others are clearly not secure because of their low coherence and also do not have sufficient evidence for classification in either the dismissing or preoccupied categories. CC transcripts reflect disorganization at a more global level because no organized strategy is in evidence, as in the following examples.

One participant idealized her relationship with her mother as "wonderful, close" before she was eight years old, despite evidence of neglect and emotional unavailability, but appeared angrily preoccupied about deficiencies that developed later. The transcript thus did not consistently reflect either a dismissing or a preoccupied state of mind with respect to attachment. Another expressed considerable anger toward her father but was extremely idealizing when speaking of her mother, and neither parental relationship was clearly dominant.

Preliminary research has found associations between CC classification in adulthood and severe adolescent psychopathology (Allen, Hauser, & Borman-Spurrell, 1996) and childhood sexual abuse (Stalker & Davies, 1995). The most disturbed individuals in a Dutch sample of personality-disordered criminal offenders (van IJzendoorn et al., 1997) had CC transcripts.

In addition to a primary classification in one of the five categories described previously, a transcript may also receive one or more secondary classifications if there is evidence for it in the transcript. In the case of an unresolved classification, the secondary classification reflects the subject's underlying state of mind with respect to attachment. For example, a mother who had been traumatized by several episodes of sexual abuse also exhibited considerable idealization and lack of recall, yielding a secondary classification of dismissing. In other instances, the secondary classification may indicate the direction in which the subject's state of mind is heading. For example, a secondary secure classification for a dismissing individual in therapy may indicate that the individual's state of mind with respect to attachment has elements of autonomous, secure thinking and may be heading in that direction.

AAI classifications have been shown to be valid in numerous studies conducted over the past decade (van IJzendoorn, 1995). AAI classifications are unrelated to social desirability, intelligence, and memory ability. Parents whose AAI transcripts are classified as secure-autonomous are more sensitive caregivers of their children. Across studies there is approximately a 75 percent concordance between adult classification on the AAI (dismissing (D), secure (F), preoccupied (E), and unresolved (U)) and infant classification in the

Strange Situation (avoidant (A), secure (B), ambivalent (C), and disorganized/disoriented (D)).

Van IJzendoorn and Bakermans-Kranenburg (1996) conducted a meta-analysis of studies using the AAI on clinical and nonclinical samples from several countries. This meta-analysis involved nine nonclinical samples and nearly 500 mothers. The distribution of AAI classifications, using the dismissing (D), secure (F), preoccupied (E), and unresolved (U) categories, was 16, 55, 9, and 19 percent respectively. The distribution of AAI classifications across five low-income samples involving 350 mothers revealed significantly fewer secure mothers and significantly more classified dismissing and unresolved/cannot classify (25, 39, 8, and 28 percent). Finally, across six clinical samples involving 165 mothers, there were fewer secure and more preoccupied and unresolved/cannot classify classifications (26, 8, 25, and 40 percent).

Results

Fifty-four cases are included in the analyses in this chapter. These included all cases with AAI transcripts coded prior to the identification of the difficult-to-engage mothers, plus five cases identified as such who were given to the coder with instructions for priority coding, but with no details about the reason for priority status. Twenty-eight were mothers who had been randomly assigned to the EHS program, and 26 had been randomly assigned to the comparison group. Of the cases identified as difficult-to-engage, one mother never

finished the baseline assessment, hence no AAI or other assessments were available for that mother.

The 28 program mothers and 26 comparison mothers were compared on all baseline measures. The results confirmed the expectation that random assignment produces equivalent groups. The groups were similar in age, estimated IQ, depressive symptoms, and reading ability. There were no differences in the distribution of AAI classifications between groups, regardless of type of AAI comparison: secure versus insecure, organized versus disorganized, or the four-category D, E, F, and U/CC.

The distributions of AAI classifications for the various samples reviewed by van IJzendoorn and Bakermans-Kranenburg (1996) were compared with the distributions in the present sample (see Table 6.1). The 54 cases had the following distribution: 35 percent dismissing (D), 24 percent secure (F), 7 percent preoccupied (E), and 33 percent unresolved or cannot classify (U/CC). As expected, this distribution was most similar to the distribution reported for low-income samples in the van IJzendoorn and Bakermans-Kranenburg (1996) meta-analysis.

The results of the baseline assessments for the difficult-to-engage mothers in the program group and the remaining mothers in the program are reported in Table 6.2. There were no differences between the difficult-to-engage group and the remaining program mothers in age, depressive symptoms, estimated IQ, and reading ability. Both groups were relatively depressed (mean CES-D scores were 18.8) and had

TABLE 6.1.

Distribution of AAI Classifications for EHS Sample, Difficult-to-Engage Program Mothers, Other Program Mothers, and Comparison Groups reported in Van IJzendoorn & Bakermans-Kranenburg (1996)

	AAI Classification			
Group	Dismissing	Secure/ Autonomous	Preoccupied	Unresolved/ Cannot Classify
EHS Sample (28 Program + 26 Comparison)	35%	24%	7%	33.3%
Difficult-to-Engage Program Mothers (n = 11)	18%	9%	9%	64%
Other Program Mothers (n = 17)	41%	29%	6%	24%
Nonclinical (n = 500)	16%	55%	9%	19%
Low-income (n = 350)	25%	39%	8%	28%
Clinical (n = 165)	26%	8%	25%	40%

TABLE 6.2

Comparison of Difficult-to-Engage Program Mothers and the Remaining Program Sample

	Hard-to-Engage (n = 11)		Remaining Program Sample (n = 17)	
	n	%	n	%
Race				
White	6	54.5	8	47.1
Black	3	27.3	4	23.5
Hispanic			1	5.9
Asian			3	17.6
Other	2	18.2	1	5.9
	M	SD	M	SD
Maternal Age	20.2	5.6	23.7	6.8
CES-D	18.8	9.7	18.8	9.7
IQ (estimated)	84.2	11.6	86.0	14.8
Reading (grade equivalent)	9.4	4.1	11.6	4.5

TABLE 6.3

Characteristics of Difficult-to-Engage Cases

Age	AAI Classification	CES-D	IQ (estimated)	WJ Reading Grade equivalent	Ethnicity
15	U1/Ds3/Ds2	18	83	7.1	White
18	Ul/Ds3/F2	27	77	7.6	Black
16	U/CC/E2	17	94	10.7	Black
21	U/CC/Ds3	12	83	5.4	Other
18	Ut/Ds3	5	94	10.7	Other
18	F1b/F2	4	83	7.6	Black
20	Ut/Ds3/CC	37	65	5.4	White
21	E2/Ut/F5	27	100	16.8	White
20	Ut/Ds2/E3	19	64	5.8	White
36	Ds3/F1	20	88	16.9	White
19	Ds1	21	90	9.7	White

Note: Key to AAI Classifications

Secure/autonomous (F)

F1	Secure, setting aside
F1a	Secure, setting aside, harshness
F1b	Secure, setting aside, poverty
F2	Secure, somewhat dismissing
F3	Autonomous
F3a	Autonomous, secure childhood
F3b	Autonomous, earned secure
F4	Secure, preoccupation
F4a	Secure, some preoccupation
F4b	Secure, preoccupation, trauma
F5	Secure, angry

Dismissing (D)

D1	Dismissive of attachment
D2	Devaluing of attachment
D3	Restricted in feeling
D4	Cut off from fear

Preoccupied (E)

E1	Preoccupied, passive
E2	Preoccupied, angry
E3	Preoccupied, fearful

Unresolved (U)

U	Unresolved
Ut	Unresolved, trauma
U1	Unresolved, loss
CC	Cannot Classify

limited verbal ability as reflected in low reading and estimated IQ scores. The only significant difference between the difficult-to-engage group and the other program mothers was the AAI classification distribution. The proportion of women in the difficult-to-engage group classified as unresolved or cannot classify versus an organized D, F, or E classification was significantly greater for the 11 difficult-to-engage mothers compared to the remaining 17 mothers in the program ($\chi^2(1) = 4.5$, p < .05). Table 6.3 lists the full AAI classifi-

cation for each difficult-to-engage mother, and other descriptive information.

The high proportion of AAI classifications that are unresolved for women whose home visitors found it very difficult to engage them in an intervention requiring frequent home visits and a relatively high intensity of services suggests that this subgroup of low-income young mothers are hard to reach because they are suffering from unresolved experiences of loss and trauma. The next section looks at the experiences of these women, as revealed in the stories they told during their Adult Attachment Interviews.

Life Experience Themes

We used the women's reports of their life experiences, as told during the AAI, to develop a qualitative database of themes and patterns characteristic of this group of difficult-to-engage mothers. The content of the AAIs was closely examined through a structured coding format. While this analysis was not grounded theory, we did borrow from the techniques of grounded theory to provide a structured, multilevel method for the analysis of the AAI content (Strauss & Corbin, 1990). These AAIs were coded inductively beginning with open coding, going line by line through all eleven transcripts. In this stage categories were constructed from the coded text, then identi-

fied and named. This structured analysis provided some initial organization of the raw data (Miles & Huberman, 1994).

The second stage of this structured analysis focused on considering, comparing, and identifying relationships between the categories generated, or axial coding. Specific phenomena and contextual elements were identified from the original raw data and reconstructed in new ways.

The final stage of structured coding involved "selecting of the core categories, systematically relating them to each other, [and] validating these relationships" (Strauss & Corbin, 1990, p. 116). This selective coding allowed common themes to be identified and defined. These themes became the foundation for telling the analytic story embedded within the AAI transcripts of our difficult-to-engage mothers.

The relationships among these themes are diagrammed in Figure 6.1. The over-

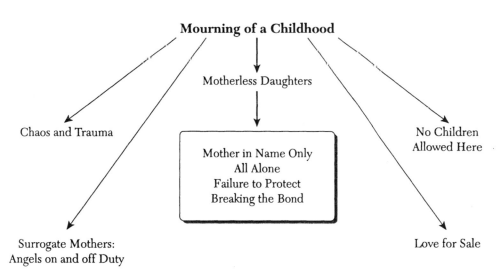

FIGURE 6.1
Themes generated from the AAIs of the Difficult-to-Engage mothers.

riding theme generated from the stories told by the AAIs was the profound sense of loss the mothers felt when they thought about their childhoods. This group of mothers began their transition into womanhood long before they had a chance to experience any resemblance of a healthy childhood. Being a child was dangerous and would have left them vulnerable. Their AAIs demonstrated that they knew this on some level of consciousness and were acting and relating to their worlds with grief over these lost childhoods.

Mourning of a Childhood

"No pain can compare to childhood, trust me." The words of this woman illustrate a childhood barren of joy, love, care, or comfort. Words like these were all too common in our group of difficult-to-engage women. The overriding theme that emerged from their words was that of loss. These women had lost a childhood and were in mourning for what never was and what would never be for them. While they all seemed to be at different stages in their grief, their mourning was apparent nonetheless. The women's words illustrate this mourning most poignantly. In this first passage the woman mixed her tenses of past and present, suggesting her mourning continues to be strong.

> All I ever wanted was somebody who came home and asked me how my day was . . . to say that *I have been* a good child. It *won't have* to be milk and cookies because I didn't want a Leave it To Beaver mom. But you know, all I wanted was somebody who actually, really cared. Who not only bought me toys but would sit and play with me . . . and

talk to me and tell me stories. My mother wouldn't do those things . . . I was never good enough.

> I had to fight to stay alive and I couldn't be a kid. Couldn't play . . . didn't have any toys . . . didn't have nothing. I just . . . I was never a kid. I would see all these other kids down the block . . . playing and . . . having fun . . . and I was always worried about if I was going to live . . . the next day.

> Every little kid or little girl, they all dream about having this nice family where nothing bad ever goes on. I am angry at my family because they chose to do all this stuff to innocent children.

The confusion, rejection, and self-blame were evident in their stories. The women spoke of trying to figure out why other kids had these great parents and they did not. They clarified it was not that they *felt* rejected, they *were* rejected. One woman summed up her feelings when she stated:

> The only thing I ever did was to hope someone would care . . . they were hurtful . . . I always thought I was a bad girl.

Motherless Daughters

The most pronounced theme within this mourning was that these women were all motherless daughters. Although all the women in this group had biological mothers with whom they had all lived with for some portion of their early lives, it became apparent that the mothers these women had were not really mothers. As one woman stated, "She just didn't act like a mother . . . she wasn't."

MOTHERS IN NAME ONLY

Many of these mothers were mothers in name only. One daughter described her mother as "not a motherly, nurturing person at all." Another described her mother as "very, oh very cold." A third woman said her mother did not act like a parental figure. "I just didn't trust her." For some women their mothers had even told them they had made a mistake in becoming parents.

LEFT ALL ALONE

Abandonment and being left alone by their mothers was clearly threaded through the lives of many of the women in this group. Frequently women would report being left alone by their mothers, sometimes for hours, sometimes for days. Women described worrying that their mothers would ever return. One mother disappeared for four days after she had said she was going to a school conference. Many reported their mothers sneaking out of the house after they were supposed to be asleep. As children many of these women learned to take care of themselves and their siblings to make up for their absent mothers. One young woman credits her independence to the fact that her mother "was never around." The aloneness of their abandonment echoes in their memories:

> My mom used to leave . . . she used to go out a lot. I used to be at home alone, all the time. With nobody to talk to, and no phone, no TV. I used to . . . I'd be sad. I'd go to bed early. I would just sit and stay in the house.

> On the Fourth of July . . . she went out and left me. And after I had used all my fireworks I went into the house and there was nothing to do except for . . . I stood on the back porch and watched the fireworks from the park . . . by myself and she didn't get home till late that night.

> I mean it was just an every night experience . . . we were alone. We felt alone because we were really little, we were too young to be by ourselves.

FAILURE TO PROTECT

Another frequent theme was mothers' failure to protect their daughters from others who were hurtful to them. Two women shared that their mothers forced them to go on visits to their fathers' homes, in spite of repeated rapes and other abusive behaviors. One woman's mother not only failed to protect her but purposely put her in harm's way, trading the use of her young daughter's body for drugs. This particular woman, in recalling her feelings of defenselessness, also remembered her mother punishing her for not performing "just right" for the men who would "mess with me all the time." The following words illustrate the anger and pain that still remain when mothers had failed to protect:

> She was really selfish. Because instead of putting . . . you know . . . if she would have stepped in then she would have to be beat. So she would of rather us get abused instead of her . . . and that's not what being a mother is about. You don't you put yourself behind your kid.

BREAKING THE BOND

A final common characteristic in this group of motherless daughters was the seemingly

187

purposeful intent by some mothers to break or destroy any bonding they did share with their daughters. Messages of rejection were common. Being told they were disappointments, they would never amount to anything, they would never do anything with their lives, and that they were ruining their mothers' lives were frequently reported. The attacks by the mothers were more than verbal abuse and criticism. Their words seem to have actually weakened the women's egos and chiseled away at the fragile attachments they may have had. Examples of the impact many of the mothers had on their daughters can be seen in the following passages:

> It is like everything I cared about she destroyed.

> She always made us feel like we were burdens.

While mothers were most often identified as purposely breaking the bonds with their daughters, fathers were not exempt from these attempts. One woman described her father in the following manner:

> He took my virginity. He took my pride. He's taken everything away from me. Everything. . . . He made me feel worthless. He made me feel like nobody would ever love me.

Chaos and Trauma

Chaos and trauma were clearly evident within the texts of these women's stories. Chaos was a way of life and trauma an all too familiar companion. The chaos and trauma these women experienced is described in the next section.

THE CHAOTIC EARLY YEARS

It is clear that the early lives of these women were characterized by unpredictability and inconsistency throughout several aspects of their lives. The consistency and predictability yearned for by infants and children were placed high out of reach. Many were cared for by people who experienced rapid, frequent, and surprising mood swings, often to the point of violence. What set off the mood swings never seemed to be clear to any of the women; their confusion continues in their adult perceptions. Some of the women described these caregivers in the following words:

> One minute my mom is a sweet loving mother and the next minute she is spitting fire out of her eyes . . . she's just like that . . . it's really weird.

> I would describe my dad as "flip-flop." It was like his attitude would . . . like . . . hop . . . it would skip back and forth, one minute he would be nice, the next minute he would be mean. I don't understand that. . . . A little kid wouldn't understand that.

Other caregivers appeared to live chaotic and unpredictable lives themselves, impacting their children with their behaviors. One woman reports that she and her sister had been kidnapped by drug dealers until their parents paid off the owed money. Another woman reports being used sexually in trade for her mother's drugs, when she was between the ages of three and five. Several women described mothers having multiple boyfriends or fathers with multiple girlfriends. One woman shared, "She would have a different boyfriend every month." Another woman reported, "My dad fathered eleven children between all the women he had." Two women reported their mothers prostituting and others living with gang members. One woman described her life with her mother as follows:

> My mom started doing drugs, things started you know . . . everything just out of control . . . we had parties in our house every night . . . boys could come over and spend the night . . . mom was dating guys who got younger and younger . . . that would just trip me out.

The lives of the women we interviewed were plagued with multiple moves, not only between houses but between families and caregivers as well. As children they were often forced to live with relatives due to their parents' drug or alcohol problems, or sometimes maternal mental illness. Several women reported living in foster homes intermittently throughout their childhoods, some being placed in multiple foster homes (five different foster homes for one mother). Homelessness was also apparent in some of their lives. The chaos in their home lives is represented in the following passages:

> We moved in with this guy, my mom's boyfriend, and I told my mom I wanted to go home and my mom said, "We are home," and I said, "No we are not." And then we went back to our old house for a week, then back to this other house, and it was like, "Mom, where do we live?"

We got evicted from our house, because they didn't pay the rent. I mean we were low income anyway and they didn't pay the rent . . . it was the drugs you know . . . their minds were just shot. We had to sleep in this truck . . . and we slept in the woods, behind our friend's house. My mom went and stayed with my grandma and we stayed at my mom's friend's.

The childhoods of these women are definitely representative of unpredictability. The safety of a consistent caregiver and a predictable environment was shattered with each chaotic event they experienced. The sadness and bewilderment of their words suggest mourning the loss of the consistency and predictability infants and young children yearn for, continued into their adult lives.

TRAUMATIC LOSS

The women in this group not only experienced the natural loss of elderly relatives, they also experienced multiple traumatic losses throughout their early lives. In addition to the multiple losses of their own childhoods, innocence, safety, and dependable attachment figures, these women experienced more than their share of loss to tragic death. Out of the 11 cases reviewed, there were two boyfriends, one sibling, nine friends, one aunt, and one infant child who died tragically and unexpectedly. Within this group of deaths there were three drinking-related automobile accidents, five murders by shooting, three murders by beating, one suicide, one peer who died of an aneurysm, and one SIDS death. In all of these cases the victims were same-age peers of the women or young relatives. The women often characterized these deaths with a continued sense of disbelief of not only the death itself but the senselessness of the circumstances surrounding the death. The words of these women illustrate the tragedy and lack of resolution in the losses incurred:

> His cousin shot him when he was trying to rob him. He didn't die right away . . . so his cousin let him lie there and bleed to death for two hours to make sure he was dead . . . it's still hard to talk about . . . my feelings haven't changed . . . I'm still as *hurted* as the day I heard he's dead.

> They [the gang] took my friend and shot him . . . they dumped his body three days later off on some highway. They had taken his shoes.

In addition to these tragic deaths, the majority of the women also reported grandparents who died of natural causes. Often these were the only people who the women identified as being their shelters from their stormy lives. Many of the women also described multiple miscarriages and abortions, reporting many instances of abortions being "forced on them" by boyfriends, parents, or their life situations. For example, one of the women reported having to choose between having an abortion or being kicked out on the streets by her mother.

No Children Allowed Here

The stories these women told had no room for children. It was as if a sign was posted over each of their front doors reading, "No Children Allowed Here." These women were not allowed to be children. Developmentally, they were punished for being normal. Three of the women shared stories of being severely punished for wetting their beds or pants as young children. These examples also support the unpredictability they experienced.

> I remember peeing my pants a few times when he'd go off like that, throwing things and screaming.

> When we were little kids and we peed the bed, my mom wouldn't sit down and say, "This is not what you do" or "You need to use the bathroom." She would never do that, she would fill the bathtub up with straight hot water and put us in it. And say, "this is what your are going to get if you pee your pants or pee the bed again."

> You know how kids that have problems, they wet the bed and stuff and my mom didn't understand that. So she would do things like tie my hands behind my back and tying my ankles together and putting me in a diaper and setting me in the tub, overnight—I had pissed the bed. I remember that. For a long time I was so afraid of water because of drops of water from the shower. . . .

They were shamed for crying the tears of a child.

> I was always crying. My aunt used to say my tears were like water works as if it were turned on . . . as if they were fake . . . they were never fake.

They were taught they could not trust anyone, and many had no friends.

A lot of the mental abuse made me shy, made me . . . you now, like when people wanted to be my friend I didn't know how to accept that because I was always told that I was nothing, and I didn't have, I didn't know why they wanted to be my friend, you know?

They worried about things children should not have to worry about, when they would get their dinner or, even more significantly, whether they would live until tomorrow.

Every day, I was worried about what time we were going to eat at night because my dad would go out and party and my mother wouldn't cook until he got there and said it was okay for her to cook. You know, and I was worried about getting hit. I was worried about getting yelled at, all on a daily basis.

Every day . . . every day I worried . . . I was afraid for my life . . . I didn't know if I was going to see tomorrow . . . or if I was going to live . . . if I was going to die or . . . I didn't know.

Many of the women in this group learned to be "substitute mommies" very early on. Many report having to care for younger siblings. One woman stated she became an instant mother at age five when her sister was born and her mom was too drugged up. Some described their relationships with their siblings as a "mother-daughter relationship" and feeling that "It was almost like I was her mother." Some women extended this caretaking role to include taking care of their own mothers, especially those who had mothers with mental illness and/or drug and alcohol problems. Caretaking seemed

to be one area where they were able to establish some type of relationship in which they were not directly being victimized.

Surrogate Mothers: Angels on and off Duty

The emotional and physical voids left by having mothers who were essentially absent from their lives facilitated the informal adoption of surrogate mothers for some of these women. Many of these difficult-to-engage mothers described other persons who came into their lives and seemed to fulfill certain aspects of having a mother-daughter relationship. They could describe these other people in positive terms such as patient, understanding, wonderful to be around, warm, and willing to be there for everybody. These people were most often grandmothers, aunts, uncles, and occasionally a stepfather. Two women described older women friends they had met who have seemed to fill the void they experienced with their biological mothers:

Now I have somebody—that I met here, even calls me her daughter, and my son her grandson. I feel she is more like a mother just in the few months I've known her.

She's my mother . . . not really my mother but I think of her as my mother . . . my ex-boyfriend's mother . . . he's passed away but I still go over there . . . I see her every Fourth of July. She's like the mom I never had.

Although the contacts may be infrequent or the relationships fairly new, the significance of these relationships for these women seems apparent. Some women only saw these surrogate mothers only once a year, but the emotional ties were characterized as strong and highly valued.

Unfortunately, however, not all the surrogate mothers were very different from the mothers for which they substituted. Interestingly, even in retrospect, women continued to see the good in these people even though they may have allowed abuse and terror to continue in these women's young lives.

> My stepmom she never raised a hand to me never hurt me in anyway she was always there to protect me she was my angel.

> She was my angel . . . during my life. She saved me, saved me a lot of times . . . think she was godsent. Somebody was watching over me.

The angel this woman speaks of was not on duty during most of her childhood. This woman endured six years of torture at the hands of her father:

> I was molested. Raped, beaten, burned, stabbed—you name it, it's happened to me from my father over six years . . . every day . . . every night.

In spite of the duration of the abuse, she still views her stepmother as her angel. Somehow, this angel was able to be the guardian of hope for this woman, but she never protected her.

In some cases the surrogate mothers or significant caretakers not only failed to protect, but they became perpetrators of abuse as well. Many of these woman were sexually abused and/or physically abused by their fathers, stepfathers, aunts, uncles, and baby-sitters. Oftentimes, these women had been placed into the homes of these caretakers as a safe haven from the abuse and neglect they had experienced with their mothers. In a sense some of what they endured was institutionally sanctioned. Women report refusing to go on visits or running away in order to avoid these people, only to be forced into the situations by the courts or social workers who ordered it.

Another interesting piece to this part of the puzzle is what was missing from these women's stories. Not one woman mentioned a teacher, counselor, social worker, neighbor, or even a friend who they could identify as someone who cared for them or had a meaningful impact on their lives. These women's childhoods often seem void of any caring individuals. While some of these women were able to find angels willing to do their jobs in protecting and caring, most encountered angels who fell short of fulfilling their job requirements.

Love for Sale

Another theme that emerged from the stories of the women was that of the shaping of a very materialistic quality to the relationships they encountered. Part of the Adult Attachment Interview requires that the person give descriptors of their relationship with each primary caretaker, and then they are asked to share a memory, story, or example of why that particular descriptor would apply. The descriptions of even some of the most inattentive, neglectful, or hurtful mothers, fathers, or other caregivers often included something positive such as loving, caring, nice, or happy. When memories or stories were shared, however, these descriptors equated with the provision of some type of goods. It was as if any affection or love these women did feel could be bought or traded for by the adults in their young lives. It was love for sale. Women used the following memories to illustrate these words:

Loving

- I asked him for a hundred dollars, and he gave it to me.
- He would give me money all the time.
- She spoiled me a whole lot . . . gave me what I wanted all or most of the time.
- She gave me what I wanted most of my life.
- Every day in the store I would keep bugging her, and she would say okay, one thing . . . to this day she is very loving and supportive.

Nice

- She would buy me things and buy me clothes.
- She would just give things to me; she was nice to me.

Happy

- We went shopping, and my mom bought me stuff.
- She used to give me what I wanted.
- He'd give me things that I wanted or asked for . . . I remember he got me the Barbie I wanted.
- Him and his girlfriend bought me a sweatshirt.

Caring

- She bought us lots of presents.
- Whatever we wanted, he always gave it

to us; he always wanted his kids to be happy no matter what.

Several other women described incidents where materialism was a factor. One woman described that she had recently renewed contact with her parents after "they got some money from the trusts coming." Another shared how her father controlled her with "things." "He would give me what I wanted to keep me quiet." Another woman describes being coaxed with tickets to a local amusement park in exchange for sexual perpetration. One woman was able to describe the effect some of the materialism had on her. "I know it is only monetary not emotional, but it has had an impact on me."

Summary

It is evident through this analysis of the AAIs that there are many common threads running throughout the life fabric of these women. Grief, loss, shame, self-blame, chaos, and trauma were frequently described and illustrated. Some women also shared their despair, wondering why so much pain would come their way—why they had been denied a childhood. One women summed this up in an extremely sad but poignant way when she questioned her life experiences in the following passage:

I struggled not to believe in God, because, if there was a God, why would he hurt somebody so bad? Like me? And let me go through what I had gone through at that point?

193

Perspectives from Home Visitors

Following the initial identification of families, the home visitors who were assigned to the families were interviewed. The home visitors were asked about their interactions, feelings, and responses to working with the hard-to-reach or difficult-to-engage families. The analysis of the interviews with the home visitors revealed several additional dimensions that identified families as difficult-to-engage. These dimensions were: (1) the patterns of interaction and communication during the home visit, (2) the social environment in which the home visit occurred, and (3) the heightened awareness that the home visitor had to risk factors and the potential for neglect in some families.

Patterns of Interaction
and Communication

The interaction during the home visit was determined more by the mother than the home visitor. The mothers often set a boundary in not being home at the time of a scheduled visit, controlling the amount of time spent during a home visit, or not attending to any topic and appearing distracted. The obvious boundary setting was missing appointments. The difficult-to-engage families varied, but some missed two or as many as 24 home visits. There were intervals of two to five months when some families did not receive services. Family and program factors contributed to periods when no home visits occurred. Several families moved more than once. Families did not have telephones, which

would have made it easier to maintain contact. In addition to the instabilities in the families' housing, two parents were absent and unreachable for two days to one week at a time. The home visitors attempted weekly contact with the families but occasionally could not make those contacts due to staff training, sick leave, or schedule conflicts.

The less obvious boundary setting was the mother limiting the time spent on the home visit. The "time's up" limit was described by a home visitor who stated that the parent stood up and left the room and on at least one visit dressed the infant and put on her own coat to prepare to leave the apartment without making any comments or closure with the home visitor. Another home visitor took the cue that time was up when the mother left the room without any comment. Not all of the difficult-to-engage parents were so abrupt in ending a planned home visit. Many of the home visits lasted 45 minutes or longer, but home visits to other program families averaged 62 to 76 minutes.

The other dimension of boundary setting was inattention described by home visitors as the mother being physically present but totally unreceptive during the home visit. When asked to describe what it was like to visit with one young parent, the home visitor remarked, "She will just sit there and not say anything so I don't really know if she is getting it or just waiting for me to leave." Two other parents were described as withdrawn, and they never initiated any topic of conversation or asked any questions of the home visitor.

The home visitors also indicated that

some parents did not take any interest in reading or doing activities with the child between the scheduled home visits. Several home visitors indicated that if they asked the mother what activities she would like to do, the parents did not respond at all. One home visitor asked a mother if she ever read to her child and the mother stated she "didn't like to read and didn't have books around." The home visitors interpreted the parents' lack of interest in following through with a parent-child activity as part of the parents' inattention to the home visit and to the program services in general.

Social Environment

The distinctions that the home visitors made in describing difficult-to-engage families became more apparent when the home visitors talked about other families who were easy to engage and who consistently participated in home visits. Several home visitors developed contrasts between the difficult-to-engage families and other families who they thought of as easier-to-engage families. The families who were easier to engage did not go through selection based on criteria, but the home visitors identified them and volunteered their perceptions of these easier-to-engage families. The easy-to-engage families differed from the difficult-to-engage families in the welcoming home environment that the former created. The easy-to-engage families were ready to interact socially in the context of their homes, gave a positive reception to the home visitor, initiated conversations, asked questions, or referred to an activity from a prior home visit.

The easy-to-engage parents were nearly always home for scheduled visits or called to change appointments. The easy-to-engage families were physically more ready for a parent-child activity with the home visitors as they positioned themselves in proximity to the home visitors at a table or in the living room. The easy-to-engage mothers acted pleased to see their home visitors, as the home visitors described that they were often greeted at the door by the parents and the children. Typically, the home visitors heard the parents remark, "I'm glad you're here. I want to show you what my child has done," or "I want to tell you what happened this week."

The willingness of the easy-to-engage families to initiate conversations sharply contrasted to the difficult-to-engage families, who were described as "distracted and not initiating conversation." The home visitors indicated that not only were some of the difficult-to-engage families slow to respond to questions, but they also did not initiate any of the common everyday greetings or pleasantries of social exchange that individuals often do upon meeting each other. That is, the home visitors described an absence of any friendly chatter (e.g., changes in weather, being busy) on the part of difficult-to-engage parents. The easy-to-engage families usually offered the home visitor a place to sit as well as a beverage. One family asked the home visitor to stay for a dinner that was prepared from recipes suggested by the home visitor during a prior home visit discussion on nutrition. The home visitors remarked that with the difficult-to-engage families they did not feel welcome, and none could recall being offered any food or beverage in the course of home visits. The easy-to-engage families were more hospitable and social in welcoming, greeting, and ending the home visit.

Risk Factors in the Home

The home visitors identified that in difficult-to-engage families, the parents demonstrated strict limit setting with their very young children or expressed very inflexible expectations for their children's behavior. One home visitor described how the mother moved furniture out of the room so the child would not climb at all on any furniture. The mother did not want the toddler to sit on the sofa at any time. Two other mothers were away from their respective houses for unexplained absences so the children were left in the care of their fathers. There were 3 of 12 families in the difficult-to-engage group who were referred (by an outside agency other than the program) to Children's Protective Services for failing to protect the child or for being inattentive or neglectful.

In addition to observing that in some difficult-to-engage families the parents had unrealistic expectations for the child's behavior and some parents were inexplicably absent from the home, the home visitors described another common situation in several difficult-to-engage families. The home visitors described how in four families the majority of the caregiving was provided by a family member other than the parent. Grandparents, an aunt and uncle, and great-grandparents provided full-time care to the focus child while the parents ei-

ther worked full time or attended school full time. The home visitors felt that some mothers were hesitant in assuming caregiving responsibilities, that is, they left the child in the care of the other family members for extended periods even when they were home and might have taken over primary responsibility. This heightened the home visitors' awareness of the child at risk for potential neglect.

Interpreting the Pattern of Interaction with Difficult-to-Engage Families

One finding that emerges from the identification of the difficult-to-engage families is the lack of social interaction between the home visitor and the parent during the home visit. The lack of social exchange hinders the relationship from the perspective of the home visitor so the home visitor doubts if the mother actually hears any information presented and assumes the mother merely tolerates the presence of the home visitor. In the absence of any feedback from the parent about information that is offered or any approaches that are discussed, the home visitors developed some self-doubts that led to questioning whether they had any positive impact for the time and effort spent with the family. The home visitors did not express guilt over these limited patterns of interaction with the difficult-to-engage parents, nor did they express responsibility for the nature of the relationship (or lack of apparent relationship). However, the home visitors were far more willing to go on home visits to the families who were more actively involved and willingly participated during the home visits. This was evident in the home visitors' verbal and nonverbal behavior as they prepared for home visits. In anticipation of an attempted visit to a difficult-to-engage family, the home visitor might announce that she expected to return soon as the mother always cut the visit short. In contrast, the home visitors planned the visits to the easier-to-engage families late in the afternoon for the family's convenience but also because the visit was expected to last longer and they allowed more time for interaction.

One home visitor thought the young mother's hesitation to care for her child explained the mother's pattern of missing appointments and not engaging in the home visits. Since the mother was not spending waking hours and any significant time with the child, she did not see the relevance of discussing parent-child activities, so she appeared very distracted and unreceptive during home visits. Two difficult-to-engage mothers were described by the home visitors as overwhelmed in getting to work on time or in getting to school and completing class assignments. For these young women, the activities associated with the program, described in the next section, were simply too demanding of what little time and energy they had remaining after struggling to make it in the world of work.

The Program

In the Children's Home Society South King County Early Head Start Program (CHSEHS) in Kent, Washington, the four cornerstones are the foundation of services provided. The original conceptualization of the CHSEHS program was as a home-visiting model. The home visitors have a background in child development and work in collaboration with public health nurses. In addition to the home visits, there are vocational counseling, stress management and mental health services, and assistance in finding child care available to the family based on individual need and interest. Once a family is enrolled, home visits occur on a weekly basis. The program was planned to work with the parent both on their own life course issues as well as focus on supporting their parenting skills and parent-child interaction. There are three linked elements of the home visiting program: (1) developing family goals, (2) developmental assessment and intervention based on the Hawaii Early Learning Program Model (HELP), and (3) Parent-Child Communication Coaching developed by the partnership researchers (Kathryn Barnard, Joanne Solchany, Colleen Morisset Huebner, and Susan Spieker). Only the Parent-Child Communication Coaching element is described in this chapter, since it was specifically developed to address the parent-child relationship and attachment.

In partnership with the South King County Families First Early Head Start Program, we created the intervention called Parent-Child Communication Coaching that begins in pregnancy and continues with age-specific interventions through the second year. In developing the intervention, we have adapted or developed methods others have suggested or based our approach on empirical evidence demonstrating a benefit for parent-child communication, interaction, and or attachment (Acredelo & Goodwin, 1995; Anisfeld, Casper, Nozyce, & Cunningham, 1990; Brazelton, Tronick, Adamson, Als, & Wise, 1975; Barnard et al., 1987; Barnard, Morisset, & Spieker, 1993; Booth, Mitchell, Barnard, & Spieker, 1989; Emde 1980; Koniak-Griffin, Verzemnieks, & Cahill, 1992; Kushner, 1987; Lawhon, 1994; Mercer, 1985; McDonough, 1993; Morisset, 1994; Rich, 1991; Rubin, 1984; Sander, 1964; Whitehurst et al., 1988). The set of interventions listed are carried out by the home visitors who visit the mothers on a weekly basis if the mother is not working or monthly if she is working.

- Pregnancy—Maternal tasks of recognizing fetus, gaining acceptance for infant within the family, trying on the maternal role and "attachment moments."
- Newborn to three months—Acquainting the parent with the infant's states, behavioral cues, and a close physical proximal environment.
- Four to eight months—The importance of learning to read the infant's emotional and verbal expressions and responding in a contingent manner.
- Nine to 24 months—The value of using natural and developing gestures to aid the parent-child communication before verbal language; encouraging preverbal activities such as book sharing, combining action and words on trips to the store, zoo, or playground.

- Twenty-four to 36 months—Book reading where the parent encourages the child to participate in communication about the book, identifying objects, and responding to parent's questions to elaborate actions of the story from the pictures.

Videotaping of the parent-child interaction is incorporated into these activities. Examples of recommended videotaping activities are feeding at one month, imitation of the baby at four to five months, eliciting emotions at six to eight months, making nonverbal gestures at 12 months, and reading at 26 to 28 months. The videotaping is done by the home visitor, and a review with the mother elicits her observations of the interaction based on the developmental emphases, such as what cues the baby gives in the feeding and what her responses are to those cues. The home visitor gives the observations a positive frame.

This chapter is not intended to report on the outcome of using the Parent-Child Communication Coaching intervention. We do know that parents for the most part engaged in the activities. There was less engagement by the mothers who are the subjects of this chapter, the difficult-to-engage mothers. Often their activities were approached in their simplest interpretation, and the mothers appeared to engage with the child with somewhat less intentionality.

In reviewing the case records of the women who were nominated as difficult-to-engage, it was surprising that all had evidence of considerable service delivery since their enrollment in the EHS program. The actual number of home visits ranged from 20 to 39 during their 9 to 15 months of enrollment in the program. About one-half of the mothers had enrolled during pregnancy. They had an average of twice per month home visits, although the program plan was for weekly home visits. The "not home" percentage ranged from 6 to 54 percent with the mode being that about 30 percent of the time the mother did not keep her scheduled home visit appointment.

There was some inconsistent recording of what was accomplished during the home visits, but the available recording suggested that home visitors focused on child development issues and family system issues about equally. There was documentation for each case that the Parent-Child Communication Coaching activities had been dealt with. However, there was no specific information about the mother's reaction or whether the specific activity, such as keeping track of fetal movement, tracing the support available for the pregnancy and the new baby, preparing a birth plan, learning the nonverbal cues of the infant, imitating the baby's behaviors, or recognizing the infant's emotions, was accomplished.

The home visitors conducted child development assessment and family assessment on most of the contacts. Only one of the 11 difficult-to-engage mothers went to the available parent classes. Few instances of dealing with crises in the family were recorded. Noted were a moderate amount of other support services, such as counseling, food, transportation, and so on, ranging from none to 12 instances for individuals over the 9-to-15 month period. Therefore, the nonengagement in the program was not evident in the service delivery documentation, except for a fairly frequent pattern of not being home for the planned visit. Because it seems that such families are receiving services, the question becomes the utility of the services in meeting the mothers' needs. It appears from our analysis of the mothers' records that there is some question about the assimilation of the EHS program based on the mothers' reactions during the actual visits when they are reported to be Nonattentive and communicate very little with the home visitor. This style, in turn, is discouraging to the home visitor, who then develops the impression that nothing is getting through and that the parent and child are making little progress.

Difficult-to-engage mothers may actually be ill-served by the type of program we designed. We believe the kinds of program activities that we planned for the pregnancy and early infancy period may be especially threatening for women who received inadequate early nurturing and remain unresolved with respect to attachment-related trauma. Further, staff who are not trained in mental health are extremely unprepared to deal with the responses from these mothers that the home visits and planned activities might elicit. For example, the pregnancy and infancy protocols we use to direct mothers' attention to the attachment needs of her infant may trigger emotional reactions in some of these mothers that home visitors are not trained to handle in a sensitive and clinically appropriate manner. The result can be an interaction for the mother wherein she feels unaccepted and possibly rejected. After such an experience the mother becomes even more distant from the home visitor and the program, continuing the cycle of nonengagement. The home visitor, who does not necessarily have the clinical skills to understand the mother's reaction to her and the topics she raises in her aim to promote the well-being of the infant, may be more comfortable with nonengagement as well. She may also experience anger and frustration in response to what she perceives as rejection by the mother of what the home visitor has to offer (a relationship with the home visitor and activities on behalf of the infant), thereby further perpetuating the cycle of nonengagement.

Conclusion

Our findings support the conclusion that a substantial minority of low-income families cannot use the services typically offered by two-generational, family support, and child development programs because the mothers have unmet mental health needs, related trauma, and loss in their lives. The questions we need to ask are: How can we identify these women early on, and what can be done to help them be more receptive to programs designed to enhance their child's development?

Certain mental health needs are clearly high in both the difficult-to-engage mothers and the remaining mothers. Depres-

sion is common in both groups. Fifty-seven percent of the sample (64 percent of the difficult-to-engage) were above the cutoff for clinical depression on the CES-D. In addition, we hypothesize that the difficult-to-engage mothers have higher rates of Post-Traumatic Stress Disorder (PTSD) and PTSD symptoms, due to the high incidence of traumatic events in their lives. We further hypothesize that activated PTSD symptoms contribute to the classification of the these mothers' AAIs as unresolved or cannot classify.

PTSD reactions are characterized by the experience of reliving the trauma, usually through intrusive thoughts and dreams, alternating with numbing of emotions and detachment from others. Other symptoms include irritability, outbursts of anger, difficulty concentrating, elevated autonomic activity, hyperalertness, and dissociative episodes. Children experience PTSD (Famularo, Fenton, Augustyn, & Zuckerman, 1996) as a result of severe abuse and neglect, and the symptoms for many of them persist for years after the termination of the abusive situation. These early experiences can affect brain development, such that individuals with a history of childhood abuse and neglect can have a vulnerability in certain neurotransmitter systems that can be activated under stress (van der Kolk, 1994). Chronic PTSD in adults has been associated with abuse and neglect in childhood (van der Kolk, 1987) and appears to play a role in the transmission of maltreatment across generations (Egeland & Susman-Stillman, 1996).

Lifetime prevalence of PTSD in young women has been reported to be 13.8 percent in a stratified, random sample of mothers of children participating in a study of child outcomes by birthweight (Breslau, Davis, Peterson, & Schultz, 1997). Exposure to trauma and subsequent PTSD were higher in mothers who were single and had not completed high school. In a study of 426 Head Start families from 64 classrooms in the same geographic region, Webster-Stratton and Hammond (1998) found that 25 percent of the mothers had experienced severe physical punishment as children (being kicked, punched, choked, severely beaten, hit with objects, tied up, and actions requiring medical attention), and 26 percent had experienced sexual abuse as children (percentages not mutually exclusive). Thus, it is quite likely that for many of the low-income families in this study, the mother-child relationship is at risk because of the mother's history of maltreatment and trauma and current PTSD. This risk is above and beyond the risk to the child of living in poverty.

While the experience of trauma was a common theme in our difficult-to-engage mothers, one woman in particular provides us with a strong example of the effects of PTSD related to the abuse and trauma of her childhood. This woman had lived her early life with her mother who was a prostitute and who often abandoned this woman and her brother for days at a time during their preschool years. Following eventual removal by child protective services, the children were placed with their father. It was at the hands of the father that this woman endured over six years of sexual and physical abuse, including being beaten with chains and stabbed, as well as being the victim of a nightly rape. She describes how these childhood experiences still affect her today.

> When I see people that look like my father, I get scared and freaky. It scares me. I have bad dreams about people trying to kill me and people going after me. My dad had threatened me that if I told anybody, he would kill me. He said this every day. I have nightmares. I still have them. I wake up scared every night.

This woman also bolted the doors of her apartment and kept the curtains closed at all times. She distrusted everyone.

This difficult-to-engage mother was also able to describe how these early experiences affect the mothering of her child.

> My boyfriend [the baby's father] doesn't even give [the baby] a bath . . . I won't let him. I give her a bath. I watch everyone . . . my boyfriend . . . my brother . . . I watch everyone that picks up my baby. I make sure that they don't hurt her, or fondle her, or do anything bad to her. I'm always there, just to look and see what's going on.

In addition, this difficult-to-engage mother never held her baby when she fed her. By six months of age the baby had been trained not to raise her arms during a feeding that was routinely done with the child in the car seat and the mother holding the bottle without touching the baby. This mother was also instrumental in preventing her boyfriend from playing with the baby or interacting with her on any level of playfulness or intimacy. At 14 months the baby had a Bayley MDI of 61. In the laboratory visit she was aimless and uninterested in the toys and activities.

Our findings and conclusions are no surprise to those who have studied child development in the context of poverty and family support services for low-income families (e.g., Halpern, 1993a, 1993b). Halpern (1993b) analyzes the historical context of support services for families in poverty. "The idea that providing scientific expert information to poor parents might improve their child-rearing patterns and, thereby, affect their children's futures underlies much parent-focused early intervention to this day" (p. 162). Family support services have become the principal vehicle for addressing our society's most basic problems. Family support services have come to promise to ameliorate all kinds of social problems to obtain funding, and we have lost sight of what are realistic goals for these programs. We want programs to reduce infant mortality, low birthweight, child abuse and neglect, teen pregnancy, school failure, juvenile delinquency, and welfare dependence in the next generation. In reality, programs "increasingly find that the global objective of supporting parents in their child-rearing efforts does not provide adequate guidance in working with families in which the parent-child relationship itself is at risk" (p. 163). Halpern points out that a growing number of young adults are embarking on parenthood "with personal histories marked by adversity in many spheres of life—by material deprivation, disruptions in caregiving, inadequate nurturing and/or rejection, family violence (including sexual abuse), and often a sense of failure in most areas outside family life as

well" (p. 164). Halpern could be talking about the difficult-to-engage families described in this chapter. In congruence with the goals of this chapter he states, "As policy and practice for supportive services evolve, it will be important to distinguish this increasing group of young families with multiple problems from their relatively less vulnerable peers" (p. 165). Halpern believes neither "parent education per se (as traditionally conceived) nor social support per se (as reflected in the typical family support program) provides an adequate theoretical structure for working with these families" (p. 166). He recommends an infant mental health orientation to complement the assumptions and purposes of parent education, child development, and family support programs.

A variety of infant mental health service models have been practiced on a small scale or in research settings for many years. Lojkasek, Cohen, and Muir (1994) review the literature on intervention models for changing troubled mother-infant relationships. Some models of intervention aim to change the relationship indirectly by working primarily with the mother. These methods, which vary in intensity, include support and psychotherapy. Other models influence the relationship directly by focusing on the dyad. Examples of this approach are developmental and relational guidance and infant-led interventions.

Supportive interventions are generally found in two-generational prevention models. They involve assisting mothers to access community resources and solve problems. The support provider may be a professional or paraprofessional, but rarely are they mental health professionals. Support may also be provided within a relationship where psychotherapy is the main goal (Fraiberg, Shapiro, & Cherniss, 1983). Psychotherapeutic approaches have their roots in psychoanalytic theory, with the idea that the mother's dysfunctional relationships with her own early caregivers influence her relationship with her infant. The aim is for the mother to gain insight into these earlier issues so as to choose not to have them interfere with her parenting.

Selma Fraiberg and her colleagues pioneered maternal psychotherapy with the infant present over 20 years ago in a series of articles on psychoanalytic treatment approaches for mothers who had suffered severe deprivation and losses in their own childhoods and their infants who had been identified as at extreme risk for abandonment, abuse, and neglect (e.g., Fraiberg, Adelson, & Shapiro, 1975; Adelson & Fraiberg, 1977). The method has been described more recently by Lieberman and Pawl (1993).

The setting for Fraiberg's therapy is not the professional's office but the family home. With the baby present, the mother is encouraged to remember, examine the past in the present, and to recognize the baby as a symbol of her painful past. In addition, the therapist provides what Fraiberg termed developmental guidance, "in which the therapist becomes a non-didactic educator of the mother as to the physical and emotional needs of her baby and the ways in which a mother can provide these needs. It is guidance in nutrition and in child development, and it is unobtrusively introduced into every session" (p.

60). The therapist may also provide concrete help or crisis intervention such as emergency aid, drives to the doctor, or mediation with other service providers.

Developmental guidance and crisis intervention all occur within the "transference cycle" that is at the heart of the therapeutic alliance in infant-parent psychotherapy. Frequently there are instances of negative transference whereby the mother sees the therapist as the hurtful, untrustworthy parent in her past. The mother is helped to see how she contributes to the repetition of the past by seeing the therapist this way. Positive transference is nourished in the trusting relationship that is painstakingly built with the therapist. The mother is psychologically nurtured in this context and becomes able to nurture her baby in turn, with the help of developmental guidance that teaches her to read the baby's cues and comprehend the baby's needs.

The three treatment modalities described by Fraiberg et al. (1983), parent-infant psychotherapy, developmental guidance, and support and crisis intervention, are fluidly and flexibly interwoven by a skilled professional. Other approaches, however, focus more exclusively on developmental or relational guidance.

Developmental guidance emerges from the tradition of infant stimulation programs for medically compromised infants. Developmental guidance focuses on increasing maternal knowledge of developmental milestones and solutions to practical caregiving problems. Instruction is fairly structured and usually not focused on the individual infant per se. However, relational guidance does focus on the mother with her infant in the context of spontaneous interactions (Bakermans-Kranenburg, Juffer, & van IJzendoorn, 1998; Juffer, van IJzendoorn, & Bakermans-Kranenburg, 1997; McDonough, 1993; Van den Boom, 1994, 1995). The approach involves videotaping the mother and infant and then using feedback sessions with the mother to reinforce positive features of the interaction and support the mother's skill in reading infant cues.

Infant-led psychotherapy is a relatively recent approach that involves "the setting aside of a regular period in which the spontaneous and undirected activity of the infant is acknowledged by the mother in much the same way as the therapist does with an adult patient" (Lojkasek et al., 1994, p. 214). The goal is to enhance mutual sensitivity in the dyad by supporting the mother's role as an observer of her infant. The presence of the psychotherapist is not to comment or focus on specific behaviors, as in relational guidance, but to provide a secure base for the mother to be a nonpassive, nonintrusive observer of her infant.

Research investigating these various methods has been summarized elsewhere (Fonagy, 1998; Lojkasek et al., 1994; Van IJzendoorn, Juffer, & Duyvesteyn, 1995). In general, there is promise in approaches that focus on infant mental health to promote caregiver-infant relationships as a context for healthy infant development. All of these methods help some dyads some of the time, but more needs to be understood about what works for whom under what circumstances. Furthermore, in reality pure intervention types do not exist. Cramer (1998) found that psychotherapists and therapists using relational guidance both use techniques supposedly typical of the other's domain. It is also interesting that short, focused interventions are reported to be more effective than longer programs (Fonagy, 1998; Van IJzendoorn et al., 1995).

Despite the promise of a range of preventive interventions based on an infant mental health perspective, it is obvious those who refuse the program, who drop out before the intervention is fully implemented, or who are otherwise difficult to engage in the program will not benefit. As stated at the beginning of this section, what is needed to assure that the developmental needs of all children are met is a way to identify families who qualify for participation in a prevention program but who are unlikely to engage in it because of parental risk factors and then to provide mental health treatment and a therapeutic relationship in order to bring them to the point where it would be possible for them to engage in the program. Our evidence suggests that mothers who have experienced multiple losses and traumas in their own childhoods, usually at the hands of caregivers, would be candidates for this alternative type of pre–prevention program treatment.

New Directions

One component of an integrated service delivery system for very young children would be the assessment of risk factors for poor outcomes. Ideally, identification of risk factors would occur before birth during universal prenatal care visits, with particular attention to first-time mothers. At an early prenatal visit, all first-time mothers would be screened by a primary health care provider who had been sensitized to mothers' emotional tasks during pregnancy. These providers would identify mothers with histories of abuse, trauma, loss, and current family violence. The presence of these risk factors would qualify the mothers for further assessment. Additional instruments would be used to assess depressive and PTSD symptoms, other mental illness, and substance abuse. Treatment for these risk conditions would be provided by mental health professionals with additional training in infant mental health, so that the professional could take advantage of "attachment moments" (Barnard, 1998) early in the mother-child relationship. The aim would be for fairly brief but effective psychotherapy that would relieve the worst of the symptomatology and also provide support during the mother's transition to a less intensive prevention program, such as one using a protocol like Parent-Child Communication Coaching. Infant mental health ideas need to be central in such a program.

Halpern (1993b) suggests that home visitors and other program helpers need not be clinically trained, but if a program is to incorporate infant mental health ideas, the staff should be highly trained in listening to and forming relationships with families. Staff would have ongoing training and supervision with a very experienced senior

staff person who would provide frequent opportunities to discuss and reflect on the home visitor's experience. In effect, the supervisor would provide the kind of trusting relationship with the home visitor that the home visitor was attempting to build with program families.

A second characteristic of home visiting programs that incorporate an infant mental health orientation would be visits that are flexible as to content and duration. The home visitor, empowered with the theoretical orientation of infant mental health, would be equipped with a variety of intervention strategies that could be employed selectively and flexibly. Promoting infant-parent attachment within the context of a particular family is the overarching framework for decisions about what is covered in a visit.

Staff would need special training to work with women experiencing symptoms of PTSD. Sable (1995) suggests that attachment theory provides some useful guidelines for clinicians. The treatment involves acknowledging the impact of the traumatic event or events and helping the individual make a coherent narrative out of the experience. Someone who is not specifically trained to hold and contain the distress of the PTSD individual would be unlikely to be able to respond appropriately when the subject of traumatic experiences comes up.

Finally, it is clear that some families would not be helped in time to be able to provide the type of nurturing that infants need to assure good development in the first critical years of life. In that situation, intensive services, in the form of full-time therapeutic day care or full-time experiences with nurturing alternate caregivers, need to be available for the children. Attention to the relationship the mother develops with a trusted mental health professional will increase the probability that she will then entrust her child to such an alternative setting during these critical early years.

Implementing these services for all who are eligible would be expensive but very likely cost-effective when compared to the expenses that could be incurred later in these children's lifetimes. It is also an opportunity to break the intergenerational cycle of abuse and neglect that produced the young, traumatized mothers whose story we have told in this chapter.

References

Acredelo, L., & Goodwyn, S. (1995, December). *Baby signs and child language outcomes.* Presented at the Zero to Three National Center Conference, Atlanta, GA.

Adelson, E., & Fraiberg, S. (1977). An abandoned mother, an abandoned baby. *Bulletin of the Menninger Clinic, 41,* 162–180.

Advisory Committee on Services for Families with Infants and Toddlers. (1994). *Statement of the Advisory Committee on Services for Families with Infants and Toddlers.* Washington, DC: U.S. Department of Health and Human Services.

Allen, J. P., Hauser, S. T., & Borman-Spurrell, E. (1996). Attachment theory as a framework for understanding sequelae of severe adolescent psychopathology: An 11-year follow-up study. *Journal of Consulting and Clinical Psychology, 64,* 254–263.

Anisfeld, E., Casper, V., Nozyce, M., & Cunningham, N. (1990). Does infant carrying promote attachment: An experimental study of the effects of increased physical contact on the development of attachment. *Child Development, 61,* 1617–1627.

Bakermans-Kranenburg, M. J., Juffer, F., & van IJzendoorn, M. H. (1998). Interventions with video feedback and attachment discussions: Does type of maternal insecurity make a difference? *Infant Mental Health Journal, 19,* 202–219.

Barnard, K. E. (1998). Developing, implementing, and documenting interventions with parents, infants, and very young children. *Zero to Three, 18,* 23–29.

Barnard, K. E., Hammond, M. A., Sumner, G. A., Kang, R., Johnson-Crowley, N., Snyder, C., Spietz, A., Blackburn, S., Brandt, P., & Magyary, D. (1987). Helping parents with preterm infants: Field test of a protocol. *Early Child Development and Care, 27,* 256–290.

Barnard, K. E., Morisset, C. E., & Spieker, S. J. (1993). Preventive interventions: Enhancing parent-infant relationships. In C. Zeanah (Ed.), *Handbook on infant mental health* (pp. 386–401). New York: Guilford.

Booth, C. L., Mitchell, S. K., Barnard, K. E., & Spieker, S. J. (1989). Development of maternal social skills in multi-problem families: Effects on the mother-child relationship. *Developmental Psychology, 25,* 403–412.

Breslau, N., Davis, G. C., Peterson, E. L., & Schultz, L. (1997). Psychiatric sequelae of Posttraumatic Stress Disorder in women. *Archives of General Psychiatry, 54,* 81–87.

Brazelton, T. B., Tronick, E., Adamson, L., & Wise, S. (1975). Early mother-infant reciprocity. *Ciba Foundation Symposium, 33 (new series)*, 137–54.

Campbell, F. A., & Ramey, C. T. (1994). Effects of early intervention on intellectual and academic achievement: A follow-up study of children from low-income families. *Child Development, 65,* 684–698.

Carnegie Task Force on Meeting the Needs of Young Children. (1994). *Starting points: Meeting the needs of our youngest children.* New York: Carnegie Corporation.

Cramer, B. (1998). Mother-infant psychotherapies: A widening scope in technique. *Infant Mental Health Journal, 19,* 151–167.

Delvaney, B. L., Ellwood, M. R., & Love, J. M. (1997). Programs that mitigate the effects of poverty on children. *The Future of Children, 7,* 88–112.

Egeland, B., & Susman-Stillman, A. (1996). Dissociation as a mediator of child abuse across generations. *Child Abuse and Neglect, 20,* 1123–1132.

Emde, R. N. (1980). Emotional availability: A reciprocal reward system for infants and parents with implications for prevention of psychosocial disorders. In P. M. Taylor (Ed.), *Parent-infant relationships* (pp. 87–115). Orlando, FL: Grune & Stratton.

Fraiberg, S., Adelson, E., & Shapiro, V. (1975). Ghosts in the nursery. *Journal of the American Academy of Child Psychiatry, 14,* 387–421.

Fraiberg, S., Shapiro, V., & Cherniss, D. (1983). Treatment modalities. In J. D. Call, E. Galenson, & R. L. Tyson (Eds.), *Frontiers of infant psychiatry* (pp. 56–73). New York: Basic Books.

Fonagy, P. (1998). Prevention, the appropriate target of infant psychotherapy. *Infant Mental Health Journal, 19,* 124–150.

Famularo, R., Fenton, T., Augustyn, M., &

Zuckerman, B. (1996). Persistence of pediatric post traumatic stress disorder after 2 years. *Child Abuse & Neglect, 20,* 1245–1248.

George, C., Kaplan, N., & Main, M. (1985). *Adult Attachment Interview.* Unpublished manuscript, University of California, Berkeley.

George, C., Kaplan, N., & Main, M. (1996). *Adult Attachment Interview* (3rd ed.). Unpublished manuscript, University of California, Berkeley.

Gomby, D. S., Larner, M. B., Stevenson, C. S., Lewit, E. M., & Behrman, R. E. (1995). Long-term outcomes of early childhood programs: Analysis and recommendations. *The Future of Children, 5,* 6–24.

Gomby, D. S., Larson, C. S., Lewit, E. M., & Behrman, R. E. (1993). Home visiting: Analysis and recommendations. *The Future of Children, 3,* 6–22.

Halpern, R. (1993a). Poverty and infant development. In C. H. Zeanah (Ed.), *Handbook of infant mental health* (pp. 73–86). New York: Guilford.

Halpern, R. (1993b). The societal context of home visiting and related services for families in poverty. *The Future of Children, 3,* 158–171.

Hesse, H. (1996). Discourse, memory, and the Adult Attachment Interview: A note with emphasis on the emerging cannot classify category. *Infant Mental Health Journal, 17,* 4–11.

Juffer, F., Van IJzendoorn, M. H., & Bakermans-Kranenburg, M. J. (1997). Intervention in transmission of insecure attachment: A case study. *Psychological Reports, 80,* 531–543.

Koniak-Griffin, D., Verzemnieks, I., & Cahill, D. (1992). Using videotape instruction and feedback to improve adolescents' mothering behaviors. *Journal of Adolescent Health, 13,* 570–575.

Kushner, K. (1987). *The effect of infant state modulation on parent-infant reciprocity: Impact of a nursing program.* Unpublished master's thesis, University of Washington, Seattle.

Lawhon, G. (1994). *Facilitation of parenting within the newborn intensive care unit.* Unpublished doctoral dissertation, University of Washington, Seattle.

Leiberman, A. F., & Pawl, J. H. (1993). Infant-parent psychotherapy. In C. H. Zeanah (Ed.), *Handbook of infant mental health* (pp. 437–442). New York: Guilford.

Lojkasek, M., Cohen, N. J., & Muir, E. (1994). Where is the infant in infant intervention? A review of the literature on changing troubled mother-infant relationships. *Psychotherapy, 31,* 208–220.

Main, M. (1995). Recent studies in attachment: Overview, with selected implications for clinical work. In S. Goldberg, R. Muir, & J. Kerr (Eds.), *Attachment theory: Social, developmental, and clinical perspectives.* Hillsdale, NJ: Analytic Press.

McDonough, S. C. (1993). Interaction guidance: Understanding and treating early infant-caregiver relationship disturbances. In C. H. Zeanah (Ed.), *Handbook of infant mental health* (pp. 414–426). New York: Guilford.

Mercer, R. T. (1985). The process of maternal role attainment of the first year. *Nursing Research, 34,* 198–204.

Miles, M. B., & Huberman, A. M. (1994). *Qualitative data analysis.* Thousand Oaks, CA: Sage.

Morisset, C. E. (1994). *Promoting toddler's language development through community based intervention.* Unpublished master's thesis, University of Washington, Seattle.

Radloff, L. (1977). The CES-D Scale: A self-report depression scale for research in the general population. *Applied Psychological Measurement, 1,* 385–410.

Ramey, S. L., & Ramey, C. T. (1992). Early educational intervention with disadvantaged children—To what effect? *Applied and Preventive Psychology, 1,* 131–140.

Rich, O. J. (1991). Maternal-infant bonding in homeless adolescents and their families. *Maternal-Child Nursing, 19,* 195–210.

Rubin, R. (1984). *Maternal identity and maternal experience.* New York: Springer.

Sable, P. (1995). Attachment theory and post-traumatic stress disorder. *Journal of Analytic Social Work, 2,* 89–109.

Sander, L. W. (1964). Adaptive relationships in early mother-child interaction. *Journal of the American Academy of Child Psychiatry, 3,* 231–264.

St. Pierre, R. G., Layzer, J. I., & Barnes, H. V. (1995). Two generation programs: Design, cost, and short term effectiveness. *The Future of Children, 5,* 76–93.

Stalker, C. A., & Davies, F. (1995). Attachment organization and adaptation in sexually-abused women. *Canadian Journal of Psychiatry, 40,* 234–240.

Strauss, A., & Corbin, J. (1990). *Basics of qualitative research.* Newbury Park, CA: Sage.

Van den Boom, D. C. (1994). The influence of temperament and mothering on attachment and exploration: An experimental manipulation of sensitive responsiveness among lower-class mothers with irritable infants. *Child Development, 65,* 1457–1477.

Van den Boom, D. C. (1995). Do first-year intervention effects endure? Follow-up during toddlerhood of a sample of Dutch irritable infants. *Child Development, 66,* 1798–1816.

Van der Kolk, B. A. (1987). *Psychological trauma.* Washington, DC: American Psychiatric Press.

Van der Kolk, B. A. (1994). Biological considerations about emotions, trauma, memory and the brain. In S. L. Ablon, D. Brown, E. J. Khantzian, & J. E. Mack (Eds.), *Human feelings* (pp. 220–240). Hillsdale, NJ: Analytic Press.

van IJzendoorn, M. H. (1995). Adult attachment representations, parental responsiveness, and infant attachment: A meta-analysis on the predictive validity of the Adult Attachment Interview. *Psychological Bulletin, 117,* 387–403.

van IJzendoorn, M. H., & Bakermans-Kranenburg, M. J. (1996). Attachment representations in mothers, fathers, adolescents, and clinical groups: A meta-analytic search for normative data. *Journal of Consulting and Clinical Psychology, 64,* 8–21.

van IJzendoorn, M. H., Feldbrugge, J. T. T. M., Derks, F. C. H., de Ruiter, C., Verhagen, M. F. M., Plilipse, M. W. G., van der Staak, C. P. F., & Riksen-Walraven, J. M. A. (1997). Attachment representations of personality-disordered criminal offenders. *American Journal of Orthopsychiatry, 67,* 449–459.

van IJzendoorn, M. H., Juffer, F., & Duyvesteyn, M. G. C. (1995). Breaking the intergenerational cycle of insecure attachment: A review of the effects of attachment-based interventions on maternal sensitivity and infant security. *Journal of Child Psychology and Psychiatry, 36,* 225–248.

Wasik, B. H., Ramey, C. T., Bryant, D. M., & Sparling, J. J. (1990). A longitudinal study of two early intervention strategies: Project CARE. *Child Development, 61,* 1682–1696.

Webster-Stratton, C., & Hammond, M. (1998). Conduct problems and level of social competence in Head Start children: Prevalence, pervasiveness, and associated risk factors. *Clinical, Child, and Family Psychology Review, 1,* 101–124.

Wechsler, D. (1981). *Manual for the Wechsler Adult Intelligence Scale—Revised.* San Antonio, TX: The Psychological Corporation.

Whitehurst, G. J., Falco, F. L., Lonigan, C. J., Fischel, J. E., DeBaryshe, B. D., Valdez-Menchaca, M. C., & Caulfield, M. (1988). Accelerating language development through picture book reading. *Developmental Psychology, 24,* 552–559.

Woodcock, R. W., & Mather, N. (1989). *Manual for the Woodcock-Johnson Psycho-Educational Battery—Revised (WJ-R).* Chicago: Riverside Publishing.

Zigler, E., & Styfco, S. J. (1993). An earlier Head Start: Planning an intervention program for economically disadvantaged families and children ages zero to three. *Zero to Three, 14,* 25–28.

Zigler, E., & Styfco, S. J. (1998). Applying the findings of developmental psychology to improve early childhood intervention. In S. G. Paris & H. M. Wellman (Eds.), *Global prospects for education, development, culture, and schooling* (pp. 345–365). Washington, DC: American Psychological Association.

7

Parenting Infants

Marc H. Bornstein

7

Introduction

Nothing rivets the attention or stirs the emotions of adults more than the birth of a child. By their very coming into existence, infants forever alter the sleeping, eating, and working habits of their parents. They change who parents are and how parents define themselves. Infants keep parents up late into the night or cause them to abandon late nights to accommodate early waking. They require parents to give up a rewarding career to care for them or take a second job to support them. They lead parents to make new circles of friends with others in similar situations and sometimes cause parents to lose or abandon old friends who are not. Parenting an infant is also a 168-hour-per-week job. That is because the human infant is totally dependent on parents for survival. Unlike the newborn foal that is on its feet within minutes of birth or the newborn chick that forages on its own more or less immediately, the human infant cannot walk, talk, or even ingest food without the aid of a competent caregiver. In a given year, approximately four million new babies are born in the United States, and worldwide each day more than three-quarter million adults experience the joys, heartaches, challenges, and rewards of becoming new parents (National Center for Health Statistics, 1994; Population Reference Bureau, 1993). Every day 11,000 babies are born in the United States—a number equivalent to the population of a small town—and every one is unquestionably unique and special (Bornstein, 1995a).

Infancy defines the period of life between birth and the emergence of language approximately one and one-half to two years later. Our generic terms *infant* and *baby* both have their origins in language-related concepts. The word *infant* derives from the Latin *in* + *fans*, translated literally as *nonspeaker* and the word *baby*

This chapter summarizes selected aspects of my research, and portions of the text have appeared in previous scientific publications cited in the references. I thank V. Lewis and B. Wright for assistance. Requests for reprints should be sent to Marc H. Bornstein, Section on Child and Family Research, Laboratory of Comparative Ethology, National Institute of Child Health and Human Development, National Institutes of Health, Building 31—Room B2B15, 9000 Rockville Pike, Bethesda MD 20892-2030, U.S.A. E-mail: Marc_H_Bornstein@nih.gov. This chapter is based upon "Parenting Infants," my chapter in *The Handbook of Parenting* (Mahwah, NJ: Erlbaum, 1995). Portions of that chapter are reprinted with the permission of Lawrence Erlbaum Associates, Publishers.

shares a Middle English root with *babble*. However, our *newborn* and *infant* are for the Chagga of Tanganyika *mnangu* (the "incomplete one") and *mkoku* ("one who fills lap"). For the Alor of the Lesser Sundra Islands, a first stage of life lasts from birth to the first smile, and a second stage lasts from the smile to the time when the child can sit alone or begins to crawl (Mead & Newton, 1967, in Fogel, 1984).

Infancy encompasses only a small fraction of the average person's life expectancy, but it is a period highly attended to and invested in by parents all over the world. Parenting responsibilities are greatest during infancy, when the child is most dependent on caregiving and the ability to cope alone is minimal. But infants also "pull" for parenting. Not by chance, infants' physiognomic structure is especially attractive to adults. Infants engender responsibility, and they make undeniable demands. Infants are fun to observe, talk to, and play with. Infants do not know how to be agonistic, deceitful, or malicious. Further, infancy is a period of rapid development in practically all spheres of human expression, and people are perennially fascinated by the dramatic ways in which the helpless and disorganized newborn human transforms into the competent and curious, frustrating and frustrated child.

Reciprocally, infants may profit most from parental care. Infancy is the phase of the life cycle when adult caregiving is thought to exert extremely salient influences. Not only does caregiving occur at its most intense levels, but infants are thought to be particularly susceptible and respon-

sive to experience. The sheer amount of interaction between parent and child is greatest in infancy. Parents spend more than twice as much time with their infants as they do with older children (Hill & Stafford, 1980). Indeed, adult (or other more mature) caregivers determine most, if not all, of infants' earliest experiences. It is the particular and continuing task of parents to prepare children for the physical, economic, and psychosocial situations that are characteristic of the culture where they are to survive and thrive (Benedict, 1938; Bornstein, 1991; LeVine, 1988). Parents everywhere appear highly motivated to carry out this task, and infants are likewise invested in their parents. At a very early age, they appear to recognize and prefer the sights, sounds, and smells of their caregivers, and over the course of the first year develop deep and lifelong attachments to them.

At their best, parent and infant activities are characterized by intricate patterns of synchronous interactions and sensitive mutual understandings (Bornstein, 1989a; Bornstein & Tamis-LeMonda, 1990; Kaye, 1982). In one study, two- to four-month-olds were observed with their mothers (Murray & Trevarthen, 1985). Infants first viewed real-time images of their mothers interacting with them via closed-circuit television, and during this period infants reacted with normal interest and pleasure. Immediately afterward, infants watched a videotape recording of those same images. This time, however, the infants exhibited signs of distress. The negative reactions were considered to arise out of the lack of synchrony that these babies experienced.

Even one-month-old infants are sensitive to the presence or absence of appropriate parenting interactions.

In this chapter, some salient features of parenting infants are presented. First, a brief history of parenting infants is provided, followed by a discussion of the theoretical significance attached to parenting infants. Next, characteristics of infants and infant development that are especially meaningful for parenting are described. Then, the chapter reviews principles of parenting infants, including direct and indirect effects, parenting behaviors and beliefs, and parenting and the mechanisms of action of these parenting principles. Multiple forces that shape parenting during infancy are outlined from an ecological systems view. Finally, differences between mothers and fathers and nonparental (i.e., sibling, familial, and nonfamilial) infant caregiving are discussed.

A Brief History of Parenting Infants

Infancy is an easily definable stage of life, based on biological and mental data as well as social convention. Infants creep and crawl, whereas the young and old walk and run. Infants do not speak, whereas the young and old do. Harkness and Super (1983, p. 223) observed that "All cultures . . . recognize infancy as a stage of human development." Infancy seems to have achieved recognition as an independent and significant period in the life cycle in pre-Classical times. When the Romans depicted the ca-reer of a typical man on "biographical" sarcophagi, they included infancy. Indeed, artists everywhere and throughout the ages have represented infancy as typically a first age or stage in the life span (Bornstein, in preparation-a). Iconographically, infants symbolize origins and beginnings.

Informal interest and concerns for parenting infants have been driven by perennial questions about the relative roles of heredity and experience on the course of child development. Plato (ca. 355 B.C.) theorized about the significance of infancy in this respect. The formal study of parenting infants had its beginnings in attempts by philosopher, educator, or scientist parents to do systematically what parents around the world do naturally every day—simply observe their babies. The first studies of children were diary descriptions of infants in their natural settings written by their own parents—"baby biographies" (see Jaeger, 1985, and Wallace, Franklin, & Keegan, 1994). Darwin published observations he made in the early 1840s on his first-born son William Erasmus, nicknamed "Doddy." Darwin's (1877) "Biographical Sketch of an Infant" gave great impetus to infancy studies (Dixon & Lerner, 1992). In succeeding years, baby biographies grew in popularity around the world—whether they were scientific documents, parents' private personal records, or illustrations of educational practices—and they still appear today (e.g., Mendelson, 1990; Stern, 1990). Perhaps the most influential of the modern baby biographers was Piaget (e.g., 1952), whose writings and theorizing refer chiefly to observations of his own young children.

These systematic observations of infancy heightened awareness in parents and provoked formal studies of how to guide infant development, that is, of parenting infants. Historians and sociologists contend that because of high rates of infant mortality (e.g., Beales, 1985), parents in early times may have cared for but resisted emotional investment in the very young (Dye & Smith, 1986; Slater, 1977–1978), a point of view that persists where especially dire circumstances reign (Scheper-Hughes, 1989). Parents seem to have generally improved in their orientation to and treatment of the very young because parents have, through successive generations, improved in their ability to identify and empathize with the special qualities of early childhood (deMause, 1975). Today, advice on parenting infants can be found in massive professional compendia, such as *Effective Care in Pregnancy and Childbirth* (Chalmers, Enkin, & Keirse, 1989), in classic how-to books, such as *Dr. Spock's Baby and Child Care* (Spock & Rothenberg, 1996), *Babyhood,* and *Your Baby and Child* (Leach, 1983, 1997), as well as in numerous popular periodicals.

The Theoretical Significance Attached to Parenting during Infancy

Infancy has opened formal studies of parenting in part because of two provocative debates, one concerning nature and nurture and the other concerning the significance of events occurring in infancy to later development. As to the second, proponents of one viewpoint argue that infancy is not particularly influential because experiences and habits of infancy have little (if any) long-term predictive significance in the life course. Embryologists and behavior geneticists have been prominent on this side of the argument. Others contend that the social orientations, personality styles, and intellectual predilections established at the start fix enduring patterns. Psychoanalysis, behaviorism, and ethology are schools prominent on this side. However, theoreticians and researchers alike have found it surprisingly difficult to confirm or refute the significance of the child's earliest experiences to the course and eventual outcome of development.

Infancy is the first phase of extrauterine life, and the characteristics developed and acquired then may be formative and fundamental in the sense that they endure or (at least) constitute features that later developments or experiences build on or modify. Infancy is only one phase in the life span, however, and so development will also be shaped by experiences after infancy. Parenting the infant does not fix the course or outcome of development, but it makes sense that effects have causes and that the start exerts an impact on the end. Parenting is central to infancy, development, and long-term investment in children. Indeed, social anthropological inquiry has almost always included reports of adults' first efforts at parenting (Bornstein, 1991; French, 1995). Parents are fundamentally invested in infants: their survival, socialization, and education.

Implications for Parenting of Characteristics Peculiar to Infancy and Infant Development

For parents and professionals alike, the pervasiveness, rapidity, and clarity of changes in infancy engender both fascination and action. During infancy, the child is transformed from an immature being unable to move his or her limbs in a coordinated manner to one who controls complicated sequences of muscle contractions and flections in order to walk, reach, or grasp and from one who can only cry or babble to one who verbally communicates needs and desires. The most remarkable of these domains of change involve the growing complexity of the nervous system, alterations in the shape and capacity of the body and its muscles, sharpening of sensory and perceptual capacity, increases in the ability to make sense of, understand, and master the object world, acquisition of communication skills, formation of specific social bonds, and emergence of characteristic personal and interpersonal styles. Parents escort their children through all these dramatic firsts. Not surprisingly, all of these developmental dynamics are closely tracked by parents, all shape parenting, and all are, in turn, shaped by parents. Significant developments in different domains in infancy influence and are influenced by parenting (Osofsky, 1987).

Developing Domains in Infancy

Infants vary in how soon they establish a predictable schedule of behavioral states (Parmelee & Sigman, 1983), and their reg-

ularity or lack thereof has critical implications for infant care and development as well as for parental well-being. State determines how infants present themselves. Much of what infants learn about people, their own abilities, and the object world is acquired during periods of quiet alertness and attentiveness. Infants who are temperamentally fretful elicit different patterns of care than do infants who cry only infrequently (Sanson & Rothbart, 1995). The amount of time infants spend in different states even determines whether they are alone or with their parents.

Infancy is the stage of greatest physical and nervous system development. On average, the newborn measures about 20 inches (51 cm) and weighs about 7½ pounds (3.2 kg). In the year after birth, the baby's length grows by one-half, and the baby's weight triples. These physical changes are paralleled by numerous advances in motor skills. Consider the eagerness with which parents await their child's first step. This achievement signifies an important stage in infant independence, permitting new means of exploring the surroundings and determining when and how much time infants spend near their parents. By walking, the baby asserts individuality, maturity, and self-mindedness. These changes, in turn, affect the ways that parents treat the child.

During infancy the capacities to take in information through the major sensory channels, make sense of the environment, and attribute meaning to information improve dramatically (see Bornstein & Lamb, 1992). Infancy culminates with the development of representational thinking and language. Maternal language and play influence infant language and play (Bornstein, Haynes, O'Reilly, & Painter, 1996; Užgiris & Raeff, 1995), and cross-cultural comparisons confirm that in cultures where parents emphasize particular types of language and play very young children tend to engage in those types of language and play (Bornstein, Haynes, Pascual, Painter, & Galperín, 1998).

Although infants communicate by means of emotional expressions (like crying), they quickly display the capacity to organize speech sounds, as indicated by babbling. The comprehension of speech combined with the generation of unique utterances rank among the major cognitive achievements of the infancy period, but the motivation to acquire language is personal and social and is born in interaction, usually with parents (Bloom, 1993; Bornstein, Haynes, & Painter, 1998). That is, the acquisition of first language reflects the child's early and rich exposure to the parent-provided target language environment as much as it does competencies that are an inborn part of a child. Language learning is active, but always embedded in the larger context of adult-infant social communication.

Emotional expressions give evidence about how babies respond to events, and new parents pay special attention to infants' emotions in their efforts to manage and modify them. The advent of emotional reactions—whether the first elicited smiles or the earliest indications of stranger wariness—cue meaningful transitions for caregivers. Infants deliberately search for and use others' (parents') emotional (facial, vocal, gestural) expressions to help clarify uncertain and evaluate novel events, a phenomenon called social referencing (Campos & Stenberg, 1981). Infants look to mothers and fathers for emotional cues and are influenced by both positive and negative adult expressions. Beyond emotional exchange, infants influence parenting by their individuality of temperament. Variation in activity level, mood, soothability, and emotional intensity define dimensions of temperamental individuality that parents typically use to characterize their infants. Just as parents and caregivers try to interpret, respond to, and manage infants' emotional states, they also devote considerable energy to identifying, adapting to, and channeling the temperament of their infants (Bornstein, 1998; Sanson & Rothbart, 1995). Just as in other spheres of infant life, cultural differences in ideology influence context and help to determine the interaction between emotional expression or temperament and parenting. No doubt some temperament proclivities of the infant transcend culture: Some smiles are more equal than others, and an infant's smile is first among equals. But adults from different backgrounds socialize the emotional displays of their infants by responding in accordance with culture-specific requirements or interpretations of infants' expressions and emotions (Super & Harkness, 1986). For example, infants universally respond to separation from parents in characteristic ways, but mothers may perceive and interpret their reactions differently according to cultural values. Thus, the meaning of infant behavior for parents is a complex function of act and context.

Infancy encompasses the gradual dawning of social awareness and is characterized by babies taking increasing responsibility for maintaining sequences of social interaction. The development of emotional relationships with other people—mainly parents—constitutes one of the most important aspects of social development in infancy. Once infants develop the capacity to recognize specific people, they begin to interact preferentially and gradually form attachments to those adults who have been consistently and reliably accessible during their first months of life. Attachment formation is a product of the convergence of built-in tendencies on the part of infants and propensities of adults to respond in certain ways to infants' cues and needs (Ainsworth, Blehar, Waters, & Wall, 1978; Bowlby, 1969).

The developmental changes that take place in individuals during the 2 ½ years after their conception—the prenatal and infancy periods—are more dramatic and thorough than any others in the life span. The body, mind, and ability to operate meaningfully in and on the world all develop with intensity. That dynamism, in turn, engages the world, for infants do not grow in a vacuum. Every facet of the world they touch as they develop influences them. These reciprocal relations ultimately cast parenting in a featured role.

Developmental Change in Infancy

Understanding dynamic change in the context of individual variation in infancy challenges all new parents. Infant development involves parallel and rapid biological, psychological, and sociological events, and infancy is synonymous with structural change. Crying in six-month-olds and behavioral inhibition in 18-month-olds may look different, but the underlying source construct of fear may be the same. Moreover, normal development in some spheres of infancy may be nonlinear in nature, stalling sometimes, or even regressing temporarily (Bever, 1982; Strauss & Stavy, 1981). Parents need to know about these infant complications and subtleties.

The number of notable developmental achievements occurring during infancy is amazing (especially when infancy is viewed as a proportion of the entire life span), but normal variability in the timing of these achievements is equally compelling. Every infant is original. Interest in the origins and expression of this variability occupies a central position in thinking about infant development and parenting. The ages at which individual infants achieve a given developmental milestone typically vary enormously, just as infants of a given age vary dramatically among themselves on nearly every index of development. When and how their toddlers talk or walk exercises a psychological impact on parents, even if the long-term significance of a given child's performance is meaningful only for extreme cases.

Parenting an infant is akin to trying to hit a moving target, the ever-changing infant developing in fits and starts at his or her own pace. Parents need to interpret aspects of infant function unambiguously, and they must accomplish this in spite of changes and fluctuations in state. Perhaps the major problem faced by parents of infants is that, at base, they are constantly trying to divine what is "inside the baby's head"—what infants want, what they know, how they feel, what they will do next about the people and things around them, and whether they understand and are affected by those same people and things. Thus, parents of infants seem constantly in search of patterns, often even on the basis of single transient instances. New parents have the job of disambiguating novel, complex, and rapidly emerging uncertain information and, at the same time, are called on to parent appropriately and effectively. Most face the formidable challenges of infancy with stunning psychological naiveté. But parents do not meet these tests totally unprepared. Beyond blind biodeterminism, culture generally equips parents for understanding and interpreting the developing domains of infancy and its vicissitudes.

Principles of Parenting Infants

Infants do not and cannot grow up as solitary individuals. Parenting constitutes an initial and all-encompassing ecology of infant development. Mothers, fathers, and others guide the development of infants via many direct and indirect means. Biological parents contribute to the genetic makeup of their infants. All parents and caregivers shape infants' experiences. Parents also influence their infants by virtue of each partner's influence on the other. Parents and others affect infant development by both their behaviors and their beliefs. In this re-

spect, similarities as well as differences in mothers' and fathers' actions and attitudes touch the nature and course of infant development, and they do so according to different mechanisms and following different models.

Direct and Indirect Effects

Mothers and fathers contribute directly to the nature and development of their infants by passing on biological characteristics. Modern behavior genetics indicates that characteristics of offspring in a host of different realms—including height and weight, intelligence and temperament—reflect inheritance to a substantial degree (e.g., Bouchard, Lykken, McGue, Segal, & Tellegen, 1990).

Although parental genes certainly contribute to infant proclivities and abilities in different domains, all prominent theories of development put experience in the world as either the principal source of individual growth or as a major contributing component (Dixon & Lerner, 1992). Studies of infants with genetic backgrounds that differ from those of their nurturing families provide a powerful means of evaluating the impact of heredity and experience on infant development (e.g., Ho, 1987). In (ideal) natural experiments of adoption, the child shares genes but little if any of the same environment with biological parents, and the child shares an environment but few if any genes with adoptive parents. Studies of one-year-olds, their biological parents, and their adoptive parents show that the rate of development of communicative competence and cognitive abilities, for example, relates to the general intelligence of the baby's biological mother (IQ) and also to the behavior of the adoptive mother (imitating and responding contingently to infant vocalization). These results point to direct roles for both heredity and experience in parenting infants (Hardy-Brown, 1983). Empirical research also attests to the short- and long-term influences of parent-provided experiences in infant development.

Indirect effects are more subtle and less noticeable than direct effects, but perhaps no less meaningful. An example of this type of effect is marital support and communication. Parents' attitudes about themselves and their marriages influence the quality of their interactions with their children and, in turn, their children's development (Cowan & Cowan, 1992).

Research shows both direct and indirect effects of parenting on infants. In addition, parents' behaviors and beliefs both matter.

Parenting Behaviors

Perhaps most salient in the phenomenology of the infant are actual experiences provided by mothers, fathers, and others. Before children are old enough to enter informal or formal social learning situations, such as play groups and school, much of their worldly experience stems directly from interactions they have within the family. In that context (at least in Western cultures), two adult caregiving figures are responsible for determining most, if not all, of infants' experiences. A small number of domains of parenting interactions have been identified as a common core of parental care.

In infrahuman primates, the majority of maternal behaviors consist simply in biologically requisite feeding, grooming, protecting, and the like (Bard, 1995). The content of parent-infant interactions is more dynamic, varied, and arbitrary in human beings. Moreover, there is initially asymmetry in parent and child contributions to interactions and control: Postinfancy, children play more active and anticipatory roles in interaction, whereas initial responsibility for adaptation in child development lies unambiguously with the parent.

Four superordinate categories of human parental caregiving (and reciprocally for the infant, experiences) can be identified: nurturant, material, social, and didactic. These categories apply to the infancy period and normal caregiving. Although these modes of caregiving are conceptually and operationally distinct, in practice caregiver-infant interaction is intricate and multidimensional, and infant caregivers regularly engage in combinations of them. Together, these modes are the most prominent of caregivers' activities with babies, and they are perhaps universal, even if their instantiation or emphases in terms of frequency or duration vary across cultures (Bornstein, in preparation-b). For their part, human infants are reared in, influenced by, and adapt to a physical and social ecology commonly characterized by the elements in this taxonomy.

Nurturant caregiving meets the physical requirements of the infant. Infant mortality is a perennial concern, and parents are responsible for promoting infants' wellness and preventing their illness from the moment of conception—or even earlier. Material caregiving includes those ways that parents provision and organize the infant's physical world. They are responsible for the number and variety of inanimate objects available to the infant, level of ambient stimulation, limits on physical freedom, and overall physical dimensions of babies' experiences. Social caregiving includes the variety of visual, verbal, affective, and physical behaviors parents use in engaging infants in interpersonal exchanges. Rocking, kissing, tactile comforting, smiling, vocalizing, and playful face-to-face contact are illustrative of interpersonal social interactions. Parental displays of warmth toward children peak in infancy. Social caregiving includes the regulation of affect as well as the management of infants' social relations with others, including relatives, nonfamilial caregivers, and peers. Didactic caregiving consists of the variety of strategies parents use in stimulating infants to engage and understand the environment outside the dyad. Didactics include introducing, mediating, and interpreting the external world, describing and demonstrating as well as provoking or providing opportunities to observe, imitate, and learn.

Adults differ considerably among themselves in their caregiving behaviors, even when they come from the same culture and socioeconomically homogeneous groups. Although individual parents do not vary much in their activities from day to day, parenting activities change over longer periods and in response to children's development. Some parenting activities are stable and continuous as infants age. Others are stable and discontinuous, showing either a general developmental increase or a decrease. Some activities are stable and continuous, whereas others are unstable and discontinuous, showing either a general developmental increase or decrease. Sensitive parents tailor their behaviors to match their infants' progress. Indeed, parents express sensitivity both to infant age and infant capacity or performance.

Classical authorities, including psychoanalysts and ethologists, once conceptualized maternal behavior as a more or less unitary construct—denoted as good, sensitive, warm, or adequate—despite the wide range of activities mothers naturally engage in with infants (e.g., Ainsworth et al., 1978; Mahler, Pine, & Bergman, 1975; Rohner, 1985; Winnicott, 1957). The thinking was that parents behave in consistent ways across domains of interaction, time, and context. The four domains of parenting infants described constitute coherent but mutually distinctive constructs, and parents vary among them.

Infant caregiving is further differentiated by responsibility and lead. In Western industrialized cultures, parents are generally acknowledged to take principal responsibility for structuring exchanges: They engage infants in early game play as well as in verbal turn-taking. To a considerable degree, however, parenting is a two-way street. Surely, infants cry to be fed and changed, and when they wake they are ready to play. Sometimes parents' initiatives are proactive. Often, however, they are reactive and interactive.

Responsiveness is a major issue in parenting infants (Ainsworth et al., 1978; Bornstein, 1989b). Parents who respond promptly, reliably, and appropriately to their babies' signals give babies a good message from the start. They tell their children that they can trust their parents to be there for them, and they give their children a sense of control and of self. Responsiveness has been observed as typical for mothers in different parts of the world (Bornstein et al., 1992a). However, some types of responsiveness in mothers are similar, and some types vary relative to divergent cultural goals of parenting.

In everyday life, parenting infants does not always go well and right, unfortunately (e.g., Fitzgerald, Lester, & Zuckerman, 1995). Infanticide was practiced historically (French, 1995), and it is very rare (although not unknown) today (Eisenberg, 1990). Short of such outright pathology, numerous other risks alter postnatal parenting and compromise the innocent infant (Carnegie Corporation of New York, 1994). More than one-quarter of births in the United States occur to unmarried mothers . . . more than one-quarter of children under three live below the federal poverty level . . . one in three victims of physical abuse is a baby . . . in the inner city, nearly one baby in two is born to a woman who tested positive for cocaine use at the time of delivery . . . fewer than one-half of American two-year-olds are fully immunized.

Parenting Beliefs

Parents' beliefs—or, more generally, their ideas, knowledge, understanding, and attitudes—hold a consistently popular place in the study of parent-infant relationships (Goodnow & Collins, 1990; Holden, 1995).

Parental beliefs are conceived to serve many functions. They may generate and shape parental behaviors, mediate the effectiveness of parenting, or help to organize parenting because they affect parents' sense of self and competence (Darling & Steinberg, 1993; McGillicuddy-De Lisi & Sigel, 1995). Observing and understanding child-rearing beliefs can lead us to determine how and why parents behave in the ways they do.

A determinative role of parental beliefs is in reports about infants. Based on their long-term, intimate experience with them, parents surely know their own infants better than anyone else does. For that reason, parents (or other close caregivers) are believed to provide valid and insightful reports about them (Thomas, Chess, Birch, Hertzig, & Korn, 1963). However, parental reporting invites problems of bias owing, for example, to parents' subjective viewpoint, personality disposition, unique experiences, and other factors. One study compared maternal and observer ratings of infant activity (operationalized in terms of explicit motor behaviors) when infants were by themselves, with their mothers, and with the observer, on two different occasions, each time in different situations (Bornstein, Gaughran, & Seguí, 1991). Mother-observer assessments agreed but only moderately, and historically, evaluations of convergence between maternal reports and assessments of infants by (significant) others (father, caregiver, or observer) have yielded only moderate levels of agreement. Apparently, different observers have different amounts of information about the baby, and they carry with them unique perspectives that have been shaped by their own idiosyncratic experiences. These perspectives influence their judgments of infants.

Nonetheless, parents' perceptions are still valuable in their own right, that is, as contributors to understanding parenting forces at work in infant development. Mothers who see their infants as being difficult, for example, are less likely to pay attention or respond to their children's positive overtures. In this way, parental perceptions per se may foster temperamental difficulty because they lead adults to treat children more negatively.

Significantly, parents of infants in different cultures may cling to different ideas about the meaning and significance of their own parenting behaviors and the behaviors of their infants. Parents then act on culturally defined beliefs as much as or more than on what their senses tell them. Parents in Samoa think of young children as having an angry and willful character, and independent of what children might actually say, parents universally report that the infant's first word is "tae"—Samoan for "shit" (Ochs, 1988). Parents who believe that they can or cannot affect their infants' temperament or intelligence modify their parenting accordingly. That is, the ways in which parents (choose to) interact with their infants appear to relate to the parents' general belief systems.

Mechanisms of Parenting Effects on Infants

Parents' behaviors and beliefs influence infants and infant development via different paths. A common assumption in parenting is that the overall level of parental involvement or stimulation affects the infant's overall level of development (see Maccoby & Martin, 1983). Increasing evidence suggests, however, that sophisticated mechanisms function in differentiated ways in explaining parenting effects. First, specific (rather than general) parental activities appear to relate concurrently and predictively to specific (rather than general) aspects of infant competence or performance, and second, parent and infant mutually influence one another through time. Infants influence which experiences they will be exposed to as well as how they interpret those experiences and how those experiences might affect them. Infant and parent bring distinctive characteristics to, and each is believed to be changed as a result of, every interaction; both then enter the next round of interaction as "different" individuals. These principles of specificity and transaction together propel development from infancy onward. The working model of parenting infants and infant development is that specific experiences at specific times affect specific aspects of the child's growth in specific ways and specific infant abilities and proclivities affect specific experiences and specific aspects of development.

Parenting behaviors and beliefs also appear to affect development in infancy via different pathways. A parent-provided experience may influence the infant at a particular time, and the consequence for the infant endures, independent of earlier or later parenting (and, perhaps, independent of any contribution of the infant). Alternatively, parent-provided experiences might influence infant development cumulatively. That is, no parent-provided experience at any one time necessarily exceeds an effective threshold in affecting the infant, but meaningful longitudinal relations are structured by similar parenting interactions continually repeating and aggregating through time. Furthermore, parenting of specific sorts might affect development monistically, but different behaviors certainly also often combine in conditional ways. Parenting affects development over both short and long periods. Some parenting effects may be immediate, and others may need to aggregate. Some may be direct, and others may be indirect.

Forces That Shape Parenting Infants

A key step toward fully understanding parenting infants is to evaluate the forces that shape it. The origins of individual variation in maternal and paternal caregiving—whether behaviors or beliefs—are extremely complex and multiply determined, but certain factors seem to be of paramount importance. They include actual or perceived characteristics of infants, biological determinants, personality characteristics, social situational factors, experiences of parents, and socioeconomic status and culture (Belsky, 1984; Bornstein, 1995b). Typically, determinants of parenting have been studied in isolation from one another, and few studies have evaluated multiple influences simultaneously. Thus, the overlap

of different determinants and the unique contribution that each may make to parenting are essentially unexplored.

Systems theorists have, however, emphasized the importance of considering the possible independence and interdependence of different domains in predicting psychological status (see Bronfenbrenner & Crouter, 1983; Lerner, Castellino, Terry, Villarruel, & McKinney, 1995). Consistent with an ecological model, cultural, sociodemographic, and personal factors and child characteristics doubtless exist in increasing predictive relation to parenting, and each exerts direct as well as indirect effects on mothers' mothering and fathers' fathering. The following discussion moves from distal determinants of parenting to more proximal ones. Proximal factors exert direct effects and/or mediate effects of distal factors on parenting.

First, cultural variation in behavior is always impressive, whether observed among different ethnic groups in one society or among groups in different parts of the world. Cross-cultural comparisons show that virtually all aspects of parenting infants—whether behaviors or beliefs—are informed by cultural practices. In some places, infants are reared in extended families where care is provided by many relatives, while in others, mothers and babies are isolated from almost all social contexts. In some groups, fathers are assigned complex responsibilities for children, while in others, fathers are treated as irrelevant social objects. Culture influences parenting patterns and child development from very early in infancy through variation in when and how parents care for infants, the extent to which parents permit infants freedom to explore, how nurturant or restrictive parents are, which behaviors parents emphasize, and so forth (Benedict, 1938; Bornstein, 1991; Erikson, 1950; Whiting, 1981). The infant-rearing practices of one's own context may seem natural, but may actually be idiosyncratic when compared with those of other groups. Cultural ideology makes for subtle, but potentially meaningful, differences in patterns of parent behaviors and beliefs toward infants.

Parents in different cultures show some striking similarities vis-à-vis their infants as well. Whether converging patterns in mothers reflect an inherent truism of caregiving across certain societies, the historical convergence of parenting styles, or the increasing prevalence of a single child-rearing pattern through migration or dissemination via mass media is difficult to determine. In the end, different peoples (presumably) wish to promote similar general competencies in their young. Some do so in manifestly similar ways. Others appear to do so in different ways, and of course, culture-specific patterns of child-rearing are adapted to each specific society's settings and needs (Bornstein, 1991).

Few nations in the world are characterized by cultural homogeneity. Class differences within Western industrialized countries color parenting attitudes and actions just as surely as larger cross-cultural differences do. Parents in different socioeconomic status (SES) groupings behave similarly in certain ways. However, SES also orders the home environment and other behaviors of parents toward infants (Hoff-Ginsberg & Tardif, 1995). Middle-SES parents, compared to lower SES parents, typically provide more opportunities for variety in daily stimulation, more appropriate play materials, and more total stimulation (Gottfried, 1984). Social class and culture pervasively influence the complexity and resourcefulness with which parents view infant development (Sameroff & Feil, 1985).

Certain choices new parents make and situations they find themselves in also exert enormous influences over parenting. About one-half of new mothers in the United States have not finished high school, are not married, or are teenagers when their baby is born (Center for the Study of Social Policy, 1993; Honig, 1995). Financial and social stresses adversely affect general well-being and health in parents and demand attention and emotional energy from them. This, in turn, may reduce parents' attentiveness, patience, and tolerance toward their children (Crnic & Acevedo, 1995). Well-supported mothers are less restrictive and punitive with their infants than less well-supported mothers, and frequency of contacts with significant others improves the quality of parent-child relationships as well as the parents' sense of their own effectiveness and competence (Abernathy, 1973). Intimate support from husbands (those indirect effects mentioned earlier) has the most general positive consequences for maternal competence (Crnic, Greenberg, Ragozin, Robinson, & Basham, 1983).

Infant parenting is also influenced by family configuration, level of parental stress, and status of parents, among other social-situational factors. For example, about one-half of the babies born in a given year are firstborns, and primiparas devote more attention and better care to infants and toddlers than do multiparas (Furman, 1995). The births of later children alter the roles of each family member and forever affect the ways in which each interacts with all others. Parents of a secondborn infant are in many ways, therefore, not the same as parents of a firstborn infant in terms of behaviors or beliefs, and the mere presence of older or younger siblings puts its own stamp on parent-infant interactions. Even though the absolute frequency of daily problems reported by parents of infants is about the same as for children of other ages, new parents do not rate the intensity and salience of problems as high (Crnic & Booth, 1991). Infancy may well represent a "honeymoon period" wherein parents recognize the difficulty of parenting chores and choose not to make stressful attributions about them.

Closer to the individual, parenting reflects enduring personality traits (Belsky, 1984). Features of personality favorable to good parenting probably include empathic awareness, predictability, responsiveness, emotional availability, and perceived effectiveness. Within the normal range, characteristics such as self-centeredness and adaptability may be especially pertinent to infant caregiving. Adult adaptability may be vital in the first few months when infants' activities appear unpredictable and disorganized, their cues less distinct and well-differentiated, and infants themselves generally less "readable."

Negative characteristics of personality, whether transient or permanent, are likely to affect parenting infants adversely. Self-centeredness can lead to difficulties when adults fail to put infants' needs before their own. Depression, whether an enduring psychological characteristic or fleeting as in response to economic circumstances or even following the birth the baby, may cause mothers to fail to experience and convey to their infants much happiness with life. Such feelings no doubt diminish the responsiveness of or discoordinate mother-infant interactions (Tronick & Gianino, 1986), and so depressed parenting may have short-term as well as long-term consequences for infants (Field, 1995).

Basic physiology is mobilized to support parenting (Corter & Fleming, 1995), and parenting tendencies normally first arise out of biological processes associated with pregnancy and parturition. Prenatal biological events such as parental age, diet, and stress, and other factors including contraction of disease, exposure to environmental toxins, and even anesthetics also affect postnatal parenting. Papoušek and Papoušek (1995) developed the idea that some infant caregiving practices are biologically "wired" into human beings. "Intuitive parenting" involves responses that are developmentally suited to the age and abilities of the child, and they often have the goal of enhancing infant adaptation and development. Parents also regularly enact such parenting programs in an unconscious fashion, so that they do not require the time and effort typical of conscious decision-making and, being more rapid and efficient, utilize less attentional reserve.

Parents can reach very different conclusions about their parenting, despite similarities in parenting per se, because of the differing physical, cognitive, emotional, or social characteristics of their children (Sanson & Rothbart, 1995). Thus, manifest as well as subtle characteristics of infants can be expected to influence parenting (and, in turn, infant development). Some so-called infant effects are universal and common to all infants; others include effects unique to a particular infant or situation. Some key physical features of infancy probably affect parents everywhere in similar ways. By the conclusion of the first trimester, fetuses are felt to move in utero, and soon after (with support) fetuses may survive outside the womb. These are significant markers in the life of the child and in the lives and psyches of the child's parents. After birth, infants' nature as well as certain of their actions are likely to influence parenting uniformly. Lorenz (1935/1970) argued that certain physiognomic features of "babyishness" provoke adults to express reflexively nurturant and solicitous reactions toward their offspring. Under ordinary conditions, specific infant behaviors also elicit predictable caregiving or other specific responses from parents (Bell & Harper, 1977; Bornstein et al., 1992a). From conception through birth and after, babies exercise several effective signals that are at their disposal. Crying, for example, will motivate adults to approach and soothe, and smiling will encourage adults to stay near.

Other structural characteristics of infants manifestly affect parenting and the quality of parent-infant interaction. Health status, gender, and age are three significant factors. Preterm infants, for example, are more passive and reactive than are term infants of comparable age, and their mothers are more active and directive (Goldberg & DiVitto, 1995). Parental patterns of interaction with infant girls and boys are a more complicated infant effect. There is evidence that parenting infant girls and boys is surprisingly similar (Fagot, 1995; Lytton & Romney, 1991). However, newborn nurseries provide color-coded blankets, diapers, and so forth. Beginning with the baby shower, gifts are carefully selected by sex, and infants are uniformly dressed in sex-typed clothing (Shakin, Shakin, & Sternglanz, 1985). Infant gender fundamentally organizes parents' descriptions, impressions, and expectations (Hildebrandt & Fitzgerald, 1977; Rubin, Provenzano, & Luria, 1974). Finally, infant development per se exerts pervasive control over parental behavior. Over the second half of the first year of life, as infants begin to achieve verbal and other competencies, parents appear to expect that their infants need and can process more information about themselves and their surroundings. Cross-cultural data on maternal speech in this period, for example, show clearly that mothers of younger infants favor affect-laden speech, but as infants achieve more sophisticated levels of motor exploration and cognitive comprehension, mothers everywhere increasingly orient, comment, and prepare their babies for the world outside the dyad by using more information-laden speech (Bornstein et al., 1992b).

Still other characteristics of infants may be idiosyncratic but no less stimulating to parents. Goldberg (1977) pointed out that salient infant characteristics of responsiveness, readability, and predictability affect parents in broad ways. Infant temperament also influences adults and the effectiveness of adult ministrations. By virtue of their temperament and the quality and contingency of their own responsiveness, infants have a major impact on how parents behave and how parents perceive their own effectiveness. Having a temperamentally easy baby (one who is relatively happy, predictable, soothable, and sociable) may enhance a mother's feelings that she is efficacious, good, and competent. Perceptions alone are critical. Mothers who perceive their babies as temperamentally easy consider themselves to be better mothers than mothers who see their babies as difficult.

Biology, personality, and perceptions of role responsibilities constitute factors that influence parenting from the start. But societal factors also channel behaviors and beliefs of infants' parents. Social situation, economic class, and culture encourage divergent patterns of parenting perceptions and practices. Parenting is thus the confluence of many complex tributaries of influence; some arise within the individual, whereas others have external sources. Some reactions felt toward babies may be reflexive and universal; others are idiosyncratic and vary with personality, society, class, and culture.

Mothers, Fathers, Others, and Infants

Mothers normally play the central role in children's development, especially in infancy (Barnard & Martell, 1995), even if historically fathers' social and legal claims and responsibilities on children were preeminent (French, 1995). Cross-cultural surveys attest to the primacy of biological mothers in caregiving (e.g., Leiderman, Tulkin, & Rosenfeld, 1977), and theorists, researchers, and clinicians have largely been concerned with mothering rather than parenting in recognition of this fact. Western industrialized nations have witnessed increases in the amount of time fathers spend with their young children. In reality, however, fathers typically assume little or no responsibility for infant care and rearing, and fathers are primarily helpers (Young, 1991). On average, mothers spend between 65 and 80 percent more time than fathers do in direct one-to-one interaction with their infants (Parke, 1995). Fathers are neither inept nor uninterested in interacting with their infants, however. Although fathers are capable of performing sensitively, they tend to yield responsibility for infant and child rearing to their wives when not asked to demonstrate their competence.

Normally, mothers and fathers interact with and care for their infants in complementary ways. That is, they tend to share the labor of caregiving and engage infants emphasizing different types of interactions. Mothers tend to be rhythmic and containing, whereas fathers provide staccato bursts of both physical and social stimulation. Mothers are more likely to hold their infants in the course of caregiving, whereas fathers are more likely to do so when playing with babies or in response to infants' requests to be held. In general, mothers are associated with caregiving, whereas fathers are identified with playful interactions (Clarke-Stewart, 1980).

Historically, direct infant care by a biological parent is more the exception than the rule. In cultures around the world, especially in non-Western nonindustrialized countries, infants may be found in the care of older sisters or brothers (Weisner, 1982; Zukow-Goldring, 1995). In such situations, siblings typically spend most of their child-tending time involved in unskilled nurturant caregiving thereby freeing adults for necessary or more rewarding economic activities. In Western and industrialized societies, by contrast, siblings are seldom entrusted with much responsibility for parenting infants per se and are themselves engaged in activities preparatory for maturity. Where they exist, sibling-infant relationships display features of both adult-infant and peer-infant systems. Sibling-infant dyads share common interests and have more similar behavioral repertoires than do adult-infant dyads. However, sibling pairs resemble adult-infant pairs to the extent that they differ in experience and levels of both cognitive and social ability.

In different locales now and in the past infants have also been tended by other non-parental care providers—aunts, grandmothers, nurses, slaves, day care providers, and metapelets—whether in family day care at home, day care facilities, village centers, or fields. Many of these individuals parent infants. In most societies, multiple caregiving is natural (e.g., Bornstein, Maital, & Tal, 1997), and infants commonly encounter a social world that extends beyond the immediate family. Today, the majority of infants in the United States are cared for on a regular basis by someone other than a parent. Families of all kinds have need for supplementary care for infants. A common form of nonparental familial care involves relatives such as grandparents (Smith, 1995). Another form of nonparental familial care involves nonrelated family day care providers: women who provide care in their own homes, in the baby's own home, or in day care centers (Clarke-Stewart, Allhusen, & Clements, 1995).

Siblings, grandparents, and various nonparents play salient roles in infant care, offering degrees of nurturing, stimulation, and entertainment that vary depending on a variety of factors including age, gender, age gap, quality of attachment, personality, and so forth. Often infants' caregivers behave in a complementary fashion to one another, dividing the full labor of infant caregiving among themselves by individually emphasizing differing parenting responsibilities and activities (Bornstein et al., 1997). Still unclear, however, are the implications of these diverse patterns of early parenting relationships for infant development.

Conclusion

Because of the nature of the infant as well as the range, magnitude, and implications of developmental change that occurs early in life, infancy is intensely fascinating and undeniably appealing but challenging and formidable in the extreme for parents. The popular belief that parent-provided experiences during infancy exert powerful influences on later development has been fostered from many quarters. Nevertheless, human behavior is malleable, and plasticity remains a feature of adaptation long after infancy. Although not all infant experiences are critical later, and single events are rarely formative, some infant experiences doubtless have enduring effects. Certainly, little and big consistencies of parenting aggregate over infancy to construct the person.

Parents intend much in their interactions with their infants. They promote their infants' mental development through the structures they create and the meanings they place on those structures, and they foster emotional understanding and development of self through the models they portray and the values they display. The complex of parent behaviors with infants is divisible into domains, and parents tend to show consistency over time in certain of those domains. Some aspects of parenting are frequent or significant from the beginning and decrease afterward; others wax over the course of infancy. The types of interactions that infants have with their parents also vary. Mothers typically assume primary responsibility for child care within the family, and mother-infant interactions are characterized by nurturant and verbal activities; less frequent, father-infant interactions are dominated by play. As a result, infants' relationships with their two parents are distinctive from a very early age. The interactive and intersubjective aspects of parent and infant activities also have telling consequences for the development of the child after infancy. Researchers and

theoreticians do not ask whether parenting affects infant development but which parent-provided experiences affect what aspects of development when and how, and they are interested also to learn the ways in which individual children are so affected, as well as the ways individual children affect their own development.

A full understanding of what it means to parent infants depends on the ecologies where that parenting takes place. Within-family experiences appear to have a major impact during the first years of life. The nuclear family triad—infant, mother, and father—constitutes the primary context within which infants grow and develop. Family constitution, social class, and cultural variation affect patterns of child rearing and exert salient influences on the ways that infants are reared and what is expected of them as they grow. Infants also form relationships with siblings and grandparents as well as nonfamilial caregivers. Large numbers of infants have significant experiences outside the family—often through enrollment in alternative care settings—and the consequences of out-of-home care vary depending on its type and quality, as well as on characteristics of infants and their families. These early relationships with mothers, fathers, siblings, and others all ensure that the parenting the young infant experiences is rich and multifaceted.

Biology, personality, beliefs and intuitions, aspects of economic, social, and cultural circumstances, and quality of intimate relationships all play important roles in determining the nature of parenting infants. Of course, infants themselves bring unique social styles and an active mental life to everyday interactions with adults that shape their caregiving experiences. Infants alter the environment as they interact with it, and they interpret the environment in their own ways. The transactional principle asserts that parent and infant convey distinctive characteristics to every interaction, and both are affected as a result. In brief, parent and infant actively coconstruct one another through time.

Infancy is a distinctive period, a major transition, and a formative phase in human development. Infants assume few responsibilities and are not at all self-reliant. Rather, parents have central roles to play in infants' physical maturation, cognitive development, emotional maturity, and social growth. With the birth of a baby, a parent's life is forever changed. The patterns that those changes follow, in turn, shape the experiences of the infant and, with time, the person to be. Parent and infant chart that course together. Infancy is a starting point of life for both infant and parent.

References

Abernathy, V. (1973). Social network and response to the maternal role. *International Journal of Sociology of the Family, 3,* 86–96.

Ainsworth, M. D. S., Blehar, M. D., Waters, E., & Wall, S. (1978). *Patterns of attach-ment: A psychological study of the Strange Situation.* Hillsdale, NJ: Erlbaum.

Bard, K. A. (1995). Parenting in primates. In M. H. Bornstein (Ed.), *Handbook of parenting* (Vol. 2, pp. 27–58). Mahwah, NJ: Erlbaum.

Barnard, K. E., & Martell, L. K. (1995). Mothering. In M. H. Bornstein (Ed.), *Handbook of parenting* (Vol. 3; pp. 3–26). Mahwah, NJ: Erlbaum.

Beales, R. W. (1985). The child in seventeenth-century America. In J. M. Hawes & N. R. Hiner (Eds.), *American childhood* (pp. 3–56). Westport, CT: Greenwood Press.

Bell, R. Q., & Harper, L. (1977). *Child effects on adults.* Hillsdale, NJ: Erlbaum.

Belsky, J. (1984). The determinants of parenting: A process model. *Child Development, 55,* 83–96.

Benedict, R. (1938). Continuities and discontinuities in cultural conditioning. *Psychiatry, 1,* 161–167.

Bever, T. G. (1982). *Regressions in mental development.* Hillsdale, NJ: Erlbaum.

Bloom, L. (1993). *The transition from infancy to language: Acquiring the power of expression.* Cambridge: Cambridge University Press.

Bornstein, M. H. (1989a). Between caretakers and their young: Two modes of interaction and their consequences for cognitive growth. In M. H. Bornstein & J. S. Bruner (Eds.), *Interaction in human development* (pp. 197–214). Hillsdale, NJ: Erlbaum.

Bornstein, M. H. (Ed.). (1989b). *Maternal responsiveness: Characteristics and consequences.* San Francisco: Jossey-Bass.

Bornstein, M. H. (1991). Approaches to parenting in culture. In M. H. Bornstein (Ed.), *Cultural approaches to parenting* (pp. 3–19). Hillsdale, NJ: Erlbaum.

Bornstein, M. H. (1995a). Parenting infants. In M. H. Bornstein (Ed.), *Handbook of parenting* (Vol. 1; pp. 3–39). Mahwah, NJ: Erlbaum.

Bornstein, M. H. (Ed.). (1995b). *Handbook of parenting* (Vols. 1–4). Mahwah, NJ: Erlbaum.

Bornstein, M. H. (1998). Infancy: Social and emotional development. In A. E. Kazdin (Ed.), *The encyclopedia of psychology.* New York: American Psychological Association and Oxford University Press.

Bornstein, M. H. (in preparation-a). *Infancy as a stage of life.* Unpublished manuscript, National Institute of Child Health and Human Development.

Bornstein, M. H. (in preparation-b). Intracultural comparisons of child development in cross-cultural contexts. *Monographs of the Society for Research in Child Development.*

Bornstein, M. H., Gaughran, J. M., & Seguí, I. (1991). Multimethod assessment of infant temperament: Mother questionnaire and mother and observer reports evaluated and compared at 5 months using the Infant Temperament Measure. *International Journal of Behavioral Development, 14,* 131–151.

Bornstein, M. H., Haynes, O. M., O'Reilly, A. W., & Painter, K. (1996). Solitary and collaborative pretense play in early childhood: Sources of individual variation in the development of representational competence. *Child Development, 67,* 2910–2929.

Bornstein, M. H., Haynes, O. M., & Painter, K. M. (1998). Sources of child vocabulary competence: A multivariate model. *Journal of Child Language.*

Bornstein, M. H., Haynes, O. M., Pascual, L., Painter, K. M., & Galperín, C. (1998). *Play in two cultures: Pervasiveness of process, specificity of structure.*

Bornstein, M. H., & Lamb, M. E. (1992). *Development in infancy: An introduction* (3rd ed.). New York: McGraw-Hill.

Bornstein, M. H., Maital, S., & Tal, J. (1997). Contexts of collaboration in caregiving: Infant interactions with Israeli kibbutz mothers and caregivers. *Early Child Development and Care, 135,* 145–171.

Bornstein, M. H., Tal, J., Rahn, C., Galperín, C. Z., Pêcheux, M.-G., Lamour, M., Azuma, H., Toda, S., Ogino, M., & Tamis-LeMonda, C. S. (1992b). Functional analysis of the contents of maternal speech to infants of 5 and 13 months in four cultures: Argentina, France, Japan, and the United States. *Developmental Psychology, 28,* 593–603.

Bornstein, M. H., & Tamis-LeMonda, C. S. (1990). Activities and interactions of mothers and their firstborn infants in the first six months of life: Covariation, stability, continuity, correspondence, and prediction. *Child Development, 61,* 1206–1217.

Bornstein, M. H., Tamis-LeMonda, C. S., Tal, J., Ludemann, P., Toda, S., Rahn, C. W., Pêcheux, M.-G., Azuma, H., & Vardi, D. (1992a). Maternal responsiveness to infants in three societies: The United States, France, and Japan. *Child Development, 63,* 808–821.

Bouchard, T. J., Lykken, D. T., McGue, M., Segal, N. L., & Tellegen, A. (1990). Sources of human psychological differences: The Minnesota study of twins reared apart. *Science, 250,* 223–228.

Bowlby, J. (1969). *Attachment and loss.* New York: Basic Books.

Bronfenbrenner, U., & Crouter, A. C. (1983). The evolution of environmental models in developmental research. In W. Kessen (Ed.), P. H. Mussen (Series Ed.),

Handbook of child psychology: Vol. 1. History, theory, and methods (pp. 357–414). New York: Wiley.

Campos, J. J., & Stenberg, C. R. (1981). Perception, appraisal and emotion: The onset of social referencing. In M. E. Lamb & L. R. Sherrod (Eds.), *Infant social cognition: Empirical and theoretical considerations* (pp. 273–314). Hillsdale, NJ: Erlbaum.

Carnegie Corporation of New York. (1994). *Starting points: Meeting the needs of our youngest children.* New York: Author.

Center for the Study of Social Policy. (1993). *Kids count data book: State profiles of child well-being.* Washington, DC: Annie E. Casey Foundation.

Chalmers, I., Enkin, M., & Keirse, M. J. N. C. (Eds.). (1989). *Effective care in pregnancy and childbirth.* New York: Oxford University Press.

Clarke-Stewart, K. A. (1980) The father's contribution to children's cognitive and social development in early childhood. In F. A. Pedersen (Ed.), *The father-infant relationship: Observational studies in the family setting* (pp. 111–146). New York: Praeger.

Clarke-Stewart, K. A., Allhusen, V. D., & Clements, D. C. (1995). Nonparental caregiving. In M. H. Bornstein (Ed.), *Handbook of parenting* (Vol. 3; pp. 151–176). Mahwah, NJ: Erlbaum.

Corter, C. M., & Fleming, A. S. (1995). Psychobiology of maternal behavior in human beings. In M. H. Bornstein (Ed.), *Handbook of parenting* (Vol. 2; pp. 87–116). Mahwah, NJ: Erlbaum.

Cowan, C. P., & Cowan, P. A. (1992). *When partners become parents.* New York: Basic Books.

Crnic, K., & Acevedo, M. (1995). Everyday stresses and parenting. In M. H. Born-stein (Ed.), *Handbook of parenting* (Vol. 4; pp. 277–297). Mahwah, NJ: Erlbaum.

Crnic, K. A., & Booth, C. L. (1991). Mothers' and fathers' perceptions of daily hassles of parenting across early childhood. *Journal of Marriage and the Family, 53,* 1042–1050.

Crnic, K. A., Greenberg, M. T., Ragozin, A. S., Robinson, N. M., & Basham, R. B. (1983). Effects of stress and social support on mothers and premature and fullterm infants. *Child Development, 54,* 209–217.

Darling, N., & Steinberg, L. (1993). Parenting style as context: An integrative model. *Psychological Bulletin, 113,* 487–496.

Darwin, C. (1877). Biographical sketch of an infant. *Mind, 2,* 285–294.

deMause, L. (1975). The evolution of childhood. In L. deMause (Ed.), *The history of childhood* (pp. 1–73). New York: Harper.

Dixon, R. A., & Lerner, R. M. (1992). A history of systems in developmental psychology. In M. H. Bornstein & M. E. Lamb (Eds.), *Developmental psychology: An advanced textbook* (3rd. ed., pp. 3–58). Hillsdale, NJ: Erlbaum.

Dye, N. S., & Smith, D. B. (1986). Mother love and infant death, 1750–1920. *Journal of American History, 73,* 329–353.

Eisenberg, L. (1990). The biosocial context of parenting in human families. In N. A. Krasnegor & R. S. Bridges (Eds.), *Mammalian parenting: Biochemical, neurobiological, and behavioral determinants* (pp. 9–24). New York: Oxford University Press.

Erikson, E. (1950). *Childhood and society.* New York: Norton.

Fagot, B. I. (1995). Parenting boys and girls. In M. H. Bornstein (Ed.), *Handbook of parenting* (Vol. 1; pp. 163–183). Mahwah, NJ: Erlbaum.

Field, T. (1995). Psychologically depressed

parents. In M. H. Bornstein (Ed.), *Handbook of parenting* (Vol. 4; pp. 85–99). Mahwah, NJ: Erlbaum.

Fitzgerald, H. E., Lester, B. M., & Zuckerman, B. S. (Eds.). (1995). *Children of poverty: Research, health, and policy issues*. New York: Garland Publishing.

Fogel, A. (1984). *Infancy: Infant, family, and society*. St. Paul, MN: West Publishing.

French, V. (1995). History of parenting: The ancient Mediterranean world. In M. H. Bornstein (Ed.), *Handbook of parenting* (Vol. 2; pp. 263–284). Mahwah, NJ: Erlbaum.

Furman, W. (1995). Parenting siblings. In M. H. Bornstein (Ed.), *Handbook of parenting* (Vol. 1; pp. 143–162). Mahwah, NJ: Erlbaum.

Goldberg, S. (1977). Infant development and mother-infant interaction in urban Zambia. In P. H. Leiderman, S. R. Tulkin, & A. Rosenfeld (Eds.), *Culture and infancy: Variations in the human experience* (pp. 211–245). New York: Academic.

Goldberg, S., & DiVitto, B. (1995). Parenting children born preterm. In M. H. Bornstein (Ed.), *Handbook of parenting* (Vol. 1; pp. 209–231). Mahwah, NJ: Erlbaum.

Goodnow, J. J., & Collins, W. A. (1990). *Development according to parents: The nature, sources, and consequences of parents' ideas*. Hillsdale, NJ: Erlbaum.

Gottfried, A. W. (Ed.). (1984). *Home environment and early cognitive development*. Orlando, FL: Academic.

Hardy-Brown, K. (1983). Universals in individual differences: Disentangling two approaches to the study of language acquisition. *Developmental Psychology, 19,* 610–624.

Harkness, S., & Super, C. M. (1983). The cultural construction of child development: A framework for the socialization of affect. *Ethos, 11,* 221–231.

Hildebrandt, K. A., & Fitzgerald, H. E. (1977). Gender bias in observers' perceptions of infants' sex: It's a boy most of the time! *Perceptual & Motor Skills, 45,* 472–474.

Hill, C. R., & Stafford, F. P. (1980). Parental care of children: Time diary estimate of quantity, predictability and variety. *Journal of Human Resources, 15,* 219–239.

Ho, H. Z. (1987). Interaction of early caregiving environment and infant developmental status in predicting subsequent cognitive performance. *British Journal of Developmental Psychology, 5,* 183–191.

Hoff-Ginsberg, E., & Tardif, T. (1995). Socioeconomic status and parenting. In M. H. Bornstein (Ed.), *Handbook of parenting* (Vol. 2; pp. 161–188). Mahwah, NJ: Erlbaum.

Holden, G. W. (1995). Parental attitudes toward childrearing. In M. H. Bornstein (Ed.), *Handbook of parenting* (Vol. 3; pp. 359–392). Mahwah, NJ: Erlbaum.

Honig, A. S. (1995). Choosing child care for young children. In M. H. Bornstein (Ed.), *Handbook of parenting* (Vol. 4; p. 435). Mahwah, NJ: Erlbaum.

Jaeger, S. (1985). The origin of the diary method in developmental psychology. In G. Eckhardt, W. G. Bringmann, & L. Sprung (Eds.), *Contributions to a history of developmental psychology* (pp. 63–74). Berlin: Mouton.

Kaye, K. (1982). *The mental and social life of babies*. Chicago: University of Chicago Press.

Leach, P. (1983). *Babyhood*. New York: Knopf.

Leach, P. (1997). *Your baby and child*. New York: Knopf.

Leiderman, P. H., Tulkin, S. R., & Rosenfeld, A. (Eds.). (1977). *Culture and infancy: Variations in the human experience.* New York: Academic.

Lerner, R. M., Castellino, D. R., Terry, P. A., Villarruel, F. A., & McKinney, M. H. (1995). In M. H. Bornstein (Ed.), *Handbook of parenting* (Vol. 2; pp. 285–309). Mahwah, NJ: Erlbaum.

LeVine, R. A. (1988). Human parental care: Universal goals, cultural strategies, individual behavior. In R. A. LeVine, P. M. Miller, & M. M. West (Eds.), *Parental behavior in diverse societies* (pp. 3–12). San Francisco: Jossey-Bass.

Lorenz, K. (1970). *Studies in animal and human behavior* (R. Martin, Trans.). London: Methuen. (Original work published 1935)

Lytton, H., & Romney, D. M. (1991). Parents' differential socialization of boys and girls: A meta-analysis. *Psychological Bulletin, 109,* 267–296.

Maccoby, E. E., & Martin, J. A. (1983). Socialization in the context of the family: Parent-child interaction. In P. H. Mussen (Series Ed.) & E. M. Hetherington (Ed.), *Handbook of child psychology: Vol. 4. Socialization, personality, and social development* (pp. 1–101). New York: Wiley.

Mahler, M., Pine, A., & Bergman, F. (1975). *The psychological birth of the human infant.* New York: Basic Books.

McGillicuddy-De Lisi, A. V., & Sigel, I. E. (1995). Parental beliefs. In M. H. Bornstein (Ed.), *Handbook of parenting* (Vol. 3; pp. 333–358). Mahwah, NJ: Erlbaum.

Mead, M., & Newton, N. (1967). Cultural patterning of perinatal behavior. In S. Richardson & A. Guttmacher (Eds.), *Childbearing: Its social and psychological aspects.* Baltimore, MD: Williams & Wilkins.

Mendelson, M. J. (1990). *Becoming a brother: A child learns about life, family, and self.* Cambridge, MA: MIT Press.

Murray, L., & Trevarthen, C. (1985). Emotional regulation of interactions between two-month-olds and their mothers. In T. M. Field & N. A. Fox (Eds.), *Social perception in infants* (pp. 177–197). Norwood, NJ: Ablex.

National Center for Health Statistics. (1994). *Births, marriages, divorces, and deaths for 1993* (Monthly Vital Statistics Report; Vol. 42, No. 12). Hyattsville, MD: Public Health Service.

Ochs, E. (1988). *Culture and language development: Language acquisition and language socialization in a Samoan village.* New York: Cambridge University Press.

Osofsky, J. D. (Ed.). (1987). *Handbook of infant development* (2nd ed.). New York: Wiley.

Papoušek, H., & Papoušek, M. (1995). Intuitive parenting. In M. H. Bornstein (Ed.), *Handbook of parenting* (Vol. 2; pp. 117–136). Mahwah, NJ: Erlbaum.

Parke, R. D. (1995). Fathers and families. In M. H. Bornstein (Ed.), *Handbook of parenting* (Vol. 3; pp. 27–63). Mahwah, NJ: Erlbaum.

Parmelee, A. H., & Sigman, M. D. (1983). Perinatal brain development and behavior. In P. H. Mussen (Series Ed.), M. M. Haith & J. J. Campos (Eds.), *Handbook of child psychology: Vol. 2. Infancy and developmental psychobiology* (pp. 95–155). New York: Wiley.

Piaget, J. (1952). *The origins of intelligence in children.* New York: Norton.

Plato. (1970). *The laws* (T. J. Saunders, Trans.). Harmondsworth, Middlesex,

England: Penguin. (Original work published ca. 355 B.C.)

Population Reference Bureau. (1993). *1993 world population data sheet.* Washington, DC: Author.

Rohner, R. (1985). *The warmth dimension.* Beverly Hills, CA: Sage.

Rubin, J., Provenzano, F., & Luria, Z. (1974). The eye of the beholder: Parents' view of sex of newborns. *American Journal of Orthopsychiatry, 43,* 720–731.

Sameroff, A. J., & Feil, L. A. (1985). Parental concepts of development. In I. E. Sigel (Ed.), *Parental belief systems: The psychological consequences for children* (pp. 83–100). Hillsdale, NJ: Erlbaum.

Sanson, A., & Rothbart, M. K. (1995). Child temperament and parenting. In M. H. Bornstein (Ed.), *Handbook of parenting* (Vol. 4; pp. 299–321). Mahwah, NJ: Erlbaum.

Scheper-Hughes, N. (1989). Death without weeping. *Natural History, 98,* 8–16.

Shakin, M., Shakin, D., & Sternglanz, S. H. (1985). Infant clothing: Sex labeling for strangers. *Sex Roles, 12,* 955–963.

Slater, P. G. (1977–1978). From the cradle to the coffin: Parental bereavement and the shadow of infant damnation in Puritan society. *The Psychohistory Review, 6,* 4–24.

Smith, P. K. (1995). Grandparenthood. In M. H. Bornstein (Ed.), *Handbook of parenting* (Vol. 3; pp. 89–112). Mahwah, NJ: Erlbaum.

Spock, B., & Rothenberg, M. B. (1996). *Dr. Spock's baby and child care.* New York: Pocket Books.

Stern, D. (1990). *Diary of a child.* New York: Basic Books.

Strauss, S., & Stavey, R. (1981). U-shaped behavioral growth: Implications for theories of development. In W. W. Hartup (Ed.), *Review of child development research* (Vol. 6; pp. 547–599). Chicago: University of Chicago Press.

Super, C. M., & Harkness, S. (1986). Temperament, development, and culture. In R. Plomin & J. Dunn (Eds.), *The study of temperament: Changes, continuities, and challenges* (pp. 131–149). Hillsdale, NJ: Erlbaum.

Thomas, A., Chess, S., Birch, H., Hertzig, M., & Korn, S. (1963). *Behavioral individuality in childhood.* New York: New York University Press.

Tronick, E. Z., & Gianino, A. F. (1986). The transmission of maternal disturbance to the infant. In E. Z. Tronick & T. Field (Eds.), *Maternal depression and infant disturbance* (pp. 5–11). New York: Wiley.

Užgiris, I. C., & Raeff, C. (1995). Play in parent-child interactions. In M. H. Bornstein (Ed.), *Handbook of parenting* (Vol. 4; pp. 353–376). Mahwah, NJ: Erlbaum.

Wallace, D. B., Franklin, M. B., & Keegan, R. T. (1994). The observing eye: A century of baby diaries. *Human Development, 37,* 1–29.

Weisner, T. (1982). Sibling interdependence and child caretaking: A cross-cultural view. In M. E. Lamb & B. Sutton-Smith (Eds.), *Sibling relationships* (pp. 305–327). Hillsdale, NJ: Erlbaum.

Whiting, J. W. (1981). Environmental constraints on infant care practices. In R. H. Munroe, R. L. Munroe, & B. B. Whiting (Eds.), *Handbook of cross-cultural human development* (pp. 155–179). New York: Garland STPM Press.

Winnicott, D. W. (1957). *Mother and child: A primer of first relations.* New York: Basic Books.

Young, K. T. (1991). What parents and experts think about infants. In F. S. Kessel, M. H. Bornstein, & A. J. Sameroff (Eds.), *Contemporary constructions of the child* (pp. 79–90). Hillsdale, NJ: Erlbaum.

Zukow-Goldring, P. (1995). Sibling caregiving. In M. H. Bornstein (Ed.), *Handbook of parenting* (Vol. 3; pp. 177–208). Mahwah, NJ: Erlbaum.

8

Prebirth Parent Characteristics and Early Family Development

Christoph M. Heinicke

8

Introduction

The transition to becoming a parent represents a major life change. Interest in this developmental change is universal. Professionals writing in the 1940s through the 1960s stressed the adjustments necessary to deal with the arrival and care of the infant. Global descriptions of the essence of these adjustments differed. Some authors concluded that the birth of the infant represented a crucial positive fulfillment of the developmental and psychic needs of the woman (Deutsch, 1945). Other writers characterized pregnancy and the transition to parenthood as a period of crisis (Bibring, Dwyer, Huntington, & Valenstein, 1961; Hill, 1949). Shereshefsky and Yarrow (1973) saw this developmental disequilibrium as an opportunity to facilitate positive change through intervention. They systematically assessed the impact of counseling on the adjustment to pregnancy and early infancy. One of their most important findings was that the clarity and confidence in self-visualization as future parents was found to anticipate a more adequate postnatal adjustment.

Other pioneer longitudinal studies (Grossman, Eichler, & Winikoff, 1980) stimulated detailed description of the transition to parenting and to delineation of those aspects of the family system likely to influence family development. Both for its own sake and as a guide to more effective intervention, investigators recognized the need for more specific information about the determinants of parenting.

Our own interest in the transition to and determinants of parenting grew out of our efforts in the late 1970s to define those prebirth and ongoing parent personality and support characteristics that were likely to be associated with the positive development of the child's security of attachment, autonomy, and task orientation. Once one had defined such potential paths of influence, the task of intervention would be to change not only the child's behavior and the parent-child transactions, but the functioning of the parents as well. Such an intervention was carried out with the preschool child (Heinicke, 1977) and achieved some significant changes in all of the preceding domains, but the extent of the impact on the child task orientation was not that extensive. We reasoned that intervention beginning even before the child was born might be more effective But on what prebirth parent functioning should the focus be? Longitudinal studies linking the prebirth and ongoing parent characteristics to the parent-child and child domains were needed. What would such findings suggest as to (1) the timing of the intervention, (2) what areas of parent-child and child functioning are likely to change, and (3) what areas of family functioning need to be addressed to bring about a sustained change? These questions are reviewed in the discussion section.

Within a family system framework, this chapter examines the research that is now available on delineating the impact of prebirth parent personality and relationship functioning on key areas of parent and child development. A number of propositions guide this review. The first proposition states that parent personality and marital functioning are relatively stable in the transition to parenthood. Parents functioning more adequately than other parents before the birth of their child also tend to function more adequately after the birth. Within this relatively consistent impact, it is next proposed that differences in the quality of the prebirth parent personality and experienced support are linked to differences in the parent-child and child functioning. The preceding propositions imply a focus on (1) the expectable stabilities and changes in the couples' transition to parenthood and (2) how variations in prebirth parent personality and support characteristics influence variations in future parenting. Accordingly, the two major goals of this chapter are to summarize the available evidence on (1) the stability of parent personality and support characteristics in the transition to parenting and (2) the evidence linking variations in prebirth parent personality and support characteristics to variations in family development.

Two conceptual frameworks are outlined to accomplish this task. The first is a summary of a family systems framework that provides a larger context for the research summarized here. The second focuses more specifically on the definition of the parent personality and marital and support characteristics that anticipate the parenting and child's development.

A Family Systems Model of Parenting

Cowan, Powell, and Cowan (1998) have proposed that in order to understand variations in the developing parent-child relationships and their effects on children's development, information about six domains of family functioning is needed. The six domains of family functioning are:

1. The biological and psychological characteristics of each individual in the family.
2. The quality of relationships in parents' families of origin and in the current relationships among grandparents, parents, and grandchildren.
3. The quality of the relationship between parents, with special emphasis on their division of roles, communication patterns, and roles as coparents to their children.
4. The quality of relationships between siblings.
5. The relationships between nuclear family members and key individuals or institutions outside the family (friends, peers, work, child care, school, ethnic group, government) as sources of stress, support, models, values, and beliefs.
6. The quality of the relationship between each parent and child.

In documenting the significance of one domain influencing another, including the influence over time, Cowan et al. (1998) cite associations that are particularly relevant to the findings presented in this chapter. They emphasize the central role of marital quality in family adaptation. They document that both the quality of the intimate partner relationship and whether they can successfully coparent has a significant impact on the parent-child relationship, and both are likely to be influenced negatively as the number of stresses in other domains increase.

Cowan et al. (1998) also stress the importance of one domain influencing another over time in citing evidence for the three-generational transmission of parenting patterns. To give an example, and as will be documented further, if the mother is characterized by an insecure working model of her early attachments as assessed *before* the birth of her child, then her child tends to have a less secure attachment to her. Illustrating their emphasis on considering many interacting influences, the preceding is less likely to occur if women classified as insecure had spouses who were secure.

Although it is essential to keep the concept of the interacting domains of a family system model in mind, to summarize the findings on the association between prebirth parent characteristics and early family development, the concepts being used to describe each of the domains needed to be defined more specifically. They will be used in relation to both goals: (1) to document the stability and change in the parent personality and support characteristics and

(2) to cite the evidence linking variations in prebirth personality and support characteristics to variations in family development. Accordingly, both the concepts and their operational definition are presented in the next section.

Prebirth Determinants, Parenting, and the Child's Development: A Conceptual Framework

Characterization of the mother's and father's personality has scrutinized their adaptation-competence, capacity for positive sustained relationships, and self-development. Consideration of their supportive relationships focuses on their partners (including marital) and extended family.

Characterization of parenting was defined by four parent-infant transactions (social interaction variables) and the associated components of the child's emerging self (personality variables). It is recognized that even if one limits oneself to tracing interconnections between personality and social interaction variables across the transition to family formation, the number of potential mutual influences and levels of abstraction is great. This chapter is limited to those interconnections that have actually been studied and specified.

Turning to the definition of the parent personality concepts, adaptation-competence refers to the efficient, nonanxious, persistent, and flexible approach to problem solving. It has been operationally specified as ego strength (Barron, 1953), adaptation-competence (Heinicke, Diskin, Ramsey-Klee, & Given, 1983), and more recently, as maternal competence (Teti, Gelfand, & Pompa, 1990) and the absence of task-related anger (Heinicke, 1993).

The capacity for positive sustained relationships refers to empathy and positive mutuality expressed by the parent in an ongoing relationship. It has been operationally specified in relation to parenting by the mother's and father's coherent, objective, and balanced account of their childhood relationship experiences (Fonagy, Steele, & Steele, 1991; Main & Goldwyn, 1994) and by the parent's recall of their own parenting as loving (Main & Goldwyn, 1994), low in conflict (Cowan, Cowan, Schulz, & Heming, 1994), and generally positive (Heinicke & Guthrie, 1992). It is also defined by sensitivity to others' needs (Brunnquell, Crichton, & Egeland, 1981) and trusting as opposed to being skeptical of interpersonal relationships (Pianta, Egeland, & Erickson, 1989).

Definition of the parent's self-development has involved their experienced autonomy and confidence as opposed to insecurity. It has been operationally specified in relation to parenting as the clarity and confidence in visualizing self as a parent (Heinicke et al., 1983; Shereshefsky & Yarrow, 1973). Cowan et al. (1985) assessed both the parent's self-esteem and which life roles are most important to them: partner, lover, worker, and so on. Diamond, Heinicke, and Mintz (1996) operationally defined the autonomy of each parent using concepts of individuation-separation. The link of self-development to past and current relationships is stressed by examining the relation to the family of origin, self-directed autonomous activities, and mutuality with and differentiation from the current partner.

The parent's positive experience of their partnerships (including marriage) is also central to this summary of research. Specific definitions have focused on different aspects of this experience. Cowan and Cowan (1988) stressed the importance of the partner's consensus regarding their mutual role arrangements (who does what) and the openness of their communication. Both inventories (Cowan & Cowan, 1988; Belsky et al., 1989) and interviews (Heinicke et al., 1983) have been used to define the expressed satisfaction with a partner. Direct observations of the quality of the marital interaction of parents underline the importance of both expressing negative affects and yet remaining on the task of resolving conflicts (Balaguer & Markham, 1991; Heinicke & Guthrie, 1992; Pratt, Kerig, Cowan, & Cowan, 1988).

While it has generally been assumed that the quality of support experienced in the partnership (married or not) plays a central role in family adaptation (Cowan et al., 1998; Belsky, 1984), the support received from family and friends also exerts a beneficial impact on parent-child relations (Belsky, 1984). Such support may be emotional or involve instrumental assistance. It is very likely related to the mother's adaptation-competence and capacity for relationships but has been considered as an independent influence in the research being considered here.

In defining the likely link of the prebirth parent characteristics to postnatal family development, it is most meaningful to focus on those qualities of parenting that are not only likely to link to prebirth parent characteristics, but also are a part of significant transactions defined by both parenting and child qualities. Thus, certain qualities of parenting are highlighted by relating them to the development of the child's self. The key forms of parenting are teaching and exposing the child to new cognitive experiences, responding to the needs of the infant, and promoting the autonomy and task involvement of the child. (For an operational definition of these parent-infant transactions, see Ainsworth, Blehar, Waters, & Wall, 1978; Bornstein & Tamis-LeMonda, 1989; Heinicke & Guthrie, 1992).

Consistent with Sroufe's (1989) discussion of relationships, self, and individual adaptation, components of the self are defined as emerging from the interaction of early infant characteristics and the constellation of parent characteristics and parenting relationship potentials. Self as an organization integrates the infant's adaptation and accompanying feelings and thoughts. The development of the components of the self can be related to the quality and goals of these relationships (Sroufe, 1989).

The competent self is associated with a sense of being an agent (Stern, 1985), task orientation, attention (Heinicke, 1980), and self-regulation. It emerges out of and continues in the context of the type of parental responsiveness that teaches and exposes the child to new cognitive experiences (Bornstein & Tamis-LeMonda, 1989). The emphasis on adaptive capacities includes early modes of self-regulation

or defense such as suppression, turning the passive into active, avoidance, and control. The secure self (Ainsworth et al., 1978) and the closely associated expectation of being cared for (Heinicke & Guthrie, 1992), sense of self as worthy (Sroufe, 1989), and modulation of aggression (Heinicke et al., 1986) emerge out of and continue in a relationship characterized by parents' responsiveness to the needs of the infant (Bornstein & Tamis-LeMonda, 1989). The separate self or subjective awareness of the self and other (Stern, 1985) begins in the second half of the first year of life and is seen as emerging out of and continuing in a relationship that prepares for and promotes autonomy as well as providing control (limits) for that expansion (Heinicke & Guthrie, 1992).

A summary of the research findings documenting both the stability of parental characteristics and how differences in those characteristics influence differences in family development follows.

The Stability of Parent Personality and Marital Characteristics

Review of the research literature suggests a striking consensus that a considerable number of parent personality and marital characteristics are relatively stable across the transition to parenthood and thus are likely to exert a continuing and generally consistent influence on postnatal family development. Grossman et al. (1980) showed that the mother's emotional well-being, marital adjustment, and level of anxiety and depression during pregnancy and at 2 months postpartum correlated significantly with measures of those same qualities as assessed at 12 months postpartum. Similarly, these authors demonstrated that measures of the father's marital adjustment and level of anxiety assessed during pregnancy and at 2 months postpartum anticipated assessment of that same quality at the 12-month postpartum point.

Although they delineated change in certain domains of couple functioning, Cowan and Cowan (1988) documented the relative stability of the following characteristics by citing the correlation between prebirth and 18-month assessments as follows: Marital satisfaction ranges from .50 to .70; role satisfaction is .56 for men and .62 for women; self-esteem is .75 for men and .76 for women. Similarly, Wolkind and Zajidek (1981) found that assessments of the mother's self-esteem at 4 months and 14 months after the birth of her child tended to be highly consistent. Huston and Mc-Hale (1983) compared the marital relationship of samples of families who had a child during approximately the first year after their marriage with those who did not. Couples who had children shared more joint activities (almost exclusively in child care) and also moved toward more traditional sex roles in terms of instrumental activities. Having a child did not, however, differentially affect involvement with kin and friends or the overall evaluation of and expression of affection within the marriage. Although these last two indexes of the marriage declined, the magnitude of the change in evaluation of the marriage

was not great. Consistent with these findings, Cox and Owen (1993) found that prenatal and three-month assessments of marital discord were significantly correlated.

Findings from two longitudinal studies (Heinicke & Guthrie, 1992) also support the hypothesis that measures of both personality functioning and marital quality significantly correlate even when the time interval extends from prebirth to the child's fourth birthday. Factor scores describing the mother's positive experience of the marriage based on ratings of recorded interviews with her during pregnancy and at 1, 6, 12, 24, 36, and 48 months of age were significantly correlated. With the exception of the correlation between the prebirth and six-month assessments, all intercorrelations were statistically significant.

As cited earlier, Cowan and Cowan (1988) also reported the consistency in marital functioning but noted that there is a lower correlation between pregnancy and 6 months than pregnancy and 18 months. This exception suggests the possible impact of the transition to parenthood. Indeed, there is variation in the patterns of change in marital patterns (Heinicke & Guthrie, 1992). However, the relative position of each couple within a group of families remains relatively stable from prebirth to 48 months. Indices of the mother's adaptation-competence and warmth are also significantly intercorrelated in the period from prebirth to 48 months (Heinicke & Lampl, 1988). Schaefer, Edgerton, and Hunter (1983) found similar levels of association between pregnancy and postpartum measures of a quality closely linked to adaptation-competence, namely, maternal locus of control.

The Adult Attachment Interview (AAI) categorizations (Main & Goldwyn, 1994) that assess an adult's state of mind with respect to attachment have also been found to be stable across a period of time. Most relevant to the span from pregnancy to postbirth status is the study by Benoit and Parker (1994). Using three categories to compare the AAI done during pregnancy with that administered when the mother's child was 12 months showed a 90 percent agreement. Van IJzendoorn and Baker-mans-Kranenburg (1996) have summarized the additional evidence showing the considerable stability of the AAI.

In summary, the previous findings suggest considerable stability in global indexes of marital quality and personality functioning when prebirth and postnatal assessments are compared. This stable and consistent impact on postnatal family development of both personality and marital characteristics begs the question of which of these characteristics link to emerging parent transactions with the infant and thus influence infant development.

Ideally, answers to this question would involve a particular study that includes assessments of all six domains of family functioning stipulated by the Cowan et al. (1998) family system model and, following the focus of this chapter, repeats such measures from the prebirth to postbirth period. Such studies are not currently available. At this point, the existing research is best organized by linking prebirth *maternal,* prebirth *paternal,* and prebirth *couple* characteristics to selected social-emotional parent-child and child functioning. At the risk of oversimplification but to make the findings more accessible, the findings are summarized by initial statements that are supported by those findings.

The Impact of Prebirth Parent Characteristics on Postnatal Family Development

Maternal Prebirth Functioning, Mother's Responsiveness, and the Security of Her Child

The mother's prebirth adaptive competence and capacity to sustain positive relationships (especially those with her partner) anticipate her responsiveness to the needs of her infant in the period from one month to four years of age. Moreover, these same prebirth characteristics anticipate the development of security in her child. The previous two statements can be rephrased as follows: If before the birth of her child, the mother copes well with various life issues, has the capacity to form positive, trusting relationships, and has a mutually positive relationship with her partner, then she is more likely to be responsive to her child's needs, and her child will develop greater security in the first four years of life. This reflects the fact that the transaction of parent responsiveness to need and the child's security are intercorrelated. Moreover, this transactional association is reflected in the first set of findings. Based on the review of research available at the time (Belsky, 1984; Heinicke, 1984), a hypothesized path analysis was formulated and reported in Heinicke, Diskin, Ramsey-Klee, and Oates (1986; see Figure 8.1).

Focusing on statistically significant associations relevant to the development of security, it was found that husband-wife adaptation, maternal adaptation-competence, and maternal warmth all are associated with variations in parent responsiveness to need at one month and that this one-month parent responsiveness is associated with infant fretting at three months. Three-month infant fretting, in turn, anticipates child modulation of aggression and parent responsiveness at two years. Modulation of aggression is here being used as an index of the child's security

(Heinicke et al., 1986; Heinicke & Guthrie, 1992). That is, these two research reports document the potential chain of effects from prebirth to one month, to three months, and then to two years. Suggesting the continuing influence of stable parent characteristics is the direct association (path) from prebirth husband-wife adaptation, maternal adaptation-competence, and maternal warmth to two-year modulation of aggression (see Figure 8.1).

A number of other prospective longitudinal studies starting with assessments of the parents before the birth of their first child have reported findings consistent with the aforementioned model. Belsky

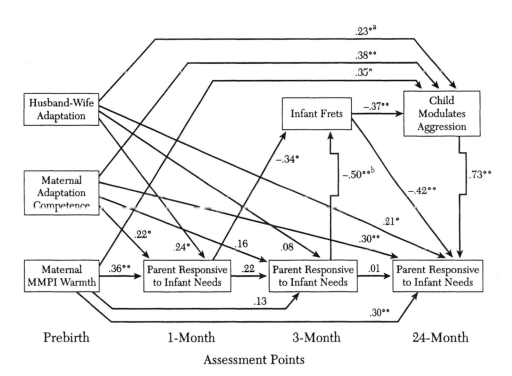

FIGURE 8.1

Path Analysis Diagram for Two Indexes of 24-month Positive Parent-Child Mutuality: Child Aggression Modulation and Parent Responsiveness to Need (N = 44). °p < .05. °°p < .01. ªBeta weights placed by across-time paths. ᵇVertical lines indicate cross-sectional correlations.

and Isabella (1986) found that mothers who scored poorly before the birth of their first child on both ego strength and interpersonal affection were likely to experience the most negative change in their marriage. In addition, these two personality characteristics, as well as the quality of the postnatal marital experience and the perceptions of their child as becoming less adaptable, all contributed to the development of an insecure infant-mother relationship at 12 months as measured by the child's reaction to separation from and reunion with the mother. Findings by Grossman et al. (1980) are also consistent with the hypotheses outlined in that parent responsiveness and infant soothability at two months are anticipated by prenatal indexes of maternal adaptation, anxiety, and marital style in the case of the firstborn child. Moreover, with respect to maternal personality, Moss (1967) demonstrated that accepting the prebirth nurturant role and viewing the care of a baby as gratifying rather than burdensome are associated with each other. Both these factors, in turn, anticipate the mother's actual responsiveness to her baby as observed at three weeks and three months.

Results from the Minnesota Mother-Child Interaction project reported by Egeland and his colleagues (Brunnquell et al., 1981; Egeland & Farber, 1984; Pianta et al., 1989) also support the power of prebirth measures of the mother's emotional stability as predictors of maternal responsive caregiving and a secure infant attachment. Thus, in this poverty at-risk sample, mothers who scored significantly higher on a prebirth factor entitled "level of personality integration" (Brunnquell et al., 1981)

met the physical and emotional needs of their children at 3 months, and their children were at 12 months more frequently classified as secure (Egeland & Farber, 1984). Level of personality integration is "composed of an amalgam of affective and intellectual elements, each of which contributes to the overall conception of the mother's recognition of her own psychological needs and process, her ability to perceive those needs and processes in others, and her ability to integrate the two sets of needs and processes." Among the measures related to this construct are IQ, locus of control, the feeling of being able to control what happens to oneself, and the Cohler Scales—such as encouragement versus discouragement of reciprocity, appropriate versus inappropriate control of the child's aggression, and acceptance versus denial of emotional complexity in child care. Further analyses of these data revealed that prebirth maternal characteristics were also associated with whether the mother anticipated and in fact found her child "difficult" as opposed to "easy" at three and six months (Vaughn, Deinard, & Egeland, 1980; Vaughn, Taraldson, Chrichten, & Egeland, 1981). The importance of the contribution of the mother's adaptation-competence and capacity for relationships to her future caregiving is supported by the fact that the best discriminator of the maltreating and inadequate caring mothers, as followed up in this sample at child age 64 months, is the emotional stability scale of the 16PF Personality test also administered at this time. Pianta et al. (1989) discussed two concepts in relation to this scale: emotional instability (impulsiveness) and being skeptical of interpersonal relationships.

In another longitudinal study, Isabella (1994) found that mothers reporting high levels of satisfaction with their marriages and high levels of family support during the prenatal period were most likely to report a higher degree of role satisfaction at four months. High levels of role satisfaction were, in turn, predictive of sensitive interactions with their infants at nine months, and these sensitive interactions contributed to the development of secure infant-mother attachments by one year as measured by the Ainsworth Strange Situation (Ainsworth, Blehar, Waters, & Wall, 1978).

One study has specifically addressed the issue of the relative contribution of three of the family system domains, namely parent, parent-infant, and infant characteristics, to the development of a secure attachment at one year of age. Del Carmen, Pedersen, Huffman, and Bryan (1993) studied the relative power of prebirth maternal anxiety, postbirth three-month maternal response to distress, and the infant characteristic of negative affect as predictors of security of attachment at one year of age. The results indicate that three-month distress management and prenatal maternal anxiety are the strongest predictors in classifying security of attachment. The authors' interpretation of these findings is consistent with the emphasis of this chapter on the importance of regulating affect. Mothers who cannot manage their own affect (distress) will have difficulty managing the distress (affect) of their three-month-old infant.

What other evidence is there that the parental adaptation-competence as well as their relationship capacity are likely to influence variation in the child's development of security? George, Kaplan, and Main (1996) showed that the classification from the Adult Attachment Interview stressing the mother's coherent, objective, and balanced account of her childhood is significantly associated with the development of security in her infant's attachment. Very relevant to predicting the transaction of parental responsiveness to the needs of the infant and the security of the child are the findings of Ward and Carlson (1995) linking the classification derived from the prebirth Adult Attachment Interview to maternal sensitivity and security of attachment in children at 15 months. Mothers classified as autonomous—as opposed to dismissing, preoccupied, or unresolved—showed higher levels of sensitivity at 3 and 9 months, and their infants were more frequently classified as secure at 15 months. However, maternal sensitivity at 3 and 9 months was not significantly associated with security of attachment at 15 months. The authors suggest that the meaning of sensitivity may have been affected by whether these adolescent mothers were the primary caretaker; many of them were not. In a similar study, Benoit and Parker (1994) found an 81 percent match between AAIs administered in pregnancy and the three-category Ainsworth Strange Situation assessment at 12 months.

As part of a meta-analysis on the predictive validity of the Adult Attachment Interview, van IJzendoorn (1995) has summarized the findings from all available studies linking three forms of maternal representations as assessed by the AAI before birth to the postbirth threefold infant security of attachment classification. He found a 69 percent correspondence for the three-way classifications. That is, his meta-analysis not only showed the significant relation between parent's attachment representations and the security of the child's attachment relationship with the parents in a large sample (N = 854), but analysis of the more limited sample specifically showed the relation of the prebirth AAI and postbirth infant security of attachment. Although not confined to the prebirth AAIs, in this same meta-analysis, van IJzendoorn (1995) also showed the power of the Adult Attachment Interview to predict the mother's responsiveness to the needs of her infant.

As the experience of classifying the responses to the attachment interview suggests, the categories being used speak as much to the issues of adaptation-competence or current ego functioning as they do to the capacity to form an empathic trusting relationship (Main & Goldwyn, 1994). A prospective study by Fonagy, Steele, and Steele (1991) linking the prebirth Parental Attachment Interview classifications to the developing security of the one-year-old permits further discussion of this question. The Adult Attachment Interview was administered to 100 mothers expecting their first child and, at one-year follow-ups, 96 mothers were again seen with their infants in the Strange Situation to assess the quality of their child's attachment. Maternal representations of attachment (autonomous vs. dismissing or preoccupied) predicted subsequent infant-mother attachment patterns (secure vs. insecure)

75 percent of the time. In addition to deriving these major classifications, each interview was also rated on eight 9-point scales describing the adult's probable childhood experience of having been parented, the current state of mind with respect to attachment, and the overall coherence of the interview. Both anxious resistant and secure, as opposed to avoidant children, had mothers who recalled their relationship with their mothers as significantly more loving and less rejecting, whereas coherence was highest among mothers of securely attached infants. Both the parent's specific positive remembrance of their own parenting and an index of ego integration (i.e., coherence) anticipate the development of a secure child attachment. The question then arises as to whether alternate measures of the mother's organizational functioning not necessarily tied to questions about her relationship history would predict her child's secure attachment. Fonagy, Steele, Steele, Moran, and Higgitt (1991) studied this issue in terms of the capacity of the mother to reflect on her mental functioning. All recorded Adult Attachment Interviews were rated on the absence or presence of reflective functions. Strong evidence of self-reflection was seen in statements indicating the subject's ability to understand psychological states, including conscious and unconscious motivations underlying their own reactions and those of others. Relating this measure of the mother's functioning to the ratings of the Adult Attachment Interview and the security of the child, it was found that the mother's self-reflection was highly correlated (.73) with the previous ratings of

quality of recall and coherence. As already noted, the coherence of the mother's interview predicted a secure child attachment, and when reflective self-function was controlled for, coherence no longer related significantly to infant security. This suggests that self-reflection is an essential component of the mother's ability to organize her relationship experiences.

Related to further search for those maternal adaptive functions that predict secure attachment and parent sensitivity to the child's need (Ainsworth et al., 1978), Teti et al. (1990) found that this sensitivity correlated with the availability and adequacy of attachment figures, marital harmony, major negative life events, daily hassles, infant difficulty, and maternal depression, but all these significant relations became nonsignificant when controlled for by maternal self-efficacy in dealing with the child. In this study, even when other family system domains were included in the design, the mother's self-efficacy was the most powerful predictor of her sensitivity.

Both the initial summary statement and the supporting research findings have focused on the association of the mother's prebirth characteristics and her responsiveness to the needs of her infant. Several other studies either focus on the father or include both mother and father.

Paternal Prebirth Functioning and Father's Positive Relationship to His Child

The father's prebirth adaptive competence and capacity to sustain positive relation-

ships (especially those with his partner) anticipate a positive relationship with his child during the first year of life as well as the security of his child. Research evidence supporting this statement is limited but consistent. Steele, Steele, and Fonagy (1996) show not only that mothers classified as secure on the prebirth Adult Attachment Interview have children who are secure in the infant-mother Strange Situation at 12 months, but fathers who are classified as secure on the AAI have children who are secure in the 18-month infant-father Strange Situation. While these associations were independent of each other, secondary analyses showed that the mother's security as derived from the AAI may also be significantly associated with the infant-father security. The authors discuss the potentially greater influence of the mother's status on the child's development of security and also consider the potential influence of the child's temperament in accounting for variations in infant security.

Other studies that support the generalization being discussed not only trace the influence of the father's competence and capacity for relationship but increasingly include measures of marital adjustment as significant predictors. Thus, Grossman et al. (1980) found that an interview measure of the father's positive relationship to his child at two months postpartum is anticipated by the following first trimester measures: the father's tendency to identify positively with his own mother and good marital adjustment. Similarly, Feldman, Nash, and Aschenbrenner (1983) showed that the father's caregiving and playfulness with his six-month-old infant and his satisfaction with fatherhood are anticipated by prebirth indices of general adjustment and marital happiness as reported by the husband and/or wife. For example, satisfaction with fatherhood was predicted by the father's empathy with his wife, few if any problems in the marriage, a match between the desired and actual sex of the baby, and a self-description low in characteristics such as gullible and childlike.

In a series of reports, Cox and her colleagues showed how prebirth measures of father and mother functioning anticipate postnatal parent responsiveness and child security. The first report (Cox, Owen, Lewis, & Henderson, 1989) used both an interview based three-month parent attitude as well as observations of sensitive parental behavior as outcome measures. Mothers had a more positive attitude toward their three-month-old infant if that infant was a son and their own prebirth psychological assessment (adaptation-competence) was adequate. Both this adequate adjustment and the positive quality of their marriage anticipated sensitive behavioral responding to their infant. Similarly, but also slightly different, both an adequate prebirth adjustment and positive marriage anticipated the father's positive attitude toward his three-month-old child. The father was likely to respond warmly if his own adjustment was adequate and his infant was a son. A second report (Cox, Owen, Henderson, & Margaund, 1992) showed that an expanded version of the previous three-month parent attitudinal and observational variables predicted the 12-month secure attachment continuum. Twelve-month infant-mother security was anticipated by the mother's positive and sensitive interaction with her infant, her physical affection, and the total amount of time spent with her infant, but not by her attitude toward her infant. Infant-father security at 12 months was anticipated by all of the aforementioned three-month variables. However, the association between time spent and infant-father security was negative. Although not easy to interpret, this last finding points to the importance of considering these variables in a total family context. Cox and Owen (1993) reported that prebirth measures of marital discord and psychological adjustment anticipated both three-month parent positive interaction/attitude and 12-month infant security. Infant-father attachment security at 12 months was anticipated directly by the father's positive interaction/attitude toward his three-month-old child and by prebirth marital discord (negatively). The father's prebirth psychological adjustment also had a significant impact on his child's security, but indirectly so, via marital discord and father positive interaction/attitude (Cox & Owen, 1993). The comprehensive analysis of the same variables predicting infant-mother security was not significant. However, significant correlations emerged when the association of variables was evaluated separately by gender. For boys, security of 12-month attachment was significantly associated with the mother's three-month parenting but was not related to marital discord or mother's adjustment. For girls, the prebirth marital relations predicted 12-month security.

In summary, in the previous two sections, it has been shown that if the mother copes well with various life issues, has the capacity to form positive and trusting relationships, and has a mutually positive relationship with her partner before the birth of her child, she is more likely to be responsive to her child's needs, and her child will develop greater security in the first two years of life. There is some evidence to suggest that similar statements also apply to the father. Most important, the studies of the impact of the individual maternal and paternal characteristics frequently included assessments of the quality of their relationship to their partner. Indeed, many studies of the association between prebirth determinants and postbirth family development are best summarized by focusing on the quality of the couple's functioning, and that is presented in the next section.

Prebirth Couple Functioning and Family Development until Kindergarten

Couples characterized by prebirth and continuing positive mutuality, partner autonomy, and the ability to confront problems and regulate negative affect are responsive to the needs of their infants, promote their autonomy, and have more secure and autonomous children as seen throughout the first four years of life. The children from these families are also more task oriented in preschool, less aggressive and shy in early kindergarten, and score higher on achievement tests at the end of kindergarten.

In tracing the link from prebirth measures of partner personality and marital functioning to the security and autonomy of the child and the subsequent academic achievement and social competence in kindergarten, Cowan et al. (1994) proceed in two longitudinal steps. The first related prebirth, 6-month, and 18-month measures of relationship functioning to observations of marital interaction and the parent's interaction with their child when the child is in preschool (or 3½ years old). A second step linked this marital interaction and parent-child interaction with measures of the child's academic achievement and social competence in late kindergarten. The first set of findings involves a self-report measure of marital satisfaction (Locke-Wallace, 1959) in pregnancy and at 18 months. The decline in marital satisfaction during this period is associated with the observed angry, cold, and competitive as opposed to warm, responsive, and cooperative marital interaction when the child is 3½ years old. This conflictual marital interaction is in turn associated with both the father and mother being less warm with their child and the father communicating less well and not being able to present the assigned tasks in a manner that helped their preschool child to manage the task. Pratt et al. (1988) showed that parents who are warm and structuring also tend to provide scaffolding for their children—to move in at the appropriate level when their children are having difficulty and back off when their children are succeeding on their own. Another prebirth measure, the Family Environment Scale (Moos, 1974) was linked to marital stress at six months, the decline in marital quality (prebirth to 18 months), and marital and parent-child interaction at 3½ years old. Parents who, during pregnancy, remember the atmosphere in the families in which they grew up as high in conflict and who experienced more stress at six months were more conflicted in their marital interaction when their child was 3½ years old. Further analyses showed that high levels of stress at six months linked directly to less adequate parenting styles and indirectly via the decline in marital satisfaction from prebirth to 18 months. As previously reported, this decline anticipated conflicted marital interaction and less responsive parenting styles when the child was 3½ years old.

Cowan et al. (1994) also documented the association between these preschool variables and children's kindergarten assessments. The kindergarten children who scored lower on the Peabody Individual Achievement Test (reading recognition, reading comprehension, spelling, mathematics, and general information) had parents who were more conflicted in their interaction with each other and less warm and encouraging of the autonomy of their preschool child. For this outcome variable (i.e., academic achievement), the prebirth to 18 months quality of relationship variables had an indirect effect via the preschool status. There were no direct links from prebirth to kindergarten.

Variation in the preschool parent and parent-child interaction also anticipated variation in the kindergarten child's shyness and aggression. Parents who were competitive and hostile in their marital interaction and did not work cooperatively in front of their preschooler tended to have children who showed more aggressive interactions or were shy and withdrawn with their classmates two years later. Further findings indicated that low levels of father and mother warmth and responsiveness at 3½ years old linked to high levels of classroom aggressiveness. However, different levels of parent structuring did not predict levels of aggression.

In contrast to the prediction of academic achievement, there were direct as well as indirect links from the prebirth family relationship to the kindergarten child's level of shyness and aggressiveness. Thus, parents who during pregnancy remembered the atmosphere in the families in which they grew up as high in conflict tended to have children who were rated shy and/or aggressive.

Evidence from the Pennsylvania State Family Development Project links a declining postnatal marital pattern to the development of an insecure attachment at one year of age. Belsky, Youngblade, Rovine, and Volling (1991) also showed the association between these declining marital patterns and observations of fathers and mothers interacting with their three-year-olds in a free-play and teaching task situation. Relevant to the parent facilitating the autonomy of the child was the finding that in declining marital relationships, fathers were more intrusive and aversive as opposed to positive and facilitative.

Path analysis diagrams (Figures 8.2 and 8.3) best summarize our own findings on the antecedents of four-year-old task orientation and modulation of aggression. Consistent with the emphasis of Cowan et al. (1994) that the prebirth and continuing

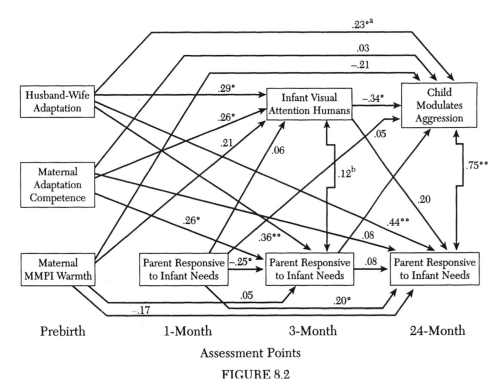

FIGURE 8.2

Path Analysis Diagram for Two Indices of 48-month Positive Parent-Child Mutuality: Child Aggression Modulation and Parent Responsiveness to Need (N = 44). °p < .05. °°p < .01. [a]Beta weights placed by across-time paths. [b]Vertical lines indicate cross-sectional correlations.

positive quality of the husband-wife adaptation is central to family adaptation, Figures 8.2 and 8.3 show that this prebirth quality is the only direct link to both aggression modulation and task orientation. Also consistent with the results reported by Cowan et al. (1994) is the finding that even when all previous influences are allowed for, both child indices are still correlated with their respective preschool transactional counterparts. Parent responsiveness to infant needs correlates with "child modulates aggression" (.75), and child task orientation correlates with "parent stimulates the child's cognitive and verbal experiences" (.34).

These same diagrams also show the indirect influence on aggression modulation of variations in early child and prebirth maternal characteristics. Thus, prebirth husband-wife adaptation and maternal adaptation-competence influence the one-month-old infant's visual attention to humans, and variation in this quality anticipate variations in aggression modulation (see Figure 8.2).

Another early infant characteristic, postnatal neurological adaptation, affects the parent responsiveness to need aspect of the transaction being discussed. At one month and 48 months, the parents' response to the needs of their infant is influ-

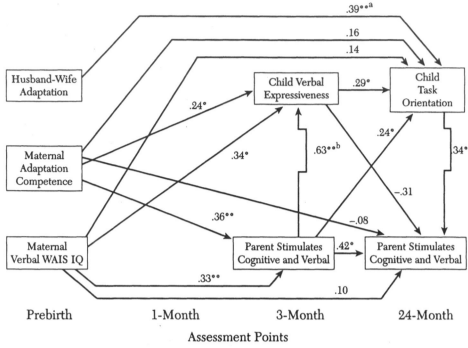

FIGURE 8.3

Path Analysis Diagram for 48-month Task Orientation and Parental Stimulation of Cognitive and Verbal: Cognitive Antecedents (N = 44). *p < .05. **p < .01. [a]Beta weights by across time paths. [b]Vertical lines indicate cross-sectional correlations.

enced not only by their prebirth marital adaptation but by the adaptive (neurological) characteristics of their infant. At one month there is a negative association. The more difficult the infant, the more responsive the parent. A form of compensation is suggested. By 48 months there is a positive link between infants who show an optimal response right after birth and optimal parent responsiveness. We assume that the compensatory behavior is not maintained and the infant's initial status has some prevailing impact on the parent-infant mutuality (see Figure 8.2).

In a similar way, 48-month task orientation is directly anticipated by husband-wife

adaptation and prior 24-month child verbal expressiveness and parent-stimulated cognitive and verbal experiences (see Figure 8.3). Each of these parts of a correlated transaction (child verbal expressiveness and parent stimulation) is anticipated by prebirth maternal adaptation-competence and maternal verbal IQ. Given all of the previous significant influences, we concluded (as did Cowan et al., 1994) that task orientation is influenced both by a social-emotional network represented by the parent's marital quality and by intellectual and adaptive antecedents such as maternal adaptation and verbal IQ.

Just as Cowan et al. (1994) analyzed the

steps in the influence of couple functioning and Belsky et al. (1991) focused on the declining marital patterns, our further analyses on a sample of 96 families included a time dimension by defining six different patterns of postnatal marital development. Three positive patterns were shown to be associated with the development of those parent-child interactions (responsiveness to need and promotion of autonomy) that enhance a secure and separate self in the first two years of life (Heinicke & Guthrie, 1992). Moreover, the more positive marital patterns were anticipated by ratings of the parent's open discussion and remembrance in the prebirth period of their own positive parenting experience and indices of maternal adaptation-competence derived from prebirth videotaped interviews with the mother and her Minnesota Multiphasic Personality Inventory (MMPI) responses. Equally striking, the overall incidence of divorce among the 96 families in the first four years of life was 17 percent, but only three divorces occurred in the 48 families with positive marital patterns, while 14 of the 25 families characterized by negative marital patterns experienced divorce (Heinicke, Guthrie, & Ruth, 1997). Cowan and Cowan (1992) also found that by child age 3½ years, 17 percent of their nonintervention families had divorced.

Because the aforementioned results are based on prebirth parent responses to self inventories and interviews, the question arises as to whether indices of the quality of the husband-wife relationship derived from direct observation of their prebirth marital interaction also anticipate variation in postnatal family development. We as-

sumed that the individual adaptation of each partner as well as their adaptation to each other when asked to resolve a conflict between them would be a valid assessment of their ability to deal with future challenges of parenting. Studies by Markman, Howes, and their colleagues (Howes & Markman, 1991) and Heinicke and Guthrie (1996) are relevant to this question. In the prebirth period, the couples of our second cohort (N = 46) were asked to discuss and resolve differences on three important issues (Heinicke & Guthrie, 1996). Systematic coding resulted in classifications contrasting those who could realistically confront the tasks and express negative feelings while maintaining a context of positive mutuality from those who could not. Those who could not resolve issues were either consistently low or decreased in their postnatal marital adjustment. As already documented, the positive patterns of postnatal marital changes were associated with the development of a secure attachment in the first child and their capacity to promote autonomy when that child was two years old. Similarly, Markman and his colleagues (Balaguer & Markman, 1991; Howes & Markman, 1991) documented an association between premarital and prebirth marital interaction measures and the development of attachment and self-concept in the child. Thus, premarital relationship problem discussions were coded and related to measures of attachment (Waters Q-sort) when the first child was between one and three years old. Correlational results indicated that avoidance of conflict and emotional invalidation in the parent's premarital relationship predicted less secure attachment relationships between mothers and their firstborns. Codes describing women as facilitating the resolution of conflict during premarital discussions predicted more secure attachment relationships between fathers and their firstborns. Howes and Markman (1991) summarized these as well as other findings by concluding that "abilities in regulating negative affect by acknowledging and addressing differences appears to be critical to both spousal and parent-child relationships" (p. 10). Similarly, Balaguer and Markman (1991) found an association between the quality of marital interaction both before marriage and before the birth of the first child and measures of the child's self-concept from ages four to seven. A mother's support of her future husband and both partners' support of each other in problem-solving marital interactions before the birth of their first child anticipate the child's experience of the self as part of positive family interaction. They stressed the importance to the child of not being exposed to destructive conflict. The additional finding that negative escalation as seen in both father and mother during prebirth interactions anticipates lower levels of the child's experience of positive self-concept is consistent with this emphasis.

In a subsequent study of the same sample (Renick & Odell, 1993), it was shown that codes of family interaction videotaped when the child was four to seven years old were associated with both the child's concurrent positive self-ratings and the couple's premarital negative escalation. That is, those families who could cooperate in a game and showed positive self-esteem

avoided negative escalation during a premarital interaction session.

In summary, it has been found that the parents' ability to confront conflictual issues, regulate their negative affect, and resolve their differences is associated with a setting in which their children develop greater security and autonomy. These results, based on observed interaction, are consistent with those based on inventory and interview data.

Conclusion and Implications

The research on the prebirth determinants of family development permits several general conclusions. Parents capable of efficient, nonanxious, flexible problem-solving, able to sustain a positive mutuality, especially with their partner, and also able to maintain their autonomy and self-esteem are more likely to provide an optimal parenting environment. In the context of the studies reviewed, this optimal parenting includes responsiveness to need, encouragement of autonomy and task orientation, and exposure to cognitive experiences. It is shown that variations in these qualities of parenting are of central significance in the family interactions enhancing security, autonomy, and task motivation in the child. These developments, in turn, are associated with higher academic achievement and less disruptive aggression in kindergarten. That is, the motivation to learn and modulation of aggression that are crucial to later academic and social development are influenced by parent and marital characteristics that are present before birth and tend to have a consistent influence in the emerging family interactions.

Although the preceding conclusions are likely to be confirmed by further research, generalizations must be viewed with some caution. The conclusion that prebirth parent characteristics have a significant impact on parenting and child development is based on the prebirth measurement and proven stability of these characteristics. These prebirth assessments reflect family system characteristics that continue and are influenced but not determined by the characteristics of the child. However, it may be possible that other influences, such as a profile of genetic determinants, could affect both prebirth and postbirth developments.

Given the findings as summarized previously, what are the implications for the design of intervention studies? Insofar as parent personality and support characteristics are stable from pregnancy onward, and given their power to predict postnatal and parent-child and child development, the earlier the intervention is initiated (as in pregnancy), the more likely it is to be effective. Less effective family system characteristics are more likely to respond to change efforts if they are not already interacting with and influencing postnatal child development.

In regard to which child outcome measures are likely to change, since security of attachment, autonomy, and task orientation were shown to be related to parent behavior that influences those developments, efforts to change such behavior as well as the child's development should have con-

siderable potential. This would contrast with child IQ as an outcome measure, since variations in child IQ are found to be influenced primarily by the genetic IQ profile of the parents and relatively less by parenting behavior (Scarr, 1985; Heinicke & Lampl, 1988; Reznick, Corley, & Robinson, 1997).

However, bringing about sustained changes in child security of attachment, autonomy, and task orientation is clearly not easily achieved. The results presented previously, showing the link of these child developments to parent personality and support characteristics, clearly argue for an intervention strategy that addresses intervention with these characteristics as well as with the parent-child and child behavior.

References

Ainsworth, M. D. S., Blehar, M. D., Waters, E., & Wall, S. (1978). *Patterns of attachment: A psychological study of the Strange Situation.* Hillsdale, NJ: Erlbaum.

Balaguer, A., & Markman, H. J. (1991). *The effects of marital communication and conflict management on child self-concept: A longitudinal perspective.* Unpublished manuscript.

Barron, F. (1953). An ego-strength scale which predicts response to psychotherapy. *Journal of Consulting Psychology, 17,* 327–333.

Belsky, J. (1984). The determinants of parenting: A process model. *Child Development, 55,* 83–96.

Belsky, J., & Isabella, R. (1986). Maternal, infant, and social-contextual determinants of attachment security. In J. Belsky &

R. Isabella (Eds.), *Clinical implications of attachment* (pp. 41–94). Hillsdale, NJ: Erlbaum.

Belsky, J., Rovine, M., & Fish, M. (1989). The developing family system. In M. Ganner & E. Thelen (Eds.), *Systems and development: Vol. 22. Minnesota Symposium on Child Psychology* (pp. 119–166). Hillsdale, NJ: Erlbaum.

Belsky, J., Youngblade, L., Rovine, M., & Volling, B. (1991). Patterns of marital change and parent-child interaction. *Journal of Marriage and the Family, 53,* 487–498.

Benoit, D., & Parker, K. (1994). Stability and transmission of attachment across three generations. *Child Development, 65,* 1444–1456.

Bibring, C. S., Dwyer, T. F., Huntington, D. S., & Valenstein, A. F. (1961). A study of the psychological processes in pregnancy and the earliest mother-child relationship. *The psychoanalytic study of the child* (Vol. 16; pp. 9–72). New York: International Universities Press.

Bornstein, M. H., & Tamis-LeMonda, C. S. (1989). Maternal responsiveness and cognitive development in children. In M. H. Bornstein (Ed.), *Maternal responsiveness: Characteristics and consequences* (pp. 49–71). San Francisco: Jossey-Bass.

Brunnquell, D., Crichton, L., & Egeland, B. (1981). Maternal personality and attitude in disturbances of child-rearing. *Journal of Orthopsychiatry, 51,* 680–691.

Cowan, C. P., & Cowan, P. A. (1992). *When partners become parents.* New York: Basic Books.

Cowan, C. P., Cowan, P. A., Heming, G., Garrett, E., Coysh, W. S., Curtis-Boles, H., & Boles, A. J. (1985). Transitions to parenthood: His, hers, and theirs. *Journal of Family Issues, 6,* 451–481.

Cowan, P. A., & Cowan, C. P. (1988). Changes in marriage during the transition to parenthood: Must we blame the baby? In G. Michaels & W. A. Goldberg (Eds.), *The transition to parenthood: Current theory and research* (pp. 114–154). Cambridge, England: Cambridge University Press.

Cowan, P. A., Cowan, C. P., Schulz, M., & Heming, G. (1994). Pre-birth to preschool family factors in children's adaptation to kindergarten. In R. Parke & S. Kellam (Eds.), *Exploring family relationships with other social contexts: Advances in Family Research* (Vol. 4; pp. 1–65). Hillsdale, NJ: Erlbaum.

Cowan, P. A., Powell, D., & Cowan, C. P. (in press). Parenting interventions: A family systems perspective. In I. E. Sigel & K. A. Renninger (Eds.), *Handbook of child psychology: Vol. 4. Child psychology in practice* (5th ed.). New York: Wiley.

Cox, M. J., & Owen, M. T. (1993). Marital conflict and conflict negotiation. *Abstracts of the Biannual Meeting of the Society for Research in Child Development, 9.*

Cox, M. J., Owen, M. T., Henderson, V. K., & Margaud, N. A. (1992). Prediction of infant-father and infant-mother attachment. *Developmental Psychology, 28,* 474–483.

Cox, M. J., Owen, M. T., Lewis, J. M., & Henderson, V. K. (1989). Marriage, adult adjustment, and early parenting. *Child Development, 60,* 1015–1024.

Del Carmen, R., Pedersen, F. A., Huffman, L. C., & Bryan, Y. E. (1993). Dyadic distress management predicts subsequent security of attachment. *Infant Behavior and Development, 16,* 131–147.

Deutsch, H. (1945). *The psychology of women: Motherhood* (Vol. 2). New York, Grune & Stratton.

Diamond, D., Heinicke, C. M., & Mintz, J. (1996). Separation-individuation as a family process in the transition to parenthood. *Infant Mental Health Journal, 17*(1), 24–42.

Egeland, B., & Farber, E. A. (1984). Infant-mother attachment: Factors related to its development and changes over time. *Child Development, 55,* 753–771.

Feldman, S. S., Nash, S. C., & Aschenbrenner, R. B. (1983). Antecedents of fathering. *Child Development, 54,* 1628–1636.

Fonagy, P., Steele, H., & Steele, M. (1991). Maternal representations of attachment during pregnancy predict the organization of infant-mother attachment at one year of age. *Child Development, 62,* 891–905.

Fonagy, P., Steele, M., Steele, H., Moran, G. S., & Higgitt, A. C. (1991). The capacity for understanding mental states: The reflective self in parent and child and its significance for security of attachment. *Infant Mental Health Journal, 13,* 200–216.

George, C., Kaplan, N., & Main, M. (1996). *Adult Attachment Interview* (3rd ed.). Unpublished manuscript, University of California, Berkeley.

Grossman, F. K., Eichler, L. W., & Winikoff, S. A. (1980). *Pregnancy, birth and parenthood.* San Francisco: Jossey-Bass.

Heinicke, C. M. (1977). *Relationship opportunities in day care and the child's task orientation* (Vols. I–II). Final report to Office of Child Development, Department of Health, Education and Welfare.

Heinicke, C. M. (1980). Continuity and discontinuity of task orientation. *Journal of the American Academy of Child Psychiatry, 19,* 637–653.

Heinicke, C. M. (1984). Impact of pre-birth parent personality and marital functioning on family development: A framework and suggestions for further study. *Developmental Psychology, 20,* 1044–1053.

Heinicke, C. M. (1993). Maternal personality, involvement in interaction, and family development. *Abstracts of the Biannual Meeting for the Society for Research in Child Development, 9,* 116.

Heinicke, C. M., Diskin, S., Ramsey-Klee, D., & Given, K. (1983). Pre-birth parent characteristics and family development in the first year of life. *Child Development, 54,* 194–208.

Heinicke, C. M., Diskin, S. D., Ramsey-Klee, D. M., & Oates, D. S. (1986). Pre- and postbirth antecedents of two-year-old attention, capacity for relationships, and verbal expressiveness. *Developmental Psychology, 22,* 777–787.

Heinicke, C. M., & Guthrie, D. (1992). Stability and change in husband-wife adaptation and the development of the positive parent-child relationship. *Infant Behavior and Development, 15,* 109–127.

Heinicke, C. M., & Guthrie, D. (1996). Prebirth marital interactions and post-birth marital development. *Infant Mental Health Journal, 17*(2), 140–151.

Heinicke, C. M., Guthrie, D., & Ruth, G. (1997). Marital adaptation, divorce, and parent-infant development: A prospective study. *Infant Mental Health Journal, 18*(3), 282–299.

Heinicke, C. M., & Lampl, E. (1988). Pre- and post-birth antecedents of 3- and 4-year-old attention, IQ, verbal expressiveness, task orientation, and capacity for relationships. *Infant Behavior and Development, 2,* 381–410.

Howes, P. W., & Markman, H. J. (1991). Longitudinal relations between premarital and prebirth adult interaction and subsequent parent-child attachment. *Abstracts of the Biannual Meeting of the*

Society for Research in Child Development, 8.

Huston, J. L., & McHale, S. M. (1983). Changes in the topography of marriage following the birth of the first child. *Abstracts of the Biannual Meeting of the Society for Research in Child Development, 4.*

Isabella, R. A. (1994). Origins of maternal role satisfaction and its influences upon maternal interactive behavior and infant-mother attachment. *Infant Behavior and Development, 17,* 381–387.

Locke, H., & Wallace, K. (1959). Short marital adjustment and prediction tests: Their reliability and validity. *Marriage and Family Living, 21,* 251–255.

Main, M., & Goldwyn, R. (in press). Interview-based adult attachment classifications: Related to infant-mother and infant-father attachment. *Developmental Psychology.*

Moos, R. H. (1974). *Family environment scale.* Palo Alto, CA: Consulting Psychologists Press.

Moss, H. (1967). Sex, age, and state as determinants of mother-infant interaction. *Merrill-Palmer Quarterly, 13,* 19–36.

Pianta, R., Egeland, B., & Erickson, M. F. (1989). The antecedents of maltreatment: Results of the Mother-Child Interaction Research Project. In D. Cichetti & V. Carlson (Eds.), *Child maltreatment: Theory and research on the causes and consequences of child abuse and neglect* (pp. 203–253). New York: Cambridge University Press.

Pratt, M. W., Kerig, P. K., Cowan, P. A., & Cowan, C. P. (1988). Mothers and fathers teaching 3-year-olds: Authoritative parenting and adults' use of the zone of proximal development. *Developmental Psychology, 24,* 832–839.

Renick, M. J., & Odell, S. (1993). Premarital communication, family interaction, and children's self-esteem. *Abstracts of the Biannual Meeting of the Society for Research in Child Development, 9,* 564.

Reznick, J. S., Corley, R., & Robinson, J. (1997). A longitudinal twin study of intelligence in the second year. *Monographs of the Society for Research in Child Development, 62*(1), 1–154.

Scarr, S. (1985). Constructing psychology: Making facts and fables for our times. *American Psychologist, 40,* 499–512.

Schaefer, F. S., Edgerton, M., & Hunter, M. (1983, August). *Childbearing and child development correlates of maternal locus of control.* Paper presented at the meeting of the American Psychological Association, Los Angeles, CA.

Shereshefsky, P. M., & Yarrow, L. J. (1973). *Psychological aspects of a first pregnancy and early postnatal adaptation.* New York: Raven.

Sroufe, L. A. (1989). Relationships and relationship disturbances. In A. J. Sameroff & R. N. Emde (Eds.), *Relationship disturbances in early childhood* (pp. 97–124). New York: Basic Books.

Steele, M., Steele, H., & Fonagy, P. (1996). Associations among attachment classifications of mothers, fathers, and their infants: Evidence for a relationship-specific perspective. *Child Development, 67,* 541–555.

Stern, O. N. (1985). *The interpersonal world of the infant.* New York: Basic Books.

Teti, D. M., Gelfand, D. M., & Pompa, J. (1990). Depressed mothers' behavioral competence with their infants: Demographic and psychosocial correlates. *Development and Psychopathology, 2,* 259–270.

van IJzendoorn, M. H. (1995). Adult attachment representations, parental responsiveness, and infant attachment: A meta-analysis on the predictive validity of the adult attachment interview. *Psychological Bulletin, 177*(3), 387–403.

van IJzendoorn, M. H., & Bakermans-Kranenburg, M. J. (1996). Attachment representations in mothers, fathers, adolescents, and clinical groups: A meta-analytic search for normative data. *Journal of Consulting and Clinical Psychology, 64*(1), 8–21.

Vaughn, B., Deinard, A., & Egeland, B. (1980). Measuring temperament in pediatric practice. *Journal of Pediatrics, 96,* 510–514.

Vaughn, B., Taraldson, B., Crichton, L., & Egeland, B. (1981). The assessment of infant temperament: A critique of the Carey infant temperament questionnaire. *Infant Behavior and Development, 4,* 1–17.

Ward, M. J., & Carlson, E. A. (1995). Associations among adult attachment representations, maternal sensitivity, and infant-mother attachment in a sample of adolescent mothers. *Child Development, 66,* 69–79.

Wolkind, S., & Zajicek, E. (1981). *Pregnancy: A psychological and social study.* London: Academic Press.

9

Fathering Infants

Wade F. Horn

9

Introduction

Two decades ago, Michael Lamb (Lamb, 1975) accurately described fathers as the "forgotten contributors to child development." In fact, for much of the twentieth century, child development theorists largely assumed that fathers were at best redundant with mothers when it came to infant development. The popular view was that the only adult with whom infants have a significant relationship is their mother. The influence of the father was largely assumed to occur, if at all, only after a child had attained the age of four or five years (e.g., Mowrer, 1950; Parsons, 1958).

What a difference two decades can make. Informed by a burgeoning research literature on the role of fathers in child development, fathers are a growing topic of interest to scholars, public policymakers, and the popular media. Far from being treated as superfluous, fathers are increasingly recognized as providing unique and irreplaceable contributions to the well-being of children beginning in infancy. Some have even described the 1990s as the decade of the father (Horn, 1998).

Paradoxically, concomitant with this growing recognition of the importance of fathers in child development is the fact that an increasing proportion of children are growing up in father-absent households. In 1960, only 17.5 percent of all children lived in households without their biological fathers. Today, that figure stands at nearly 40 percent (Hernandez, 1993; U.S. Bureau of the Census, 1993a, 1993b). Tragically, when children grow up without their fathers, they are at increased risk for a host of developmental disorders and negative outcomes (Horn, 1995, 1996). Some commentators have even described the growing problem of fatherlessness as the most compelling and consequential social crisis of our time (Blankenhorn, 1995; Popenoe, 1996).

This chapter reviews the literature on fathers and their infants. It begins with an overview of what we know about fathers' interest in and behavior toward their infants. It then describes predictors of positive father involvement with infants followed by a review of the literature on the consequences of father absence for child development. The chapter ends with recommendations for how more fathers can be encouraged to be actively involved in the lives of their infants.

Are Fathers Interested in Their Infants?

There is ample evidence to indicate that fathers do, indeed, show a keen interest in their babies beginning at birth. In an early study of first-time fathers, Greenberg and Morris (1974) observed strong paternal feelings for and involvement with newborns, something the authors termed engrossment. The fathers in this study enjoyed looking at their babies, holding them, playing with them, and touching them. These fathers also felt they could readily distinguish their baby from other babies and tended to perceive their infants as perfect. Overall, these new fathers were preoccupied with and absorbed by their newborns and described their experience as one of extreme elation, often as an emotional "high." Other studies have found that fathers of premature babies visit their hospitalized newborns frequently (Marton & Minde, 1980; Levy-Shiff, Sharir, & Mogilner, 1989) and react very similarly to mothers when first presented with their newborns (Rodholm & Larsson, 1982).

Not only do fathers show an interest in their babies, they frequently report being profoundly affected by the birth of their infants. Greenberg and Morris (1974) noted that first-time fathers often describe themselves as being bigger, more mature, and older after seeing their baby for the first time. Other studies indicate that on becoming fathers, many men report a desire to become more responsible in their own behavior. Interestingly, this shift in attitude toward more responsible and mature behavior has been found to occur even when the father did not live with the child at the time of birth, as in the case of incarcerated fathers (Palkovitz & Palm, 1997). Unfortunately, it is not well established whether shifts in attitudes toward more responsible behavior that fathers profess upon the birth of their child translate into longer term behavioral change, especially for nonresident fathers.

While most wives are apparently pleased by their husbands' positive response to their newborn, some report feeling threatened by the father's involvement with the infant. Greenberg and Morris (1974) reported that one wife became angry because her husband spent all of his time looking at the child rather than spending time interacting with her. In other cases, wives became upset because they considered infant care an area that they had staked out for themselves.

In fact, there is evidence from cross-sectional research that greater father involvement in child rearing can lead to lower overall life satisfaction in some mothers (Baruch & Barnett, 1986) and, at least for dual-earner couples, increased marital unhappiness (Crouter, Perry-Jenkins, Huston, & McHale, 1987). One possible explanation for these findings is that many American mothers have tremendous ego investment in the parenting of their infants, to prove their self-worth. When fathers take on high levels of daily infant caretaking responsibility, some mothers may interpret this as an implicit criticism of their ability to appropriately "mother" their infants, leading to resentment, low self-esteem, and marital discord.

It is possible, however, that low maternal overall life satisfaction and marital discord are the cause of higher levels of father involvement in daily child care, not the result. For example, maternal depression can lead to ineffective mothering that can, in turn, result in higher paternal involvement in daily infant care as the father attempts to compensate for the mother's ineffective caretaking. Alternatively, couples experiencing high levels of marital discord may find daily infant care activities as another battleground for expressing their dissatisfaction with each other. In the latter instances, high levels of paternal involvement in daily child care may be more a reflection of the father's desire to express dissatisfaction with his wife than a desire to be involved in infant caretaking.

Undoubtedly, whether low levels of maternal life satisfaction and marital discord are the result or the cause of higher levels of father involvement in daily child care activities will depend upon individual circumstances. But this literature does suggest that many American mothers continue to view themselves as gatekeepers to their infants and may be more ambivalent about paternal involvement in infant care than is often recognized. While it may be true that mothers in general want their husbands to be actively involved in daily child care, many may want the fathers to be involved on *their* terms—with themselves as the "field generals" and the fathers as "enlisted men." This implies that attempts to encourage father involvement in infant care should pay as much attention to the needs, feelings, and desires of the mother as to those of the father.

How Much Time Do Fathers Spend Interacting with Their Infants?

Although daily estimates of the amount of time fathers spend with their infants varies widely, it is clear that fathers' interest in their babies extends well past the newborn period. For example, in a study of 75 20-month-olds, fathers were found to spend 1.75 hours per day alone with their babies and an average of three hours per day playing with them (Easterbrooks & Goldberg, 1984). Similarly, Blair and Hardesty (1994) found that fathers of children ages zero to four years spend an average of 2.4 hours per day physically caring for their children. These estimates are considerably higher than the figure frequently cited in the popular media that the average father spends less than 12 minutes per day interacting with his children, a figure based on a single study conducted nearly 25 years ago where the amount of direct father-child interaction was measured during workdays only (see Pleck, 1992a, 1992b for a more thorough discussion and critique).

Nevertheless, fathers generally do spend significantly less time interacting with their babies than do mothers. Golinkoff and Ames (1979) reported that fathers spent 3.16 hours per day interacting with their babies compared to 8.33

hours per day for mothers. Similarly, Kotelchuck (1975) found that whereas mothers spent 9 hours per day interacting with their babies, fathers spent 3.2 hours with them.

However, as a consequence of the growing number women entering the paid labor force, fathers are spending increasingly more time as the primary caretakers of their infants. In 1993, 18.5 percent of employed mothers of preschoolers reported that the father was the primary child care provider in her absence, compared to 16.9 percent in 1988 (U.S. Bureau of the Census, 1997). For some fathers, being the primary caretaker for their infant is a matter of choice. For many, however, it may be more a matter of economic necessity, as is reflected in the fact that fathers caring for infants and preschoolers increases during times of economic hardship and declines when the economy recovers (U.S. Bureau of the Census, 1997).

Still, independent of economic factors, it is clear that American fathers are spending significantly more time interacting with their infants than did fathers two or three generations ago (Pleck, 1997). In fact, there is evidence that American culture contains a positive press toward father involvement with their infants. For example, in an observational study of 40 two-parent, Indian immigrant families rearing 18- to 44-month-old children, it was found that the fathers who were most engaged with their children, especially in teaching and disciplining, were the most assimilated fathers. Interestingly, it was not the number of years of residence in the United States that predicted fathers' involvement but the degree to which the Indian immigrant father identified with American culture (Jain & Belsky, 1997).

What Do Fathers Do When They Interact with Their Infants?

It is well established in the research literature that fathers are competent, skillful, and sensitive in their interactions with infants and young children (Belsky, 1979; Lamb, 1977; Parke & O'Leary, 1976; Parke & Sawin, 1980). For example, Parke and Sawin (1977) found that fathers and mothers were equally responsive to infant cues during feedings. In addition, fathers as well as mothers alter their speech patterns when interacting with infants by speaking more slowly, using shorter phrases, increasing their pitch, and repeating themselves frequently, a distinctive pattern of speech that infants find particularly interesting and enjoyable (Dalton-Hummel, 1982, 1979; Rondal, 1980).

American fathers are generally characterized as playmates with their infants (Crawley & Sherrod, 1984; Jain, Belsky, & Crnic, 1996; Roopnarine, Ahmeduzzaman, Hossain, & Riegraf, 1992). For example, in a naturalistic observational study of 40 White fathers and their firstborn infants ranging in age from 5.5 to 15 months, it was found that fathers were more involved in social activities, particularly play and affective physical contact, than in physical caretaking (Rendina & Dickerscheid, 1976). This tendency for fathers to play with their infants, as opposed to engaging in caretaking activities such as feeding and diapering, has been reported not only for middle-class, White fathers, but for African American fathers as well (Hossain & Roopnarine, 1994). The father's role as social playmate also tends to increase over time, with fathers engaging in more play periods in the average day than mothers by the time children attain 2½ years of age (Clarke-Stewart, 1978).

Fathers have also been found to spend more time interacting with their sons than with their daughters (Kotelchuck, 1976; Lamb, 1977; Parke & Sawin, 1980). In a study of 75 White, middle-class, 20-month-olds where all of the fathers and two-thirds of the mothers were employed outside the home, fathers spent 3.81 hours per day interacting with their daughters and 4.33 hours per day interacting with their sons (Easterbrooks & Goldberg, 1984). There is even evidence that at approximately the child's first birthday, fathers tend to withdraw from interaction with their daughters in favor of interaction with their sons. Indeed, throughout the second year of life, fathers have been found to spend as much as twice the amount of time interacting with their sons as with their daughters, while their wives are equally active with children of either sex (Lamb & Lamb, 1976). Given that fathers concentrate a good deal of their time engaging their sons in play, it is not surprising that by early in the second year of life, sons frequently prefer their fathers as playmates over their mothers (Clarke-Stewart, 1978; Lamb, 1977).

Do Fathers Interact Differently with Their Infants Than Do Mothers?

In general, research indicates that while there are certainly similarities in the way that mothers and fathers interact with their infants, fathers are not merely redundant to mothers in their interactions with their infants. Indeed, differences in father-child and mother-child interaction are well documented, even when fathers assume active caregiving roles (Clarke-Stewart, 1980; Lamb, 1976).

For example, in an early study of 7- to 13-month-old infants, Lamb and Lamb (1976) found that whereas mothers more often engaged in conventional games, such as pat-a-cake, and in games involving stimulation of their children with toys, fathers were more likely to engage in vigorous, physically stimulating games or in unusual and unpredictable types of play—the types of play that many infants find most enjoyable. Furthermore, mothers most often held their babies for caretaking purposes and to restrict the babies' exploration, whereas fathers were more likely to hold the babies just to play with them or because the babies wanted to be held. Other research confirms that compared to mothers, fathers engage in less talking to infants (Rebelsky & Hanks, 1971), engage in more playful and less containing and caretaking behaviors (Lamb, 1977; Yogman, Dixon, Tronick, Adamson, Als, & Brazelton, 1976), praise their infants more during social-physical play (Clarke-Steward, 1978), and engage in more poking and mimicry of prespeech grimaces (Trevarthen, 1974).

There is also evidence that fathers and mothers tend to react differently to sons and daughters. For example, in a study of 84 10-month-old healthy, full-term infants, mothers of females rated themselves as expressing more positive affect than mothers of males. For fathers, the opposite was true. Fathers of males reported that they expressed more positive affect toward their infants than fathers of females (Stifter & Grant, 1993).

Interestingly, mother-father differences in how they interact with infants have been found to occur not only in the United States but in other cultures as well. For example, Sun and Roopnarine (1996) found that Taiwanese mothers held their infants more than did Taiwanese fathers and were more likely to feed, smile at, vocalize to, and engage in object play than were fathers. Taiwanese fathers, in contrast, engaged in more rough play than did mothers. Thus, differences in how mothers and fathers interact with infants do not appear to be exclusive to the culture of the United States or the West at large.

While it is well established that there are differences in the father-infant and mother-infant behavior, it is less clear whether these differences are due to being a father versus being a mother or due to differences in being a secondary versus a primary caretaker. At least according to one study of 36 four-month-old infants (Field, 1979), the answer appears to be both. Specifically, this study found that both primary and secondary caretaker fathers engaged in less holding of the infant's limbs and in more game playing and poking than did primary caretaking mothers, indicating that some mother-father differences are independent of whether the father was the primary caretaker. However, the study also found that both primary caretaking fathers and primary caretaking mothers exhibited less laughing and more smiling, imitative grimaces and high-pitched imitative vocalizations than did secondary caretaking fathers.

Thus, while fathers as a group did interact with their infants differently than did mothers, the magnitude of the father-mother differences was reduced but not eliminated when comparing primary caretaking fathers with primary caretaking mothers. This suggests that as both mothers and fathers become increasingly familiar with their infant, they engage in more infantile imitative behaviors because they have learned that their infants both enjoy being imitated and more readily imitate infantile parent behaviors.

Fathers have also been described as being more preoccupied than mothers with the sex role development of their children (Biller, 1971, 1974). For example, when asked to describe certain personality traits to newborn infants, fathers attributed characteristics such as "delicate" to infants they are told are female and "strong" to supposedly male infants even though they had no opportunity to interact with the infants and the male and female infants did not differ in birthweight, length, or Apgar scores (Rubin, Provenzano, & Luria, 1974). In addition, fathers have generally been found to be more punitive and restrictive in their behavior toward their sons, whereas they are more permissive toward their daughters. It has been suggested that fathers' greater punitiveness toward boys may be a result of their belief that girls are physically weaker than boys and therefore less able to cope with punishment.

Snow, Jacklin, and Maccoby (1983) attempted to tease out just how much of the differential behavior fathers show toward their infant sons and daughters is a function of the father and how much is a reaction to behavioral differences on the part of boy and girl infants. One hundred and seven father-infant dyads were observed in a waiting room with a variety of toys and were given the instruction that they could not play with one particularly tempting toy. In accordance with the results of investigations of fathers of older children, fathers were significantly more likely to use physical and verbal prohibitions with their sons than with their daughters. However, the boy infants were significantly more likely to touch the toy designated by the experimenter to be tempting but off-limits. Indeed, when boy-girl differences in rule-breaking behavior were covaried, there were no differences in the number of prohibitions the fathers gave to their infant sons and daughters. Thus, it appears the reason that fathers give their sons more prohibitions is less a function of sex role stereotyping than it is a reaction to gender differences in rule-breaking behavior in infants that have emerged as early as 12 months of age.

This same study also found that fathers were more likely to hold their infant daughters and remain in close proximity, compared to their infant sons. But again, this difference in father-infant behavior seemed to be the result of differences in infant behavior, in that the girl infants initiated more proximity and holding than did the boy infants.

Finally, although fathers were found to be more likely to give toys to girls overall, they were significantly less likely to give dolls to boys. But even this difference was found to be related to the behavior of the child in that girl infants requested and played with the dolls more frequently than did the boy infants. Interestingly, fathers were equally likely to give trucks, a shovel, or a toy vacuum cleaner to boy and girl infants. In fact, the boy infants were more likely to play with the vacuum cleaner than were the girl infants, suggesting that as early as 12 months of age, boys already are more interested than girls in activities that involve the use of gross motor skills, a sex difference that has also been found at later ages.

Thus, the differential behavior that fathers show toward male and female infants may be more the result of their sensitivity to differences in infant behavior than to attempts by the father to impose rigid sex role stereotypes on their children. In fact, more recent studies have not shown fathers to be particularly involved in the promotion of rigid sex stereotypes (Caldera, Huston, & O'Brien, 1989; Fagot & Hagan, 1991; Lytton & Romney, 1991). Indeed, when it comes to rough and tumble play—one of the hallmarks of father-infant interaction—fathers have been found to engage in equivalent amounts of such roughhouse play with boy and girl infants (Rendina & Dickerscheid, 1976).

Do Infants Develop Attachments with Their Fathers?

Given that fathers not only have an interest in their babies but spend substantial amounts of time per day interacting with them, it should not be surprising that infants can and frequently do develop discriminating and focused attachments to their fathers beginning at approximately six or seven months of age. In an early home observational study of father-infant attachment in two-parent households, Lamb (1977) found that by seven months of age infants clearly differentiated both their mother and father from strangers, and the degree of preference for both their father and mother over a stranger widened over the six-month period of this study. Thus, as early as seven months of age, infants have already formed attachment relationships with their fathers as well as their mothers. Later studies have consistently confirmed that in-home fathers frequently form strong attachment bonds with their infants. In fact, this finding is quite robust, occurring across a range of samples and methodologies, including both naturalistic home observations and experimental laboratory manipulations (Cohen & Campos, 1974; Feldman & Ingham, 1975; Kotelchuck, 1976; Lamb, 1976, 1981; Willemsen, Flaherty, Heaton, & Ritchey, 1974).

The attachments that in-home fathers form with their infants also seem to develop as regularly and be as secure as those that mothers form with their infants. For example, Easterbrooks and Goldberg (1984), in a study of 75 White, middle-class, 20-month-olds, where all of the fathers and two-thirds of the mothers were employed outside the home, found two-thirds of the children were observed to have secure attachments with their fathers whereas one-third were found to be insecurely attached. This distribution in the quality of father-infant attachment is comparable to norms concerning the quality of attachment for mothers and infants in middle-class populations. Similarly, Lamb (1976) found that infants fussed to their fathers as often as they did to their mothers and were soothed by their fathers in times of distress as readily as they were by their mothers.

Furthermore, several studies have found that infants ranging in age from seven months to two years show no preference for either parent over the other in stress-free situations (Feldman & Ingham, 1975; Lamb, 1975, 1976; Willemsen, Flaherty, Heaton, & Ritchey, 1974), although one early study did find a preference for mothers in 10- to 16-month-old infants (Cohen & Campos, 1974). Neither do most infants protest separation from either parent more often in either the home (Ross, Kagan, Zelazo, & Kotelchuck, 1975) or structured laboratory settings (Kotelchuck, Zelazo, Kagan, & Spelke, 1975; Spelke, Zelazo, Kagan, & Kotelchuck, 1973). In stressful situations when infants are alone with the father, infants tend to restrict interaction with unfamiliar persons and are motivated to achieve and maintain proximity to and contact with their father in the same way that they do when they are alone with their mothers (Feldman & Ingham, 1975; Lamb, 1975; Willemsen, Flaherty, Heaton, & Ritchey, 1974).

However, when both parents are available in a stressful situation, infants seem to prefer their mothers. For example, using the Strange Situation paradigm (a semi-structured laboratory procedure designed to assess differences in the quality of parent-infant attachment; see Ainsworth, Blehar, Waters, & Wall, 1978, for a more complete description of this procedure), several studies have found that when the stranger enters the room and both parents are available, the infant tends to seek proximity and contact with his or her mother preferentially over his or her father (Lamb, 1975, 1976). This suggests that while fathers do frequently establish secure attachments with their infants, mothers are seen as stronger comforting figures by their infants.

Recently several authors have argued for the need to move beyond the study of individual fathering behaviors, such as feeding, play, and stimulation, and instead use individual fathers as the unit of analysis (e.g. Magnusson, 1995). In this view, the father "forest" has been lost by an overemphasis on observing individual fathering behavior "trees." Using cluster analysis, Jain, Belsky, and Crnic (1996) identified four interpretable types of fathers: caretakers (those fathers who engaged their sons mainly in routine and basic care activities, feeding, dressing, and comforting), playmates-teachers (those fathers primarily engaged in playful interactions and instructional activities with their infants), disciplinarians (those fathers engaged more in disciplining, controlling, and socializing the child than in caretaking, playing, or teaching activities), and disengaged fathers (those who remained aloof from the child and did not participate in many father-infant interactions). It was found that the caretaker and playmate-teacher fathers were more educated, had more prestigious occupations, and were less anxious, hostile, and irritable compared to the disciplinarians and disengaged fathers. Interestingly, neither child temperament nor marital quality discriminated between the different groups of fathers, indicating that fathering style is more a function of intrapersonal, rather than interpersonal, factors. It is not yet known, however, whether this typology of fathers is replicable in other samples or whether these different father groups predict different child outcomes.

What Predicts Secure Father-Infant Attachments?

Research attempting to predict the strength and quality of the father-infant attachment from specific fathering behaviors is somewhat contradictory. Belsky (1983), in attempting to relate measures of fathering obtained during naturalistic observations of mother-father-infant interaction at one, three, and nine months to classifications of infant-father attachment security at 13 months, found no significant associations. Volling and Belsky (1992) studying a similar but different sample and employing comparable observational measures obtained at six and nine months, also found no significant associations. Similarly, Caldera, Huston, and O'Brien (1995) did not find an association between sensitivity of paternal interaction at six months and attachment security at 18 months as measured by the Strange Situation or at 30 months using a Q-sort security measurement, though infants who were classified as insecure in the Strange Situation did have fathers who, one year earlier, had behaved in a more detached fashion during a semistructured play interaction.

In contrast, Cox, Owen, Henderson, and Margand (1992) found that infants who were more securely attached at 12 months of age had fathers who, nine months earlier, had engaged in more sensitive, warm, reciprocally playful, active, and appropriately encouraging and positive interactions during a 15-minute structured interaction than those who were more insecurely attached. Similarly, Spelke, Zelazo, Kagan, and Kotelchuck (1973) found that qualitative and quantitative aspects of father-child interactions—parental attitudes, responsiveness, and amount of time spent with the child—were positively related to infant sociability with strangers.

Although results are mixed as to the usefulness of specific fathering behaviors as predictors of the quality of father-infant attachment, numerous studies have found that children growing up in families with better functioning marriages are more likely to establish secure attachments to their mothers (Goldberg & Easterbrooks, 1984; Howes & Markman, 1989; Isabella & Belsky, 1985), and in at least in the case of daughters, marital harmony has been found to be positively related to infant-father security as well (Goldberg & Easterbrooks, 1984). This suggests that the development of secure parent-infant attachment is predicted better by an understanding of broader social-contextual factors than dyadic factors alone. Indeed, in a study of 126 firstborn sons in maritally intact, middle-class and working-class Caucasian families, fathers of more securely attached infants tended to have more positive marriages and experienced more harmony and support in both work and family (Belsky, 1996). Similarly, Jarvis and Creasey (1991) reported that father-infant attachments are most likely to be insecure when fathers experience high levels of stress.

What Are the Consequences of Father Involvement for Infant Development?

There is evidence that infants who develop secure attachments to both parents function more competently than infants who develop only one or no secure attachments (Belsky, Garduque, & Hrncir, 1984; Main & Weston, 1981) and that the quality of a father's engagement with his infant is predictive of better child outcomes. For example, in a study of 75 20-month-olds in White, middle-class families, Easterbrooks and Goldberg (1984) reported that the amount of time a father spent interacting with his children was associated with children's problem-solving ability, and the fathers' behavioral sensitivity, lack of aggravation about the child, and not feeling bothered about lack of parenting knowledge were consistently related to optimal toddler development. Interestingly, a father's participation in caregiving activities (such as feeding, diapering, arranging babysitting) was less strongly related to variations in child development than was the amount of time the infant and the father spent together. Similarly, Kromelow, Harding, and Touris (1990) found that boy infants who were securely attached to their father were significantly more sociable with strangers than were boys with an insecure father-infant attachment.

Conversely, there is evidence that infant development falters when the father is not actively engaged with his infant. In a study of 55 low–socioeconomic status (SES), Black infants (age five to six months) living in the inner city, Pedersen, Rubenstein, and Yarrow (1979) found that male infants, but not female infants, who had experienced minimal interaction with their fathers scored significantly lower on the Bayley Mental Developmental Index and on measures of social responsiveness, secondary circular reactions, and preferences for novel stimuli. Of note is that this study did not define father absence by marital status but by mother's response to questions regarding household members (some fathers were out of town for protracted periods because of military service or other employ-

ment, as well as separations due to family discord and conflict), and father involvement was defined by mother's report of the amount of interaction the father actually had with the infant.

One possible explanation for the poorer performance of infants living in a father-absent home relates to the number of adults in the household. It is possible that the father is simply another source of adult stimulation to the infant, providing nothing particularly more unique than any other adult in the home. Indeed, if father-absent households are significantly smaller than father-present households, then differences in infant development might be explained by the number of adults in the household without imputing any special significance to the father. At least in the aforementioned Pedersen et al. (1979) study, this was not found to be the case, in that there was no difference in the number of adults in the household as a function of father presence and father absence. Thus, given that the number of adults who are potential sources of stimulation were comparable, it appears that the father has an impact that is qualitatively different from that of other adults.

It is also important to distinguish between the direct effects of a father's interaction with his infant and the indirect effects a father may have on infant development due to his relationship with other important caretakers in the infant's life, especially the mother. That is, the father may influence infant development both through his interactions with his infant and through the effect he has on the quality of the interaction between the infant and the infant's mother. In the Pedersen et al. (1979) study, however, there was no evidence that the mother-infant social interaction was influenced by the quality of the father-infant relationship. This suggests that, at least for this sample of low-income, African American fathers, it is the father's direct interaction with his son that most significantly influences infant development.

This does not mean that there are no indirect father effects on infant development. Indeed, there is a substantial body of research indicating that the quality of the marital relationship is one of the best predictors of later child adjustment. For example, in a study of over 1,300 children and their families, children conceived by and born to parents with a difficult marital relationship were five times more fearful and jumpy than the offspring of parents with happier marital relationships. At four or five years of age, these same children were also more likely to be undersized, timid, and emotionally overdependent upon their mothers (Stott, 1973, 1977). Other studies have found that mothers with supportive husbands adjust better to their pregnancies, have more positive birth experiences, and give birth to less temperamentally difficult babies compared to mothers whose husbands are uninvolved in the pregnancy (Nicholson, Gist, Klein, & Standley, 1983).

Marital quality has also been found to be predictive of the ability of mothers to enjoy and be affectionate with their infants (Price, 1977) as well as maternal skill in feeding four-month-old infants (Pedersen, 1975). In addition, marital quality has consistently been found to affect the frequency and quality of fathers' interactions with their infants (Belsky, 1990; Belsky, Gilstrap, & Rovine, 1984; Lamb & Elster, 1985). For example, Feldman, Nash, and Aschenbrenner (1983) found that fathers with higher marital satisfaction were more involved with their infants. Similarly, Voling and Belsky (1991) reported that higher levels of marital conflict were associated with less responsive and stimulating fathering. Thus, while the quality of the father-infant relationship may not predict the quality of the mother-infant relationship, the quality of the marital relationship clearly affects the quality of mother-child interactions, frequency and quality of father-child interactions, and overall child development.

Finally, there is substantial evidence that a father's absence is particularly predictive of poor outcomes for children. Compared to children who grow up in intact, two-parent families, children who grow up without their fathers are more likely to fail at school or drop out (Dawson, 1991; National Center for Health Statistics, 1993), experience behavioral or emotional problems requiring psychiatric treatment (National Center for Health Statistics, 1988), engage in early sexual activity (Garfinkel & McLanahan, 1986; Newcomer & Udry, 1987), and develop drug and alcohol problems (National Center for Health Statistics, 1993). Children who grow up without fathers are also three times more likely to commit suicide as adolescents (McCall & Land, 1994) and be victims of child abuse or neglect (Malkin & Lamb, 1994).

These data have led noted developmental psychologist Urie Bronfenbrenner to conclude:

> Controlling for factors such as low income, children growing up in [father absent] households are at a greater risk for experiencing a variety of behavioral and educational problems, including extremes of hyperactivity and withdrawal; lack of attentiveness in the classroom; difficulty in deferring gratification; impaired academic achievement; school misbehavior; absenteeism; dropping out; involvement in socially alienated peer groups, and the so-called "teenage syndrome" of behaviors that tend to hang together—smoking, drinking, early and frequent sexual experience, and in the more extreme cases, drugs, suicide, vandalism, violence, and criminal acts.

Thus, not only do fathers provide a distinct social context for infants, but the quality of the father-infant attachment is predictive of important aspects of child development. It should not be surprising, then, that infants devoid of contact with an involved, sensitive, and skilled father are at risk for poorer developmental outcomes. Some authors have suggested that father absence beginning in infancy is particularly debilitating for children (Blanchard & Biller, 1971; Burton, 1972; Heatherington & Deur, 1971), and that boys are more likely than girls to experience negative consequences as a result of father absence at all ages (Lamb & Lamb, 1976; Persen, Rubenstein, & Yarrow, 1979).

What Do We Know about the Growing Trend toward Fatherlessness?

Unfortunately, the most significant trend in fatherhood today is not the increasing involvement of fathers with their infants, but the father's growing absence from the home. In 1960, the total number of children in the United States living in father-absent families was less than 10 million. Today, that number stands at over 24 million (Horn, 1998). This means that nearly four out of every 10 children in the United States reside in a home in which their biological father does not live. By some estimates, this figure is likely to rise to 60 percent of children born in the 1990s (Furstenberg & Cherlin, 1991).

For nearly one million children each year, the pathway to a fatherless family is divorce (National Center for Health Statistics, 1991). Between 1960 and 1980, the divorce rate nearly tripled before leveling off and declining slightly (U.S. Bureau of the Census, 1993). Today, 40 out of every 100 first marriages now end in divorce, compared to 16 out of every 100 first marriages in 1960. No other country has a higher divorce rate (National Commission on Children, 1993).

The second pathway to a fatherless family is out-of-wedlock fathering. In 1960, about 5 percent of all births were out of wedlock. That number increased to 10.7 percent in 1970, 18.4 percent in 1980, 28 percent in 1990, and nearly 33 percent in 1994 (Horn, 1996; U.S. House of Representatives, Committee on Ways and Means

1996). Currently, over 1.2 million children are born out of wedlock each year. On an annual basis, the number of children fathered out of wedlock now surpasses the number of children whose parents divorce.

African Americans are disproportionately affected by the problem of father absence. In fact, 62 percent of African American children live in father-absent homes. But fatherlessness is by no means restricted to African Americans. Indeed, the absolute number of father-absent families is larger—and the rate of father absence is growing the fastest—in the White community (U.S. Bureau of the Census, 1994a). Currently, over 13 million White children reside in father-absent homes, compared to approximately 6.5 million African-American children (U.S. Bureau of the Census, 1994b).

There are, of course, many reasons for the growing problem of fatherlessness. Transformation from an agrarian to a modern industrialized society separated fathers from the home for extended periods of time and led to the view that the contribution fathers make to families is primarily, if not exclusively, economic. In addition, both the 1960s sexual revolution and the introduction and widespread use of contraception helped to decouple human sexual activity and childbearing. There is also evidence that welfare policy has operated to push low-income fathers out of the home (Horn & Bush, 1997). But perhaps the most important factor leading to the rise in the number of children being reared without fathers is the cultural retreat from marriage as the institution within which one is expected to bear and rear children.

Why Is Marriage Important to Involved Fatherhood?

The available evidence suggests that the most effective pathway to involved, committed, and responsible fatherhood is marriage. Research has consistently found that unmarried fathers, whether through divorce or out-of-wedlock fathering, tend over time to become disconnected, both financially and psychologically, from their children. According to research by Furstenberg and Nord (1985), about 40 percent of children in father-absent homes have not seen their father in at least one year. Of the remaining 60 percent, only one in five sleeps even one night per month in the father's home. Overall, only one in six sees their father an average of once or more per week. More than one-half of all children who do not live with their fathers have never even been in their father's home (Furstenberg & Cherlin, 1991).

Unwed fathers are particularly unlikely to stay connected to their children over time. For example, Lerman and Ooms (1993) found that whereas 57 percent of unwed fathers are visiting their child at least once per week during the first two years of their child's life, by the time their child reaches 7½ years of age, that percentage drops to less than 25 percent. Furthermore, approximately 75 percent of men who are not living with their children at the time of their birth never subsequently live with them. Even when unwed fathers are cohabiting with the mother at the time of their child's birth, they are very unlikely to stay involved in their children's lives over the long term. Although one-quarter of nonmarital births occur to cohabiting couples, six out of ten cohabiting couples never go on to marry, and those that do marry are more likely to eventually divorce than those couples who bear children within the context of marriage (Moore, 1995). Remarriage or, in the case of an unwed father, marriage to someone other than the child's mother, makes it especially unlikely that a noncustodial father will remain in contact with his children (Stephens, 1996).

There are at least two possible reasons why marriage is important to both children and fatherhood. First, it has been suggested that much of a father's influence on child development is mediated through maternal attitudes and behaviors. That is, much of the father's importance to children is exerted indirectly through the provision of emotional, practical, and economic support to the mother (Feiring & Lews, 1978; Petersen, Anderson, & Cain, 1980). It is reasonable to assume that, on average, unmarried fathers are less likely than married fathers to provide such consistent and sustained emotional, practical, and economic support of the mother.

Second, a variety of ethological attachment theorists (e.g., Ainsworth, Blehar, Waters, & Wall, 1978; Bowlby, 1969; Lamb, Thompson, Gardner, & Carnov, 1985; Mackey & Day, 1995) have proposed that human infants are biologically predisposed to engage in certain behaviors, such as crying and smiling, to which both male and female adults are predisposed to respond. Given enough reciprocal, sensitive interactions between the infant and the caretaker, a special attachment relationship forms. Unmarried fathers, due to the fact that they are unlikely to consistently coreside with their infants, have far fewer opportunities to interact with their infants, reducing the likelihood of their developing a secure early attachment relationship with them. In essence, marriage maximizes opportunities for the father and infant to engage in this biologically driven father-infant "dance," that appears necessary for the formation of a healthy attachment relationship. Given the importance of the development of secure, early attachment relationships to optimal child development, it should not be surprising that marriage is predictive of both secure father-infant attachments and positive child development.

In fact, there is evidence that fathers who have more opportunities to interact with their newborns and infants develop more secure and lasting attachment relationships with them. For example, Keller, Hildebrandt, and Richards (1985) found that fathers who witnessed the birth of their children and engaged in extensive postpartum interaction with them while in the hospital were more involved with their infants later on than those who had not. Similarly, Peterson, Mehl, and Leiderman (1979) reported that fathers who participated in the birth of their baby and had a positive attitude toward participation in the birth evidenced better attachments to their infants. In addition, divorced fathers (who presumably had more opportunity to interact with their children when they were infants) communicate with and visit their children more often than do never-married fathers (McKenry et al., 1996).

Of course, all marriages between biological parents are not ideal. Domestic violence and other irreconcilable differences will, at times, necessitate single-parent families. There are certainly many instances where both divorced and unwed fathers are intimately involved with their children. But the reality is that without marriage, high levels of father engagement with their infants are less likely to occur. This seems particularly true when the father is not married to the mother at the time the child is born.

What Can Be Done to Encourage More Fathers to Be Involved with Their Infants?

Given that the quality of a father's engagement in his infant's daily life has both short-term and long-term consequences for the well-being of the child, what can be done to encourage more fathers to get and stay involved with their infants?

First, our culture needs to develop a clearer sense of what we want fathers to do, especially in infancy. Much of the research on fathers has suffered from an inadequate conceptualization of what it means to be a father. When it comes to in-home fathers, instead of developing an independent standard for paternal involvement, fathers are frequently assessed on standards originally developed for assessing the behavior of mothers. Hence, the preoccupation of many researchers with asking how much time fathers spend doing housework and changing diapers, while neglecting to ask them how much time they spend securing economic support for their families—a task that many men believe is their major contribution to their children's well-being.

Curiously, when it comes to studying physically absent fathers, the opposite is true. Here, the preoccupation is not with how much time a father spends doing housework or performing child care duties but how much financial support he provides. Thus, the message our culture sends to fathers is: When in the home, pay attention to your kids; when out of it, just pay.

What is needed is a broader conceptualization of the fathering role, one that recognizes both the economic and noneconomic contributions that fathers make to the well-being of their families and their children. Michael Lamb and his colleagues (1985) have delineated a particularly helpful model consisting of three components to paternal involvement: (1) paternal engagement (direct interaction with the child in the form of caretaking or play), (2) accessibility (or availability to the child), and (3) responsibility for the care of the child as distinct from the performance of care. This model seems particularly helpful for informing both researchers and fatherhood promotion activities. Unfortunately, most research and fatherhood promotion activities have thus far only focused on the first aspect of this fathering component, direct father-infant interaction and caretaking.

Second, the father role, beginning in infancy, needs to receive more widespread support and encouragement from the broader culture. Unfortunately, many fathers retreat from the world of the newborn, believing that women are more innately suited to care for infants and that there is little they can do during pregnancy or infancy to enhance their child's development, other than to be supportive of the mother (Biller & Trotter, 1994). These beliefs on the part of new fathers need to be countered by publicizing the myriad of unique ways that infants can and are influenced by direct interactions with their fathers.

There is, for example, increasing recognition that the rough and tumble play of fathers, far from being irrelevant to child development, is helpful in encouraging the development of self-regulation and recognition of emotional cues (Parke, 1995). Yet, the unique aspects of father involvement, especially play, are often downplayed even by fatherhood advocates. For example, Michael O'Donnell, executive director of the Center for Fathering at Abilene Christian University, was quoted in an article appearing in the June 14, 1996 issue of *The Chronicle of Higher Education* as saying, "When we're talking about being involved, we're not talking just about playing. We're talking about changing diapers and feeding the kids—things that used to be seen as woman's work" (Mangan, 1996). Similarly, Will Jordan, in a paper published at the behest of the Center for Fathers and Families asserted that fathers can no longer be "permitted to simply be their child's playmates" (p. 6).

But, as Michael Lamb (1977) points out, "[b]abies [form] attachments to those with whom they interacted regularly; involvement in caretaking seem[s] insignificant" (p. 13). The implication is that for fathers to have a positive impact on infants, fathers need not merely duplicate the work of mothers. Indeed, as reviewed earlier, simply increasing amounts of direct child care by fathers may even result in the unintended consequence of increased marital conflict. Thus, effective fatherhood promotion means highlighting the fact that far from being simply part-time, substitute mothers, fathers can and do make unique contributions to the well-being of their infants.

Third, our culture needs to reestablish the expectation that men should father children only in the context of committed and legal marriages. While men (and women) nearly universally expect that someday they will have children and get married, there is a decreasing belief that there needs to be an order to these two events. Unfortunately, the available data indicate that when men father children out of wedlock, they are unlikely to be involved and committed fathers in either the short or long term. All of society needs to help couples build strong marriages before having children.

Fourth, public and private organizations need to engage in more aggressive outreach to support men who desire to be good and committed fathers. Civic and religious organizations, in particular, should offer new fathers support and, where needed, training through workshops and mentoring programs. Employers also need to place a higher value on fatherhood by implementing father-friendly workplaces in which father employees are encouraged and not discouraged to take time off to be with their children, especially during pregnancy, birth, and the first few years of life.

Unfortunately, thus far there is little empirical evidence from well-designed studies with adequate experimental controls that short-term interventions for new fathers significantly improve either their functional competence or actual involvement with their infants (Belsky, 1985; Pannabecker, Emde, & Austin, 1982; Parke & Beitch, 1986). The dearth of empirical evidence should not, however, dissuade others from implementing fatherhood promotion activities but rather challenge them to develop more effective models for enhancing father-infant involvement.

Finally, public policy must begin to encourage, not discourage, marriage and responsible fatherhood. The U.S. tax code currently punishes most two-earner couples when they marry (Steuerle, 1997). Given the high likelihood that out-of-wedlock fathers will not stay committed to their children in the long run, such anti-marriage tax policies are counterproductive to improving the well-being of children. In addition, the welfare system has frequently operated to punish and not reward father involvement (Horn & Bush, 1997). There are, for example, instances where rents in public housing skyrocket when a single mother chooses to marry or if there is a "man in the house." In addition, welfare rules in the United States often prevent a woman from receiving full benefits if the father is at home and has an employment record or works more than 100 hours per month. Wherever such perverse incentives exist that drive fathers out of the home, they need to be eliminated.

Conclusion

This review of the literature on fathers and infants clearly indicates that: (1) Fathers can—and frequently do—become as attached to their infants as mothers; (2) fathers are neither uninterested nor inept in interaction with their newborns; (3) fathers and mothers differ in the ways they tend to parent infants, and as a result, infants tend to respond differentially to fathers and mothers; (4) the quality of the marital relationship affects the quality of mother-child interactions, the quality of father-child interactions, and the quality of the child's development; and (5) active father involvement with his infant is predictive of better development outcomes for the child.

Still, many questions remain unanswered. First, too few studies have examined the broader social-cultural contexts wherein fathers fulfill or fail to fulfill their role as social fathers. As a result, we have an inadequate understanding of the factors within families, communities, workplaces, social institutions, and the broader culture that support or undermine fathering for different groups of fathers in different circumstances.

Second, because most studies of fathers and their infants have been conducted with White, middle-class families, we have only a limited understanding of differences that may exist between fathers from different ethnic groups. Do, for example, African American and Hispanic fathers interact similarly with their infants to White, middle-class fathers? If there are differences, are these differences more a matter of ethnicity or social class? This kind of information would seem to be particularly helpful when designing outreach, skills building, and support programs targeted to fathers of different ethnic and socioeconomic backgrounds. More work also needs to be done to identify subgroups of fathers, rather than merely studying individual fathering behaviors, and correlate father subgroups with relevant sociocultural factors and developmental outcomes for children.

Third, although it is clear that increasing numbers of fathers are abandoning their role as social father, it is unclear exactly why this is happening. Some posit that it is the loss of a clear fatherhood ideal (Blankenhorn, 1996). Others stress economic factors (Mincy & Pouncy, 1996). Still others emphasize the retreat from marriage as a cultural ideal (Popenoe, 1997). Exactly which of these factors or combination of factors is operative for which fathers and under what circumstances is unknown.

Finally, we are only beginning to evaluate the effectiveness of programs and initiatives designed to increase the positive involvement of fathers with their infants. Little is known as to what types of approaches are most effective with which groups of fathers and under what circumstances. Hence, much of the activity in this area is being driven more by supposition than empirical data. There is a pressing need to bring these activities under increasing scientific scrutiny so that we have a better knowledge base concerning which types of intervention programs work best for whom and under what circumstances.

Nevertheless, what we do know is that fathers matter to their infants and that they matter a whole lot more than has been assumed for much of this century. Unfortunately, this knowledge comes at a time when increasing numbers of infants can no longer count on their fathers' being there throughout their childhood. The challenge is to continue to accumulate knowledge about the unique ways that fathers contribute to infant development, while at the same time persuading more fathers to actually make those contributions.

References

Ainsworth, M. D. S., Blehar, M. C., Waters, E., & Wall, S. (1978). *Patterns of attachment.* Hillsdale, NJ: Erlbaum.

Baruch, G. K., & Barnett, R. D. (1986). Consequences of fathers' participation in family work: Parents' role strain and well-being. *Journal of Personality and Social Psychology, 51,* 983–992.

Belsky, J. (1979). Mother-father-infant interaction: A naturalistic observational study. *Developmental Psychology, 15,* 601–607.

Belsky, J. (1983). *Father-infant interaction and security attachment: No relationship.* Unpublished manuscript, Pennsylvania State University.

Belsky, J. (1985). Experimenting with the family in the newborn period. *Child Development, 56,* 407–414.

Belsky, J. (1990). Parental and nonparental care and children's socioemotional development: A decade in review. *Journal of Marriage and the Family, 52,* 885–903.

Belsky, J. (1996). Parent, infant and social-contextual antecedents of father-son attachment security. *Developmental Psychology, 32,* 905–913.

Belsky, J., Garduque, L., & Hrncir, E. (1984). Assessing performance, competence, and executive capacity in infant play: Relations to home environment and security of attachment. *Developmental Psychology, 20,* 406–417.

Belsky, J., Gilstrap, B., & Rovine, M. (1984). The Pennsylvania Infant and Family Development Project, I: Stability and change in mother-infant and father-infant interaction in a family setting at one, three, and nine months. *Child Development, 55,* 692–705.

Biller, H. B. (1971). *Father, child and sex role.* Lexington, MA: Heath.

Biller, H. B. (1974). *Paternal deprivation: Family, school, sexuality and society.* Lexington, MA: Heath.

Biller, H. B., & Trotter, R. J. (1994). *The father factor: What you need to know to make a difference.* New York: Pocket Books.

Blanchard, R. W., & Biller, H. B. (1971). Father availability and academic performance among third grade boys. *Developmental Psychology, 4,* 301–305.

Blankenhorn, D. (1995). *Fatherless America: Confronting our most urgent social problem.* New York: Basic Books.

Bowlby, J. (1969). *Attachment and loss: Vol. 1. Attachment.* New York: Basic Books.

Bronfenbrenner, U. (1991, Winter/Spring). What do families do? *Family Affairs,* p. 1–6.

Burton, R. V. (1972). Cross-sex identity in Barbados. *Developmental Psychology, 6,* 365–374.

Caldera, Y. M., Huston, A. C., & O'Brien, M. (1989). Social interactions and play patterns of parents and toddlers with feminine, masculine, and neutral boys. *Child Development, 49,* 466–478.

Caldera, Y., Huston, A., & O'Brien, M. (1995, April). *Antecedents of father-infant attachment: A longitudinal study.* Paper presented at the Biennial Meeting of the Society for Research in Child Development, Indianapolis, IN.

Clarke-Stewart, K. A. (1978). And daddy makes three: The father's impact on mother and young child. *Child Development, 55,* 1–7.

Clarke-Stewart, K. A. (1980). The father's contribution to children's cognitive and social development in early childhood. In F. A. Pedersen (Ed.), *The father-infant relationship: Observational studies in the family setting* (pp. 111–146). New York: Praeger.

Cohen, L., & Campos, J. (1974). Father, mother, and stranger as elicitors of attachment behaviors in infancy. *Developmental Psychology, 10,* 146–154.

Cox, M., Owen, M., Henderson, V., & Margand, N. (1992). Prediction of infant-father and infant-mother attachment. *Developmental Psychology, 28,* 474–483.

Crouter, A. C., Perry-Jenkins, M., Huston, T. L., & McHale, S. M. (1987). Process underlying father-involvement in dual-earner and single-earner families. *Developmental Psychology, 23,* 431–440.

Crawley, S. B., & Sherrod, K. B. (1984). Parent-infant play during the first year of life. *Infant Behavior and Development, 7,* 65–75.

Dalton-Hummel, D. (1982). Father-infant interaction and parent stress with healthy and medically compromised infants. *Infant Behavior and Development, 17,* 3–14.

Dawson, D. (1991). Family structure and children's health and well-being: Data from the 1988 National Health Interview

Survey on Child Health. *Journal of Marriage and the Family, 53,* 573–582.

Easterbrooks, M. A., & Goldberg, W. A. (1984). Toddler development in the family: Impact of father involvement and parenting characteristics. *Child Development, 55,* 740–752.

Fagot, B. I., & Hagan, R. (1991). Observations of parent reactions to sex-stereotyped behaviors: Age and sex effects. *Child Development, 62,* 617–628.

Feiring, C., & Lewis, M. (1978). The child as a member of the family system. *Behavioral Science, 23,* 225–233.

Feldman, S. S., & Ingham, M. E. (1975). Attachment behavior: A validation study in two age groups. *Child Development, 46,* 319–330.

Feldman, S. S., Nash, S. C., & Aschenbrenner, S. (1983). Antecedents of fathering. *Child Development, 54,* 1628–1636.

Furstenberg, F. F., & Cherlin, A. J. (1991). *Divided families: What happens to children when parents part.* Cambridge, MA: Harvard University Press.

Furstenberg, F. F., & Nord, C. W. (1985). Parenting apart: Patterns of child rearing after marital disruption. *Journal of Marriage and the Family, 47,* 893–904.

Garfinkel, I., & McLanahan, S. (1986). *Single mothers and their children.* Washington, DC: Urban Institute Press.

Goldberg, W. A., & Easterbrooks, M. A. (1984). The role of marital quality in toddler development. *Developmental Psychology, 20,* 504–514.

Golinkoff, R. M., & Ames, G. J. (1979). A comparison of fathers' and mothers' speech with their young children. *Child Development, 50,* 28–32.

Greenberg, M., & Morris, N. (1974). Engrossment: The newborn's impact upon the father. *American Journal of Orthopsychiatry, 44,* 520–531.

Heatherington, E. M., & Deur, J. L. (1971). The effects of father absence on child development. *Young Children,* 233–248.

Hernandez, D. J. (1993). *America's children: Resources from family, government and the economy.* New York: Russell Sage Foundation.

Horn, W. F. (1995). *Father facts.* Lancaster, PA: The National Fatherhood Initiative.

Horn, W. F. (1996). *Father facts 2.* Lancaster, PA: The National Fatherhood Initiative.

Horn, W. F. (1998). *Father facts third edition.* Gaithersburg, MD: The National Fatherhood Initiative.

Horn, W. F., & Bush, A. (1997). *Fathers, marriage and welfare reform.* Indianapolis, IN: The Hudson Institute.

Hossain, Z., & Roopnarine, J. L. (1994). African-American fathers' involvement with infants: Relationship to their functional style, support, education, and income. *Infant Behavior and Development, 17,* 175–184.

Howes, P., & Markman, H. J. (1989). Marital quality and child functioning: A longitudinal investigation. *Child Development, 60,* 1044–1051.

Isabella, R., & Belsky, J. (1985). Marital change during the transition to parenthood and security of infant-parent attachment. *Journal of Family Issues, 6,* 505–522.

Jain, A., & Belsky, J. (1997). Fathering and acculturation: Immigrant Indian families with young children. *Journal of Marriage and the Family, 59,* 873–883.

Jain, A., Belsky, J., & Crnic, K. (1996). Beyond fathering behaviors: Types of dads. *Journal of Family Psychology, 10,* 431–442.

Jarvis, P. A., & Creasey, G. L. (1991). Parental stress, coping, and attachment in families with an 18-month-old infant. *Infant Behavior and Development, 14,* 383–395.

Jordon, W. (1997, October). *Role transitions: A review of the literature.* Paper presented at the Role Transitions Roundtable, National Center on Fathers and Families, Philadelphia, PA.

Keller, W. D., Hildebrandt, K. A., & Richards, M. E. (1985). Effects of extended father-infant contact during the newborn period. *Infant Behavior and Development, 8,* 337–350.

Kotelchuck, M. (1975, September). *Father caretaking characteristics and their influence on infant father interaction.* Paper presented at the meeting of the American Psychological Association, Chicago, IL. As cited in Lamb, M. E., The development of father-infant relationships. In M. E. Lamb (Ed.), *The role of the father in child development* (pp. 104–120). New York: Wiley.

Kotelchuck, M. (1976). The infant's relationship to the father: Experimental evidence. In M. E. Lamb (Ed.), *The role of the father in child development* (pp. 161–192). New York: Wiley.

Kotelchuck, M., Zelazo, P., Kagan, J., & Spelke, E. (1975). Infant reactions to parental separations when left with familiar and unfamiliar adults. *Journal of Genetic Psychology, 126,* 255–262.

Kromelow, S., Harding, C., & Touris, M. (1990). The role of the father in the development of stranger sociability during the second year. *American Journal of Orthopsychiatry, 60,* 521–530.

Lamb, M. E. (1975a). Effects of stress and cohort on mother- and father-infant interaction. *Developmental Psychology, 12,* 435–443.

Lamb, M. E. (1975b). Fathers: Forgotten contributors to child development. *Human Development, 18,* 245–266.

Lamb, M. E. (1976a). *The role of the father in child development.* New York: Wiley.

Lamb, M. E. (1976b). Twelve-month-olds and their parents: Interaction in a laboratory playroom. *Developmental Psychology, 12,* 237–244.

Lamb, M. E. (1977a). The development of father-infant relationships. In M. E. Lamb (Ed.), *The role of the father in child development* (pp. 104–120). New York: Wiley.

Lamb, M. E. (1977b). The development of mother-infant and father-infant attachments in the second year of life. *Developmental Psychology, 13,* 637–648.

Lamb, M. E. (1977c). Father-infant and mother-infant interaction in the first year of life. *Child Development, 48,* 167–181.

Lamb, M. E. (1981). The development of father-infant relationships. In M. E. Lamb (Ed.), *The role of the father in child development* (pp. 459–488). New York: Wiley.

Lamb, M. E., & Elster, A. B. (1985). Adolescent mother-infant-father relationships. *Developmental Psychology, 21,* 768–773.

Lamb, M. E., & Lamb, E. (1976, October). The nature and importance of the father-infant relationship. *The Family Coordinator,* pp. 379–385.

Lamb, M. E., Thompson, R. A., Gardner, W., & Charnov, E. L. (1985). *Infant-mother attachment: The origins and developmental significance of individual differences in Strange Situation behavior.* Hillsdale, NJ: Erlbaum.

Lerman, R., & Ooms, T. (1993). *Young unwed fathers: Changing roles and emerging policies.* Philadelphia, PA: Temple University Press.

Levy-Shiff, R., Sharir, H., & Mogilner,

M. B. (1989). Mother- and father-preterm infant relationship in the hospital preterm nursery. *Child Development, 60,* 93–102.

Lytton, H., & Romney, D. M. (1991). Parents' differential socialization of boys and girls: A meta-analysis. *Psychological Bulletin, 109,* 267–296.

Mackey, W. C., & Day, R. (1995). A test of the man-child bond: The predictive potency of the teeter-totter effect. *Genetic, Social, and General Psychology Monographs, 121,* 425–444.

Magnusson, D. (1995). Individual development: A holistic integrated model. In P. Moen, G. H. Elder, & K. Luscher (Eds.), *Linking lives and contexts: Perspectives on the ecology of human development* (pp. 19–60). Washington, DC: American Psychological Association.

Main, M., & Weston, D. (1981). The quality of the toddler's relationship to mother and father: Related to conflict behavior and readiness to establish new relationships. *Child Development, 52,* 932–940.

Mangan, K. S. (1996, June 14). Reforming "phantom fathers": Teaching men to become better parents. *The Chronicle of Higher Education,* p. A6.

Marton, P. L., & Minde, K. (1980, April). *Paternal and maternal behavior with premature infants.* Paper presented at the meeting of the American Orthopsychiatric Association, Toronto, Canada. As cited in Lamb, M. E., The development of father-infant relationships. In M. E. Lamb (Ed.), *The role of the father in child development* (pp. 104–120). New York: Wiley.

McCall, P. L., & Land, K. C. (1994). Trends in White male adolescent young-adult and elderly suicide: Are there common underlying structural factors? *Social Science Research, 23,* 57–81.

Mincy, R. B., & Pouncy, H. (1996, October). *There must be fifty ways to start a family: Social policy and the fragile families of low-income, non-custodial fathers.* Paper presented at a symposium of the Center of the American Experiment, Minneapolis, MN.

Moore, K. A. (1995). Non-marital childbearing in the United States. In *Report to Congress on out-of-wedlock childbearing* (p. vii). Washington, DC: U.S. Department of Health and Human Services.

Mowrer, O. H. (1950). Identification: A link between learning theory and psychotherapy. In O. H. Mowrer (Ed.), *Learning theory and personality dynamics.* New York: Ronald.

National Center for Health Statistics. (1988). *National health interview survey.* Hyattsville, MD: U.S. Department of Health and Human Services.

National Center for Health Statistics. (1993). *Survey of child health.* Washington, DC: U.S. Department of Health and Human Services.

National Commission on Children. (1993). *Just the facts: A summary of recent information on America's children and their families.* Washington, DC: U.S. Government Printing Office.

Newcomer, S., & Udry, J. R. (1987). Parental marital status effects on adolescent behavior. *Journal of Marriage and the Family,* May, 235–240.

Nicholson, J., Gist, N. F., Klein, R. P., & Standley, K. (1983). Outcomes of father involvement in pregnancy and birth. *Birth: Issues in Perinatal Care and Education, 10,* 5–9.

Palkovitz, R., & Palm, G. (1997, November). *Fatherhood and faith in formation: The developmental effects of fathering on religiosity and values.* Paper presented at the meeting of the National Council on Family Relations, Arlington, VA.

Pannabecker, B., Emde, R. N., & Austin, B. (1982). The effect of early extended contact on father-newborn interaction. *Journal of Genetic Psychology, 141,* 7–17.

Parke, R. D. (1995). Fathers and families. In M. Bornstein (Ed.), *Handbook of parenting.* Hillsdale, NJ: Erlbaum.

Parke, R. D., & Beitch, A. (1986). Hospital-based intervention for fathers. In M. E. Lamb (Ed.), *The father's role: Applied perspectives* (pp. 293–323). New York: Wiley.

Parke, R. D., & O'Leary, S. (1976). Family interaction in the newborn period: Some findings, some observations, and some unresolved issues. In K. Riegel & J. Meacham (Eds.), *The developing individual in a changing world: Vol. 2. Social and environmental issues* (pp. 49–62). The Hague: Mouton.

Parke, R. D., & Sawin, D. (1977, March). *The family in early infancy: Social interactional and attitudinal analyses.* Paper presented at the meeting of the Society for Research in Child Development, New Orleans. As cited in Lamb, M. E., The development of father-infant relationships. In M. E. Lamb (Ed.), *The role of the father in child development.* New York: Wiley.

Parke, R. D., & Sawin, D. (1980). The family in early infancy: Social interactions and attitudinal analyses. In F. Pedersen (Ed.), *The father-infant relationship: Observational studies in the family setting* (pp. 44–70). New York: Praeger.

Parsons, T. (1958). Social structure and the development of personality: Freud's contribution to the integration of psychology and sociology. *Psychiatry, 21,* 321–340.

Pedersen, F. A., Anderson, B. J., & Cain, R. L. (1980). Parent-infant and husband-wife interactions observed at five months. In F. A. Pedersen (Ed.), *The father-infant relationship: Observational studies in the family setting* (pp. 71–86). New York: Plenum.

Pedersen, F. A., Rubenstein, J. L., & Yarrow, L. J. (1979). Infant development in father-absent families. *The Journal of Genetic Psychology, 135,* 51–61.

Peterson, G. H., Mehl, L. E., & Leiderman, P. H. (1979). The role of some birth-related variables in father attachment. *American Journal of Orthopsychiatry, 49,* 330–338.

Pleck, J. H. (1992a). Families and work: Small changes with big implications. *Qualitative Sociology, 15,* 427–432.

Pleck, J. H. (1992b). Work-family policies in the United States. In H. Kahne & J. Z. Giele (Eds.), *Women's work and women's lives: The continuing struggle worldwide* (pp. 248–275). Boulder, CO: Westview.

Pleck, J. H. (1997). Paternal involvement: Levels, sources, and consequences. In M. E. Lamb (Ed.), *The role of the father in child development* (pp. 66–103). New York: Wiley.

Popenoe, D. (1996). *Life without father: Compelling new evidence that fatherhood and marriage are indispensable for the good of children and society.* New York: The Free Press.

Price, G. (1977, March). *Factors influencing reciprocity in early mother-infant interaction.* Paper presented at the meeting of the Society for Research in Child Development, New Orleans. As cited in Lamb, M. E., The Development of father-infant relationships. In M. E. Lamb (Ed.), *The role of the father in child development* (pp. 104–120). New York: Wiley.

Rebelsky, F., & Hanks, C. (1971). Father's

verbal interaction with infants in the first three months of life. *Child Development, 42,* 63–68.

Rendina, R., & Dickerscheid, J. D. (1976, October 25). Father involvement with first-born infants. *The Family Coordinator,* pp. 373–379.

Rodholm, M., & Larsson, K. (1979). Father-infant interaction at the first contact after delivery. *Early Human Development, 3,* 21–27.

Rondal, J. A. (1980). Fathers' and mothers' speech in early language development. *Journal of Child Language, 7,* 353–369.

Roopnarine, J., Ahmeduzzaman, M., Hossain, Z., & Riegraf, B. (1992). Parent-infant rough play: Its cultural specificity. *Early Education and Development, 3,* 298–311.

Ross, G., Kagan, J., Zelazo, P., & Kotelchuck, M. (1975). Separation protest in infants in home and laboratory. *Developmental Psychology, 11,* 256–257.

Rubin, J. Z., Provenzano, F. J., & Luria, Z. (1974). The eye of the beholder: Parents' view on sex of newborn. *American Journal of Orthopsychiatry, 44,* 512–519.

Snow, M. E., Jacklin, C. N., & Maccoby, E. E. (1983). Sex-of-child differences in father-child interaction at one year of age. *Child Development, 54,* 227–232.

Spelke, E., Zelazo, P., Kagan, J., & Kotelchuck, M. (1973). Father interaction and separation protest. *Developmental Psychology, 9,* 83–90.

Stephens, L. S. (1996). Will Johnny see Daddy this week? An empirical test of three theoretical perspectives of post-divorce contact. *Journal of Family Issues, 17,* 466–494.

Steuerle, C. E. (1997, June). *The effects of tax and welfare policies on family formation.*

Paper presented at a meeting of the Family Impact Seminar, Washington, DC.

Stifter, C. A., & Grant, W. (1993). Infant responses to frustration: Individual differences in the expression of negative affect. *Journal of Nonverbal Behavior, 17,* 187–204.

Stott, D. (1973). Follow-up study from birth of the effects of prenatal stresses. *Developmental Medicine and Child Neurology, 15,* 770–787.

Stott, D. (1977). Children in the womb: The effects of stress. *New Society, 19,* 329–331.

Sun, L, & Roopnarine, J. L. (1996). Mother-infant, father-infant interaction and involvement in childcare and household labor among Taiwanese families. *Infant Behavior and Development, 19,* 121–129.

Trevarthen, C. (1974, May 2). Conversations with a 2-month-old. *New Scientist,* pp. 230–235.

U.S. Bureau of the Census, Department of Commerce. (1993a). *Marriage, divorce and remarriage in the 1990s* (Current Population Reports, P–23, No. 180). Washington, DC: Author.

U.S. Bureau of the Census, Department of Commerce. (1993b). *Marital status and living arrangements: March 1990* (Current Population Reports, P–20, No. 450). Washington, DC: Author.

U.S. Bureau of the Census, Department of Commerce. (1993c). *Statistical abstract of the United States, 1993.* Washington, DC: U.S. Government Printing Office.

U.S. Bureau of the Census, Department of Commerce. (1994a). *Marital status and living arrangements: March 1993* (Current Population Reports, Population Characteristics, 20–478). Washington, DC: Author.

U.S. Bureau of the Census, Department of Commerce. (1994b). *Diverse living arrangement of children: Summer 1991* (Current Population Reports, Household Economic Studies). Washington, DC: Author.

U.S. Bureau of the Census, Department of Commerce. (1997, September). *My daddy takes care of me! Fathers as care providers* (Current Population Reports, P–70, No. 59). Washington, DC: Author.

U.S. Department of Health and Human Services, National Center for Health Statistics. (1991). *Advance report of final divorce statistics, 1988* (Monthly Vital Statistics Report, Vol. 39). Washington, DC: U.S. Government Printing Office.

U.S. House of Representatives, Committee on Ways and Means. (1996). *1996 green book.* Washington, DC: U.S. Government Printing Office.

Volling, B., & Belsky, J. (1992). Infant, father, and marital antecedents of infant-father attachment security in dual-earner and single-earner families. *International Journal of Behavioral Development, 15,* 83–100.

Willemsen, E., Flaherty, D., Heaton, C., & Ritchey, G. (1974). Attachment behavior of one-year-olds as a function of mother vs. father, sex of child, session, and toys. *Psychology Monographs, 90,* 305–324.

Yogman, M. W., Dixon, S., Tronick, E., Adamson, L., Als, H., & Brazelton, T. B. (1976, April). *Development of infant social interaction with fathers.* Paper presented at the meeting of the Eastern Psychological Association, New York.

10

Intuitive Parenting

Hanuš Papoušek

10

The Changing Interpretation of Human Infancy

Recent contributions to our knowledge of infant mental development and health have reached levels of technological sophistication and objective evidence that diminish the necessity of using speculative interpretations, unlike in the not very distant past, of the care for infant mental health.

Even the dilemma between monistic and dualistic views on the regulation of immune versus mental processes—that is, the body-mind problem—appears in a new light in relation to recent neuroscientific discoveries. Introduction of methods for investigating entire neuronal populations as dynamic systems and the detection of humoral modulators of action potentials at synaptic levels have led to surprising evidence of a narrow, bilateral coregulation between the central nervous system and the seemingly independent immune system. The participation of immune cells in the production of neurotransmitters or endorphin serves as an example of that complex coregulation (Cupps & Fanci, 1982; McEwen & Stellar, 1993).

Similarly, the growing understanding of the genetic regulation of developmental processes makes it obvious how irrational it was to deny the significance of this regulation in ecological adaptation. Perhaps still controversial and less influenced by recent neuroscientific findings remains the interpretation of interrelationships between emotional regulation and integrative processes (learning and cognition). In human infancy research, it was shown rather early (Papoušek, 1967, 1969) that the former views of infants as subjects responding to environmental stimulation predominantly with emotional responses were erroneous. Not only was learning demonstrated in newborns and premature infants prior to postconceptual maturity, but also a close, bilateral interdependence between learning parameters and behavioral/emotional states appeared evident as early as in newborns. The behavioral/emotional state preceding learning trials significantly affected the course of learning. However, the outcome of learning—successful or unsuccessful coping with the learning task—influenced successive emotional behavior.

Recently, advanced neuroscientific studies have detected some of the coregulation pathways indicating how problematic it is to view integrative and emotional processes as autonomous and independent from each other. For example, exposure to the nipple, the first learning situation, activates the endogenous opioid system affecting emotional functions in newborn rats (Robinson, Arnold, Spear, & Smotherman, 1993; Blass & Ciaramitaro, 1994). For another example, detailed analyses of responses to emotional events in primate models have also confirmed inseparable forms of interdependence between cognitive and emotional subsystems (Ledoux, 1995; Rolls, 1995; Weinberger, 1995).

Emotional bonding represents the most universal component of parent-offspring interactions in the mammalian world whereby other components have evolved in an increasing number from paleomammalian species—marsupials or rodents—

to neomammalian species, such as carnivores or primates. Thus, to study parent-infant bonding in humans and neglect human-specific perspectives has proved insufficient. Researchers of human bonding have often shown more interest in its similarities with bonding in other species than in differences. Doubtless, similarities justify conceptual verifications of nonspecific aspects of human bonding in animal models. However, differences may point out the evolutionary avenues leading to human-specific forms of bonding.

Considering the most substantial capacities that may have differentiated humans from all other mammalian species and proved most effective as means of evolutionary adaptation, von Bertalanffy (1968) has drawn attention to the capacity of using representational symbols that stand for real objects, subjects, or events but can be created by every individual freely and independently of biological or physical determinants. Such symbols enable internal mental operations to communicate with external realities independently of physical or any other constraints and thus facilitate intended physical operations with them. In this symbolic capacity, humankind has gained the primary basis for verbal communication, internal representation, rational thinking, self-consciousness, and a high level of moral and cultural values.

Speaking of the significance of symbolic capacities for the emergence of human culture, von Bertalanffy warned that, due to their independence of evolutionary laws, they can develop in problematic directions and lead to dangerous consequences. For example, humans, in contrast to all other animals, are capable of committing suicides or murders and organizing wars or extinction of other species for mere symbolic, biologically meaningless values of their culture.

Although the significance of von Bertalanffy's arguments is undeniable, the development of symbolic capacities, the first levels of which appear during early infancy, and the effects of environmental factors on them have remained insufficiently investigated. In spite of concentrated efforts, neuroscientists have not yet been able to identify brain structures or humoral factors of consciousness in representational symbols (Gazzaniga, 1995). Perhaps, in terms of the theory of dynamic systems, they may per exclusion come to the conclusion that it is the complexity of multimodal and multidimensional experience that leads to the emergence of new functional qualities, including consciousness. However, since the per exclusion way is far from easy, an interdisciplinary attention to the earliest forms of symbolic capacities could provide supportive evidence as in several cases in the past.

The neuroscientists' increased interest in conscious regulation of human behavior has also brought about evidence that many everyday decisions in humans occur on the nonconscious level rather than on the basis of rational, fully conscious mental processes (Gazzaniga, 1995).

Developmental neurologists and neurophysiologists have come to the conclusion that even the first year of infancy is to be viewed as a phasic developmental process, characterized by periods of distinct transformations in the modularity of the central nervous system and by corresponding shifts in the development of observable behaviors or experimentally detectable integrative capacities. As explained in the next section of this chapter, infants' caregivers do not miss these observable shifts but respond, albeit unaware, with adaptive, phasic shifts in intuitive forms of parental caregiving. The intimate interplay between phases in either infantile competencies or their intuitive parental support are best interpretable as an outcome of a coevolution of predispositions for the development of species-specific and particularly effective means of adaptation (Papoušek & Papoušek, 1991). Probably due to their nonconscious character, such interpretation had long remained unconsidered in concepts of early human development.

Consequently, the contemporary views on intrinsic motivational, sociobiological, sociocultural, and contextual factors of early human development offer interpretations that evidently contradict premises of former, for instance, psychodynamic theories or remind of missing aspects in other, for example, behavioristic or emotionalistic theories. With respect to further potential discoveries, it seems advisable in general to keep theoretical concepts open-ended and revise them periodically in relation to the interdisciplinary progress in sciences.

In this chapter, the reader's attention is concentrated on the role of intuitive forms of caregiving in the infant's mental development and health and interactional disorders that are often associated with failures in intuitive parenting that may begin as in-

conspicuous deviations and yet lead to serious disturbances that might have been prevented with early therapeutic interventions.

Intuitive Forms of Parental Rearing

Extensive experimental research beginning in the 1960s has elucidated a complex mental competence of human infants (for survey see Sameroff & Cavanaugh, 1979; Harris, 1983). They are capable of processing informational input, for instance, maternal voice (DeCasper & Fifer, 1980), as early as during the later months of intrauterine life. Since the earliest postpartum months, they show not only simple forms of learning, but also intentional and goal-directed forms of instrumental acts (Papoušek, 1967). At the age of three to four months, infants are capable of detecting rules in environmental events, conceptualizing them under the given contextual conditions, and accordingly adjusting their behaviors (Papoušek & Bernstein, 1969). Similarly, they can process preverbal categorical messages in infant-directed speech (Papoušek, Bornstein, Nuzzo, Papoušek, & Symmes, 1990). Before they reach the age of one year, most of them become confronted with the first culture-dependent representational symbols: They learn the first words. Thus, the human infant, who used to be considered altricial due to slow locomotor development, achieves the prestige of precocity among other mammals in terms of symbolic capacities (Papoušek & Papoušek, 1989).

However, the discovery of infant mental competence has also raised puzzling questions. What does laboratory performance mean in everyday family situations where parents, according to interviews or questionnaires, are unaware of infant competencies and their potential benefits to rearing practices? Particularly striking was parental inability to explain whether or how they might support speech acquisition in their infants. For some time, the infant's predispositions for the use of representational symbols—the crucial criterion of humankind according to von Bertalanffy (see the preceding section)—seemed to miss any systematic social support, no matter how unusual this circumstance might be from the viewpoint of comparative biology.

Conversely, researchers of infant integrative capacities were aware of the fact that they—almost like teachers—had to follow some didactic principles in order to conduct experiments successfully. For instance, they had to select or with adequate interventions induce optimal behavioral/emotional states in infants for the sake of their successful coping with learning tasks. In experiments applying successive series of various learning tasks, a sequence of easy tasks preceding more difficult tasks significantly facilitated the rate of coping with difficult tasks (Papoušek & Papoušek, 1989).

With this in mind, I spent two years observing and audiovisually recording parent-infant interactions in German families in order to find out whether and how frequently spontaneous learning situations occur under everyday life conditions. I concluded that some learning situations occasionally appear dependent on physical events in the infant's environment, in contrast to an abundant number of learning situations regularly associated with caregiver-infant interactions (Papoušek & Papoušek, 1977, 1984).

Moreover, caregivers appeared to arrange supportive interventions rather systematically and in accordance with the infant's momentary progress in development. However, focused interviews revealed that caregivers were unaware of their capacity to specifically and didactically support infants' mental development. In later analyses of latent periods in parental responses to infant cue signals (Papoušek & Papoušek, 1992), parents were shown to respond within 200 to 400 milliseconds in some cases, although a minimum of 500 milliseconds of uninterrupted stimulation of the brain cortex is necessary for a mere conscious perception, according to Vander, Sherman, and Luciano (1990).

Because of the human specific capacity for representational symbolization, particular attention was then paid to the significance of intuitive parenting for the infant's communicative and integrative abilities (Papoušek, 1992, 1994a; see also M. Papoušek's Chapter 11 in Volume 4; Papoušek & Papoušek, 1982, 1987). With an increasing clarity, intuitive parenting, initially outlined at the World Congress of Ethology in 1977 (Papoušek & Papoušek, 1978), has emerged as a modular subsystem in the regulation of caregiving behaviors in humans subserving crucial aspects of the care for progeny.

Primarily, intuitive interventions enable parents and caregivers, in general, to support the development of symbolic capacities, representational thinking, and verbal communication, in particular during infancy, and seem to be elicited by specific infant cues, such as the babyish appearance of infants under one year of age. According to recent reports, infant-directed forms of intuitive parenting also function in interactions with older children who have already lost babyish features but have not yet proceeded in communication beyond preverbal forms (Papoušek, Rothaug, & Flehmig, April 1995), or temporarily lost the ability to speak, for example, in case of an apallic syndrome (Rodny, 1998).

The intuitive support of the development of symbolic capacities is embedded in a set of intuitive behaviors serving more general purposes in caregiving, such as interventions related to the infant's general behavioral/emotional state and its circadian cycling (feeding schedule, rituals of sleeping habits, smooth transitions between active waking and quiet sleep that avoid transitional periods of fussing and upsetness) or short fluctuations (soothing, removing causes of discomfort, activating and maintaining attention). While doing so, caregivers follow cue signals coming with infants' vocal or nonvocal behaviors. In infants under two months of age whose vocal and bodily displays are not yet sufficiently expressive, caregivers attempt to elicit observable signals on their own, for example, by testing the infant's muscle tone in the perioral or hand areas (for detailed descriptions of the intuitive repertoire, see Papoušek & Papoušek, 1987).

In analyses of caregivers' intuitive repertoire concerning the beginning of symbolization that are based not only on a longitudinal study of preverbal vocalization (Papoušek, Papoušek, & Bornstein, 1985; Papoušek, 1994a), but also on a rich literature of caregivers' infant-directed speech (Ferguson, 1964; Fernald, 1992; Remick, 1976; Snow, 1972), it has become evident how systematically and didactically parents (mothers, in most studies) lead infants in a steplike process toward symbolization and speech acquisition.

During the first six to eight postpartum weeks, the newborn successfully copes with the transition from intrauterine to extrauterine environment, a revolution surpassing the extent of environmental oscillations to a degree that could be fatal to adults. The neonatal organism, preoccupied with complex reorganization of regulatory processes related to metabolism, oxygen and water supply, chronobiologically adjusts to the night/day cyclicity in the environment, while the immune system is coping with the microbial invasion of skin, mucous membranes, and gastrointestinal tract. Thus, merely limited reserves and waking time are left for involvement in social interchanges and play.

The newborn is provided with innate predispositions for the development of language-related structures in the neocortex. However, the neocortex is exposed to considerable risks during labor, and thus, it may have been adaptive during evolution to postpone structural differentiation and retain plasticity for reorganizing language-related structures in case some of them have been damaged. Such a remarkable plasticity is available only to very young organisms. Moreover, the postponement of verbal competence brings about the possibility of tuning the corresponding structures to the specific characteristics of the infant's cultural environment as evident in studies on perceptual-motor mapping of speech in the brain (Kuhl & Meltzoff, 1996).

Unlike other primates, human parents strongly tend to imitate infants' facial and vocal displays. They are the first to imitate; as evident in parent-newborn interactions, they encourage infants in various ways for imitating, reward imitations with expressions of pleasure, and simultaneously offer models for improving the displays in the direction of further steps in the process of speech acquisition (Papoušek & Papoušek, 1987). Because parental imitation is also contingent on infant behavior, imitative interchanges may act as early opportunities for infants to learn controlling contingent events.

Newborns' and young infants' capacity of imitating has been studied in relation to facial or manual behaviors with no participation of auditory signals (Field, Woodson, Greenberg, & Cohen, 1982; Maratos, 1973; Meltzoff & Moore, 1977). Vocal imitation allows comparing the product of imitation with the model sound and thus concerns the development of perceptual, integrative, and communicative processes concurrently and mostly in combination with pleasant, mutually rewarding emotional experience (Papoušek & Papoušek, 1987). Obviously, dialogic interchanges rather early and with an increasing complexity activate neuronal subsystems in various directions.

The crucial minimum of communicative capacities that allows the caregiver to locate, identify, and help the newborn involves neonatal crying. It is vital to and universal among all mammals (Newman & Goedeking, 1992) and safely organized from low parts of the brain stem that are less vulnerable than the cortex. Acoustic features of crying function as a powerful means of personal identification (Gustafson, Green, & Cleland, 1994) but do not leave enough freedom for expressions of the infant's motivational states (Green, Gustafson, Irwin, Kalinowski, & Wood, 1995).

However, human newborns are unique in having parents who have evolved to experts in metacommunication and can communicate even with nonhuman species. Whether the newborn intends to express something is not as important as the caregiver's supreme effort to detect information in neonatal behavior and establish a dialogue, wherein they perceive cry acoustics in unity with dynamic parameters and context (Hadjistavropoulos, Craig, Grunau, & Johnston, 1994) and interpret even nonvocal forms of the infant's behavior as intentional communicative feedback (Papoušek & Papoušek, 1987). Such holistic constellations seem to characterize preverbal parent-infant communication in general.

In its earliest postpartum forms, human crying is part of autonomic or vagal self-regulation. Soon, however, crying may become intentional, due to operant or instrumental conditioning, if it repeatedly elicits contingent responses from the caregiver. In addition to the primary, tonic form of crying, a new, purposeful form develops at approximately the age of seven months, and the dynamic parameters of crying acquire the phasic character of intentional communication signals (Papoušek, Papoušek, & Koester, 1986) prior to the appearance of the first word.

Prior to eight weeks, the initial, quiet vocal sounds merely appear as isolated utterances without differentiated spectrographic patterning. The newborn is unable to prolong expiration for the sake of noncry vocalizations. Pattern-like vocalizations are caused by the rhythm of respiration that changes with the infant's behavioral state and is passively subordinated to ongoing activities. The limited modulation of acoustic parameters in crying is caused by a high and prominent position of larynx, particularly the entrance to air passage, in the throat. This position facilitates proper coordination of sucking, swallowing, and breathing without suffocation during breast-feeding (Bu'Lock, Woolridge, & Baum, 1990). The newborn masters this coordination with a competence unparalleled in older subjects. However, too little resonance space is left for voiced sounds between the larynx and the cranial base (Lieberman, 1984).

At the time when newborns cannot even prolongate breathing for quiet noncry vocalizations, parental guidance is based on the display of strikingly prolonged vowels in infant-directed speech and expressive signs of pleasure rewarding the infant for imitation of the displayed models. The exaggerated display of vowels also seems to help infants setting the mind for prototypical sounds of their culture, a perceptual process that has been demonstrated in preverbal infants by Kuhl (1983) in relation to her concept of "native language magnets"

involved in perceptual-motor mapping of speech in the brain (Kuhl & Meltzoff, 1996). The delay in infant walking maximizes the probability of face-to-face interactions during which parents can display models for sound production and infants can imitate and learn them. The delay may have been selected for the merit of an early head start in speech acquisition (Papoušek & Papoušek, 1992) with which no other animal can compete.

At the age of two months, the resonance space increases, allowing for a larger heterogeneity of spectrographic parameters in voice, the control of breathing improves, and the coordination of specific tongue movements changes (Eishima, 1991) within a major transformation of brain functions (Prechtl, 1984). Prolonged sounds are indicative of the first variations, and facial expressions indicate signs of interest and/or pleasure that have been noted by most observers as features of vocal play (Lewis, 1975; Stark, 1980; Wolff, 1969). In fact, a considerable proportion of early mother-infant vocal interchanges seem to serve no other purpose than having an obvious pleasure of coactivities, mutual duetting, reciprocal alternations in quasi-dialogues, or mutual imitations.

At the age of two to three months, learning of goal-directed movements distinctly accelerates (Papoušek, 1977), and affective facial displays accompanying the course of learning or problem-solving become more expressive (Papoušek, 1967). The caregivers can more easily read feedback cues in facial expressions and hand gestures—the two areas predisposed in primates for nonvocal communication—

that indicate how far the infant processes interactional experience. The content of caregivers' comments in infant-directed speech suggests that caregivers start viewing the infant as a competent social partner. Infants who, as newborns, have been able to imitate only oral activities and facial expressions start imitating vocal sounds. Interactions between caregivers and infants increasingly acquire a dialogic character (Papoušek, 1994b).

Pitch contours that are rather monotonous in caregivers' adult-directed speech and serve mainly syntactic purposes (giving a sentence the character of statement, question, warning, etc.) fulfill a different role in caregivers' infant-directed speech. They are strikingly expanded independently of lexicon or syntax. Their acoustic properties and the modes in which they are displayed (repetitiveness, slow tempo, contingency on infant behaviors) may help the infant to detect, categorize, and abstract elementary holistic units in the flow of speech. They also seem to represent language-independent sources of information (Bolinger, 1989; Crystal, 1986; Papoušek & Papoušek, 1981; Papoušek, 1994b). Interactional analyses in German mother-infant dyads revealed significant form-function relations between particular categories of melodic contours in six out of eight interactional contexts under investigation. Analogous results of analyses in American and Mandarin Chinese dyads indicate cross-cultural universality of contour-context relations (Papoušek, Papoušek, & Symmes, 1991) and confirm anew that melodic contours may function as both the earliest categorical messages (Papoušek, Papoušek, &

Bornstein, 1985) and the means of didactic guidance, for example, in the sense of encouraging or discouraging messages.

The effect of such guidance was demonstrated in four-month-olds in an infant-controlled auditory preference study. Infants appropriately responded to a contrastive pair of approving/disapproving bell-shaped contours, looked longer at one of two identical slides associated with an approving contour, and reduced their looking behavior at the slide associated with a disapproving contour (Papoušek, Bornstein, Nuzzo, Papoušek, & Symmes, 1990).

Between three and six months of age, vocal imitation is increasingly incorporated in nursery games initiated by mothers and in infants' vocal play (Pawlby, 1977; Uzgiris, 1984). Such complex engagement has much in common with interpretations of the roles of imitation and play in cognitive development (Harkins, & Uzgiris, 1991; Piaget, 1962; Uzgiris, 1989). The reciprocal nature of imitative sequences indicates that each partner can take either modeling or matching turns in vocal dialogues. Between two and five months of age, infants have been experimentally shown to proceed from sporadic to systematic or quasi-intentional imitation of sounds corresponding to the infant's repertoire (Piaget, 1962; Uzgiris, 1981; Uzgiris, Benson, Kruper, & Vasek, 1989) and imitate absolute pitch (Kessen, Levine, & Wendrich, 1979) as well as, occasionally, vowels or melodic patterns (Kuhl & Meltzoff, 1982; Legerstee, 1990). At the age of five months, they can imitate the vowel sounds "a" (uh), "i" (ee), and "u" (oo; Kuhl & Meltzoff, 1996).

During the second trimester, the first precursors of consonants appear in the infant's vocalization, and the parent responds in two distinct ways: first, with displaying adequate models of consonants, alluring the infant into their imitations, and rewarding the imitations, and second, with introduction of rhythmic games into the repertoire of interchanges. The infant learns to segment expiration so as to produce several consecutive syllables within one breath.

A detailed analysis of rhythms occurring in maternal interactions with three-month-old infants (Koester, Papoušek, & Papoušek, 1989) has revealed a high frequency of rhythmical patterns (occupying 48.3 percent of three-minute interactions) and a variability of rhythms that is independent of any inherent pacemaker but reflects the ongoing dynamics of the interaction and the type of movements involved. Their average rhythm is 2.64 bps and is thus comparable to the rhythm of the infant's canonical syllables appearing at approximately seven months of age. According to Kelso, Tuller, and Harris (1983) or Oller and Eilers (1992), the "minimal rhythmic units" in nursery games, fingertapping, or syllables in various languages are remarkably similar, apparently due to general human timing tendencies (Turner, 1985).

From seven months of age on, discrete patterns become evident in repetitive babbling, and melodic variations are superimposed upon these patterns. These variations may often be interrupted or may end with laughter or joyful squeals. The significant increase in the frequency of similar expressions has been shown in a detailed analysis of the development of emotionality by Papoušek, Papoušek, and Koester (1986). Infants' intrinsic motivation for vocal performances is clearly observable both in signs of pleasure accompanying vocal interchanges with partners and/or in the increasing amount of time spent in vocal monologues by waking infants in the absence of social partners.

In a long-term analysis of vocal interchanges between infants and mothers, Papoušek (1994a) found that such rhythmical games appear in the repertoire of maternal interventions at three months of age, culminate at seven months of age, and then gradually decrease in frequency at the end of the first year (Figure 10.1). The peak overlaps with the beginning of reduplicated, canonical syllables as if the use of rhythmical games were to support the infant's ability to segment breath in this particular rhythm.

The distinct and striking new element in the vocal expertise of seven-month-old infants—reduplicated syllables—coincides with a new didactic strategy in parents. Parents utilize each pair of canonical syllables as a potential protoword, assign it a lexical meaning, and start teaching the infant to associate it with the corresponding informational content (Papoušek & Papoušek, 1981; Papoušek, 1994a). This turning point marks the transition from procedural to declarative aspects of symbolic representation.

One or two months later, the infant becomes capable of combining unequal syllables in one word and learning regular words, which represents a crucial step in the direction of cultural integration. On

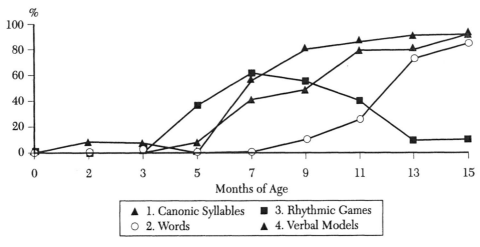

FIGURE 10.1

Transition from Procedural to Declarative Integration of Interactional Experience
Infants' Phonetic and Linguistic Competence: 1st canonic syllables; 2nd words
Maternal Didactic Interventions: 3rd rhythmical games; 4th verbal models.

From M. Papoušek (1994a). Vom ersten Schrei zum ersten Wort; Anfänge der Sprachentwicklung in der Vorsprachlichen Kommunikation (pp. 89–90). Bern: Huber.

the infant's side, the appearance of reduplicated, canonical syllables occurs simultaneously with other symptoms indicating a progress in the functioning of the speech-dominant hemisphere (de Schonen & Mathivet, 1989). On the parental side, the new intervening strategy is a part of intuitive parenting. Thus, the avenue leading to cultural integration seems to be paved with biological predispositions and influenced by coevolution of interplaying determinants on both infantile and parental sides.

The biological origins of intuitive parenting are not easy to prove. The use of social isolation allowing a direct experimental evidence of innateness of concerned behaviors in laboratory animals is not thinkable in studies of humans. Genetic screening in human subjects lacking capacities for intuitive parenting has not yet been reported, according to the evidence. Therefore, concepts depend on indirect pieces of evidence (Papoušek & Papoušek, 1987), such as:

1. Functional involvement of the concerned behavioral patterns in species-specific means of evolutionary adaptation.
2. High probability of occurrence in response to cue elicitors or within given interactional contexts.
3. Universality of the pattern across sex, age, culture, or species.
4. Early emergence during ontogeny.
5. Minimal awareness and rational control of the given behavioral pattern in subjects carrying out the pattern.

6. Coevolution of counterparts to the pattern in conspecifics.
7. Presence of the pattern in cases where environmental influence was for some reason seriously restricted or eliminated.
8. Conceptual integrity in best-fitting interpretations of determinants of the given pattern with respect to other functionally interrelated behavioral patterns.

The deeper the evolutionary roots of intuitive parenting may reach, the more powerful may be the intrinsic motivation related to it, and the more attention should be paid to this motivation in interpretations of infant needs or in clinical considerations on pathogenetic factors of early behavioral disorders. In the many recommendations for parents, integrative and communicative needs of infants have seldom found a place next to hygienic and emotional needs. Similarly, insufficient satiation of these needs only gradually finds recognition in the list of factors causing deviations in infant mental health.

Pathogenetic Significance of Interactional Disorders

In infants involved in long-term investigations on integrative abilities (Papoušek, 1967), observed participation of emotional behaviors indicated that the need to accumulate and integrate experience with environmental events was based on a strong intrinsic motivation. Infants showed a distinct pleasure on successful coping with experimental tasks and just as evident frustration, fussiness, and rejective behaviors in cases of difficult coping or violation of expectancies. Infants younger than two months tended to answer such frustrating situations with a sudden change of behavioral state in the form of "playing possum"—motionless and unresponsive state with slow heart rate and slow, regular breathing like in sleep but with widely open eyes without convergence (staring) for 20 to 30 seconds. Hopkins and van Wulften Palthe (1985) confirmed that similar patterns occur under comparable conditions in infants reared at home.

Infants older than two or three months of age responded to similar frustrating situations with more dynamic changes in behavior. Four phases could typically be differentiated: (1) signs of surprise and attentive observation, (2) attempts to regain the lost control over environment (social, in particular) with the help of activated or, eventually, overactivated behavioral patterns (facial displays and hand gestures, in particular) that used to affect the environment before, (3) signs of frustration and disappointment, and (4) depressed mood, turning away (reminding of "learned helplessness"), or during social interactions, rejection of the partner, the mother included.

Rather dramatic examples of such phasic changes in the behavior of four-month-olds were observed in experimental situations where mothers were repeatedly leaving infants for short periods of time while they were experimentally prevented from displaying their typical farewell rituals (Papoušek & Papoušek, 1975). Infants tolerated repeated absences of their mothers as long as mothers were allowed to use their farewell rituals, but otherwise, they started refusing mothers with protest crying after three or four trials. Mothers found infantile rejections very annoying, although infants calmed down in a few minutes after the end of experiments.

From the aforementioned experimental and corresponding clinical observations (see also M. Papoušek's Chapter 11 in Volume 4) we attempted to form a concept regarding the participation of interactional processes in the pathogeny of mental disorders in any of the interacting partners (Figure 10.2, according to Papoušek & Papoušek, 1979). As in all living organisms, social interactions between human parents and infants are embedded in variable physical and organic environments creating mutually beneficial circumstances in some cases and antagonistic circumstances in others.

The same may be true about interrelationships between parents and infants. In their interactions, a strong biological motivation for the survival of the species may be confronted with an equally important sociocultural motivation favoring family interests or individual achievements. As long as no disturbing deviations interfere, parent-infant interactions function as reliable sources of human happiness and may facilitate both partners' successful coping with adverse organic or social phenomena (the compensatory circuit in Figure 10.2). However, in the sense of the dynamic systems theory, even an inconspicuous deviation may disturb the course of parent-infant interactions and cause a switch in the direction of increasing difficulties in either the course of the interactions or in coping with adverse environmental conditions (the vicious circle in Figure 10.2).

An assumption that, due to biological determination, intuitive forms of parent-

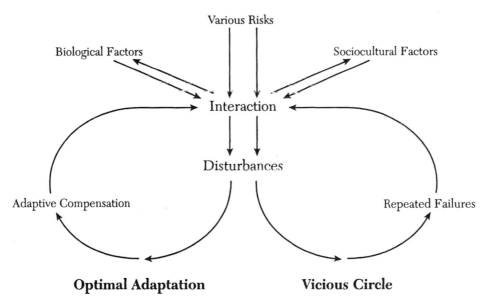

Optimal Adaptation   **Vicious Circle**

FIGURE 10.2
Course of mother-infant interactions

ing are particularly resistant against disturbances contradicts clinical experience. They may belong to relatively young phenomena in evolutionary terms and, therefore, be fragile. According to clinical experience, they require certain conditions to function successfully. For example, according to Bastick (1982), their functioning depends on a cultural and intimate social atmosphere, the immediate situation, and, particularly, a relaxed, stress-free state of mind. However, these fundamental requirements have been heavily violated by present sociocultural conditions.

Under the influence of various theoretical speculations, mothers have been burdened with exclusive responsibility for the infant's proper development without being advised or supported in coping with the burden. The increasing number of fatherless families living under adverse conditions with no available help from grandparents or neighbors and no adequate accommodation has often been associated with problematic and conflicting attempts to manipulate parenthood rationally: one trying to prevent overpopulation and the other prohibiting contraception. Consequently, women's identification with the maternal role has become increasingly questionable. Conversely, frequent juvenile motherhood indicates a lack of education concerning parental roles.

Bastick (1982) also reported on the adverse effect of exaggerated rational guidance on the functioning of intuitive behaviors. This effect is exemplified by the flood of unverified recommendations for infant rearing from commercial agencies. Generally, the contemporary sociocultural situation includes many risk factors that can dangerously inhibit intuitive parenting.

As explained earlier in this chapter, intuitive parental interventions result from a dialogic communication between parents and infants. This communication suffers if the expressivity of vocal or body signals is diminished on any side: in infants, due to muscle hypotonia or hypertonia due to birth complications; in mothers, for example, due to postpartum depression; and in fathers, due to initial absence or inability to spend a sufficient amount of time with the newborn and learn profiting from innate parental predispositions for communication with infants. Perinatal complications often raise the infant's perceptual thresholds and thus reduce infant responsivity to parental stimulation. Occasionally, a parent may be misled by the infant's sick appearance and may carefully use such a low voice, tactile or proprioceptive stimulation that the infant cannot perceive and answer them. The resulting mismatch between infant needs and parental tendencies may jeopardize the development of communication and lead to an interactional failure (Papoušek, Rothaug, & Flehmig, April, 1995).

Insofar as similar unfavorable factors often accumulate, the complex system of dynamic interrelationships suggested in Figure 10.2 can frequently deviate in the direction of vicious circles and lead to serious consequences. For example, an unwanted pregnancy frequently occurs with parental alcoholism, marital problems, and additional difficulties in the social environment, as pointed out by Papoušek and Papoušek (1992). The resulting stress can lead to deficient intrauterine development of the fetus, perinatal complications, and/or various deviations in infant behaviors. The intuitive parental predispositions that develop and become adjusted to each individual infant by additional learning, under normal conditions, are inhibited instead, due to accumulation of unfavorable circumstances. The mother may then be unable to establish satisfactory communication with the infant, misses the rewarding emotional experience, and finds no support in her social environment. Additional difficulties come with the infant's increased frequency of crying, sleep or feeding disorders, and superimposed infections. Such a vicious circle can lead to child abuse, maternal rejection, or disorders in infant mental health.

For practical reasons, Papoušek and Papoušek (1992, p. 51) divided the most frequent forms of disorders that can threaten infant mental health and are interrelated to intuitive parenting into the following categories:

1. Missed experience in initial communication. For various reasons, one or both parents miss the first chance of interacting with the infant and orchestrating intuitive predispositions for parenting in accordance with the newborn's individuality. Fathers, in particular, may be absent and find no early chance for interactions with infants. Mothers may be separated from newborns due to perinatal complications. Premature newborns are sometimes isolated due to intensive medical care. Similar situations may arise if parents adopt an older in-

fant. In such cases, a lack of mutual adjustment and development of communicative predispositions may cause communicative difficulties that most parents overcome. However, some parents may be discouraged by initial failures, particularly if infants keep answering them as strangers.

2. Initial discouragement due to infant handicaps. Postpartum complications, such as muscular hypotonia or hyperbilirubinemic hypersomnia, may temporarily decrease infant responsivity and communicative expressiveness. Prior to infant recovery, unsuccessful parental attempts to initiate interchanges and absent or deviant feedback signals from the infant may inhibit intuitive predispositions for communication in parents. Parents then may fail to be effective interactive partners at the time when the infant recovers and might be capable of his or her first interchanges.

3. Mismatch between parental and infantile predispositions. In some cases, parental predispositions, adaptive under other conditions, may be inappropriate and cause communicative failures. For instance, an infant's perceptual thresholds may be elevated due to various nervous system disorders. Although this infant would still respond to stimuli of increased intensity, a parent's impression of being confronted with a sick and fragile infant may lead to the use of careful and tender stimulation that is too weak for the infant to perceive. A thorough assessment of partial nervous handicaps helps disclose the

reasons for mismatch and suggests appropriate forms of therapy.

4. Major prolongation in the need for preverbal forms of communication. Some children, retarded children in particular, have difficulty acquiring speech during the first several years. During that time period, they lose the features of babyishness that elicit intuitive support to speech acquisition. These children still need the kind of support parents give to preverbal infants, but the elicitors of preverbal support are no longer present. The parents' original competence may have been inhibited due to frustrations of previous efforts.

Conclusion

Thus far, clinical experience together with valuable contributions from several centers, particularly the Child Development Center in Hamburg (Dr. Inge Flehmig, director), the Rehabilitation Center in Landstuhl/Pfalz (Dr. Andreas Fröhlich, director), and the Child Center of the Maximilian University in Munich, Department of Social Pediatrics (Dr. Hubertus von Voss, director, successor to Dr. Theodor Hellbrügge), have confirmed the relevance of attention paid to the participation of intuitive parenting in both the pathogeny or the prevention of disorders in infant mental development and health. With respect to further clinical application, a few recommendations are mentioned.

First, a careful assessment of the preverbal communication between the infant and the caregiver, the mother in particular, should be part of the diagnostic tools as it is a sensitive indicator of the functionality of the aforementioned forms of intuitive caregiving. Direct observations of interacting partners can hardly be replaced by fast and simple tests.

Second, preventive care for the proper development of communication as well as therapy for detected communicative disorders should be part of the regular therapeutic plan, including careful guidance with respect to preverbal parent-infant interactions.

Third, it is important to understand that intuitive parental support for infant development is based on nonconscious interventions that cannot be entirely controlled by rational decisions. Therefore, the parent will not be helped by detailed recommendations of interactional behavioral patterns that should be used in individual interactional contexts. However, the parent can be encouraged to establish convenient situations for stress-free dialogues and play with the infant. Once the interchange begins, the first signs of attention and responsivity from the infant can prime intuitive predispositions in the parent for further interchanges. The intentional start may thus open a way for unintentional, intuitive interchanges whereby the parent may regain self-confidence and motivation for further interactions while the infant perceives the necessary communicative experience. The first perceived success may then motivate both partners for further attempts.

Better understanding of nonconscious behavioral regulations has sharpened attention to biological origins of human behavior. Modern cultures have often misinterpreted and underestimated their significance, considering some of them to be outdated evolutionary relics in behavioral tendencies. However, as to intuitive parenting, the presently high frequency of failures in early social interactions indicates how risky it might be to disregard those predispositions that have been selected for the sake of our progeny during thousands of generations and try to replace them with unverified rational recommendations.

References

Bastick, T. (1982). *Intuition: How we think and act.* New York: Wiley.

Blass, E. M., & Ciaramitaro, V. (1994). A new look at some old mechanisms in human newborns: Taste and tactile determinants of state, affect, and action. *Monographs of the Society for Research in Child Development, 59*(1), Serial No. 239.

Bolinger, D. (1989). *Intonation and its uses.* Stanford, CA: Stanford University Press.

Bu'Lock, F., Woolridge, M. W., & Baum, J. D. (1990). Development of co-ordination of sucking, swallowing and breathing: Ultrasound study of term and preterm infants. *Developmental Medicine and Child Neurology, 32,* 669–678.

Crystal, D. (1986). Prosodic development. In P. Fletcher & M. Garman (Eds.), *Language acquisition* (pp. 174–197). Cambridge, UK: Cambridge University Press.

Cupps, T., & Fauci, A. (1982). Corticosteroid-mediated immunoregulation in man. *Immunological Review, 65,* 134–140.

DeCasper, A. J., & Fifer, W. P. (1980). Of human bonding: Newborns prefer their mothers' voices. *Science, 208,* 1174–1176.

de Schonen, S., & Mathivet, E. (1989). First come, first served: A scenario about the development of hemispheric specialization in face recognition during infancy. *Cahiers de Psychologie Cognitive, 9,* 3–44.

Eishima, K. (1991). The analysis of sucking behavior in newborn infants. *Early Human Development, 27,* 163–173.

Ferguson, C. A. (1964). Babytalk in six languages. *American Anthropologist, 66,* 103–114.

Fernald, A. (1992). Meaningful melodies in mothers' speech to infants. In H. Papoušek, U. Jürgens, & M. Papoušek (Eds.), *Nonverbal vocal communication: Comparative and developmental approaches* (pp. 262–282). New York: Cambridge University Press.

Field, T., Woodson, R., Greenberg, R., & Cohen, D. (1982). Discrimination and imitation of facial expressions by neonates. *Science, 218,* 179–181.

Gazzaniga, M. S. (1995). Consciousness and the cerebral hemispheres. In M. S. Gazzaniga (Ed.), *The cognitive neurosciences* (pp. 1391–1400). Cambridge, MA: MIT Press.

Green, J. A., Gustafson, G. E., Irwin, J. R., Kalinowski, L. L., & Wood, R. M. (1995). Infant crying: Acoustics, perception and communication. In R. G. Barr (Ed.), Crying in context. *Early Development and Parenting, 4*(4), 161–175.

Gustafson, G. E., Green, J. A., & Cleland, J. W. (1994). Robustness of individual identity in the cries of human infants. *Developmental Psychobiology, 27,* 1–9.

Hadjistavropoulos, H. D., Craig, K. D., Grunau, R. V. E., & Johnston, C. C.

(1994). Judging pain in newborns: Facial and cry determinants. *Journal of Pediatric Psychology, 19,* 485–491.

Harkins, D. A., & Uzgiris, I. C. (1991). Hand-use matching between mothers and infants during the first year. *Infant Behavior and Development, 14,* 289–298.

Harris, P. L. (1983). Infant cognition. In M. Haith & J. J. Campos (Eds.), Infancy and developmental psychobiology (pp. 689–782). In P. H. Mussen (Gen. Ed.), *Handbook of child psychology* (Vol 2). New York: Wiley.

Hopkins, B., & van Wulften Palthe, T. (1985). Staring in infancy. *Early Human Development, 12,* 261–267.

Kelso, J. A. S., Tuller, B., & Harris, K. S. (1983). A dynamic pattern perspective on the control and coordination of movement. In P. F. MacNeilage (Ed.), *The production of speech* (pp. 137–173). New York: Springer.

Kessen, W., Levine, J., & Wendrich, K. (1979). The imitation of pitch in infants. *Infant Behavior and Development, 2,* 93–99.

Koester, L. S., Papoušek, H., & Papoušek, M. (1989). Patterns of rhythmic stimulation by mothers with three-month-olds: A cross-modal comparison. *International Journal of Behavioural Development, 12,* 143–154.

Kuhl, P. K. (1983). Perception of auditory equivalence classes for speech in early infancy. *Infant Behavior and Development, 6,* 263–285.

Kuhl, P. K., & Meltzoff, A. N. (1982). The bimodal perception of speech in infancy. *Science, 218,* 1138–1141.

Kuhl, P. K., & Meltzoff, A. N. (1996). Infant vocalizations in response to speech: Vocal imitation and developmental change. *Journal of Acoustical Society of America, 100*(4), 2425–2438.

Ledoux, J. E. (1995). In search of an emotional system in the brain: Leaping from fear to emotion and consciousness. In M. S. Gazzaniga (Ed.), *The cognitive neurosciences* (pp. 1049–1061). Cambridge, MA: MIT Press.

Legerstee, M. (1990). Infants use multimodal information to imitate speech sounds. *Infant Behavior and Development, 13,* 343–354.

Lewis, M. M. (1975). *Infant speech: A study of the beginnings of language.* New York: Arno Press.

Lieberman, P. (1984). *The biology and evolution of language.* Cambridge, MA: Harvard University Press.

Maratos, O. (1973). *The origin and development of imitation in the first six months of life.* Unpublished doctoral dissertation, University of Geneva.

McEwen, B. S., & Stellar, E. (1993). Stress and the individual: Mechanisms leading to disease. *Archives of Internal Medicine, 153,* 2093–2101.

Meltzoff, A. N., & Moore, M. K. (1977). Imitation of facial and manual gestures by human neonates. *Science, 198,* 75–78.

Newman, J. D., & Goedeking, P. (1992). Noncategorical vocal communication in primates: The example of common marmoset phee calls. In H. Papoušek, U. Jürgens, & M. Papoušek (Eds.), *Nonverbal vocal communication: Comparative and developmental approaches* (pp. 87–101). Cambridge, UK: Cambridge University Press.

Oller, D. K., & Eilers, R. E. (1992). Development of vocal signaling in human infants: Toward a methodology for cross-species vocalization comparisons. In H. Papoušek, U. Jürgens, & M. Papoušek (Eds.), *Nonverbal vocal communication: Comparative and developmental approaches* (pp. 174–191). Cambridge, UK: Cambridge University Press.

Papoušek, H. (1967). Experimental studies of appetitional behavior in human newborns and infants. In H. W. Stevenson, E. H. Hess, & H. L. Rheingold (Eds.), *Early behavior: Comparative and developmental approaches* (pp. 249–277). New York: Wiley.

Papoušek, H. (1969). Individual variability in learned responses during early post-natal development. In R. J. Robinson (Ed.), *Brain and early behavior: Development in the fetus and infant* (pp. 229–252). London: Academic.

Papoušek, H. (1977). Entwicklung der Lernfähigkeit im Säuglingsalter. In G. Nissen (Ed.), *Intelligenz, Lernen und Lernstörungen* (pp. 89–197). Berlin: Springer-Verlag.

Papoušek, H., & Bernstein, P. (1969). The functions of conditioning stimulation in human neonates and infants. In A. Ambrose (Ed.), *Stimulation in early infancy* (pp. 229–252). London: Academic.

Papoušek, H., & Papoušek, M. (1975). Cognitive aspects of preverbal social interaction between human infants and adults. In *Parent-Infant Interaction,* Ciba Foundation Symposium 33 (New Series), 241–260. Amsterdam: Elsevier.

Papoušek, H., & Papoušek, M. (1978). Interdisciplinary parallels in studies of early human behavior: From physical to cognitive needs, from attachment to dyadic education. *International Journal of Behavioral Development, 1,* 37–49.

Papoušek, H., & Papoušek, M. (1979). Care of the normal and high risk newborn: A psychobiological view of parental behavior. In S. Harel (Ed.), *The at risk infant.* International Congress Series No. 492 (pp. 368–371). Amsterdam: Excerpta Medica.

Papoušek, H., & Papoušek, M. (1982). Integration into the social world: Survey of research. In P. M. Stratton (Ed.), *Psychobiology of the human newborn* (pp. 367–390). London: Wiley.

Papoušek, H., & Papoušek, M. (1984). Learning and cognition in the everyday life of human infants. In J. S. Rosenblatt, C. Beer, M. C. Busnel, & P. J. B. Slater (Eds.), *Advances in the study of behavior* (Vol. 14, pp. 127–163). New York: Academic.

Papoušek, H., & Papoušek, M. (1987). Intuitive parenting: A dialectic counterpart to the infant's integrative competence. In J. D. Osofsky (Ed.), *Handbook of infant development* (2nd ed., pp. 669–720). New York: Wiley.

Papoušek, H., & Papoušek, M. (1989a). Intuitive parenting: Aspects related to educational psychology. In B. Hopkins, M. G. Pecheux, & H. Papoušek (Eds.), Infancy and education: Psychological considerations. *European Journal of Psychology of Education, 4*(2, Special Issue), 201–210.

Papoušek, H., & Papoušek, M. (1991). Innate and cultural guidance of infants' integrative competencies: China, the United States, and Germany. In M. H. Bornstein (Ed.), *Cultural approaches to parenting* (pp. 23–44). Hillsdale, NJ: Erlbaum.

Papoušek, H., & Papoušek, M. (1992). Beyond emotional bonding: The role of preverbal communication in mental growth and health. *Infant Mental Health Journal, 13,* 43–53.

Papoušek, H., Papoušek, M., & Koester, L. S. (1986). Sharing emotionality and sharing knowledge: A microanalytic approach to parent-infant communication. In C. E. Izard & P. Read (Eds.), *Measuring emotions in infants and children* (Vol. 2; pp.

93–123). Cambridge: Cambridge University Press.

Papoušek, H., Rothaug, M., & Flehmig, I. (April, 1995). The role of bodily (tactile, proprioceptive, and vestibular) communication in preverbal caregiver-infant/child interactions. Paper presented at the Biennial Meeting of the Society for Research in Child Development, Indianapolis, IN.

Papoušek, M. (1992). Early ontogeny of vocal communication in parent-infant interactions. In H. Papoušek, U. Jürgens, & M. Papoušek (Eds.), *Nonverbal vocal communication: Comparative and developmental aspects* (pp. 230–261). New York: Cambridge University Press.

Papoušek, M. (1994a). *Vom ersten Schrei zum ersten Wort: Anfänge der Sprachentwicklung in der vorsprachlichen Kommunikation* [From the first cry to the first word: The beginnings of speech development in preverbal communication]. Bern: Huber.

Papoušek, M. (1994b). Melodies in caregivers' speech: A species-specific guidance toward language. In H. Papoušek (Ed.), Intuitive parenting: Comparative and clinical approaches. *Early Development and Parenting, 3*(1), 5–17.

Papoušek, M., Bornstein, M. H., Nuzzo, C., Papoušek, H., & Symmes, D. (1990). Infant responses to prototypical melodic contours in parental speech. *Infant Behavior and Development, 13,* 539–545.

Papoušek, M., & Papoušek, H. (1981). Musical elements in the infant's vocalizations: Their significance for communication, cognition and creativity. In L. P. Lipsitt (Ed.), *Advances in infancy research* (Vol. 1, pp. 163–224). Norwood, NJ: Ablex.

Papoušek, M., & Papoušek, H. (1989b). Forms and functions of vocal matching in precanonical mother-infant interactions. *First Language, 9,* 137–158.

Papoušek, M., Papoušek, H., & Bornstein, M. H. (1985). The naturalistic vocal environment of young infants: On the significance of homogeneity and variability in parental speech. In T. Field & N. Fox (Eds.), *Social perception in infants* (pp. 269–297). Norwood, NJ: Ablex.

Papoušek, M., Papoušek, H., & Haekel, M. (1987). Didactic adjustments in fathers' and mothers' speech to their three-month-old infants. *Journal of Psycholinguistic Research, 16,* 491–516.

Papoušek, M., Papoušek, H., & Symmes, D. (1991). The meanings of melodies in motherese in tone and stress languages. *Infant Behavior and Development, 14,* 414–440.

Pawlby, S. J. (1977). Imitative interaction. In H. R. Schaffer (Ed.), *Studies in mother-infant interaction* (pp. 203–224). London: Academic.

Piaget, J. (1962). *Play, dreams, and imitation in childhood.* New York: Norton.

Prechtl, H. F. R. (1984). Continuity and change in early neural development. In H. F. R. Prechtl (Ed.), *Continuity in neural functions from prenatal to postnatal life* (pp. 1–15). Oxford: Blackwell Scientific Publications.

Remick, H. L. N. (1976). Maternal speech to children during language acquisition. In W. von Raffler-Engel & Y. Lebrun (Eds.), *Baby talk and infant speech* (pp. 223–233). Lisse, Holland: Swets & Zeitlinger.

Robinson, S. R., Arnold, H. M., Spear, N. E., & Smotherman, W. P. (1993). Experience with milk and an artificial nipple promotes conditioned opioid activity in the rat fetus. *Developmental Psychobiology, 26,* 375–387.

Rolls, E. T. (1995). A theory of emotion and consciousness and its application to understanding the neural basis of emotion.

In M. S. Gazzaniga (Ed.), *The cognitive neurosciences* (pp. 1091–1106). Cambridge, MA: MIT Press.

Sameroff, A. J., & Cavanaugh, P. J. (1979). Learning in infancy: A developmental perspective. In J. D. Osofsky (Ed.), *Handbook of infant development* (pp. 344–392). New York: Wiley.

Snow, C. E. (1972). Mothers' speech to children learning language. *Child Development, 43,* 549–565.

Stark, R. E. (1980). Stages of speech development in the first year of life. In G. H. Yeni-Komshian, J. F. Kavanagh, & C. A. Ferguson (Eds.), *Child phonology: Vol. 1. Production* (pp. 73–92). New York: Academic.

Turner, F. (1985). *Natural classicism.* New York: Paragon.

Uzgiris, I. C. (1981). Two functions of imitation during infancy. *International Journal of Behavioural Development, 4,* 1–12.

Uzgiris, I. C. (1984). Imitation in infancy: Its interpersonal aspects. In M. Perlmutter (Ed.), *The Minnesota Symposia on Child Psychology* (Vol. 17, pp. 1–32). Hillsdale, NJ: Erlbaum.

Uzgiris, I. C. (1989). Infants in relation: Performers, pupils, and partners. In W. Damon (Ed.), *Child development today and tomorrow* (pp. 288–311). San Francisco, CA: Jossey-Bass.

Uzgiris, I. C., Benson, J. B., Kruper, J. C., & Vasek, M. E. (1989). Contextual influences on imitative interactions between mothers and infants. In J. L. Lockman & N. L. Hazen (Eds.), *Action in social context: Perspectives on early development* (pp. 103–127). New York: Plenum.

Vander, A. J., Sherman, J. H., & Luciano, D. S. (1990). *Human physiology: The mechanisms of body functions* (5th ed.). New York: McGraw-Hill.

von Bertalanffy, L. (1968). *Organismic psychology theory.* Barre, MA: Clark University.

Weinberger, N. M. (1995). Retuning the brain by fear conditioning. In M. S. Gazzaniga (Ed.), *The cognitive neurosciences* (pp. 1071–1089). Cambridge, MA: MIT Press.

Wolff, P. H. (1969). The natural history of crying and other vocalizations in early infancy. In B. Foss (Ed.), *Determinants of infant behavior* (Vol. 4, pp. 81–109). London: Methuen.

11

Toward an Integrated Theory of Maternal Caregiving

Judith Solomon and Carol George

11

[Bruno Bettelheim] scoffed at the notion of a maternal instinct: "Of course there is none, otherwise there would not have been the many children who needed my professional services."

(Merkin, 1997)

When one considers what we may call the vicissitudes of mothering, including neonatal abandonment, child abuse and neglect, infanticide, and child homicide (not to mention the perennial complaints against the mother by the neurotic in the clinician's office), it is hard to argue with Bettelheim's dour conclusion. Even turning from what many would view as signs of frank pathology to the broader cross-cultural literature, the variability in caregiving is so great as to confound simple notions of a species-characteristic maternal instinct. These variations include culturally sanctioned and, in some cases, systematic abandonment of disabled or ailing infants and toddlers (Hrdy, 1992; Miller, 1987; Scheper-Hughes, 1987, 1990), nursing and provision of basic care from the earliest days of life by multiple, nonrelated caregivers (Tronick, Morelli, & Winn, 1987), and physical contact ranging from virtually continuous carrying to isolation of the swaddled infant through the first year of life (Howrigan, 1988).

Despite what appears to be nearly limitless variation in patterns of maternal care, Bornstein (1995) identified a common biological species-characteristic core of maternal functions that includes feeding, thermoregulation, protection, communication, stimulation, and affect regulation. Recently, we have attempted to articulate a framework for understanding the organization of maternal caregiving (George & Solomon, 1996, 1999; in press, Solomon & George, 1996). This framework takes as its starting point Bowlby's provocative, but relatively undeveloped, hypothesis that there exists within the mother a caregiving behavioral system that is reciprocal to the attachment behavioral system within the infant (Bowlby 1969/1982, 1973). It is derived directly from ethological analysis of behavior systems and draws upon and attempts to integrate data from attachment theory, clinical and developmental psychology, evolutionary biology, comparative and biological psychology, anthropology, and our own study of caregivers in normative and high-risk samples (George, 1989; George & Solomon, 1996; Solomon & George, 1999, in press-a) The purpose of this chapter is to summarize and extend this thinking in ways that may be helpful to the field of infant mental health.

What is the value of such a model? A recent previous attempt to place maternal behavior on a biological footing, Klaus and

Kennell's theory of early maternal bonding (1976), has met with strong criticism (Lamb, 1982; Scheper-Hughes, 1987, 1990) and has in a number of studies been disconfirmed, at least in regard to long-term effects of early mother-infant interaction. The plasticity of human behavior, especially adult behavior, the multiply-determined nature of behavior at the level of proximate causality, and the well-known pitfalls of applying functional, evolutionary thinking to human psychology (Hinde, 1982b) all suggest that such an attempt is, at best, a risky enterprise.

We believe that this attempt is worthwhile, even necessary, for several reasons. First, we need to understand the mother in order to comprehend her infant's development. It is by now axiomatic that the infant must be understood in the context of his or her early relationships, indeed that social and emotional development is organized from the earliest moments by the nature and quality of relationships with primary caregivers. Although the mother is seen as pivotal in the unfolding of this relationship, interest has focused on what she does for the infant and how well she does it, but the mother herself is largely unknown.

Within the domain of attachment theory, the mother's sensitive and prompt response to infant signals has been shown to be the most important predictor of infant attachment security (Ainsworth, Blehar, Waters, & Wall, 1978; Isabella, 1993). In developmental psychology more generally, the mother's skill in promoting affect regulation in the infant and providing appropriate scaffolding and socialization have been major areas of study. In an attempt to explicate the factors that determine adequate versus inadequate mothering, psychologists have focused on variables such as socioeconomic conditions, culture, social and marital support, and the mother's psychological health and developmental history. Within the empirical equation where these variables are the input and maternal behavior and infant development are the outputs, the mother as caretaker is the proverbial black box. Little attention has been given to the psychological substrates or mechanisms that may regulate and integrate these various inputs and thereby mediate maternal behavior. We have proposed that this mediating mechanism is the caregiving system, a goal-corrected system that is organized around protection of the infant and functions in dynamic balance with other behavioral systems within the mother (George & Solomon, 1999, in press; Solomon & George, 1996). We suggest that this system, once fully organized, gives rise to the compelling motivation within the mother to respond protectively to the young infant and to buffer him or her from sources of stress and harm. We are reminded here of one mother's description of herself in our recent study of infants in divorced and separated families. Enmeshed in intense conflict with her husband, ill herself, and with a sick and therefore needy and demanding infant, she described how she studied for an exam, far into the night, with the infant cradled in one arm and her textbook in the other.

A second and related reason to focus on the caregiver is the need for greater understanding of the conditions under which the mother-infant relationship may be placed at risk. Developmental and psychoanalytic theories have placed strong, sometimes exclusive, emphasis on the mother's own attachment (object relations) history and/or on maternal psychopathology as determinants of later optimal versus deficient caregiving. There is increasing evidence, however, that contemporaneous factors, such as recent loss and miscarriage, infant disability, family violence, and high-conflict divorce predispose the dyad toward the development of troubled early relationships (Pianta, Marvin, Britner, & Borowitz, 1996; Osofsky, 1997; Pianta, Marvin, & Morog, 1999; Slade et al., 1995; Solomon & George, 1998a). Clearly, a model of caregiving and its development must take into account these factors as well as those from the past. As discussed later, our model leads us to suggest that such circumstances may be viewed as direct assaults on the caregiving system, a system that we see as developmentally linked to attachment but with its own developmental pathway and set of determinants. This view, which places the caregiving system rather than the parent's attachment system in the forefront of our understanding of maternal behavior, has clear and unique implications for both research and intervention.

The third and final reason for expanding our understanding of the caregiving system is to elucidate the caregiver's experience as a phenomenon in its own right. Parenthood is one of the most emotionally intense, potentially transforming, and long-lasting experiences of adult life. Caregiving must be viewed as one of the major goals and great achievements of adult development. Its centrality with respect to the mother's reproductive success almost certainly implies that particular elements of caregiving behavior and its overall organization have been subject to natural selection. Given its fundamental importance in human life, it is curious that so much of what psychologists have learned about the caregiver has been from the point of view of the infant and child rather than from the mother. Bettelheim's well-known disparagement of mothers stemmed, intellectually at any rate, from his stance as an advocate for the needs of the child (Merkin, 1997). Although he is one of the more controversial figures in modern child psychology, it is fair to say that his stance has been characteristic of many researchers and practioners. Putting aside the issue of what some might consider political or cultural biases in favor of the vulnerable child, it is understandable that developmentalists would focus on the needs of the developing youngster and view the mother, helpful or otherwise, as an adjunct or variable in the explanatory enterprise. The traditional focus of developmental psychology has been almost exclusively on the development of the child through adolescence. The empirical study of adult development, on the other hand, with the exception of some aspects of personality and cognitive development, continues to be the domain of life span developmental psychology, a branch of psychology that adheres to different theoretical models and, generally, does not address issues of continuity or coherence from childhood to adulthood. While the study of the caregiver from the perspective of the needs, imperatives, and development of the mother has been a minor theme in psychology, other disciplines, such as anthropology and biological and comparative psychology, have treated the mother as a focus of study. These disciplines provide divergent models and a wealth of information about parenting that, in general, have not been integrated into the developmental perspective.

Infant mental health practioners, including Bowlby (1984), Selma Fraiberg (1980), and more recently Stern (1995), in their work with infants inevitably have drawn closer to the parents and have been among the strongest voices calling for a systematic, as well as sympathetic, look at the experiences and internal mental organization of the parent as a caregiver. At present, there are only a handful of empirical studies that have focused on the links between infant development and the mother's subjective experiences, goals, and internal representation of the relationship with the child (Aber, Slade, Cohen, & Meyer, 1989; Aber, Belsky, Slade, & Crnic, 1998; Benoit, Parker, & Zeanah, 1997; Benoit, Zeanah, Parker, Nicholson, & Coolbear, 1997; Bretherton, Biringen, Ridgeway, Maslin, & Sherman, 1989; Cox, Owen, Henderson, & Margand, 1992; Cramer et al., 1990; Fonagy, Steele, & Steele, 1991; Pianta & Marvin, 1992; Slade, Belsky, Aber, & Phelps, 1998; Zeanah & Barton, 1989; Zeanah, Benoit, Hirshberg, Barton, & Regan, 1994). These studies have provided important insight into child attachment, parental perceptions and attitudes, and developmental risk but have not focused on articulating the mother's unique point of view. Our hope is that the model of caregiving that we are developing will provide a

broader context, new questions, and new approaches to understanding the complex interaction that exists between the developmental agendas and experiences of both mother and child.

We begin by defining the caregiving system from a behavioral systems perspective (Bowlby, 1969/1982; Hinde, 1982a). Our primary focus is on that aspect of caregiving that is represented by the coadapted axis of maternal protection and infant and child attachment. This reflects our own interest in attachment and the place that it has been given in academic and clinical circles as one of the core organizing constructs in development (Sroufe & Waters, 1977). It reflects, as well, our belief that a wide variety of caregiving functions (e.g., feeding, cognitive stimulation) are coordinated at the behavioral and physiological levels with respect to the mother's overarching goal of ensuring the survival of offspring. Although this goal is not always conscious, the desire to protect her child has a subjective immediacy and urgency to the mother, especially under conditions of danger or threat and even in circumstances where she chooses or feels compelled to behave in ways that undermine the child's welfare. Next, we briefly summarize what is known about causal mechanisms and normative influences in the expression of caregiving, followed by a discussion of alternative caregiving strategies as related to infant and child attachment. The chapter concludes with the introduction of the construct of assaults to the caregiving system, that is, perturbations in the immediate caregiving context that may disable caregiving, and a consideration of the implications of our model for infant mental health practioners.

Defining the Caregiving Behavioral System

Bowlby's theory of attachment introduced mainstream psychology and psychoanalysis to the ethological construct of behavioral systems. This construct permits us to understand motivated or goal-directed behavior without relying on scientifically outdated models of drive. In addition, it encourages us to understand behavior as arising from the action of particular motivational systems that may compete with or be integrated with others and yet retain unique, internally consistent organizational properties. According to ethologists, much of the behavioral repertoire in humans and other species is guided by behavioral systems. They comprise behaviors that are coordinated to achieve a specific goal and adaptive function. Further, behavioral systems are goal-corrected; that is, the behaviors recruited to achieve the system goal are adjusted flexibly to a wide range of circumstances and the development of the individual.

Our working assumption, following Bowlby, is that the caregiving system is reciprocal to and evolved in parallel with the attachment system. Thus, it is reasonable to assume that the adaptive function of caregiving, as is that of attachment, is *protection of the young*. From the point of view of natural selection, protective behavior can be readily understood as conferring a selective advantage to the mother, that is, it enhances her reproductive fitness. Following ethological theory and paralleling Bowlby's (1969/1982) discussion of attachment, the *behavioral goal*, that is, the goal around which protective behaviors are selected, carried out, and internally organized, is proximity to the child or, at the level of appraisal or affect, felt safety or protection of the child.

Central to Bowlby's theory was his identification of factors involved in the activation, termination, and regulation of the child's attachment system (Bowlby, 1969/1982). Internal or external cues or stimuli associated with situations that the child perceives as frightening, dangerous, or stressful are known to activate the attachment system. With regard to the caregiving system, internal or external cues associated with situations that the *caregiver* perceives as frightening, dangerous, or stressful *for the child* should activate the caregiving system. These situations include, but are not limited to, separation, threats to the child or child endangerment, the child's verbal and nonverbal signals of discomfort and distress, and direct signals for approach or retrieval from the child.

Once activated, the caregiver can call upon a repertoire of behaviors. The goal of these behaviors, including retrieval, maintaining proximity, carrying, following, signaling the child to follow, calling, looking, and in humans, smiling, is to ensure proximity to, comforting of, and ultimately, protection of the child. The child's attachment system is deactivated by proximity and/or physical contact or psychological reassurance. We suggest that in a parallel manner, the parent's caregiving system should be deactivated by physical or psychological proximity to the child, signs that the child is comforted, contented, or satisfied, or a change in the environment signaling that danger has passed. An important feature of the attachment and caregiving systems, often overlooked in theoretical discussions and research, is that they depend on a continual and active monitoring and assessment of the environment. The importance of the mother's appraisal of the environment can be easily underemphasized or even overlooked. This is especially the case when one is focusing on early mother-infant interaction, before the infant is mobile, and when observing behavior in the relatively protected indoor environment. In fact, the success of both the attachment and caregiving systems requires that the mother be able to integrate information available to her about the physical and social environment with the infant's signals in order to achieve the goal of protection.

The importance of the mother's protective behavior as the foundation to attachment security emerges clearly in a recent study by Kondo-Ikemura and Waters (1995), who observed free-ranging rhesus macaque mothers and their youngsters. They found that the strongest maternal correlates of secure rhesus infant behavior were the mother's attention, vigilance, and protectiveness rather than general measures of responsiveness or tenderness. We suggest that observations of human mothers with their toddlers in an environment such as an outdoor park or airport would indicate the universality of the tendency to approach and retrieve the infant, even in the absence of any direct signal on the part of the infant. A situation that the mother deems to be dangerous may be even more likely to result in maternal approach and retrieval than infant signals. Indeed, the mother's goal of protection may sometimes be at odds with the infant's appraisal of his or her needs. The fact that the mother is, if only by virtue of more advanced cognitive development, in a different and often better position to judge environmental risks provides ample basis for conflicts between child and mother, especially once the infant is mobile. It is probably also natural for the mother to judge the safety of a situation based on her affective appraisal of a situation. This can result in at least transitory difficulties for mother and child. More enduring difficulties may arise when the mother relies entirely on her appraisal of circumstances and is impervious to the infant's or child's reading of the situation. This difference in perspectives is, in our view, one of the values of considering the organization of caregiving in its own right.

The goal-corrected nature of behavioral systems potentially allows for maximum behavioral flexibility. This feature permits the specific type and range of caregiving behavior to vary depending upon context, age, and experiences of parent or child. For example, paralleling the well-known phenomenon that infants or toddlers can range widely in familiar or interesting environments but insist on proximity when frightened (Anderson, 1972), the mother may be comfortable about leaving her infant with an alternate caregiver with whom she is comfortable but unwilling to leave the infant with a caregiver with whom she is unfamiliar or has reason to mistrust. Additionally, the mother may adjust her behavior to the child's development, for example, allowing the child free range over the neighborhood once she is certain he or she can safely cross streets and is capable of carrying out a plan (e.g., calling a policeman) should an emergency arise (Solomon, George, & Silverman, in press).

The notion of a goal-corrected system is key to understanding the wide cultural variation that exists in patterns of infant care, for it permits the smooth functioning and integration of diverse maternal behaviors as long as the mother can be satisfied that these behaviors achieve an internal standard of safety or protection for her child. Observers of mother-infant interaction in Africa and Central America have noted how quickly mothers respond even to minor infant distress signals and how much close physical contact these mothers provide in contrast to Western mothers (Ainsworth, 1977; Brazelton, 1977; DeVore & Konner, 1974). For example, Bell and Ainsworth (1972) found that the median number of cries ignored by a group of 23 middle-class mothers was 46 percent, while !Kung San Bushman mothers are said to respond promptly to all signals (DeVore & Konner, 1974). Additionally, non-Western mothers are very likely to respond to all signals of distress with nursing, while the type of intervention provided by Western mothers is highly variable. As a result, for non-Western infants nursing behavior becomes inextricably intertwined with attachment behavior and weaning can be emotionally disturbing (Ainsworth, 1977). In contrast, Western mothers as a group

appear to be more protective regarding the use of alternate caregivers. Leaving a young child in the care of a preadolescent caregiver is against the law in California (although not systematically enforced), and there is continued concern in the United States about the use of day care for young infants. In contrast, the extensive use of alternative caregivers, including preadolescent older siblings, is common in some non-Western cultures (e.g., Tronick et al., 1987; Zukow-Goldring, 1995). These cultural differences in maternal behavior appear to reflect differences in the probability of various dangers such as high infant mortality from thirst and dehydration, dangers underfoot such as cooking fires and snakes in the home (Levine, 1977; True, 1994), steep terrain (Kaplan, 1987), or in our own culture, the unavailability of alternate caregivers in the family and the perception of a high probability of maltreatment from nonmaternal caregivers.

Affect plays a central role in the regulation of behavioral systems. Bowlby (1969/1982) assigned a secondary role to affect—affect was considered a byproduct of cognitive appraisal mechanisms. It is clear, however, that affect can play a regulatory role as well, motivating mothers to prolong or repeat behavior (pleasure), overcome obstacles (anger, guilt), and, if necessary, relinquish their goal of protection when it is impossible to achieve (despair). Indeed, caregivers' affective experiences with their infants and children are among the most intense and compelling in adult life. Commonalities in the range and quality of maternal feelings may arguably constitute evidence for an underlying core or substrate for caregiving at least as convincing as universalities in maternal behavior.

Physiological Substrates

We presume, as with the attachment system, that the goal-corrected organization of caregiving is regulated by neurological systems in the brain. There has been relatively little study of these substrates in humans, however (Corter & Fleming, 1995). This is in contrast to the well-studied caregiving system in the rat, wherein maternal hormonal state or experience prime the caregiver for well-organized behavioral responses to auditory, tactile, visual, and olfactory cues from the pup, leading to rapid onset of maternal behavior and timely and behaviorally appropriate responsiveness to the changing physiological and development requirements of offspring (Rosenblatt, 1995; Fleming & Corter, 1995). In the last two decades researchers have demonstrated links between infant signals and stimuli and maternal responses, such as identification of one's own neonate's odor, that may be mediated or enhanced by the mother's hormonal condition at the time of parturition (Corter & Fleming, 1995). The largest body of research exists for responsiveness to infant cries that lead to attentional responses, changes in galvanic skin response and heart rate in adult females as well as adult males (Boukydis & Burgess, 1982; Frodi & Lamb, 1978a, 1978b). The probability that infant cries will elicit maternal retrieval (picking up),

approach, or even proximity, however, is highly variable depending, for example, on the intensity of the cry and identification of the infant as one's own (Corter & Fleming, 1995). Infant visual, tactile, and olfactory cues have also been shown to evoke maternal responsiveness and form a basis for maternal recognition of the infant (Fleming et al., 1993; Weisenfeld & Klorman, 1978). Paralleling the data on crying, these cues do not appear to have a simple "releaser" effect on caregiving behavior such as has been found in the rat. Rather, they may be thought of as having physiological orienting and arousing properties (Furedy et al., 1989) or the capability to lower the threshold for exhibiting caregiving behavior or raise the threshold for incompatible responses (Rosenblatt, 1995).

The relative openness of the human caregiving system highlights the importance of developmental processes and cognitive control mechanisms for the orchestration of caregiving behavior. These topics will again be considered later in the chapter.

The Caregiving System in Context

Up to this point we have discussed normative aspects of the caregiving system with an emphasis on the manner whereby caregiving becomes organized around the developing infant in such a way as to promote his or her current and future welfare. In our communal, idealized portrait of mother and infant, there is complete harmony or complementarity. But the needs and goals of caregivers and their infants can never overlap completely. It is a well-accepted proposition within evolutionary biology that although parent and child share common goals, there are also inherent and inevitable conflicts of interest between them (Clutton-Brock, 1991; Trivers, 1974). This is explained by the fact that natural selection acts upon the individual rather than the mother-infant dyad or some other social or population group. The evolutionary success of the individual is therefore determined by his or her own reproductive success (fitness). The mother's fitness is determined by the reproductive success of all her offspring, while the child's reproductive success is more closely tied to his or her own survival and ultimate reproductive success. Broadly speaking, any savings the mother can gain from providing less care to a particular child can be invested in herself, allowing her to reproduce again, or invested in another child. From the perspective of the growing field of life history theory in biology, the reproductive costs and benefits to mother and child of various patterns of parental care must ultimately be a function of the interaction between species' biology and ecological niche (Clutton-Brock, 1991; Kaplan, 1996). Further, many species are capable of differing or conditional strategies depending upon environmental and cultural circumstances. Indeed, this kind of behavioral flexibility is the hallmark of human adaptation. We emphasize that we are speaking of the effects of natural selection on those aspects of caregiving that may have a biological or instinctual basis or

component. The effects of natural selection on caregiving might be quite specific, for example, effects on neurological or hormonal substrates, or fairly broad, for example, the capacity to read relevant environmental or other conditions either directly or indirectly and respond differentially to them.

The analysis of human caregiving patterns at the evolutionary level of analysis is still new, but the limited data that are available suggest that variations in maternal care may ultimately be traced to adaptations to constellations of economic and social factors and sources of threat or danger to offspring at various developmental phases (Kaplan, 1996; Levine, 1977). For example, Burton Jones, Hawkes, and Draper (1994) described two groups of African hunter-gatherers, the !Kung Bushmen and the Hazda, who are characterized by different caregiving patterns. In the environment of the !Kung, food-gathering activities of young children are discouraged by parents because food sources are dispersed and children may easily get lost if they pursue them. In contrast, food sources are more easily reached in the Hazda environment, and the terrain is highly navigable. The investigators proposed that this constellation of factors contributes to higher fertility, greater parental demands for children's labor, and more relaxed child protectiveness among the Hazda in comparison to the !Kung. For a somewhat different but related view of attachment/caregiving adaptations, see Belsky (1991; 1999).

In some situations, mothers may be profoundly and painfully conscious of this fundamental caregiving equation (investment in one child at a cost to others or to the self), while in others, they may be entirely unaware of such calculations, in part the product of cultural norms and taboos. Whether conscious or not, however, it seems that the underlying realism of maternal caregiving strategies is promoted by proximate psychological mechanisms that may be thought of as opposing influences or dampers to the factors that activate caregiving that were discussed in the previous section. We presume that these mechanisms are also, fundamentally, products of natural selection.

We propose that the first of these arises from the interaction of and competition between caregiving and other behavioral systems within the mother. The caregiving system is only one of many behavioral systems within the individual that may interact with or directly compete with the expression of caregiving behavior (Hinde, 1982a; Stevenson-Hinde, 1994). When we consider parents' roles in terms of other behavioral systems, in addition to being a caregiver to one child, a parent may be a caregiver for other children, friend (affiliative system), sexual partner (sexual system), worker (the exploratory system and others), or child to his or her own parents (attachment system). Further, parents' relationships, especially with other adults, may combine any number of behavior systems (e.g., a combination of attachment, caregiving, affiliative, and sexual systems in a long-term romantic relationship). In the well-studied maternal rat, the balance among competing behavioral systems is regulated in part by parturitional hor-

mones that not only prime the dam's responsiveness to pups but reduce her interest in sexual behavior, diminish her sexual attractiveness, and increase her aggressiveness, facilitating physical protection of the young (Fleming et al., 1995; Rosenblatt, 1995). The more flexible control of caregiving in the human mother permits her to adapt her caregiving to her immediate social and physical circumstances but also requires gatekeeping of potentially competing behavioral systems.

These other behavioral systems, of course, are at the interface between the mother and the broader physical and social context wherein she functions, and these contextual factors may be sources of support or additional resources for the mother or may interfere with or deplete her caregiving resources. In some cultures, family and community interactions appear to be organized to minimize interference from other behavioral systems and maximize support for the mother (and infant). For example, in Levine's description of the sub-Saharan Gusii, a pastoral culture, husbands and wives refrain from sexual relations until the infant is weaned or nearly weaned at age two, thus avoiding the mother's need to divert food and attention away from the first infant (this practice may of course have other social functions as well). In addition, the involvement of other mothers, older siblings, relatives, or, in some cases, hired help as alternate caregivers is a routine feature of the caregiving context, permitting the mother to engage in out-of-home economic activities (Levine, 1994). In our own culture, external supports for maternal investment in the infant and child are far less systematized, and the sources and intensity of stress (or interference) may also vary greatly.

There is now a considerable body of literature demonstrating the effects of the social and economic context on caregiving and infant attachment. Lack of social and marital support, as well as poverty conditions, are all associated with decreases in infant attachment security and with less child-centered, especially authoritarian child-rearing styles (Belsky, 1984; Belsky, Rosenberger, & Crnic, 1995a, 1995b; Hoff-Ginsburg & Tardif, 1995; Lyons-Ruth, Connell, Gruenbaum, & Botein, 1990; Sroufe, 1983; Vondra, Hommerding, & Shaw, 1996). Contextual factors do not have simple linear effects on attachment and caregiving. Crockenberg (1981) found that infant irritability was associated with anxious attachment only when mothers were lacking social support. Belsky and colleagues, in their study of over 200 middle-class mothers and infants, found no significant effects of contextual factors such as marital and social support along with measures of infant temperament and maternal personality on infant attachment when these variables were analyzed separately. They were able to demonstrate cumulative (but not linear) effects, however, such that when three or more stressors were present, the probability of secure infant attachment was halved. The investigators interpreted this finding as evidence that "parenting is a well-buffered system" (Belsky et al., 1995a, p. 121). We suggest that a primary source of this buffering *is* the caregiving behavioral system that, as we have noted, motivates the mother to organize her be-

havior and draw upon her internal and external resources as necessary in order to maximize her protection of the infant. As these resources become more strained and/or mutually conflictual, however, the mother is more likely to compromise her availability to the infant (Hrdy, 1992).

A second set of mechanisms that mothers appear to use to determine their overall caregiving strategy are aversive responses to or negative evaluations of the child. Virgin female rats, in the absence of hormonal priming, tend to find newborn pups aversive and may avoid them (Rosenblatt, 1995). In what may be a parallel process, human mothers at the time of parturition seem to undergo a period of "maternal strangeness," that is, a slowness to respond to the infant or an aversive response. DeVries (1987) has proposed that this period permits the mother to evaluate the viability of her infant and to reject him or her if necessary. It is reasonably well-documented that the infant's physical unattractiveness can interfere with caregiving responses (e.g., Langlois, 1988; Langlois, Ritter, Casey, & Sawin, 1995). Not only the neonate's and infant's appearance but his or her behavior (e.g., lethargic, difficult to console, unable to self-soothe) may also be used as an index of lack of viability in at least some cultures (Scheper-Hughes, 1990). The underlying psychological mechanism for rejection of the infant whose behavior is deviant may be very basic indeed. Murray (1985) noted that adult responses to infant distress cries may be described by a U-shaped function, with responsiveness and sympathy increasing until the cries are very intense or persistent, at which point they are experienced as aversive and may lead to self-protective ("egoistic") responses such as anger or withdrawal. Frodi & Lamb (1980) found that abusing mothers have a lower threshold for this aversive response as measured by physiological indices, and it is tempting to speculate that differences in reactivity and threshold contribute to variation in caregiving across the range of caregiving strategies. We simply propose that one of the most potent sources of positive or negative evaluations of the infant may be founded on the mother's subjective experience of how responsive the infant is to her caregiving, resulting in a greater tendency to reject the infant who is (or is perceived to be) more difficult to care for or manage.

Alternative Caregiving Strategies

Maternal infanticide, viewed as pathological or criminal in our own society, represents in *evolutionary* perspective, the most extreme expression of parent-infant conflict. Circumstances where these practices are culturally sanctioned or tolerated tend to be characterized by a combination of greatly distressed or limited maternal resources and infant disability, illness, or gender, rendering the child extraordinarily costly to raise and/or severely limiting the chances of the child's ultimate viability or reproductive success (e.g., Hrdy, 1992; Miller, 1987; Scheper-Hughes, 1987, 1990). This same combination of factors may be at work in cases of maltreatment or infanticide in our own society as well (Belsky, 1993), suggesting that the tendency to

reject the infant or child under extreme circumstances is a very general one and may have an evolutionary basis.

Between the harmonious mother-infant ideal and infanticide there exists a broad range of maternal caregiving patterns. Based on the still limited number of cross-cultural studies available, it would appear that the three major patterns of infant attachment codified by Ainsworth (secure, insecure-avoidant, insecure-ambivalent) capture the range of organized attachment strategies available to infants. Secure patterns of infant attachment are normative in all societies studied to date, including the United States and Western Europe, Japan, Israel, and two samples of African mothers and infants (Ainsworth, et al., 1978; Belsky, Campbell, Cohn, & Moore, 1996; Grossman & Grossman, 1990; Kermoian & Lie derman, 1986; Miyake, Chen, & Campos, 1985; True, 1994; Sagi, 1990). Main (1990) argued that the secure pattern represents the primary infant attachment strategy and that avoidant and ambivalent attachment are conditional patterns that allow the child to maintain proximity to the mother under less than optimal conditions. These attachment patterns have been systematically linked to variations in maternal sensitivity to infant cues and signals (deWolff & van IJzendoorn, 1997). Since Ainsworth's original presentation of her findings, there has been an implication that the relatively insensitive mothers of insecurely attached infants are grossly inadequate and may be thereby placing their infants at developmental risk (Sroufe, 1988). Accumulating research indicates that the latter assumption is unwarranted. Infants and children whose attachment strategies are *disorganized,* but not those whose attachments are organized but insecure, are at greater risk for psychopathology as well as disturbances in cognitive and academic functioning (Carlson, 1998; Craig & George, 1998; Lyons-Ruth, 1996; Jacobsen, Edelstein, & Hofmann, 1994; Moss, Parent, Gosselin, Rousseau, & St. Laurent, 1996; Moss, Rousseau, Parent, St. Laurent, & Saintonge, 1998; Solomon, George, & De Jong, 1995; Solomon & George, in press-b).

The distributions of the types of insecure dyads vary greatly cross-culturally and across socioeconomic levels, suggesting that they may be linked to cultural differences in child-rearing values and practices (which are themselves related to economic conditions; Ainsworth et al., 1978; Belsky, Campbell, Cohn, & Moore, 1996; Duncan, Brooks-Gunn, & Klebanov, 1994; Grossman & Grossman, 1990; Kermoian & Liederman, 1986; Miyake, Chen, & Campos, 1985; True, 1994; Sagi, 1990). We have proposed, therefore, that the standard infant attachment patterns broadly reflect the range of adequate ("good enough") caregiving strategies and reflect different maternal solutions to the problem of protecting the infant under varying cultural and environmental circumstances (Solomon & George, 1996). Following the preceding discussion, we suggest that these alternative patterns reflect the mother's appraisal of her own caregiving resources and her child's current needs as well as her beliefs and experiences about what will be effective with a particular child.

We have described the pattern of maternal care associated with secure infant attachment as one of *flexible care.* This flexibility is founded upon the mother's ability to attend to and balance cues both from the child (including developmental cues) and the environment (sources of physical and social risk or danger) in order to determine when protection is and is not needed (Ainsworth et al., 1978; Belsky & Isabella, 1988; Isabella, 1993; Solomon, George, & Silverman, in press). As long as the mother is satisfied that her child is safe, she is free to pursue other goals, while continuing to monitor the infant and the environment to determine when her care will be needed again. This characterization, of course, corresponds to (but is not identical to) Ainsworth's description of the sensitive care of mothers of securely attached infants. Note that sensitive care is contingent upon infant cues but is not entirely dependent upon them. The mother also selectively ignores cues or intervenes in her infant's behavior on her own initiative, for example, by preventing him or her from wiggling off the changing table or prohibiting him or her from touching a cooking fire or electrical sockets. Yet, even in this context she remains sensitive to infant cues, being tactful and mild in her interventions when possible or at least remaining available to repair the relationship when there is a true conflict of wills (Biringen, Emde, & Pipp-Siegal, 1997).

Mothers of avoidant infants tend to rebuff the infant's bids for close contact (although in nonemergency situations they may encourage it). They are also less cooperative with their infants, that is, they are likely to intervene abruptly with the infant's exploration, based on their own assessment of the danger or desirability of the infant's behavior. Note that this suggests that the mothers are reasonably protective but are not inclined to coordinate their interventions with the infant's own wishes. We have also observed that mothers of avoidant children may be particularly skilled in setting up the environment to be stimulating yet safe (Solomon, George, & Silverman, in press). This frees them from direct supervision and involvement with the infant while ensuring his or her physical safety. Mothers of ambivalent infants, while inconsistent in their response to infant distress, initiate and encourage close affective tracking between themselves and their infants (Slade et al., 1995) and appear to avoid direct expressions of anger or disapproval (Solomon et al., in press). We have described the caregiving strategy associated with infant avoidance as "protection from a distance," while the caregiving pattern associated with ambivalence can be described as "close protection." Under conditions where it is desirable from the mother's perspective to give somewhat greater priority to her own needs and other activities and limit her responsiveness to the infant, providing care "from a distance" may be more advantageous. Under conditions of limited resources, mothers may also choose to defer or deny noncaregiving activities and attend closely (maintain close proximity) to the child. This latter strategy, which is very taxing to the mother, may actually result in a pattern of inconsistent and delayed maternal responsiveness to the infant's cues because the mother cannot in fact maintain a high level of responsiveness

when her personal resources are limited or strained.

Flexible caregiving is founded on openness to and integration of a full range of internal and external cues. Alternative caregiving strategies, however, appear to require the mother to selectively ignore certain cues—cues from the infant or the environment that might normally activate her caregiving system or internal cues that might otherwise lead the mother to ignore or reject a child whom she believes requires extraordinary care. Thus, we can expect the various maternal caregiving strategies to be associated with different perceptions of the self and infant and individual differences in the psychological processing of cognitive information and affective experience relevant to caregiving.

Representational Models of Caregiving

Once we begin to consider the subjective experience of the caregiver and the importance of bias or defensive exclusion in the mother's perception of her child and herself as caregiver, we are entering territory that is more familiar to infant mental health practitioners. It is increasingly understood that individuals construct inner representational models of significant relationships and that such models function to organize and regulate thought, affect, memory, and behavior. Representational models are inherently conservative, since they permit the individual to judge present circumstances in the light of the past, and yet, they are capable of being updated and reworked to permit adaptation to changes in development and novel situations. These models are believed to comprise both specific and generalized schemes of the self and other(s) and information-processing rules related to access and integration of memories and perception (Bretherton, 1985; Main, Kaplan, & Cassidy, 1985; Stern, 1995). Adapting the construct of representational or working models from cognitive psychology, Bowlby (1969/1982) proposed that they serve to regulate behavioral systems, thus providing the cognitive interface between the individual's experience and underlying instinctual (goal-corrected) systems. More recently, Stern (1995) has elaborated this construct, focusing on the multiple pathways through which clinical intervention can modify the mother's and the infant's representations of one another and, thereby, enduring qualities of their relationship.

The development of the Adult Attachment Interview (AAI; George, Kaplan, & Main, 1984/1985/1996), a semistructured interview focusing on the adult's attachment experiences, has given rise to a major shift in attachment research and a new emphasis on exploring the links between parents' representation of (or state of mind with respect to) their past and the security of their own child's attachment to them (van IJzendoorn, 1995). This approach has provided an assessment model for a growing number of researchers who are interested in the links between the mother's mental representations of the child and variations in maternal sensitivity and child attachment security. Following the semi-

structured style of the AAI, these researchers developed interviews wherein parents are asked to describe their perceptions and subjective experiences of their child, interactions with their child, and their relationship (Aber, Slade, Cohen, & Meyer, 1989; Bretherton, Biringen, Ridgeway, Maslin, & Sherman, 1989; Bretherton, Ridgeway, & Cassidy, 1990; Cox, Owen, Henderson, & Margand, 1992; Cramer et al., 1990; Pianta & Marvin, 1992; Zeanah & Barton, 1989). Unlike the more typical, structured self-report format that tends to closely guide and contain parents' descriptions of themselves as caregivers, the open-ended interview leaves room for the parent to construe questions and frame answers in a very individual way. The researcher is thus able to observe the parent as she constructs a model of her relationship with the child *in the moment* and take note of what she emphasizes, what she omits, and her specific choice of words. Parental representations in these studies have been analyzed in terms of constructs derived from studies of adult attachment (e.g., coherence, insight, lack of resolution) or from observation of mother-infant or child interaction (e.g., sensitivity, acceptance, anger, intensity of involvement). Researchers have been successful in describing individual differences in parental attributions and perceptions of the child as related to the child's attachment (Benoit, et al., 1997; Zeanah et al., 1994; Bretherton et al., 1989; Marvin & Pianta, 1996), the child's behavior (Aber et al., 1998; Benoit et al., 1997; Slade et al., 1998; Slade & Cohen, 1996), and the mother's adult attachment classification (Benoit, et al., 1997;

Slade et al., 1997; Slade & Cohen, 1996). This research has provided important insight into child attachment and parental perceptions and attitudes.

Our approach to this work has differed from the preceding studies in that we have attempted to infer from these interviews something of the structure of the mother's representation of caregiving, especially the mother's underlying propositions relating to the self as caregiver and the child as the recipient of care, and her characteristic style of information processing (or defensive processes) regarding the relationship. This approach has given us a vivid picture of the mother's experience of caring for a particular child and allowed us to develop rating scales that in turn differentiate mothers of children classified as secure, avoidant, ambivalent, and disorganized/controlling (George & Solomon, 1989; George & Solomon, 1996). These ratings are based primarily on the mother's evaluations of her own and her child's feelings, thoughts, and behaviors in situations that pose physical and psychological threats to the child (e.g., separation, safety, stress).

Following we briefly summarize pertinent findings from our studies of two normative samples of mothers of kindergartners and a sample of married, separated, and divorced mothers of one-year-olds comprised of many families who are considered high risk (see George & Solomon, 1996; Solomon & George, 1998a, 1999 for more details about these samples). Mothers of securely attached children and infants were distinguished by their positive evaluations of themselves as willing and effective caregivers, especially with regard to consoling their child. They evaluated their child as responding positively to them (e.g., "When I pick her up [after a fall]—I don't have to say a word to her, and it's OK. I'm there, and she trusts that I will make whatever is wrong—she trusts that I will *know* what is wrong—and make it OK"). Paralleling findings by other investigators, these mothers were sensitive in the sense that they based their actions on a detailed and quite individualized picture of their child. We found that these mothers were also flexible and resourceful, especially when trying to resolve conflicts of will or conflicts between their need or desire to engage in other activities and the child's emotional needs. It is important to emphasize that even for the mothers of secure children, regardless of the child's age or the mother's marital situation, this balancing act was difficult to achieve. Most mothers of secure children described unhappy, distressed, frustrated, or angry scenes involving the child. Nevertheless, they were explicitly committed to the child and, despite their own distress, remained emotionally available and responsive.

Mothers of avoidant and ambivalent children appeared to have developed conditional representational models of caregiving. Mothers of avoidant children and infants described strategies of protecting the child from a distance, guided at the representational level by mild rejection. They evaluated the self and child as slightly unwilling and unworthy individuals and tended to emphasize the negative aspects of their interactions. Mental representations of these rejecting mothers were characterized by cognitive *deactivation,* that is, they dismissed or devalued their child's attachment needs ("She just wanted attention" or "They really know how to get around you") and emphasized their commitment to the role of mother rather than to the emotional relationship with the child. Although these mothers never actually allowed the child to be unsafe (indeed, they seemed especially concerned about the child's physical safety) or experience intense distress, they were unwilling to provide the personal attention that was required. For example, one mother put several "distance" caregiving strategies into place, including providing swimming lessons and putting the child's older sibling in charge rather than staying in proximity when the child was in the pool. When these mothers found themselves in conflict with their child or when there were conflicts between other activities and caring for their child, these mothers described themselves as considerably less flexible and cooperative. They were often resentful or eager for a time when the child would be more independent.

In contrast to mothers of avoidant children, mothers of ambivalent children were characterized by uncertainty in their experience, in their reported behavior, and at the representational level. They often described themselves as unsure about how to calm or manage their infant or child and ambivalent about whether to respond to him or her or require greater independence. In terms of defensive processes, these mothers were characterized by cognitive *disconnection,* as revealed by their inability to integrate positive and negative, good and bad, and desirable and undesirable in their descriptions of their child or themselves. This mental position appeared to result in handling of the child that was hesitant, delayed, or vacillating. Uncertain mothers enjoyed their children, especially the more nurturant and intimate aspects of the relationship, and wished to delay the child's independence ("And sometimes I wish I could just stop her from growing, cause she's just this really schnugable [sic] size"). They also tended to overinterpret their child's distress and need for them ("I'm afraid he'll feel abandoned"). As a result, these mothers often sacrificed their own comfort or peace of mind unnecessarily, for example, by being unwilling to ask for assistance from others or going out of their way to avoid separation from the child even for minor errands or to fulfill legitimate personal needs (e.g., school, exercise). As a reaction to this level of self-enforced deprivation, they sometimes literally fled from the child or failed to respond due to a combination of resentment, the belated desire to promote autonomy, and emotional depletion (e.g., "At times I'll have to run upstairs to get something . . . and she'll wait at the bottom of the stairs and cry until I come down, and then I sort of ignore her and walk past her [laugh] . . . just because I don't want her making a big deal out of it").

The Disabled Caregiving System

Although secure attachments are generally recognized as the normative infant or child-mother relationship, with normative defined as most common and most theoretically expected (based on attachment theory), we have suggested that the avoidant and ambivalent relationships are "good enough" or "normatively" insecure. This is reflected, we believe, not only in the fact that infants and children who receive such attachment classifications tend not to exhibit behavioral pathologies (for reviews see Lyons-Ruth & Jacobvitz, 1999; Solomon & George, in press-b) but from a consideration of the mother's representation of the relationship. If we picture actual relationships as a kind of sine wave between the poles of psychological and physical protection and fulfillment of the mother's competing needs, the mothers of secure infants appear to maintain their behavior (and the child) within fairly regular and narrow limits, while the mothers of avoidant and ambivalent children might be represented by larger, perhaps more irregular sine waves arising from the mothers' struggles to balance caregiving with their other needs. Nevertheless, the caregiving representations of mothers of avoidant and ambivalent children reveal an essential organization around the child and an approximation of behavioral systems integration, and this organization is mirrored in the behavioral organization of attachment as observed in their children.

It is increasingly clear that in very high-risk caregiving contexts, such as maltreatment, alcoholism, and some kinds of maternal psychopathology, infant and child attachments are more likely to fall outside the behavioral guidelines of the three standard categories, and the infant's attach-

ment behavior typically is classified as disorganized (Lyons-Ruth & Jacobvitz, 1999; Solomon & George, 1999). This classification is given when attachment behavior is inherently paradoxical or contradictory, that is, the infant seems unable to maintain a coherent attachment strategy with respect to the parent (Main & Solomon, 1990). By at least kindergarten age, many of these children can be observed to engage in role-reversed behavior during laboratory reunions with the mother, behaving either in a punitive or caregiving manner to her (Main & Cassidy, 1988). Main and Hesse (1990) have developed the compelling theory that the infant's attachment behavior becomes disorganized because he or she has experienced the mother as either frightening or frightened. This places the infant in an unresolvable conflict because the same individual who is a source of threat or alarm is also his or her haven of safety. Although we are lacking extensive observations of disorganized infants and their mothers at home in the first year of life, more focused home observations have confirmed that some mothers of disorganized infants display signs of fear or threat during interaction with their infants, although sometimes these indices are very subtle (Liotti, in press; Lyons-Ruth, in press; Jacobvitz, Hazen, & Riggs, 1997; Schengal, van IJzendoorn, Bakersman-Kranenburg, & Blom, in press). Although some frankly disturbed mothers have infants or children whose attachment to them is disorganized, maternal psychopathology does not appear to be a necessary condition for these caregiving problems. Especially in normative samples, a number of mothers of children who are classified as disorganized have experienced early loss of an attachment figure and are thought to become momentarily disoriented or disorganized in their thinking about the loss, but they are not otherwise clearly at risk in the quality of their caregiving skills (Main & Hesse, 1990). Due to the many unresolved questions about this group and its clinical significance, we have given special attention to the representational caregiving models of the mothers of disorganized infants and their kindergarten-age counterparts.

We have found that the discriminating feature among these mothers is at least intermittent *abdication of caregiving*, that is, a failure of protection, and this is so both for mothers of infants and older children, where role reversal has already been established in the mother-child relationship. These mothers evaluate themselves as helpless in protecting their child (and sometimes themselves as well) from threats and danger, including and sometimes especially, danger from the mother herself. Their discussion of interactions with the child emphasized strong themes of inadequacy, helplessness, losing control, and, in some cases, a somewhat sexualized dissolution of parent-child boundaries (Egeland, Jacobvitz, & Sroufe, 1988; e.g., "Even though F is out here with him, I really worry that a car's going to come and F isn't going to see it . . . and I couldn't even lay there in bed [with the flu] . . . I had to sit there [at the window] and watch him"). The majority of mothers in this group described how they lacked effective and appropriate resources to handle everyday situations, and as a result, they placed the infant in extreme, unrelieved distress ("I'm running late, put on my clothes . . . I have to get her (the baby) ready . . . I had to just let her . . . cry . . . over there and get myself together, and locked her out of the bathroom . . . Uh, came out of the shower . . . she was right by the door . . . I had to pick her up because if I didn't she would just scream and scream and scream"). In other instances they described serious failures to provide reassurance to a frightened child because of external stresses such as court-imposed overnight visitation with the father ("When I would get [the baby] back from his dad . . . he was incredibly fussy and I couldn't handle it . . . I remember just leaving [the baby] in his room for while and I'd shut the door and . . . [say] 'Fine'"). Certainly in some of these instances, the mother could be described as frightening or frightened with respect to the child. Their own descriptions and their subjective experience, however, was of being totally helpless or on the verge of losing control and a nearly complete failure to feel like the "older and wiser" protective figure.

Descriptions of the child generally paralleled descriptions of the self. He or she was out of control—for example, wild, acting like a "maniac," strong-willed, defiant, or hysterical—and the self was helpless to combat or organize the child's behavior. Some mothers, however, viewed their child as the complete opposite of the self, as precocious and serenely in control of the situation, themselves, or others. The child was especially sensitive (e.g., a skilled caregiver), possessed extraordinary gifts, or was described in glorified, spiritual terms.

Even these exceptionally positive descriptions suggest abdication of the caregiving position because the mother evaluated her own caregiving as relatively unimportant or ineffective. Oblivious to the needs of the child, she was relieved that the child was so advanced. Finally, for some mothers, caregiving and control were not in the forefront of their thinking because of their "special" understanding or relationship with their child. These mothers described the child and the self as psychologically merged ("we're like two peas in a pod") so that special care and protection were deemed unnecessary.

In contrast to the interviews of mothers of insecure-avoidant and ambivalent children, the interviews of mothers of disorganized children failed to reveal any predominant defensive processing strategies. Rather, they described the *failure* of defensive processes such as mild rejection (deactivation) or mild denial of their children's strength or aggressiveness (cognitive disconnection) and an inability to select, evaluate, or modify their own behavior or that of their child. Evaluations of the self or child as helpless were clearly associated with powerful emotions and affective dysregulation.

We propose that the mother's experience is both a cause and a signal of a disabled caregiving system and a *disorganized* and dysfunctional form of providing care (Solomon & George, 1996a). Rather than behaving protectively toward their infants and children, these mothers were themselves disoriented, childlike, or frightened, harshly punitive, or abandoned the child to his or her own intense distress. Of equal or greater significance from the perspective of the child's attachment, we believe, was that the mother was at these times impermeable to the infant's or child's cues, so that the repair of the relationship that is available to other dyads under stress seems unavailable to the infant or child in these cases. From the perspective of the caregiving system, however, it seems that the mother's experience of helplessness evokes her acute responses to threat (Perry, Pollard, Blakley, Baker, & Vigilante, 1995), which strongly interfere with or block the caregiving system, preventing the mother from responding protectively to her defenseless offspring. We have stressed elsewhere that it is the infant's subjective experience of the mother as helpless and abdicating care that may be frightening the infant (George & Solomon, in press).

The Development of Caregiving

The body of research previously described documents the way that the mother's representation of caregiving, including her predominant information-processing or defensive style, strongly parallels her child's attachment behavior and her child's representational model of attachment to her (George & Solomon, 1996; Slade et al., 1995; Steele & Steele, 1994). There is also significant correspondence between these measures and classifications of the mother's state of mind with respect to (her own) attachment relationships (Aber et al., 1989; Ainsworth & Eichberg, 1991; Benoit

& Parker, 1994; Bus & van IJzendoorn, 1992; Crowell & Feldman, 1988; Fonagy, Steele, & Steele, 1991; Grossman, Fremmer-Bombik, Rudolph, & Grossman, 1988; Haft & Slade, 1989; Main et al., 1985; Slade et al., 1995; van IJzendoorn, 1995; Ward & Carlson, 1991), providing some support for a fundamental axiom of psychoanalytic, social learning, and attachment theories that the individual's caregiving style or pattern reflects her own early experiences of receiving care (Benedek, 1959; Bowlby, 1973, 1980; Bretherton, 1985; Fonagy, Steele, & Steele, 1994; Fraiberg, 1980; Sroufe & Fleeson, 1986). Stability across generations may provide one route by which the individual can read and adapt to prevailing social and economic conditions and thus may be an outgrowth of natural selection for conditional or alternative caregiving patterns (see also Belsky, 1999).

Although these data suggest common origins, many researchers have, in our view, overemphasized the degree of stability and minimized the evidence of lack of correspondence and intimations of change over time. Cross-sectional studies suggest that concordance for mother and child attachment is found predominantly when mothers are judged secure. Within this group, apparently, are both mothers who very likely experienced secure and supportive attachment relationships in childhood and those whose security is "earned" following unpromising beginnings (Main et al., 1985; Fonagy et al., 1985). Concordance is lowest for insecure mothers, particularly when the mother is judged to be unresolved about early loss.

Not all infants and children of unresolved mothers develop a disorganized or role-reversed relationship to mother, and mothers whose representation of their own attachments are secure or insecure but organized may also promote attachment disorganization in their relationships with their children (Main et al., 1985; van IJzendoorn, 1985; George & Solomon, 1998). Studies that have assessed mothers' representations of their own attachments prenatally have resulted in a similar pattern of findings. Maternal security predicts infant attachment security, but prediction is moderate to poor for mothers judged insecure prenatally. Further, in cases where there is discordance between the maternal measure and later infant attachment, the movement is predominantly toward security. Differences between mother and infant attachment classifications and within mothers across time raise the larger question: What factors across development, from infancy through adulthood, contribute to the mother's capacity to provide flexible protection to her child, and what factors foreclose development and change and, in particular, lead to abdication of caregiving?

There is surprisingly little systematic, developmental information about caregiving in humans. The information that currently exists suggests, however, that the caregiving system has a unique developmental trajectory and characteristic mental organization that distinguishes it from other behavioral systems, including the attachment system. Caregiving appears to mature slowly and be open to a variety of influences at many points in development.

There is good reason to believe that the experience of being mothered is a necessary condition for the organized expression of caregiving behavior both in humans and in primates, in general (Fleming et al., 1995; Pryce, 1995). The developmental links between actual caregiving experiences and individual differences in later caregiving have yet to be directly demonstrated, however (Solomon & George, 1996). Young children's enactments of attachment-relevant themes using sets of family dolls predict their own attachment behavior following laboratory separations from the mother (Bretherton, Ridgeway, & Cassidy, 1990; George & Solomon, 1998; Solomon, George, & De Jong, 1995), and children's empathically motivated helpfulness seems to vary with maternal sensitivity to them (Zahn-Waxler, Friedman, & Cummings, 1983; Main & George, 1980). These findings suggest that young children internalize qualitative differences in caregiving (see also Sroufe & Fleeson, 1986). They do not necessarily tell us, however, how children will behave when they are placed in the role of the caregiver.

We have proposed that this shift in perspective—from the one who is attached to the one who must provide care and protection—is fundamental to assuming the role of caregiver (Solomon & George, 1996). Once this transformation is accomplished, situations of danger and risk to the child should activate caregiving behavior and motivate the parent to organize her psychological and behavioral strategies to provide protection for her dependent young. Furthermore, adequate protection requires that the parent sustain herself and/or appeal to others should the situation activate her own attachment system.

We believe (George & Solomon, 1999, in press) that this shift in perspective may be facilitated by caretaking experiences in childhood. "Play-mothering" is common among juveniles in primate species, especially females (Pryce, 1995), and Bard (1995) has suggested that these activities are necessary experiences for the later expression of appropriate maternal behavior among apes. In our view, however, the most significant developmental shift occurs primarily at the level of mental representation and reflects a fundamental reorganization of the self around the protected particular child.

We have proposed that this process of developmental transformation gathers momentum in adolescence and culminates in the period known as the transition to parenthood—pregnancy through the birth of the child and for some time thereafter. The period is a time when behavioral systems mature and the child begins to construct a coherent sense of agency and identity. An inextricable part of this process is an adolescent review of relationships with his or her own parents that may precipitate both the development of new models or narratives of past attachments and the emergence of new models of appropriate caregiving. It is interesting in this vein to consider Fruchtman's (1995) finding that adolescents who engaged in sexual behavior and became pregnant, as opposed to those who used birth control, were more likely to show a distinct lack of memory about their own past attachment relationships as revealed in response to the AAI.

347

The transition to parenthood proper, at the biological level, is accompanied by intense hormonal and neurological changes that especially influence the hypothalamus and the limbic system (Pryce, 1995). Coincident with these changes, researchers have noted an enormous upsurge in thoughts, doubts, and worries about the self as a parent, the spouse, and the past in this period that some have suggested is essential for a reorganization of the self as a caregiver (Ammaniti, 1994; Benedek, 1959; Bibring, Dwyer, Huntington, & Valenstein, 1961; Brazelton, 1981; Cowan, 1991; Deutscher, 1971; Lee, 1995; Liefer, 1980). This period of internal turmoil may function to prime the caregiving system, paralleling the way in which parturitional hormones prime the caregiving system in the rat. The mother's review of her past, ruminations about the baby-to-be, and heightened emotional vulnerability leading up to and following parturition may be critical in allowing her to accept and adapt to the infant once he or she arrives. In support of this notion, anecdotal data suggests that adolescents who engage in neonatal homicide actively and quite successfully suppress all thoughts of the coming child throughout the pregnancy.

Physiological processes at parturition may be thought of as supporting the psychological process of constructing a representation of the self as caregiver. Recent research suggests that the hormonal milieu at this time, in particular cortisol, promotes a mood of emotional calm and closeness to the newborn (Corter & Fleming, 1995). Factors surrounding the baby's birth were once thought to be critical to the development of a commitment to the new infant, but the strong interpretation of these effects has now been tempered (Klaus et al., 1995). Providing human mothers with bonding experiences (i.e., the opportunity for extended closeness and physical contact with her infant immediately following birth) has been found to enhance touching, kissing, talking to the baby, and nursing, especially for mothers at risk (e.g., those experiencing economic risk, high stress, unplanned or unwanted pregnancies) but has not been found to be related to the child's attachment security at the end of the first year of life (Rode, Change, Fisch, & Sroufe, 1981). The mother's experience of pregnancy, birth, and the early postpartum period, especially the quality of social support available to her when she is vulnerable, may directly contribute to a reorganization of the mother's representation of herself as both the caregiver and the attached (Belsky & Rovine, 1990; Cowan, Cowan, Heming, & Miller, 1991). Nonfamily members may also be important in this process. For example, Manning-Orenstein (1998) recently found that the presence of a duola at birth was significantly related to the mother's representations of herself as a committed and competent caregiver.

One of the most powerful organizing influences on the caregiving system appears to be the baby. Lorenz (1943, in Fullard & Reiling, 1976) suggested that the physical features of "babyness," a combination of the prominent features of the infant (e.g., rounded, oversized head, large eyes), evoked caregiving behavior in adults. Suomi (1995) has noted that neonatal behavioral, perceptual, and social biases, including distinctive emotional expressions, make human infants and their closest primate relatives (Old World monkeys and apes) attractive to any caregiver. Human mothers recognize and prefer their own baby's cries and odors, and their baby's vocalization elicits affectionate behavior and instrumental caretaking (Fleming et al, 1995). Somewhat later, the infant's ability to seek and hold eye contact and smile are reported by many Western mothers to lead to a deeper and warmer feeling for them (e.g., Corter & Fleming, 1995; Fraiberg, 1980). Anisfeld, Casper, Nozyce, and Cunningham (1990) found that increased physical contact with the infant by using a soft baby carrier, as compared with an infant seat, was associated with increased maternal sensitivity in early infancy and attachment security at one year, suggesting in part that the infant can guide the mother toward sensitive care. It is most likely, of course, that the influence of the baby on the caregiving system is transactional rather than linear and unidirectional (Sameroff, 1993).

To summarize, throughout the course of the child's development and culminating with the birth of and unfolding relationship with the child, the mother's caregiving representational system and, by extension, her caregiving behavioral system potentially are open to a number of influences that may condition the organization of her care and protection for the infant. We have proposed, therefore, that while the mother's caregiving representation builds upon the mother's past, once the infant is born it reflects actual experiences with the child

(Solomon & George, 1996). The unfolding mother-infant relationship is thus a process of equilibration in which the mother's expectations about herself as a mother and her particular infant are repeatedly tested and potentially confirmed or disconfirmed in ways that may lead to profound changes in mother or infant. Whatever the quality of the mother's experience, it is likely to resonate with similar experiences, hopes, or fears from the past and in this way may set into motion a psychological reworking of the mother's attachment representations of her past.

Clearly, these supportive conditions are not available to all mothers, and there are circumstances that may function to disorganize the developmental roots of caregiving and foreclose the possibilities for reorganization. The best recognized and studied of these circumstances are early attachment-related traumatic experiences. Unresolved, especially traumatic loss of a parent through death (Ainsworth & Eichberg, 1991), physical and sexual abuse, and witnessing family violence to a family member have all been linked to dysfunctional patterns of caregiving and to second-generational attachment disorganization (Bowlby, 1973, 1980; Fraiberg, 1980; Lieberman, 1996; Lyons-Ruth & Block, 1996). It has been suggested that the mother's childhood need to suppress her experience of fear and distress leads her to literally block out or misinterpret her infant's or child's cues when she is a mother (Main & Hesse, 1990). Intriguingly, when mothers speak of their own experience, they give us a different view. The mothers of disorganized infants in our sample seemed, if anything, hypersensitive to their child's attachment cues. The infant's distress and rage elicited intolerable discomfort in the mother, and it was her intense or frantic efforts to control the child or the situation in an effort to modulate her own arousal that seemed to result in the most dysfunctional interactions—extreme rejection and/or physical and psychological abandonment. Aggressive or coy behavior on the part of the infant or child, by reminding the abused mother of her own past abuse, may similarly hijack the caregiving system. The hypersensitivity and desperate (helpless) behaviors of these mothers are characteristic of traumatized individuals of any age (Perry et al., 1995). We suggest, therefore, that the timing of trauma (i.e., whether it occurred in childhood during a presumed sensitive period for the development of caregiving) is less important with respect to caregiving than whether a trauma occurred at all and the intensity of its impact on the mother (e.g., adult experiences of loss, violence, rape). In addition, we would suggest that the experience of past or present trauma need not necessarily lead to attachment disorganization unless this state continues to be evoked in the mother during interaction with the child.

Assaults to the Caregiving System

In the previous section, we considered how attachment-related traumas in the caregiver's history might undermine her ability to organize her caregiving behavior and representation coherently around protection of the infant. Here we consider examples of how three contemporaneous situations that normally are conceptualized as risks to the development of infant attachment—premature delivery of the infant, infant disability, and custody and access plans in the context of divorce—may be understood from the perspective of the caregiver. We suggest that each of these situations acts directly on the caregiving system and, under adverse conditions, is capable of disabling caregiving in ways that may parallel the effects of attachment-related trauma.

Prematurity and Disability

The effects on the mother of premature delivery are probably the best studied of assaults to the caregiving system. Consideration of the mother's reaction to her baby's premature birth reflects, in part, the contribution of developmentalists who have stressed the primacy of the caregiving context in predicting developmental sequelae to "reproductive casualties" (Sameroff & Chandler, 1975). Its has also influenced the views of medical and mental health practitioners who have witnessed the anxiety, pain, and confusion experienced by parents in these circumstances and the failure of some parents to participate in the baby's care during hospitalization or following release (Klaus & Kennell, 1976; Klaus et al., 1995). Premature infants often present immediate behavioral challenges to care and the establishment of harmonious interaction. For example, they have been described as underreactive to normal handling, leading mothers to resort to an overly stimulating style of interaction. Because the premature infant is also susceptible to behavioral disorganization, maternal overstimulation can result in further disorganization of the infant's behavior, leading to persistent feelings of uncertainty and incompetence within the mother about how to establish mutually satisfying interaction with her infants (Beckwith & Cohen, 1983; Barnard, Bee, & Hammond, 1984; Brazelton, Koslowski, & Main, 1974; Field, Widmayer, Stringer, & Ignatoff, 1980). Further, parents who experience prolonged physical separation from their premature infants may experience intense feelings of yearning for them and anxiety for their welfare (Minde, 1993). These difficulties may be conceptualized as acting directly on the caregiving behavioral system, that is, they interfere with the caregiver's ability to read the infant's signals and terminate attachment behavior appropriately.

Prematurity can and usually does have a direct effect on the caregiver's representational system, that is, on the caregiver's perception of herself as an adequate protector and of her infant as worthy of protection. Thus, the premature infant by the simple fact of his or her early birth or condition can evoke strong feelings of failure as a parent, self-blame, and guilt, feelings that are sometimes exacerbated by the response of relatives and hospital personnel (Minde, 1984, 1993).

When we look at how mothers describe the experience of premature delivery, it is clear that they indeed perceive this crisis as involving threats to the survival of the infant or to their ability to care for it. Of 114 mothers followed by Affleck, Tennen, and Rowe (1991) immediately subsequent to their infant's premature birth, about 60 percent described fears for the child's survival or eventual health as the most difficult part of their experience in the immediate postpartum period. "There was this deep and awful fear than no matter how much they did for him, he could die the very next minute" (p. 5). One-third of the mothers described the frustration and regret of being unable to care for the infant as the greatest difficulty. "I didn't really feel like a mother at all. I couldn't have him with me and do what other mothers do" (p. 6). About 10 percent of the mothers described the experience of helplessness in the face of the infant's fragility. "It was a feeling of complete helplessness. Here I am having produced this baby and I don't even have the power to keep it alive" (p. 6). Mothers' descriptions of their earliest impressions indicated that the appearance of the baby violated their expectations of a lovable and viable infant. "His head was so small I thought I could crush it just by touching it"; "He looked like those starving babies you see in Africa"; "He didn't look like he was real"; "I couldn't believe that anything that small could live"; "Actually he didn't even look like a person" (p. 4). Not surprisingly, mothers also discussed the difficulties they faced in becoming emotionally attached to their babies. "Right from the beginning, I didn't feel that I was bonded to her. I never felt that she was mine"; "I remember deciding not to visit for awhile . . . not so much because I didn't care about her, but because I just didn't want to be attached to a child who was less than I wanted her to be"; "I just didn't want to accept him as my child. The doctors were telling us that his chances weren't too good. I didn't want to become attached and then have my heart broken" (p. 5).

However devastating the mother's initial experiences are, they appear to be resolved for many mothers over the course of first year of life, reflecting the mother's capacity to generate cognitive and affective coping strategies, to marshal and benefit from social support, and the developmental resilience of the premature infant himself (Affleck et al., 1991; Crnic, Greenberg, Ragozin, Robinson, & Bradshaw, 1983; Goldberg & DiVitto, 1995; van IJzendoorn, Goldberg, Kroonenberg, & Frenkel, 1992).

In contrast, the disabled infant (irrespective of its birth status) appears to present an assault to the caregiving system that may have more profound and long-lasting consequences. When the disability reflects compromised neurological and/or motor function, it can have a direct effect on the infant's capacity to provide clear behavioral and affective signals that normally activate the caregiving system (e.g., Emde & Brown, 1978; Pianta et al., 1996; Vaughn et al., 1994). At the same time, it is clear that the infant's difficulties can also act upon the mother's representation of her infant as worthy of care and her representation of her worth as a caregiver. Pianta and his colleagues (Pianta et al., 1996; Pianta, Marvin, & Morog, 1999), as well as others, have conceptualized the process whereby the mother adapts to the disabled infant as entailing "grieving for the loss of the perfect child," that is, as reflecting an assault on the mother's representation of a viable (successful) and lovable child. These researchers suggest that individual differences in the extent to which the mother is able to resolve this grief and reorient to the present reality of the baby may predict differences in the mother's capacity to provide sensitive care to the disabled baby or young child. Paralleling our views, they have conceptualized infant disability as an assault to the caregiving system and emphasized the importance of cognitive resolution of the crisis of receiving the diagnosis. Ratings of the mother's resolution of diagnosis have been shown to predict secure versus insecure infant and child attachment in samples of infants with cerebral palsy (Barnett et al., 1999; Pianta et al., 1996, 1999). Consistent with our argument throughout this chapter, that the caregiving system is independent of the attachment system, the mother's lack of resolution with respect to her own attachment experiences apparently does not predict her resolution of her child's diagnosis of disability (Pianta et al., 1999). The challenge of grieving, that is, of accepting the loss and the new reality, is a chronic and recurring one that is reawakened with each developmental milestone missed or delayed. The fears about who will protect the child in the future, when one is no longer available to provide protection to the vulnerable child, continue to haunt the parents even when a temporarily successful adaptation to the child's limitations has been achieved.

Psychoanalytically inclined writers have framed the experience of giving birth to a disabled child as primarily a wound to the self-concept, that is, as a narcissistic injury. This view is clearly articulated in an often-quoted study of five normal couples and their disabled infants (Mintzer, Als, Tronick, & Brazelton, 1985). These authors conceptualized mothers' early attempts to distance themselves emotionally from the infant as an attempt to shore up the self, and view the therapeutic task as one of helping mothers to differentiate negative aspects of the infant from negative views of the self. As discussed earlier, attempts to distance oneself from the "imperfect" child may have a biological base (DeVries, 1987), as may the tendency for mothers to merge psychologically with the infant (Winnicott, 1958). At the same time we emphasize here that the birth of a disabled newborn is inevitably a challenge or assault to the representation of the self-as-caregiver (Is one to blame? Could one do more or better with this child?), and the mother's concerns may be equally for her infant as for herself. These caregiving concerns may resonate with or activate more global concerns about the self, ultimately compromising a reorganization of caregiving around the strengths of the child, but may be distinguished from them both theoretically and clinically.

Disputes over Custody and Visitation in the Context of Divorce and Separation

Judith Wallerstein (1991) has commented on the "diminished capacity" for parenting in the immediate aftermath of divorce, and this has typically been understood as reflecting the parents' deep personal distress and involvement in conflict with the other spouse. In this area as well, clinical investigators have conceptualized divorce as a narcissistic injury to the parent (Johnston & Campbell, 1988) and as an adaptational crisis (Rutter, 1997). In cases involving infants and toddlers, concern has focused on the effects that various custody and visitation arrangements, especially overnight visiting with the father, may have on the infant's capacity to develop a secure attachment to the mother (e.g., Hodges, 1986). Our study of the development of attachment in divorced and separated families suggests, however, that when very young children are involved, the circumstances surrounding separation and custody may constitute, from the mother's perspective, an assault to the caregiving system. Further, our data suggest that assaults to caregiving may play as great a role as the infant's vulnerability to separation in the development of attachment insecurity in these circumstances.

As part of our study of 93 mother-infant dyads wherein the parents were separated or divorcing (and 52 intact comparison families) (Solomon & George, 1999, in press-a), we interviewed parents to explore their representations of caregiving. Over 75 percent of mothers spontaneously described concerns about how the infant's visitation with the father and separation from them might threaten their infant's psychological health. Issues of physical safety were of deep concern for a somewhat smaller number of mothers (65 percent). Mothers in these circumstances articulated their concerns directly in the language of protection and safety for their infants. Many found it excruciating to be separated from their young children, others articulated concerns about the effects of separation on the infant's security, and many expressed strong doubts and fears about whether fathers were attentive to the infant's psychological and physical needs. Based on our ratings of the mother's representation of herself as providing psychological protection to the infant in these circumstances, 45 percent of mothers whose infants had overnight visits with the father but only 18 percent of mothers whose infants did not have overnight visits with the father described themselves as failing or helpless to provide psychological protection or support to the infant in the context of visits with the father. We note that mothers' fears about fathers were not necessarily veridical and, in some cases, undoubtedly were distortions fueled by distrust and animosity toward the father as well as by anxieties for the baby. Nevertheless, it is clear that many mothers experienced coparenting under these circumstances as a direct assault on their ability to care for their infants and on their representation of themselves as caregivers.

Within the group of infants with overnight visitation, those whose mothers evaluated themselves as active and effective in buffering and protecting the infant from potential ill effects of separations were likely to show an organized pattern of attachment to the mother (secure, avoidant, or resistant). In contrast, when the mother evaluated herself as helpless or fail-

ing in protection, the infant was likely have a disorganized or unclassifiable attachment strategy with respect to the mother. From the perspective of the infant's attachment and separation experiences, the latter group of mothers may have failed to provide the infant with the additional support necessary to manage the anxiety of prolonged separation from her. From the perspective of the mother's caregiving system, this finding may suggest that mothers' lack of resolution with respect to the coparenting situation, similar to lack of resolution in the case of infant disability, prevents them from adequately protecting their infants. That is, the mother's representation or expectation of how she would care for this infant—influenced by the development of caregiving strategies in the course of pregnancy and during the breakdown of the marriage or relationship and in response to infant cues and the unfolding of her relationship with the infant postpartum—tends to consolidate upon proximity with the infant, rapid responsiveness to the infant's cues, and protection from undue distress, threats, or dangers to his safety and well-being. Indeed, this may be particularly true when the marital breakup comes so early in the infant's life, since these parents tend to be particularly invested in the relationship with the infant (Heinicke, Guthrie, & Ruth, 1997). To the extent that she has not incorporated the father into this picture, and especially if she views him as incompetent or dangerous to the child, coparenting presents a challenge and an assault to her cherished views of how it would be, indeed, how she feels it *must* be to keep her infant safe. To be required to radically relinquish this representation, especially in the context of other losses, adaptations, and stresses of marital separation and divorce, may readily be likened to the experience of bereavement and loss. In this context, mothers' intense and persistent resistance to granting or increasing visitation time, indeed their intransigence to all efforts to make "reasonable" accommodations to the father and the court's requirements, is hardly surprising. The fact that nearly one-half of the mothers whose infants participated in overnight visitation with the father had clearly not made a psychological adjustment that allowed them to support and protect their infants in the changed circumstances hardly seems surprising either.

The Range of Assaults

We have described three circumstances that may be considered assaults to the caregiving system—prematurity, disability, and court-ordered visitation with the father in cases of separation and divorce. We conceive of these as assaults to caregiving because they have the capacity to disorganize mothers' representations of themselves as caregivers and their representation of the infant as worthy of protection and thus disable their capacity to organize their behavior coherently around the goal of protection of the infant. Representational models of attachment are often thought to rest upon cognitive processing. However, it is imperative to remember that these mechanisms have strong affective components that both arise from and engender in-

tensely experienced emotions. Thus, although these events may be considered to register first in the mother's representation of caregiving, they are capable of evoking in the mother a sense of personal vulnerability, panic, and despair that may be entirely parallel to the psychological context for what we may call developmental disorganization of caregiving, arising from traumatic attachment experiences.

Following this thinking, there are obviously a great many more events that may have the capacity to dysregulate maternal caregiving by overwhelming the mother's capacity to regulate her attention and modulate her emotional state in such a way as to achieve the goal of protection. In short, we proposed that any other event that engenders feelings of helplessness and vulnerability in the mother—domestic violence, environmental catastrophe, loss or threat of permanent separation from an attachment figure (her own parent or adult partner), life-threatening illness of an attachment figure or of the self, miscarriage or death of a child, depression or other mental illness—may give rise to or contribute to abdication of caregiving. Whether these events are sufficient to permanently alter the mother's caregiving representation in and of themselves or only in combination with other traumas (or lack of supports) is a matter for further investigation.

Conclusion

As compared to some models of intervention that focus only on the mother or only on the child, the hallmark of infant mental health models is the focus on the mother-child relationship. To accomplish these more complex and integrated goals, infant mental health practitioners have drawn upon an eclectic variety of theoretical models—biological, developmental, contextual, and cross-cultural—to inform their thinking. This is appropriate; in the important work of helping families and infants we cannot afford to limit our perspective to one theoretical approach or another. Here we have tried not only to emphasize the caregiver's point of view but to bring together diverse theoretical and empirical models in order to elucidate how one level of analysis interacts with others. To summarize briefly, we have proposed that both the caregiving system and alternative caregiving strategies arise, ultimately, from the action of natural selection. The caregiver is equipped to organize her behavior around the needs of the infant and at the same time adjust her behavior, in ways that may have positive or negative consequences for infant mental health, with respect to the resources available to her and her estimation of the ultimate viability of her infant. Contextual factors such as social support or interference, mediated by personal relationships and culture and characteristics of the infant, including appearance and behavior, provide important current information to the mother about the organization of her caregiving. Experiences over the course of the mother's development also provide key information to the caregiving system and, to the extent that they result in biases in perception, memory, and attitudes, may be a conservative and even a disruptive influ-

ence. Once caregiving is viewed as a system, one can readily understand why the system may be "entered" at any number of points—in terms of developmental history and representation, social or economic context, or the nature and quality of the infant's behavior—to effect a significant shift in its functioning.

In this chapter, we have expanded on our previous work by articulating the construct of assaults to the caregiving system. These experiences threaten the caregiving system by rendering the mother, for the short or long term, helpless and ineffective in providing care for a particular child. In severe form or in combination, assaults to caregiving may result in abandonment or abuse. Certainly, as we described, some problems with caregiving are the product of childhood trauma, childhood experiences that we have proposed may actually undermine the development of the caregiving system during childhood and adolescence. We stress, however, that the caregiving systems even of mothers who bring a secure attachment history to situations such as prematurity, disability, divorce, and family violence are susceptible to breakdown or disruption. Regardless of its origin, a breakdown in the caregiving system leaves the infant or child without care and protection.

We have described how the mother's desire to keep her child safe and protected is one of the fundamental mechanisms underlying maternal behavior. Clinically, the most potent benefit of this insight is that it allows us to speak to and form an alliance with the mother as caregiver. In our experience, mothers from a wide variety of cultural backgrounds and circumstances spontaneously speak in the language of safety and protection, however differently they define these terms. In contrast, constructs derived from infant studies, such as sensitivity and reciprocity, may be experienced as foreign or critical. The first question mothers ask us, in both research and clinical contexts, is whether we ourselves have children. The reason for the question is obvious. Mothers feel supported and understood when the clinician can share their perspective and especially when the clinician can appreciate that mothers may wish to protect their infants and at the same time feel overwhelmed, hostile, or even repelled by them. These are not different sides of the mother, the ego and the destructive id; they exist side by side and form the basis of painful and sometimes intractable conflict in the lives of contemporary mothers everywhere.

References

Aber, J. L., Belsky, J., Slade, A., & Crnic, K. (1997). *Stability and change in maternal representations of their toddlers: A study of first-born boys.* Manuscript submitted for publication.

Aber, J. L., Slade, A., Cohen, L., & Meyer, J. (1989, April). *Parental representations of their toddlers: Their relationship to parental history and sensitivity and toddler security.* Paper presented at the Biennial Meeting of the Society for Research in Child Development, Baltimore, MD.

Affleck, G., Tennen, H., & Rowe, J. (1991). *Infants in crisis: How parents cope with newborn intensive care and its aftermath.* New York: Springer-Verlag.

Ainsworth, M. D. S. (1977). Infant development and mother-infant interaction among Ganda and American families. In P. H. Liederman, S. R. Tulkin, & A. Rosenfeld (Eds.), *Culture and Infancy* (pp. 119–150). New York: Academic Press.

Ainsworth, M. D. S., Blehar, M. C., Waters, E., & Wall., S. (1978). *Patterns of attachment: A psychological study of the Strange Situation.* Hillsdale, NJ: Erlbaum.

Ainsworth, M. D. S., & Eichberg, C. (1991). Effects on infant-mother attachment of mother's unresolved loss of an attachment figure or other traumatic experience. In C. M. Parkes, J. Stevenson-Hinde, & P. Marris (Eds.), *Attachment across the life cycle* (pp. 160–186). New York: Routledge.

Ammaniti, M (1994). Maternal representations during pregnancy and early infant-mother interaction. In M. Ammaniti & D. S. Stern (Eds.), *Psychoanalysis and development: Representations and narratives* (pp. 79–96). New York: New York University Press.

Anderson, J. W. (1972). Attachment behavior out of doors. In N. Burton-Jones (Ed.), *Ethological studies of child behavior* (pp. 199–216). London: Cambridge University Press.

Anisfeld, E., Casper, V., Nozyce, M., & Cunningham, N. (1990). Does infant carrying promote attachment? An experimental study of the effects of increased physical contact on the development of attachment. *Child Development, 61,* 1617–1627.

Bard, K. (1995). Parenting in primates. In M. H. Bornstein (Ed.), *Handbook of parenting* (Vol. II; pp. 27–58). Hillsdale, NJ: Erlbaum.

Barnard, K., Bee, H., & Hammond, M. (1984). Developmental changes in maternal interactions with term and preterm infants. *Infant Behavior and Development, 7*, 101–113.

Barnett, D., Hunt, K. H., Butler, C., McCaskill, J., Kaplan-Estrin, M., & Pipp-Siegal, S. (in press). Indices of attachment disorganization among toddlers with neurological problems. In J. Solomon & C. George (Eds.), *Attachment disorganization.* New York: Guilford.

Bell, S. & Ainsworth, M. D. S. (1972). Infant crying and maternal responsiveness. *Child Development, 43*, 1171–1190.

Belsky, J. (1984). The determinants of parenting: A process model. *Child Development, 55*, 83–96.

Belsky, J. (1993). The etiology of child maltreatment. *Psychological Bulletin, 114*, 413–434.

Belsky, J. (1999). Modern evolutionary theory and patterns of attachment. In J. Cassidy & P. Shaver, (Eds.), *Handbook of attachment theory and research and clinical implications* (pp. 141–161). New York: Guilford.

Belsky, J., & Isabella, R. (1988). Maternal, infant, and social contextual determinants of attachment security. In J. Belsky & T. Nezworski (Eds), *Clinical implications of attachment* (pp. 41–94). Hillsdale, NJ: Erlbaum.

Belsky, J., Rosenberger, K., & Crnic, K. (1995a). The origins of attachment security: "Classical" and contextual determinants. In S. Goldberg, R. Muir, & J. Kerr (Eds.), *Attachment theory: Social, developmental, and clinical perspectives* (pp. 153–183). Hillsdale, NJ: Analytic Press.

Belsky, J., Rosenberger, K., & Crnic, K. (1995b). Maternal personality, marital quality, social support, and infant temperament: Their significance for infant-mother attachment. In C. R. Pryce, R. D. Martin, & D. Skuse (Eds.), *Motherhood in human and nonhuman primates* (pp. 115–124). Basel: Karger.

Belsky, J., & Rovine, M. (1990). Patterns of marital change across the transition to parenthood: Pregnancy to three years postpartum. *Journal of Marriage and the Family, 52*, 5–19.

Belsky, J., Steinberg, L., & Draper, P. (1991). Childhood experience, interpersonal development, and reproductive strategy: An evolutionary theory of socialization. *Child Development, 62*, 647–770.

Benedek, T. (1959). Parenthood as a developmental phase: A contribution to the libido theory. *Journal of the American Psychoanalytic Association, 7*, 389–417.

Benoit, D., & Parker, K. (1994). Stability and transmission of attachment across three generations. *Child Development, 65*, 1444–1456.

Benoit, D., Parker, K. C. H., & Zeanah, C. H. (in press). Mothers' internal representations of their infants during pregnancy: Stability over time and association with infants' attachment classifications at 12 months. *Journal of Child Psychology, Psychiatry and Allied Disciplines.*

Benoit, D., Zeanah, C. H., Parker, K. C. H., Nicholson, E., & Coolbear, J. (1997). Working model of the child interview: Infant clinical status related to maternal perceptions. *Infant Mental Health Journal, 18*, 107–121.

Biringen, Z., Emde, R. N., & Pipp-Siegal, S. (1997). Dyssynchrony, conflict, and resolution: Positive contributions to infant development. *American Journal of Orthopsychiatry, 67*, 4–19.

Bibring, G., Dwyer, T., Huntington, D., & Valenstein, A. (1961). A study of the psychological processes in pregnancy and of the earliest mother-child relationship. *Psychoanalytic Study of the Child, 16,* 9–24.

Bornstein, M. (1995). Parenting infants. In M. Bornstein (Ed.), *Handbook of parenting* (Vol. I; pp. 3–40). Hillsdale, NJ: Erlbaum.

Bowlby, J. (1969/1982). *Attachment and loss: Vol. I. Attachment.* New York: Basic Books.

Bowlby, J. (1973). *Attachment and loss: Vol. II. Separation.* New York: Basic Books.

Bowlby, J. (1980). *Attachment and loss: Vol. III. Loss.* New York: Basic Books.

Bowlby, J. (1984). Caring for the young: Influences on development. In R. S. Cohen, B. J. Cohler, & S. H. Weissman (Eds.), *Parenthood: A psychodynamic perspective* (pp. 269–284). New York: Guilford.

Boukydis, Z., & Burgess, R. (1982). Adult physiological response to infant cries: Effects of temperament of infant, parental status, and gender. *Child Development, 53,* 1291–1298.

Brazelton, T. B. (1977). Implications of infant development among the Mayan Indians of Mexico. In P. H. Liederman, S. R. Tulkin, & A. Rosenfeld (Eds.), *Culture and infancy* (pp. 151–188). New York: Academic.

Brazelton, T. B. (1981). *On becoming a family.* New York: Delacorte Press/Laurence.

Brazelton, T. B., Koslowski, B., & Main, M. (1974). The origins of reciprocity: The early mother-infant interaction. In M. Lewis & L. Rosenblum (Eds.), *The effect of the infant on its caregiver* (pp. 49–76). New York: Wiley.

Bretherton, I. (1985). Attachment theory: Retrospect and prospect. In I. Bretherton & E. Waters (Eds.), Growing points in attachment theory and research (pp. 3–35).

Monographs of the Society for Research in Child Development, 50(1–2, Serial No. 209).

Bretherton, I., Biringen, Z., Ridgeway, D., Maslin, D., & Sherman, M. (1989). Attachment: The parental perspective. *Infant Mental Health Journal, 10,* 203–221.

Bretherton, I., Ridgeway, D., & Cassidy, J. (1990). Assessing internal working models of attachment relationships: An attachment story completion task for 3-year-olds. In M. T. Greenberg, D. Cicchetti, & E. M. Cummings (Eds.), *Attachment in the preschool years* (pp. 273–308). Chicago: University of Chicago Press.

Burton Jones, N. G., Hawkes, K., & Draper, P. (1994). Differences between Hazda and !Kung children's work. Affluence or practical reason? In E. S. Burch Jr. & L. J. Ellanna (Eds.), *Key issues in hunter-gatherer research* (pp. 189–215). Oxford: Berg.

Bus, A. G., & van IJzendoorn, M. H. (1992). Patterns of attachment in frequently and infrequently reading mother-child dyads. *Journal of Genetic Psychology, 153,* 395–403.

Carlson, E. (1998). A prospective longitudinal study of consequences of attachment disorganization/disorientation. *Child Development, 69,* 1107–1128.

Clutton-Brock, T. H. (1991). *The evolution of parent care.* Princeton, NJ: Princeton University Press.

Corter, C., & Fleming, A. S. (1995). Psychobiology of maternal behavior in humans: Sensory, experiential and hormonal factors. In M. Bornstein (Ed.), *Handbook of parenting* (Vol. II; pp. 59–85). Mahwah, NJ: Erlbaum.

Coulson, W. (1995). *Disruptive caregiving strategies in mothers with symptoms of post-traumatic stress.* Unpublished undergraduate thesis, Mills College, Oakland, CA.

Cowan, C. P., Cowan, P. A., Heming, G., & Miller, N. B. (1991). Becoming a family: Marriage, parenting, and child development. In P. A. Cowan & E. M. Hetherington (Eds.), *Family transitions* (pp. 79–109). Hillsdale, NJ: Erlbaum.

Cowan, P. (1991). Individual and family life transitions: A proposal for a new definition. In P. Cowan & M. Hetherington (Eds.), *Family transitions* (Vol. 2; pp. 3–30). Hillsdale, NJ: Erlbaum.

Cowan, P. A., Cohn, D. A., Cowan, C. P., & Pearson, J. L. (1996). Parents' attachment histories and children's externalizing and internalizing behavior: Exploring family systems models of linkage. *Journal of Consulting and Clinical Psychology, 64,* 53–63.

Cox, M., Owen, M. T., Henderson, V. K., & Margand, N. A. (1992). Prediction of infant-father and infant-mother attachment. *Developmental Psychology, 28,* 474–483.

Craig, C., & George, C. (1998). *Cognitive development and attachment in three-year-olds: Does disorganized attachment and defensive dysregulation constrain symbolic reasoning?* Manuscript submitted for publication.

Cramer, B., Robert-Tissot, C., Stern, D., Serpa-Rusconi, S., De Muralt, M., Besson, G., Palacio-Espasa, F., Bachmann, J. P., Knauer, D., Berney, C., & D'Arcis, U. (1990). Outcome evaluation in brief mother-infant psychotherapy: A preliminary report. *Infant Mental Health Journal, 11,* 278–300.

Crockenburg, S. B. (1981). Infant irritability, mother responsiveness, and social support influences on the security of infant-mother attachment. *Child Development, 52,* 857–869.

Crowell, J. A., & Feldman, S. S. (1988). Mothers' internal models of relationships and children's behavioral and developmental status: A study of mother-child interaction. *Child Development, 59,* 1273–1285.

Deutscher, M. (1971). First pregnancy and family formation. In D. Milmen & G. Goldman (Eds.), *Psychoanalytic contributions to community psychology* (pp. 233–255). Springfield, IL: Charles C. Thomas.

De Vore, I., & Konner, M. (1974). Infancy in a hunter-gatherer life: An ethological perspective. In N. White (Ed.), *Ethology and psychiatry* (pp. 113–141). Toronto: University of Toronto Press.

DeVries, M. W. (1987). Alternatives to mother-infant attachment in the neonatal period. In C. M. Super (Ed.), *The role of culture in developmental disorder* (pp. 109–129). New York: Academic.

de Woolff, M. S., & van IJzendoorn, M. H. (1997). Sensitivity and attachment: A meta-analysis on parental antecedents of infant attachment. *Child Development, 68,* 571–591.

Emde, R. A., & Brown, C. (1978). Adaptation to the birth of Down syndrome infants. *Journal of the American Academy for Child Psychiatry, 17,* 299–323.

Field, T., Widmayer, S. M., Stringer, S., & Ignatoff, E. (1980). Teenage, lower class, black mothers and their preterm infants: An intervention and developmental follow-up. *Child Development, 51,* 426–436.

Fleming, A. S., & Corter, C. (1995). Psychobiology of maternal behavior in nonhuman mammals. In M. H. Bornstein, (Ed.), *Handbook of parenting* (Vol. II; pp. 59–86). Mahwah, NJ: Erlbaum.

Fleming, A. S., Corter, C., Franks, P., Surbey, M., Schneider, B. A., & Steiner, M.

(1993). Post-partum factors related to mother's attraction to newborn infant odors. *Developmental Psychobiology, 26,* 115–132.

Fleming, A. S., Corter, C., & Steiner, M. (1995). Sensory and hormonal control of maternal behavior in rat and human mothers. In C. R. Pryce, R. D. Martin, & D. Skuse (Eds.), *Motherhood in human and nonhuman primates* (pp. 106–114). Basel: Karger.

Fonagy, P., Steele, H., & Steele, M. (1991). Maternal representations of attachment during pregnancy predict organization of infant-mother attachment at one year of age. *Child Development, 62,* 891–905.

Fraiberg, S. (1980). *Clinical studies in infant mental health: The first year of life.* New York: Basic Books.

Frodi, A. M., & Lamb, M. E. (1978a). Fathers' and mothers' response to the faces and cries of normal and premature infants. *Developmental Psychology, 14,* 490–498.

Frodi, A. M., & Lamb, M. E. (1978b). Sex differences in responsiveness to infants: A developmental study of psychophysiological and behavioral responses. *Child Development, 49,* 1182–1188.

Frodi, A. M., & Lamb, M. E. (1980). Child abusers' responses to infant smiles and cries. *Child Development, 51,* 238–241.

Fruchtman, D. (1995). Attachment relationships of childbearing adolescents. Unpublished doctoral dissertation, California School for Professional Psychologists, Alameda, CA.

Fullard, W., & Reiling, A. M. (1976). An investigation of Lorenz's babyness. *Child Development, 47,* 1191–1193.

Furedy, J., Fleming, A. S., Ruble, D., Scher, H., Daly, J., Day, D., & Loewen, R. (1989). Sex differences in small-magnitude heart-rate program to sex use and input related stimuli. *Physiology and Behavior, 46,* 903–905.

George, C. (1996). A representational perspective of child abuse: Internal working models of attachment and caregiving. *Child Abuse and Neglect, 20,* 411–424.

George, C., Kaplan, N., & Main, M. (1984/1985/1996). *Adult Attachment Interview.* Unpublished interview, University of California, Berkeley.

George, C., & Solomon, J. (1989). Internal working models of caregiving and security of attachment at age six. *Infant Mental Health Journal, 10,* 222–237.

George, C., & Solomon, J. (1996). Representational models of relationships: Links between caregiving and attachment. *Infant Mental Health Journal, 17,* 198–216.

George, C., & Solomon, J. (1998, July). *Attachment disorganization at age six: Differences in doll play between punitive and caregiving children.* Paper presented at the meeting of the International Society for the Study of Behavioural Development, Berne, Switzerland.

George, C., & Solomon, J. (1999). Attachment and caregiving: The caregiving behavioral system. In J. Cassidy & P. Shaver (Eds.), *Handbook of attachment: Theory, research and clinical applications* (pp. 649–670). New York: Guilford.

George, C., & Solomon, J. (in press). The development of caregiving: A comparison of attachment and psychoanalytic approaches to mothering. *Psychoanalytic Inquiry.* Special issue: D. Diamond, S. Blatt, & D. Silver (Eds.).

Goldberg, S. (1983). Parent-infant bonding: Another look. *Child Development, 54,* 1355–1382.

Goldberg, S., & DiVitto, B. (1995). Parenting children born preterm. In M. H. Bornstein (Ed.), *Handbook of parenting* (Vol. I; pp. 209–231). Mahwah, NJ: Erlbaum.

Grossman, K., Fremmer-Bombik, E., Rudolph, J., & Grossman, K. E. (1988). Maternal representations as related to patterns of infant-mother attachment and maternal care during the first year. In R. A. Hinde & J. Stevenson-Hinde (Eds.), *Relationships within families* (pp. 241–260). Oxford: Oxford University Press.

Grossman, K. E., & Grossman, K. (1990). The wider concept of attachment in cross-cultural research. *Human Development, 33*, 31–47.

Haft, W., & Slade, A. (1989). Affect attunement and maternal attachment: A pilot study. *Infant Mental Health Journal, 10*, 157–172.

Heinicke, C. M., Guthrie, D., & Ruth, G. (1997). Marital adaptation, divorce, and parent-infant development: A prospective study. *Infant Mental Health Journal, 18*, 282–299.

Hinde, R. A. (1982a). *Ethology.* New York: Oxford University Press.

Hinde, R. A. (1982b). Attachment: Some conceptual and biological issues. In C. M. Parkes & J. Stevenson-Hinde (Eds.), *The place of attachment in human behavior* (pp. 60–78). London: Tavistock.

Hodges, W. F. (1986). *Interventions for children of divorce: Custody, access, and psychotherapy.* New York: Wiley.

Hoff-Ginsberg, E., & Tardif, T. (1995). Socioeconomic status and parenting. In M. H. Bornstein (Ed.), *Handbook of parenting* (Vol. II; pp. 161–188) Mahwah, NJ: Erlbaum.

Howrigan, G. A. (1988). Fertility, infant feeding, and change in the Yucatan. In R. A. Levine, P. M. Miller, & M. Maxwell (Eds.), *Parental behavior in diverse societies* (pp. 37–50). San Francisco: Jossey-Bass.

Hrdy, S. B. (1992). Fitness tradeoffs in the history and evolution of delegated mothering, with special references to wet-nursing, abandonment, and infanticide. *Ethology and Sociobiology, 13*, 409–442.

Isabella, R. A. (1993). Origins of attachment: Maternal interactive behavior across the first year. *Child Development, 64*, 605–621.

Jacobsen, T., Edelstein, W., & Hofman, V. (1994). A longitudinal study of the relation between representations of attachment in childhood and cognitive functioning in childhood and adolescence. *Developmental Psychology, 30*, 112–124.

Jacobvitz, D., Hazen, N. L., & Riggs, S. (1997, April). *Disorganized mental processes in mothers, frightening/frightened caregiving, and disoriented, disorganized behavior in infancy.* Paper presented at the Biennial Conference of the Society for the Research for Child Development, Washington, DC.

Johnston, J., & Campbell, L. E. G. (1987). *Impasses of divorce.* New York: Free Press.

Kaplan, H. (1996). A theory of fertility and parental investment in traditional and modern societies. *Yearbook of Physical Anthropology, 39*, 91–136.

Kaplan, H., & Dove, H. (1987). Infant development among the Ache of Eastern Paraguay. *Developmental Psychology, 23*, 190–198.

Kermoian, R., & Liederman, P. H. (1986). Infant attachment to mother and child caretaker in an East African community. *International Journal of Behavioral Development, 9*, 455–469.

Klaus, M. H., & Kennell, J. H. (1976). *Maternal-infant bonding. St. Louis, MO: Mosby.

Klaus, M. H., Kennell, J. H., & Klaus, P. H. (1995). *Bonding*. Reading, MA: Addison-Wesley.

Kondo-Ikemura, K., & Waters, E. (1995). Maternal behavior and infant security in Old World monkeys: Conceptual issues and a methodological bridge between human and nonhuman primate research. In E. Waters, B. Vaughn, G. Posada, & K. Kondo-Ikemura (Eds.), Caregiving, cultural, and cognitive perspectives on secure-base behavior and working models (pp. 97–110). *Monographs of the Society for Research in Child Development, 60* (Serial No. 244).

Lamb, M. (1982). Early contact and mother-infant bonding: One decade later. *Pediatrics, 70,* 763–768.

Langlois, J. (1988). The role of physical attractiveness in the observation of adult-child interactions: Eye of the beholder or behavioral reality? *Developmental Psychology, 24,* 254–263.

Langlois, J. H., Ritter, J. M., Cassey, R. J., & Sawin, D. B. (1995). Infant attractiveness predicts maternal behaviors and attitudes. *Developmental Psychology, 31,* 464–472.

Lee, R. E. (1995). Women look at their experience of pregnancy. *Infant Mental Health Journal, 16,* 192–205.

Levine, R. A. (1977). Child rearing as cultural adaptation. In P. H. Liederman, S. R. Tulkin, & A. Rosenfeld (Eds.), *Culture and infancy* (pp. 15–28). New York: Academic.

Levine, R. A. (1994). *Child care and culture*. London: Cambridge University Press.

Lieberman, A. (1996). Aggression and sexuality in relation to toddler attachment: Im-plications for the caregiving system. *Infant Mental Health Journal, 17,* 276–292.

Liefer, M. (1980). *Psychological effects of motherhood*. New York: Praeger.

Liotti, G. (1999). Disorganization of attachment as a model for understanding dissociative psychopathology. In J. Solomon & C. George (Eds.), *Attachment disorganization*. New York: Guilford.

Lyons-Ruth, K. (1996). Attachment relationships among children with aggressive behavior problems: The role of disorganized early attachment strategies. *Journal of Clinical and Consulting Psychology, 64,* 64–73.

Lyons-Ruth, K., & Block, D. (1996). The disturbed caregiving system: Relations among childhood trauma, maternal caregiving, and infant affect and attachment. *Infant Mental Health Journal, 17,* 257–275.

Lyons-Ruth, K, Bronfman, E. & Atwood, G. I. (1999). A relational diathesis model of hostile-helpless states of mind: Expressions in mother-infant interaction. In J. Solomon & C. George (Eds.), *Attachment disorganization*. New York: Guilford.

Lyons-Ruth, K., Connell, D. B., Grunebaum, H., & Botein, S. (1990). Infants at social risk: Maternal depression and family support services as mediators of infant development and security of attachment. *Child Development, 61,* 85–98.

Lyons-Ruth, K., & Jacobvitz, D. (1999). Attachment disorganization: Unresolved loss, relational violence, and lapses in behavioral and attentional strategies. In J. Cassidy & P. Shaver (Eds.), *Handbook of attachment: Theory, research, and clinical applications* (pp. 520–594). New York: Guilford.

Main, M. (1990). Cross-cultural studies of attachment organization: Recent studies, changing methodologies and the concept of conditional strategies. *Human Development, 33,* 48–61.

Main, M., & Cassidy, J. (1988). Categories of response to reunion with the parent at age 6: Predictable from infant attachment classifications and stable over a 1-month period. *Developmental Psychology, 24,* 415–426.

Main, M., & George, C. (1985). Responses of abused and disadvantaged toddlers to distress in agemates: A study in the day care setting. *Developmental Psychology, 21,* 407–412.

Main, M., & Hesse, E. (1990). Parents' unresolved traumatic experiences are related to infant disorganized attachment status: Is frightened and/or frightening parental behavior the linking mechanism? In M. T. Greenberg, D. Cicchetti, & E. M. Cummings (Eds.), *Attachment in the preschool years* (pp. 161–182). Chicago: University of Chicago Press.

Main, M., Kaplan, N., & Cassidy, J. (1985). Security in infancy, childhood, and adulthood: A move to the level of representation. In I. Bretherton & E. Waters (Eds.), Growing points in attachment theory and research (pp. 66–104). *Monographs of the Society for Research in Child Development, 50*(1–2, Serial No. 209).

Main, M., & Solomon, J. (1990). Procedures for identifying infants as disorganized/disoriented during the Ainsworth Strange Situation. In M. T. Greenberg, D. Cicchetti, & E. M. Cummings (Eds.), *Attachment in the preschool years* (pp. 121–160). Chicago: University of Chicago Press.

Manning-Orenstein, G. (1998). A birth intervention: Comparing the influence of doula assistance at birth versus Lamaze birth preparation on first-time mothers' working models of caregiving. *Alternative Therapies in Health and Medicine, 4,* 73–81.

Marvin, R. S., & Pianta, R. C. (1996). Mothers' reaction to their child's diagnosis: Relations with security of attachment. *Journal of Child Clinical Psychology, 25,* 436–445.

Merkin, D. (1997, March 24). The mystery of Dr. B. *The New Yorker.*

Miller, B. D. (1987). Female infanticide and child neglect in rural North India. In N. Scheper-Hughes (Ed.), *Child survival: Anthropological perspectives on the treatment and maltreatment of children* (pp. 164–181). Boston: D. Reidel.

Minde, K. (1984). The impact of prematurity on the later behavior of children and their families. *Clinics in Perinatology, 11,* 227–244.

Minde, K. (1993). Prematurity and serious medical illness in infancy: Implications for development and intervention. In C. H. Zeanah (Ed.), *Handbook of infant mental health* (pp. 87–105).

Mintzner, D., Als, H., Tronick, E. Z., & Brazelton, T. B. (1985). Parenting an infant with a birth defect: The regulation of self-esteem. *Zero to Three, V,* 390–396.

Miyake, K., Chen, S. J., & Campos, J. J. (1985). Infant temperament, mother's mode of interaction, and attachment in Japan: An interim report. In I. Bretherton & E. Waters (Eds.), Growing points in attachment theory and research (pp. 276–297). *Monographs of the Society for Research in Child Development, 50*(1–2, Serial No. 209).

Moss, E., Parent, S., Gosselin, C., Rousseau, D., & St. Laurent, D. (1996). Attachment and teacher-reported behavior problems during the preschool and early school-age period. *Development and Psychopathology, 8,* 511–525.

Moss, E., Rousseau, D., Parent, S., St. Laurent, D., & Saintonge, J. (1998). Attachment at school-age: Maternal reported stress, mother-child and behavior problems. *Child Development, 69,* 1390–1405.

Murry, A. (1985). Aversiveness is in the mind of the beholder: Perception of infant crying by adults. In B. Lester & C. Boukydis (Eds.), *Infant crying* (pp. 217–240). New York: Plenum.

Osofsky, J. D. (Ed.). (1997). *Children in a violent society.* New York: Guilford.

Perry, B. D., Pollard, R. A., Blakley, T. L., & Vigilante, D. (1995). Childhood trauma, the neurobiology of adaptation, and "use dependent" development of the brain: How "states" become "traits." *Infant Mental Health Journal, 16,* 271–289.

Pianta, R. C., Egeland, B., & Adam, E. M. (1996). Adult attachment classification and self-reported psychiatric symptomatology as assessed by the Minnesota Multiphasic Personality Inventory. *Journal of Consulting and Clinical Psychology, 64,* 273–281.

Pianta, R. C., & Marvin, R. S. (1992). *The reaction to diagnosis interview.* Unpublished interview, University of Virginia, Charlottesville, VA.

Pianta, R. C., Marvin, R., Britner, P., & Borowitz, K. (1996). Mothers' resolution of their children's diagnoses: Organized patterns of caregiving representations. *Infant Mental Health Journal, 17,* 239–256.

Pianta, P. C., Marvin, R. S., & Morog, M. C. (1999). Resolving the past and present: Relations with attachment organization. In J. Solomon & C. George (Eds.), *Attachment disorganization.* New York: Guilford.

Pryce, C. R. (1995). Determinants of motherhood in human and nonhuman primates: A biosocial model. In C. R. Pryce, R. D. Martin, & D. Skuse (Eds.), *Mother-hood in human and nonhuman primates* (pp. 1–15). Basel: Karger.

Rode, S. E., Chang, P., Fisch, R. O., & Sroufe, L. A. (1981). Attachment patterns in infants separated at birth. *Developmental Psychology, 17,* 188–191.

Rosenblatt, J. S. (1995). Hormonal basis of parenting in mammals. In M. H. Bornstein (Ed.), *Handbook of parenting* (Vol. II, pp. 3–25). Mahwah, NJ: Erlbaum.

Rutter, M. (1997). Clinical implications of attachment concepts: Retrospect and prospect. In L. Atkinson & K. J. Zucker (Eds.), *Attachment and psychopathology* (pp. 17–45). New York: Guilford.

Sameroff, A., & Chandler, M. (1975). Reproductive risk and the continuum of caretaking casualty. In F. D. Horowitz, E. M. Hetherington, S. Scarr-Salapateck, & G. Siegal (Eds.), *Review of child development research* (Vol. 4, pp. 187–244). Chicago: University of Chicago.

Sameroff, A. J. (1993). Models of development and developmental risk. In C. H. Zeanah (Ed.), *Handbook of infant mental health* (pp. 3–14). New York: Guilford Press.

Scheper-Hughes, N. (1987). Culture, scarcity and maternal thinking: Mother love and child death in Northeast Brazil. In N. Scheper-Hughes (Ed.), *Child survival: Anthropological perspectives on treatment and maltreatment of children* (pp. 291–317). Boston: D. Reidel.

Scheper-Hughes, N. (1990). Mother live and child death in Northeast Brazil. In J. W. Stigler, R. A. Shweder, & G. Herdt (Eds.), *Cultural psychology* (pp. 542–565). Cambridge: Cambridge University Press.

Schuengel, C., van IJzendoorn, M. H., Bakermans-Kranenburg, M. J., & Blom, M. (1999). Frightening, frightened, and/or dissociated behavior, unresolved loss, and infant disorganization. In J. Solomon &

C. George (Eds.), *Attachment disorganization*. New York: Guilford.

Slade, A., Belsky, J., Aber, J. L., & Phelps, J. L. (1997). *Maternal representations of their toddlers: Links to adult attachment and observed mothering.* Manuscript submitted for publication.

Slade, A., & Cohen, L. J. (1996). The process of parenting and the remembrance of things past. *Infant Mental Health Journal, 17,* 217–238.

Slade, A., Dermer, M., Gerber, J., Gibson, L., Graf, F., Siegal, N., & Tobias, K. (1995, March). *Prenatal representation, dyadic interaction, and the quality of attachment.* Paper presented at the Biennial Meeting of the Society for Research in Child Development, Indianapolis, IN.

Solomon, J., & George, C. (1996a). Defining the caregiving system: Toward a theory of caregiving. *Infant Mental Health Journal, 17,* 183–197.

Solomon, J., & George, C. (1999). The development of attachment in separated and divorced families: Effects of overnight visitation, parent, and couple variables. *Attachment and Human Development, i.*

Solomon, J., & George, C. (in press-a). The caregiving behavioral system in mothers of infants: A comparison of divorced, separated, and married mothers. *Attachment and Human Development.*

Solomon, J., & George, C. (in press-b). The place of disorganization in attachment theory: Linking classic observations with contemporary findings. In J. Solomon & C. George (Eds.), *Attachment disorganization.* New York: Guilford.

Solomon, J., George, C., & De Jong, A. (1995). Children classified as controlling at age six: Evidence of disorganized representational strategies and aggression at home and school. *Development and Psychopathology, 7,* 447–464.

Solomon, J., George, C., & Silverman, N. (in press). Maternal caregiving Q-sort: Describing age-related changes in mother-infant interaction. In E. Waters, B. Vaughn, & D. Teti (Eds.), *Patterns of attachment behavior: Q-sort perspectives in secure base behavior and caregiving in infancy and childhood.* Hillsdale, NJ: Erlbaum.

Sroufe, L. A. (1983). Infant-caregiver attachment and patterns of adaptation in preschool: The roots of maladaptation and competence. In M. Perlmutter (Ed.), *Minnesotal Symposium in Child Psychology* (Vol. 16; pp. 41–81). Hillsdale, NJ: Erlbaum.

Sroufe, L. A. (1988). The role of infant-caregiver attachment in development. In J. Belsky & T. Nezworski (Eds.), *Clinical implications of attachment* (pp. 18–38). Hillsdale, NJ: Erlbaum.

Sroufe, L. A., & Fleeson, J. (1986). Attachment and the construction of relationships. In W. Hartup & Z. Rubin (Eds.), *The nature and development of relationships* (pp. 51–71). Hillsdale, NJ: Earlbaum.

Steele, H., & Steele, M. (1994). Intergenerational patterns of attachment. *Advances in Personal Relationships, 5,* 93–120.

Stern, D. (1995) *The motherhood constellation: A unified view of parent-infant psychotherapy.* New York: Basic Books.

Stevenson-Hinde, J. (1994). An ethological perspective. *Psychological Inquiry, 5,* 62–65.

Suomi, S. J. (1995). Attachment theory and nonhuman primates. In S. Goldberg, R. Muir, & J. Kerr (Eds.), *Attachment theory: Social, developmental, and clini-*

cal perspectives (pp. 185–201). Hillsdale, NJ: Analytic.

Trivers, R. L. (1974). Parent-offspring conflict. *American Zoologist, 11,* 249–264.

Tronick, E. A., Morelli, G., & Winn, S. (1987). Multiple caretaking of Efe (Pygmy) infants. *American Anthropologist, 89,* 96–106.

True, M. (1994). *Mother-infant attachment and communication among the Dogon of Mali (West Africa).* Unpublished doctoral dissertation, University of California, Berkeley.

van IJzendoorn, M. H. (1995). Adult attachment representations, parental responsiveness, and infant attachment: A meta-analysis on the predictive validity of the Adult Attachment Interview. *Psychological Bulletin, 117,* 387–403.

van IJzendoorn, M. H., Goldberg, S., Kroonenberg, P. M., & Frenkel, O. J. (1992). The relative effects of maternal and child problems on the quality of attachment: A meta-analysis of attachment in clinical samples. *Child Development, 63,* 840–858.

Vaughn, B. E., Goldberg, S., Atkinson, L., Marcovitch, S., MacGregor, D., & Siefer, R. (1994). Quality of toddler-mother attachment in children with Down syndrome: Limit to interpretation of Strange Situation behavior. *Child Development, 65,* 95–108.

Vondra, J. I., Hommerding, K. D., & Shaw, D. S. (1996). *Stability and change in infant attachment in a low-income sample.* Unpublished manuscript, University of Pittsburgh, Pittsburgh, PA.

Wallerstein, J. (1991). The long-term effects of divorce on children: A review. *Journal of the American Academy of Adolescent Psychiatry, 30,* 349–361.

Ward, M. J. & Carlson, E. (1995). Associations among adult attachment representations, maternal sensitivity, and infant-mother attachment in a sample of adolescent mothers. *Child Development, 66,* 69–79.

Waters, E., & Deane, K. E. (1985). Defining and assessing individual differences in attachment relationships: Q-methodology and the organization of behavior in infancy and early childhood. In I. Bretherton & E. Waters (Eds.), Growing points in attachment theory and research (pp. 41–65). *Monographs of the Society for Research in Child Development, 50*(1–2, Serial No. 209).

Weisenfeld, A., & Klorman, R. (1978). The mother's psychophysiological reactions to contrasting affective expressions by her own and an unfamiliar infant. *Developmental Psychology, 14,* 294–304.

Winnicott, D. W. (1958). *Collected papers.* London: Tavistock.

Zahn-Waxler, C., Freidman, S. L., & Cummings, E. M. (1983). Children's emotions and behaviors in response to infant cries. *Child Development, 54,* 1532–1528.

Zeanah, C. H., Hirshberg, L., Danis, B. A., Brenna, M., & Miller, D. (1995, March). *On the specificity of the Adult Attachment Interview in a high risk sample.* Paper presented at the Biennial Meeting of the Society for Child Development Research, Indianapolis, IN.

12

Exploring Triangular Relationships in Infancy

Elisabeth Fivaz-Depeursinge, France Frascarolo, and Rosine Lob-Izraelski

12

Introduction

Our team has set out to study the interaction between father, mother, and infant on the grounds that, after all, this triangle is the niche in which a baby develops (when the father is absent, usually another person such as a companion or grandmother comes into play as a third party). Surely, dyadic relations between the parents and between the infant and either parent are essential. Yet the dyads also form together a triadic unit. We know from systems theory that it is not legitimate to infer the nature of this unit from these dyadic relationships (Belsky, Rovine, & Fish, 1989; Lewis, Owen, & Cox, 1988; Yogman, 1981). Thus, the triadic unit has to be observed as an entity in itself, with its specific developmental trajectory (Frascarolo, 1997; Parke, 1988; Pedersen, 1985).

Perhaps the main reason for putting off this exploration so long is the complexity of the triad in comparison with the dyad (Parke, Power, & Gottman, 1979). Indeed, whereas face-to-face dyadic relationships encompass a single configuration, face-to-face triangular relationships comprise four possible configurations: the single "three-together" that involves the partners in direct interaction and the three "two-plus-ones" that place either father, mother, or baby in a third party position with respect to the other two family members engaged in direct interaction. Therefore, the notion of triangulation as defined by psychodynamic or family clinicians extends beyond the classical notion of exclusion.

Accordingly, the WAIMH study group on interfaces has proposed a revisitation of triangulation (Emde, 1994; Fivaz-Depeursinge, Stern, Corboz-Warnery, & Bürgin, 1997; Fivaz-Depeursinge et al., 1994). We explicitly include the handling of the system of the four configurations in a triad under this heading. The goal of this process is to maintain threesome relatedness under various conditions, notably pleasure, conflict, and uncertainty. The label *interactional triangulation* applies when referring to its behavioral enactment, and the label *imaginary triangulation* applies when referring to its representational enactment. Likewise, triangulation may be conducted collectively, for example, at the family level, or individually. This new perspective requires observation of interactions of the father-mother-infant triad in the four configurations if one is to fully assess their handling of the triangular system. Moreover, it poses anew the developmental question of how and when an infant comes to master triangulation.

The first step we took to explore these issues was to elaborate a semistructured situation, the Lausanne Triadic Play (LTP; Corboz-Warnery, Fivaz-Depeursinge, Gertsch-Bettens, & Favez, 1993; Fivaz-Depeursinge, 1989; Fivaz-Depeursinge &

Corboz-Warnery, 1995, 1999). It enables a systematic observation of the father, mother, and infant in interaction. We found play trilogues, the analogue of play dialogues, to be the best choice for our purposes because direct, purely social interactions are most revealing of communication resources and difficulties (Stern, 1974). In particular, since the natural goal of trilogue play is to create moments of threesome playful affect communion, the partners have to closely coordinate their signals. Hence, it is the degree of interpartner coordination that is most critical to our assessment. We called this property the family alliance. We assume it is unique to the triadic unit, just as the dyadic alliance would be unique to a given dyadic unit.

We then elaborated three readings of these interactions: (1) a clinical reading, based on intuition and experience, which aims at detecting what appears most salient and meaningful to a clinician's eye; (2) a structural reading, based on a systematic, more micro and objective description, which detects the behavioral patterns a family generates in order to reach the goal of trilogue play; and (3) a developmental reading, which specifically focuses on the infant's development of triangular strategies and parents' responses.

We applied these readings to data of nonclinical families volunteering for a longitudinal research project, as well as with clinical families brought by their therapists to our center for expert advice. Using the three readings, we studied two samples. Sample One included 16 paired families (clinical and nonclinical) with infants ranging in age from two to nine months. Sample

Two included 12 nonclinical families observed five times over the first year and followed up at four years.

On the basis of these observations, we devised an assessment scheme of triadic interactions that involves four types of family alliances. These alliances describe functioning that ranges from optimal (cooperative) and fair (stressed) to problematic (collusive) and pathological (disordered). It is important to understand that a family alliance remains constant in spite of the changes a family traverses as the infant moves from stage to stage. Indeed, the results of our first longitudinal study indicate impressive stability in alliance over the first year (Frascarolo, Fivaz-Depeursinge, & Corboz-Warnery, 1996). The type of alliance at three months postpartum, namely at the social stage, remained stable at six months (at the object stage) and at nine months (at the intersubjective stage). At this time, we are examining whether the family alliance persists at 18 months, namely at the moral/verbal stage (Emde & Buchsbaum, 1990), as well as comparing it with what we call the prenatal family alliance (during pregnancy). As for the development of the infant's triangular strategies, our exploratory results indicate that the more functional the family alliance, the most differentiated and extensive the infant's and the parents' strategies at nine months, namely at the beginning of the intersubjective stage. We shall see that this has far-reaching implications regarding the development of threesome relatedness.

In this chapter, we introduce the three readings by means of the data on Tom and his parents, a nonclinical family. It is in many ways an ordinary family, yet it verges on the problematic in some respects. Therefore, reporting on these data will allow covering a wide range of functioning and making excursions into the optimal as well as into the problematic ranges. Most of all, it illustrates how diverging component dyadic subsystems may combine to constitute a unique triadic unit, as well as the major influence of the parental coordination. Finally, it also allows us to introduce the new concept of triangulation.

Because of the novelty of these themes, we will report and discuss the works of other authors in this new field after presenting our model and results.

The Lausanne Triadic Play Paradigm

Setting and Equipment

It is important to understand precisely how the LTP setting works for the family. Figure 12.1 illustrates the setup from an aerial view.

The three seats form an equilateral triangle. The distances between partners facilitate interaction with the infant, and the parents' seats are more oriented toward the infant's seat rather than toward one another, given that play with young infants is typically infant-centered. Although the parents are instructed not to displace their seats, they can easily rotate on them. In this way, they are able to deviate from the preset arrangement. The infant's seat is mounted

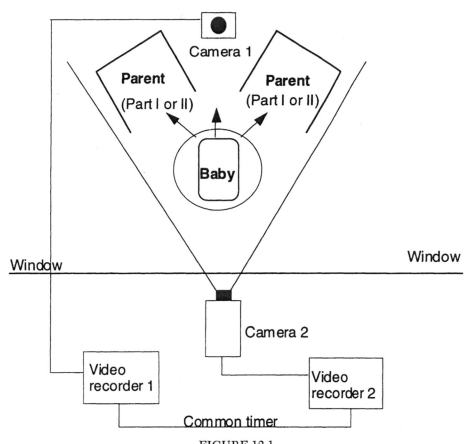

FIGURE 12.1
Aerial view of the LTP setting: observation layout.

on a table that is adjustable to three positions: toward one or the other parent or in between them. This allows the parents to designate the infant's direct partner. The infant's seat is also adjustable in size and in inclination to fit the infant's growth, thus allowing the baby to utilize all his energy for interacting. An inappropriately inclined seat would make it more difficult for the baby to engage in interaction.

The recording equipment includes at least two cameras. One of the cameras videotapes the parents at three-quarters face, from head to knees, while the other one captures the infant in a close-up, full frontal view. Two other cameras may be added to videotape the parents' faces in close-ups (split screen). The two or three records are synchronized by a timer and kept separate for adequate resolution in coding.

Task

The LTP is a semistructured situation that is appropriate from eight weeks until the child first begins walking. We will see that it can be easily adjusted to other stages of family development. It is divided in four parts that cover each of the four possible configurations of a triadic relationship listed in the introduction. They are represented in Figure 12.2.

The procedure is as follows:

1. One parent (active parent) plays with the infant while the other parent watches (third party parent).
2. The parents switch roles.

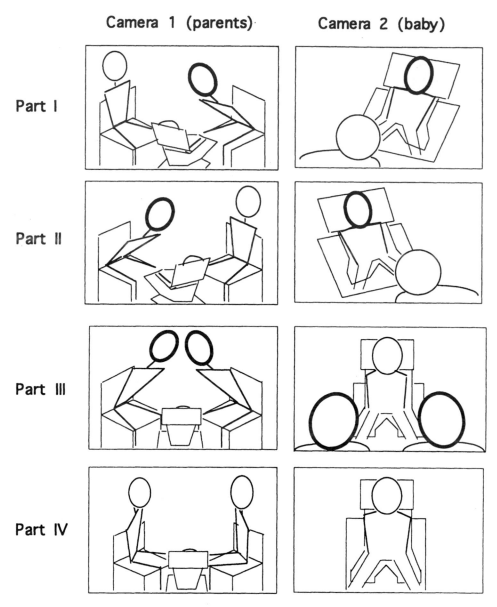

Camera 1 (parents) **Camera 2 (baby)**

Part I

Part II

Part III

Part IV

FIGURE 12.2
The four parts of the LTP: video screens.

3. Both parents play together with the infant.
4. The infant becomes the third party as the parents directly interact with one another.

On the day of the assessment, parents are shown how to incline the child's seat to comfortably fit the baby in the seat. Once the parents are seated, we give specific instructions, asking them to play as a family and explaining that the play will take place in four parts. We specify each of these parts and tell the parents that we will leave it up to them to decide how to orient the child's seat and how long to play in each part. Therefore, the timing of the four parts and the transition points are not established by the experimenters, but rather are left open to the families. Prior to nine months, the instructions also stipulate not to use objects. From nine months on, when the infants have learned to coordinate play with objects and persons, the instructions stipulate to try not to use objects, at least in the beginning. In Sample Two, we did standardize the order in which father and mother took their turns playing with the infant. Finally, immediately after the triadic play session has ended, we review the videotapes with the parents and ask them, among other things, to precisely identify the transition points between the parts.

The narratives of Tom's family's interactions will uncover in detail what is involved in such a task.

It is possible to keep the structure of the task, namely interacting in the four different configurations, while accommodating it to other developmental stages. It requires modifying the physical setting in which it takes place to fit the toddler or child and changing the content of the task to adjust to developmental issues that are pertinent. Thus, it is more appropriate to sit the toddler and his parents at a round table to allow play with objects. The negotiation of limits that comes to the fore at the moral/verbal stage naturally arises from such a physical setting. Then, as the child acquires the capacity to elaborate narratives, we ask the family to coconstruct a story, moving along the four successive configurations. As to the prenatal stage, about the sixth month of pregnancy, namely when the parents' representations of their imagined baby are at their peak (Ammaniti, 1991), we ask the parents to role-play their first encounter with their newborn. We help them enact the scene by presenting them with a doll and role-playing the beginning of the encounter with them.

We present Tom's family data at three different stages: prenatal, social, and intersubjective. More precisely, we start out with the clinical reading of the prenatal LTP. Because the corresponding structural reading is still under elaboration, we then proceed directly to the clinical and structural readings at the social and intersubjective stages. We finish with the developmental reading of Tom's triangular strategies and his parents' responses.

Note that we have conducted the clinical and microanalytical readings separately, in order to preserve their independence.

Tom's Family at the Prenatal Stage

Clinical Reading

The question we ask in the clinical reading, be it at the prenatal or postnatal stage, is straightforward: Are the parents (to be) working together and helping each other toward the LTP goal? This provides an answer regarding their family (to be) alliance. Note that it is also clinically pertinent to ask the corresponding question regarding the family and the team, namely their working alliance. Are they working together and helping each other toward the goal they share: implementing the research tasks to everyone's benefit? There are strong reasons to assume that there exists an isomorphism between these two dimensions. The external exchanges of the family strongly reflect their internal exchanges (Reiss, 1981).

Tom's parents are a middle-class couple, in their mid-twenties. The father works as an educator, and the mother works as a trainer in a fitness club. They have been recruited through their gynecologist at the time of the first echography and have volunteered for the research project.

About the fifth month of pregnancy, the facilitator who was to accompany the family across the transition to parenthood and up to 18 months postnatal met with the couple for an interview. It focused on individual and couple histories of the parents-to-be, as well as on their representations around the arrival of their first child. During this preliminary interview, we noted a set of patterns that would characterize our exchanges with this family. Whereas the spouses' dialogue with the facilitator proved their motivation and engagement to collaborate, it was interspersed with brief moments of embarrassment and silence regarding certain subjects. This occurred in particular when questions required them to anticipate unknown situations and project themselves into the future. Some questions appeared to surprise the couple. It was the wife who explicitly manifested it, as if they had never before thought of them. The facilitator sometimes had to reformulate a question, as if the wife was not ready to listen. She finally answered, yet tended to repeatedly solicit her husband's approval, in particular by turning to him while verbally addressing the facilitator.

Overall, the couple showed themselves attentive and concerned to find the appropriate answers. Trust was progressively built up between them and the facilitator. This was demonstrated by the information they provided on their couple and origin families, as well as by the quasitherapeutic comments the facilitator authorized herself to make.

Then the parents-to-be were invited into the LTP setting to role-play their first encounter with their newborn after its delivery. Playing the midwife's role, the facilitator brought them their "baby" (a doll). They expressed their discomfort before the facilitator had time to state the instructions. Again, it was the mother-to-be who solicited her spouse's help. Even though he remained reserved, she set out to begin the task. This was revealing of the type of working alliance she and her spouse established with the team: an assiduous submission.

During the first part in the two-plus-one configuration where the mother-to-be played with the doll and the father-to-be was third party, she expressed her feelings of impotence and self-depreciation in the face of this task through body and verbal signals and called her husband to her rescue. He instead referred her back to the instructions. At a loss, she gave him the signal to proceed to the second part of the play. The father-to-be's attempt was more audacious, yet short-lived. He soon gave the doll back to his wife. They skipped the three-together part, where they were supposed to play together with the doll, and put the doll back into its crib. Having expressed their disappointment at their poor performance, they called for the facilitator.

During the subsequent discussion, the parents-to-be attempted to justify their inability, and the facilitator tried to reassure them. It appears that it was the absence of anticipation of their relation with the baby-to-come that prevented these parents from engaging in the role-playing. This difficulty is in sharp contrast with the playful but authentic engagement of the parents-to-be who otherwise anticipate their relations with their future child. We will see in the discussion that these prenatal anticipations also correlate with differences in actual interactions at the postnatal stage. The family alliance between the parents-to-be was existed, yet was insufficient to allow them to effectively work together and help each other. Indeed, covert competition and disagreements coexisted with supportive actions between them. Likewise, the working

alliance between the couple and the team was also developing, yet it was revealed as insufficient to allow them to optimally work together and help each other. The parents-to-be were curious, interested, and showed great willingness to collaborate. However, their submission prevented them from openly refusing a task and compelled them to endure a situation they experienced as difficult to bear. Nevertheless, some verbal and nonverbal signals indicated an underlying passive opposition.

Tom's Family at the Social Stage

Clinical Reading

The postnatal consultation for the clinical assessment of the working and family alliances at the social stage took place when Tom was 14 weeks old. During a previous session, the family had the opportunity to familiarize themselves with the LTP task. At that time, the parents had voiced criticisms, albeit humorously, concerning the baby seat (this would remain a leitmotiv throughout the sessions). They had experienced several difficulties, some of them fairly usual at that age. Their play session lasted an exceptionally long time, much too long considering their infant's development. The baby had been fussy, and the parents had trouble coordinating their efforts to help him. They also did not dare interrupt the play and take Tom onto their laps in order to really soothe him.

The 14 weeks session started out with a feeding. In the meantime, the conversation was somewhat dull, and it was up to the facilitator to animate it. During the installation of the setting, the father jokingly complained again about the baby seat, whereas the mother hurried to help out the facilitator. Tension was distinct.

The consultant was careful to terminate the delivery of the instruction with an indication about the usual duration of play (8 to 12 minutes). She also asked the parents to please remember that after the LTP, a stranger would play with their baby, recommending that they take this into account in their timing. Yet again, confusion arose in the mother's mind on this issue, and it was father who set her straight. The mother replied by asking him not to play too long (he was to play first) and not to use up all the games. During Part I, the father succeeded in engaging Tom in a succession of games that they both enjoyed. The mother, though resonating with their pleasure, remained tense and apprehensive about her own success in the next part. It was the mother who proposed that the father terminate his play part. He acquiesced, yet delayed the transition and then moved the baby's seat quite abruptly.

During her play (Part II), the mother struggled to capture Tom's attention, which often focused on the father. She had trouble engaging him in games and expressed her disappointment. However, toward the end, she initiated a physical game with him that succeeded for a short while. However, the father unexpectedly interfered with their game by holding out his hand to support Tom's head. Tom reacted by fussing, and the game was over. The mother solicited the father's advice. The father declined, and she decided unilaterally to move to Part III.

By that time, Tom was crying. The parents did not succeed in coordinating their soothing actions. They tried in a rather disorderly way using various actions, such as moving him around, singing, changing his position in the seat, caressing him, giving him their fingers to suck on, and so on. The mother's worry over pleasing the research team was perceptible.

Growing tired and in spite of Tom's crying, the mother decided to proceed to Part IV, and the father eventually gave in, too. It is noteworthy that when they gave up working at soothing Tom to proceed to Part IV, Tom was finally able to quiet down. Yet by then, the mother was already worrying about Tom getting too tired to play with the stranger (the next task). She prematurely interrupted this part in spite of the fact that he was calm.

In summary, we recognize the very same resources and difficulties observed at the prenatal stage in working together and helping each other as a family and a team. In spite of their perceptiveness of the baby's states and their empathic stance, the parents are overly influenced by Tom's distress. Again, supportive actions between the parents coexist with covert competition between them that prevents them from coordinating their actions in an effective way. Likewise, their collaboration is tinged with passive opposition that prevents their fully engaging in the task.

Structural Reading

The structural reading captures the characteristic patterns of repeated interactions

(Fivaz-Depeursinge, Frascarolo, & Corboz-Warnery, 1996). This approach of triadic interactions parallels those developed to describe dyadic interactions, in particular under the term of "ongoing regulations" (Beebe & Lachman, 1994) or "dyadic phases" (Cohn & Tronick, 1987). The LTP model states that when partners engage in play trilogues, as in other face-to-face situations, they fulfill together four functions that constitute a nested series in which each of them constitutes a context for the next. The four functions are: (1) participation: they display their readiness to interact; (2) organization: they take on specific roles; (3) focal attention: they sustain a joint focus; and (4) affective contact: they share affects. Thus, when we assess the structure of triadic play interactions, we examine each of the four embedded functions in succession.

To carry out these functions during the LTP, the participants rely on four levels of interaction that are connected yet distinct (see Figure 12.3). Level 1 concerns the orientations of the participants' pelvises, Level 2 concerns the orientations of their torsos, Level 3 concerns the orientations of their heads and gazes, and Level 4 concerns their expressive signals, made up of facial, vocal, and gestural displays. As we progress from Level 1 to Level 4, the coordination between the participants becomes distinctly more complex and more rapid (Fivaz-Depeursinge, 1991).

The assessment of triadic interactions may appear complicated. The most critical task is to set one's mind to attending to what goes on between the interactants rather than focusing on individuals (Scheflen, 1964). Then, provided one strictly follows the procedure, examining each function in

FIGURE 12.3
The four levels of interaction in trilogue play.

turn and level by level, assessing triadic patterns becomes practicable. (The precise criteria are described in a manual that includes training tapes, the GETCEF [Fivaz-Depeursinge, Cornut-Zimmer, Borcard-Sacco, & Corboz-Warnery, 1997]. Training necessitates sessions at a center practicing the LTP.)

PARTICIPATION

We ask whether everyone is included in the play or if anyone is excluded. Mutual participation obviously is the first necessary function to fulfill in order to achieve trilogue play because, if anyone is excluded, then no trilogue play can take place. Physically, participation is displayed at the four levels of interaction.

PELVISES AND TORSOS

The orientations of the pelvises (Level 1) as well as of those of the torsos (Level 2) of the three interactants delimit a transactional space within which their exchanges will take place. When all partners have equal access to this space, everyone is included, and none are excluded. In the LTP situation, where the parents have a guiding role with respect to their child, the parents orient their bodies toward the infant's body, thus signifying their readiness to interact. If one parent orients toward the other parent, then he or she would automatically exclude the infant. Likewise, orienting outward would constitute an autoexclusion. (Note that this is often observed in disordered family alliances, where participation derails.) As for the infant, a three-month-old baby does not have sufficient control to include or exclude himself at Levels 1 and

2. It is up to the parents to substitute for him to include him, by adjusting his seat so that he sits in an appropriate position. Without proper physical support, he would be prevented from participating because of his discomfort.

During the four parts of the play, Tom is comfortably seated and his parents' pelvises and torsos are oriented toward him. Therefore, participation is implemented at Levels 1 and 2.

HEAD AND GAZE AND EXPRESSIVE LEVELS

When everyone is included at the head and gaze level (Level 3), the interactants tend to keep each other in their field of vision, at least peripherally. Therefore, exclusion at Level 3 corresponds to head and gaze aversions that cut off a partner from the peripheral vision of the others. At the expressive level (Level 4), exclusion occurs when one or the other fails to keep in touch with the others. When everyone is included, one observes the partners joining in brief moments of triadic mutual affective contact at regular intervals, whether positive or negative, such as mutual smiles, confrontations, or tensions. These moments are called triadic expressive events (TEE). When someone is excluded, there are few sufficiently coordinated TEEs.

In Tom's family, no one is visually cut off (Level 3) and everyone participates in moments of affective contact (Level 4). Even in the three-together part, when Tom fusses, he remains in touch with his parents, even though it is in a negative mode. Therefore, participation is also implemented at Levels 3 and 4.

However, as noted, the parents have difficulty coping together with Tom's irritation during Part III. This lack of coordination corresponds to a partial derailment of the next function of organization.

ORGANIZATION

After assessing the partners' participation, we begin the second assessment. Specifically, we ask whether everyone keeps to their role or does anyone abstain or interfere? Organization is, hence, the second necessary function for achieving trilogue play. Problems occur in particular when a parent who is supposed to remain third party interferes by directly engaging with the baby. In such cases, trilogue play according to the instructions cannot be achieved.

Organization is displayed from Level 2 up. According to the instructions, each partner is either active or third party. In order to coordinate these roles, it is important that everyone clearly displays by means of his or her addresses whether he or she is directly engaging, remaining in the periphery, or coengaging (in the three-together).

TORSOS AND HEADS AND GAZE LEVELS

Distance and orientation are critical for a three-month-old infant's understanding of what role is expected of him. Indeed, so-called dialogue distance and vis-à-vis orientations are known to be essential in order to establish dialogue with a young infant (Papoušek & Papoušek, 1987). Therefore, when the roles are clear, the active parent leans toward the infant, whereas the third party parent sits back. When they play to-gether, the parents align with respect to the infant in order to secure equal access for everyone. Finally, both sit back when they directly interact. Regarding orientation, when roles are clear, the infant's seat is oriented vis-à-vis the active parent in the first two parts (Parts I and II), but in between them during the three-together play and when the infant is in the third party role. It may occur that a third party parent interferes with the active one by actively interfering in the dyad's interaction, without previous consultation. Then organization is disrupted.

Whereas these distances and orientations hold for both torsos and head and gaze levels, there is a new aspect to the control of the interaction at Level 3. At three months, the infant can actively display his understanding of roles in the two first parts by orienting his head and gaze mostly at the active parent and keeping the third party parent in the periphery. Likewise, he can alternate his orientation between the two parents in the three-together or when he is third party. This is what we observe when the parents' roles are clearly displayed.

In Tom's family, the orientation of the infant seat is appropriate throughout. So are the distances between the partners during the first two parts and the last one (Levels 2 and 3). However, as noted in the clinical reading, the father's interference in the play between the mother and Tom marks a first derailment in organization. Then, during the third part (three-together), the access of the partners to each other is hindered, due to the insufficient coordination of the parents. Tom no longer addresses his gazes to either parent, orienting here and there in a disordered way. Therefore, we observe a derailment of organization in Parts I and III at Levels 2 and 3. In the last two-plus-one, with Tom in the third party position, there is too little direct interaction between the parents, so that organization derails at Level 3.

EXPRESSIVE LEVEL

When roles are clear, the partners mark them by addressing their expressive signals to the appropriate partner. In the first two-plus-one, the expressive signals, whether positive or negative, are primarily exchanged between the active parent and the infant with the third party parent remaining in the periphery and abstaining from address signals unless directly solicited. In the three-together, the partners address their expressive signals to each other. Finally, in the last two-plus-one, the parents address their signals to each other and abstain from directly addressing the infant.

This is what we observe in Tom's family except in the three-together part, where his "speaking out" of his irritation is no longer specifically addressed. Furthermore, the parents' addresses tend to interfere with each other. Therefore, we also observe a derailment of organization in the three-together part at this level. It carries over into the last part.

It is to be noted that Tom's parents have a particularly close style of interaction. This did not cause problems in this family. Yet, being too close may convey intrusion, causing the infant to orient to the third party parent, who may in turn encourage direct contact with him- or herself instead of redirecting the infant to the active parent. This is typical of the collusive alliances.

FOCAL ATTENTION

After assessing the parents' roles, we begin the third assessment. Specifically, we ask whether all family members are attending to the tasks under way. This assessment measures joint focal attention, the family's ability to share a common focus on a particular task (Bruner, 1978). Joint attention is, hence, the third necessary function for achieving trilogue play. In the LTP, the task is specifically to carry out face-to-face games. Because the instructions stipulate not to use objects, at least at three months, these games typically center on faces or body parts, in contrast to objects or external matters. It is also important that the active parent structures and diversifies the games, as well as adjusts them to the infant's momentary interests, so as to attract and sustain the infant's attention. When the infant is distressed and the focus momentarily shifts to helping him soothe himself, the criteria of focal attention change accordingly. Focal attention is displayed at Levels 3 and 4.

HEAD AND GAZE AND
EXPRESSIVE LEVELS

When the partners sustain a joint focus of attention, they are cooriented on the locus of the games (Level 3). (Note that although it is mostly visually that the partners display focal attention in tactile-kinesthetic and vocal games, the infant's inner concentration may prevent him from looking at his partner. Then criteria other than gaze are required to code for coorientations.) The games are well-contoured, with variations, and the infant actively engages in them. The TEEs specifically refer to what is happening in the games (Level 4) rather than to external matters (see following for examples).

In Tom's family, we observe a progressive weakening of focal attention. During the first part, the father and baby play rather elaborate proprioceptive games and the mother follows the action. However, some of her expressive signals betray her anxious anticipation of a failure in her own play part to come. These constitute a partial derailment of focal attention at Level 4.

During the second part, the mother indeed experiences difficulties in structuring games that capture Tom's attention (Level 3) and enlist his affective engagement (Level 4). Giving up too quickly, she also tends to overstimulate him, looming on him abruptly in a way that stresses him, thus provoking interruptions that fragment the games. The father monitors the action, yet his interference with the mother's play also contributes to fragmenting the game.

We have seen that Tom's growing irritation during the third part forced another agenda on the family, namely, helping him to regulate his emotional state. Note that this may happen for many different reasons. What counts in this assessment is whether the family focuses together on this task and whether the moments of affect sharing refer to this agenda or to external matters. Thus, the parents' difficulties in coordinating to soothe Tom also affect focal attention. For instance, at the beginning of the three-together part, the parents disagree on what to do, and each of them

tries his or her own ways. The TEEs then come to refer to the tension between them rather than to their actual agenda regarding their child. For instance, as Tom fusses, the mother proposes to sing, the father refuses, the baby fusses more, and the mother protests. This triadic event refers to the tension between the parents rather than to the interaction with Tom.

It is after several back-and-forth exchanges between the three-together and the last two-plus-one, with Tom as third party, that a focus is tentatively reestablished, namely a conversation between the parents. Interestingly, as noted, Tom quiets down under these new circumstances. However, again, the mother will interrupt the part prematurely, giving as a pretext that Tom will be too tired for the next situation. This constitutes another derailment of focal attention. Focal attention tends to weaken as the play proceeds, from Level 3 up.

AFFECTIVE CONTACT

Once focal attention has been assessed, we turn to the fourth and final assessment, asking whether everyone is in touch or whether anyone is not in tune. This last assessment concerns the function of affective contact, which we use to refer to the sharing of emotions, whether direct, empathic, or conflictual. Affective contact is hence the fourth necessary function for achieving trilogue play. Affective contact is displayed at the upper level of interaction, that of expressive signals (Level 4). Remember that the task is specifically to reach moments of threesome playful, affective communion, using the games. We know that this requires considerable work from the family: the infant in regulating his affective state and the parents in jointly supporting him in this endeavor. Therefore, we expect to observe not only TEEs that manifest playful positive communion, but also TEEs that manifest tension, confrontation, or distress. However, when the family is in touch, positivity still dominates. Indeed, in the face of the infant's inevitable moments of negativity or distress, the parents maintain an affectionate, empathic, and playful stance. Likewise, they repair their miscoordinations with each other with affection and humor. In contrast, in families where affective contact derails, the balance between positive and negative TEEs tilts toward the negative. Confrontations with the infant tend to divide the parents, and tension between them increases, undermining the family's affective contact. It may come to the point of diverting their tension into their interactions with their child (Vogel & Bell, 1960). These differences in balance between positive and negative affect may arise from the well-documented principle that regulates affect in couple interactions, as described by Gottman (1994).

In Tom's family, the balance between negative and positive does not tilt enough toward the positive, as typical in stressed alliances. More precisely, at the beginning, we observe positive TEEs. For instance, baby opens his mouth and smiles, looking at the father, whereas the father pulls on his arms and encourages him to lift himself to a sitting position. The mother, resonating, smiles. But the family's affective contact declines as they proceed from part to part.

We have observed that the transitions between the parts are particularly sensitive to tension between the parents since they require stringent coordinations. In Tom's family, each transition actually initiates a lower stage in affective contact. The foregoing example regarding focal attention, when the parents disagree on what to do in the face of Tom's irritation, precisely occurred during a transition. It also entails a derailment in affective contact. In fact, the very same event is repeated later: The mother proposes to sing, the father smiles but does not follow up, and Tom fusses more. Once these types of events occur, they tend to amplify, and it becomes difficult to revert to more positive ones.

In summary, the function of affective contact increasingly declines as play progresses, along with that of focal attention. Overall, Tom's family succeeds in fully implementing participation. Organization is adjusted, except in the three-together part. Focal attention and affective contact progressively derail.

What are the relative weights of these achievements and derailments in the categorization of family alliances? We now turn to this.

The Categorization of Family Alliances

Figure 12.4 depicts the assessment scheme of the family alliances. It shows that the four functions form a nested series. Indeed, participation is a necessary but not sufficient condition for organization. In

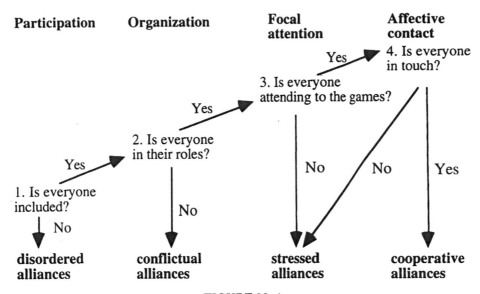

FIGURE 12. 4

The assessment scheme of family alliances.

turn, organization is a necessary but not sufficient condition for focal attention, and so on.

This principle implies that when participation is not appropriately implemented, the other functions are not appropriately implemented. Under these conditions, the family alliance would be categorized as the most problematic type, the disordered alliance. We frequently observe such alliances in clinical families with severe parental psychopathology (Frascarolo, 1997; Gertsch Bettens, Favez, Corboz-Warnery, & Fivaz-Depeursinge, 1992), although they can also exist in nonclinical families.

When participation is implemented but organization derails, focal attention and affective contact are not appropriately implemented. The family alliance would then be categorized as the next most problematic type, the collusive alliance. These alliances are seen in families, both clinical and nonclinical, in which the parents divert their marital tension into their relationships with their child (Vogel & Bell, 1960). In such "detouring coalitions" (Minuchin, Baker, Roseman, Milman, & Todd, 1975), family tensions are attributed to the child, who is often trained to accept responsibility for the family's ills (Broderick, 1993).

When participation and organization are both implemented but focal attention and/or affective contact derail, the family alliance would be categorized as the stressed type. Early results from our exploratory studies indicate that stressed alliances occur most frequently in nonclinical families.

When affective contact is fully implemented, then the four necessary functions have been fulfilled, and the family alliance would be categorized as the cooperative type. To date our observations of families confirm the theoretical premise that participation, organization, and focal attention are necessary conditions for the implementation of affective contact. We have never observed a family interaction in which affective contact was sufficiently adjusted while the other functions were maladjusted.

It follows from this scheme that Tom's family resources and difficulties during the LTP correspond to the stressed type. More precisely, the global scoring of the alliance corresponds to the lower end of this category, verging on the collusive type. We now show that, like most others in our longitudinal sample, this family conserves the same type of alliance over the first year.

Tom's Family at the Intersubjective Stage

Clinical Reading

We meet again for a new LTP session with this family six months later when Tom is nine months old. The preliminary phase will last approximately 30 minutes. It is marked by much parental hesitation as to whether to feed or to play first, and as a consequence, a back-and-forth between the LTP setting and moments of feeding results.

During the first part of the LTP, the father tries a succession of games. Tom is only mildly enthusiastic about playing. He would rather get out of the seat and turns several times toward his mother with a pick-me-up gesture. She keeps to her third party role, but in a somewhat rigid way by averting her gaze or freezing her face. Oth-

erwise, she attends to the games and resonates. We are intrigued by the fact that Tom emits brief, anxious "eh" sounds whenever he perceives the noise of the elevators. This noise is faint, and Tom's reactions denote an unusual vigilance, toned with anxiety.

The father picks out one of Tom's signals to his mother to propose the transition to the second part. The mother follows up by insisting that Tom waves good-bye to his father before beginning the play with her. Tom keeps on the lookout for the sound of the elevators. The mother, more than the father, has trouble captivating his attention except when she engages in a particularly intense peek-a-boo game. It both pleases and scares Tom. Yet suddenly out of inspiration, she abruptly interrupts it and calls the father for help.

The father delays his engagement in the three-together, in spite of mother's invitation to sing a song together. She bravely sets out to sing alone. It is only after Tom has invitingly looked at him that the father finally joins in. As the parents sing together, Tom gazes with rapt attention alternately at his father and mother. Yet, this beautiful triadic sequence is interrupted by Tom's movement at the sound of the elevators. After this interruption, the parents play separately, alternating games with their baby. It is finally the mother who signals the transition to the last part.

The parents have apparently forgotten the part of the instruction that stipulates the two of them to "be on their own." Leaving Tom on his own, they sit silently. Tom tries to enlist their attention by vocalizing to them. It is not long before the mother, uncertain, questions the father on what to do next. The father keeps to his usual wait-and-see policy. Thus, she calls out to the facilitator, asking her what to do next. The facilitator puts an end to the session after a while.

We recognize again in this session the patterns noted during the previous observations. On one hand, the parents succeed to some extent in working together and helping each other. In particular, they pick up Tom's spontaneous movements at transition points. They also succeed in organizing at least one three-together game, however brief. On the other hand, the imbalance between them is still there, with the father showing himself more effective than the mother. This is all the more striking in that mother has proved herself at moments to be quite sensitive and empathic in attending to Tom's affects. We have also seen that the family quickly reverts to working in dyads, presumably an easier way to negotiate the covert competition between the parents. Covert competition shows in particular in the mother's somewhat abrupt requests to the father, who then responds with delay or silencing reminiscent of the "chase and dodge" pattern (Beebe & Lachman, 1994). Tom's anxious hypervigilance may well provide an outlet for this tension between the parents. Furthermore, the parents' assiduous submission remains an important aspect of their working alliance with the team.

Structural Reading

In this section, we merely summarize the main points resulting from this reading,

because the principles of assessment are essentially the same as at three months. However, it is necessary to account for the changes in the balance of control between the infant and his parents. Thanks to the newly acquired ability to control his upper body, the infant can now actively include or exclude himself at Level 2, for instance by leaning his torso in or out of his seat. Likewise, he can actively address or avert from a parent by orienting his torso toward or away from him or her, thus directly affecting the implementation of organization at Level 2. Having developed skills to play with objects, he may insist that his parents introduce objects in the play. Thus, limit setting and playful negotiation become an integral part of the play. Finally, the family reaches a new depth of affective communion as the infant matures to intersubjectivity. This aspect will be fundamental in the analysis of triangular process.

In Tom's family, we recognize the previously mentioned differences in the balance of control between the parents and the infant. Thus, Tom's body movements affect the assessment of participation and organization at Level 2. For instance, his numerous torso orientations with pick-me-up gestures toward the third party mother during the play with the father tend to weaken the scoring of organization from Level 2 up. Likewise, his overvigilance toward the elevator sounds causes fragmentation in the games, impairing the implementation of focal attention and affective contact.

Yet, in spite of these changes and as with most families in the longitudinal sample, the implementation of the four functions in Tom's family at nine months is close to what it was at three months. Basically, participation is implemented at all levels. Organization is mostly appropriate during the first two-plus-one, but derails later on. In the three-together part, the parents succeed only for a brief moment in coordinating a three-together game and then revert to dyadic games. In the last two-plus-one, the parents do not engage directly with each other. As for focal attention and affective contact, they tend to decline as the play proceeds from part to part, as at three months.

Thus, the categorization of this family's alliance is again the lower end of the stressed alliance.

Conclusion Regarding the Clinical and Structural Readings of Tom's Family Alliance

Both the clinical and structural readings pick up cooperative and divisive forces in Tom's family alliance. The clinical reading brings to the fore the cooperative forces in terms of the parents' willingness to collaborate to overcome divisions for their child's sake and Tom's role in helping to unite the parents. Whereas the diverging forces are the covert competition between the parents, the crystallization of the mother's apprehensiveness and her insistent demands on a reluctant coparent result in the infant's increasing anxiety.

The structural reading brings out the cooperative forces in terms of the adjustment of the functions of participation and organization and the divisive forces in terms of the derailment of the functions of focal attention and affective contact.

Both readings stress the key role of the parental party in the family's implementation of the task. In the absence of separate observations of the dyads, we can only guess at their functioning. However, it is a real possibility that the father and mother would act differently in the absence of their coparent. In particular, according to Lauretti's study (Lauretti & McHale, 1997) showing that maritally distressed mothers interact more effectively with their baby in the absence of their husbands, one may imagine that Tom and his mother might better attune to each other in dialogue play than they did in trilogue play. In any case, the disparity in effectiveness between the father and mother in their two-plus-one play parts has to be considered in the light of the other play parts when the cooperation between the parents becomes more critical.

Finally, both readings reveal considerable continuity in time and across developmental stages, so much so that the resources and difficulties observed at the intersubjective stage were already apparent at the social and prenatal stages. Clinically, the continuity is all the more striking due to the parallels between the working and the family alliances. Structurally, the patterns remain invariant beyond development transformations. Although the structural reading of the prenatal LTP data is still in elaboration, pilot results already indicate correspondence between the prenatal and postnatal patterns that characterize the four functions. Thus, the "chase and dodge" pattern (Beebe & Lachman, 1994) between the wife and husband is transferred in their coparental interaction with respect to Tom. Likewise, the difficulties in anticipating the relations with their child-to-be that were noted in the prenatal interviews and behavioral observations translate into their interactions with the infant, preventing them from flexibly dealing with him.

Developmental Reading

Most theories consider that development proceeds from dyadic interactions that characterize the social and object stages, from approximately three months up, to triadic interactions at the intersubjective stage, from approximately nine months up. Note that by triadic interactions developmentalists specifically mean the infant and mother interacting with an object (Bakeman & Adamson, 1984). An example of triadic object interaction is an infant pointing to an object and then gazing at his mother, with a vocalization. The infant trusts his mother to understand his intention of getting her to give him the object (Bruner, 1990). Here we have in mind E. Bates's (1979) definition of intentionality: "the sender is aware, in advance, of the effect that the signal will have on the receiver, and will continue to act so as to obtain that expected goal" (p. 36). This ability to refer intentionally to third parties, albeit nonverbally, is characteristic of the intersubjective stage. What we intend to show in this section is that these referential capacities extend to persons' triangular interactions at this stage and how they substantially widen intersubjective relatedness. Then we raise

the question of their prefigurations at earlier ages.

Triangular Strategies at the Intersubjective Stage

In the realm of the infant's interactions with two persons, three processes that have been extensively described in object triadic interactions are relevant: affect sharing (Kasari, Sigman, Mundy, & Yirmya, 1990), affect signaling (Bruner, 1978), and social referencing (Klinnert, Campos, Sorce, Emde, & Svejda, 1983). However, they are more complex when they concern persons.

Affect sharing occurs when an infant, experiencing a moment of pleasure with his father, briefly turns to his mother to share his pleasure with her too. Then he resumes the game with his father. The latter behavior attests to the intentional, referential status of affect sharing. Note that, in the LTP, the mother may or may not respond positively, depending on her intuitive understanding of the infant's intention: as a way to legitimately enact a moment of threesome communion or as a violation of the two-plus-one role configuration.

In Tom's family, we observe triangular affect sharing at the beginning of the father's play. In the midst of a proprioceptive game, Tom begins to tap on the side of the seat, vocalizing and smiling at his father. The father imitates him by tapping too. Then, still tapping, Tom turns to the mother (third party), looks at her, smiling brightly, and visibly wishes to share with her too the pleasure he is experiencing in this game with his father. However, anxious to not interfere with the father's role, the mother abstains from responding as long as Tom is looking at her. (She smiles afterwards.) Tom sobers and resumes the game with his father. We shall see that this absence of ratification, here by the third party mother, is typical of stressed alliances.

We observe another triangular affect sharing where Tom's initiation triggers a change in the parents' interaction. At the very beginning of Part III, the mother is faced with the father's refusal to sing along with her. She sets out to sing alone with her son. Tom turns invitingly to his father and wins him over, so that the parents sing together, moving their hands in synchrony. Tom alternates gazing at each of them, his face rapt with concentration. Thus, his intervention has helped shift from tension between the parents to three-some affect communion.

Affect signaling occurs when an infant, having addressed a negative affect signal to the mother because he disagrees with her, intends to change this state of affairs by turning to the father with the same negative display. Again, what follows obviously depends on the father. He may confirm his baby's signal with a sorry or empathic look and defer to the mother; he may abstain from responding, afraid of transgressing his third party role; or he may give in, actually interfering with the mother's role.

In Tom's family, affect signaling occurs several times. At some point during the father's play, Tom, tired of the game, leans toward his father with a pick-me-up gesture. The father replies firmly, "No, you are supposed to remain seated!" Hence, Tom addresses the very same gesture to his mother. Again, as third party, the mother fails to confirm she has perceived Tom's request. She ignores him. The same sequence is repeated three more times in close succession.

Social referencing is usually observed when an infant experiences uncertainty. For instance, he may be surprised by an unusual movement on the father's part. Turning to his mother with a perplexed expression, he consults her face in order to understand the meaning of the event and guide his behavior according to her response. It is often under such circumstances that the mother will not only reassure the infant, but also make an affect attunement (Stern, Hofer, Haft, & Dore, 1985). Not only does she encourage the infant to trust what is going on with his father, but she also conveys to her baby that she knows his inner feeling and carries out a nonverbal translation of his display of uncertainty. In doing so, she supports the relation between the father and baby, and she establishes intersubjective communion with the infant regarding an experience that concerns his relationship with the father. Yet again, the mother may not feel authorized to respond, or she may not understand her baby's request, in which case the baby will be left alone with his uncertainty. Alternatively, she may signal that the father's behavior is indeed negative and then side with the baby against him. The point is that however the mother responds, it has an impact on the baby's relationship with the father.

In Tom's family, social referencing occurs twice during the father's play. First, during a proprioceptive game (the father caresses Tom's ears, nose, cheeks, and so on), Tom, absorbed in his sensations, gazes far away. His father calls for his attention— "Eh, ahi!"—in a loud voice that startles Tom. Tom glances at his father, then looks at his mother with a surprised expression. Again, the mother ignores him. Tom eventually turns from her. One may assume that Tom was trying to read his mother's face in order to understand the meaning of his father's call.

Later, Tom becomes intrigued by the noise of the elevators. Alerted, he searches the room, then looks at his mother with an interrogative face. The mother laughs nervously—a response indeed, yet an ambiguous one. Tom goes on searching, and the father tries to soothe him: "What is it that intrigues you so?" In other parts of the LTP, we observe a few more occurrences of affect sharing, affect signaling, and social referencing. They indicate that Tom can handle the four configurations quite aptly and that he, like most infants his age observed, actively seeks opportunities for threesome relatedness with his parents.

Yet Tom's conduct of triangular strategies diverges from those of infants in cooperative alliances in that he most frequently enrolls them under negative conditions. Out of the approximately ten occurrences of triangular strategies, only two consist of affect sharing. The remaining occurrences are equally divided between affect signaling and social referencing.

The parents' responses also diverge from those in cooperative alliances, in that, as third parties, they most often ignore or refuse his quests for threesome relatedness. Thus Tom is deprived of these moments of communion that an intersubjective infant legitimately seeks when interacting with his two parents.

To be sure, he may return to the active parent. However, the latter's response may also fail to meet his wish for affective contact. Indeed, as we know from the structural reading, the triad's affective contact progressively weakens. As tension between Tom and his parents builds up, so does the tension between the parents themselves.

Remember, it is not for lack of perceptiveness or responsivity on the part of the parents that affective contact derails. What seems evident is their failure to sufficiently support each other in coordinating their responses under conditions that stress them and their preoccupation with the researchers' demands (as they construe them).

Yet Tom's triangular strategies and his parents' responses also largely differ from those in problematic alliances. The negative conditions in this family correspond mostly to overt confrontations between Tom and his parents, even if they are tinged with ambiguities arising from the tension between the parents. But this type of negative condition hardly compares with those we observe in problematic alliances. Indeed, it is in extremely ambiguous and confusing negative contexts that infants in collusive or disordered alliances enroll triangular strategies. The infant's triangular skills are then colonized in the service of regulating the parents' conflictual relationship. Hence is threesome relatedness not only impoverished but distorted, sometimes even beyond reach.

Prefigurations of Triangular Strategies

Researchers who study early interactions are increasingly led to assume that the infant has innate propensities to interact with two persons or more. Given that social adaptation requires the infant to interact in groups, an intelligent evolution would have done well to bestow on the infant this triadic or polyadic competence. It is a fact that, but for a few exceptions (Papoušek & Papoušek, 1993), developmentalists have not questioned the infant on this issue. The classical observation paradigm has placed the infant in dyadic settings. The LTP allows challenging the infant on his triangular competence.

What would we expect of a triangular infant at the social stage in the LTP? Under favorable conditions, he would show that he differentiates the four configurations by displaying specific signals at head and gaze and expressive levels. The infant would give a greater place to the active parent in the two-plus-ones, but alternate between the father and the mother during the three-together as well as when he is third party. In particular, he would carry over his affect from one parent to the other, for instance by beginning to smile at the father and transferring the smile to the mother. These behaviors would constitute the prefiguration of affect sharing, even if not intentional. One may also assume the infant may display prefigurations of affect signaling and social referencing by turning from one parent to the other under conditions of tension or uncertainty.

In Tom's family, where the conditions offered by the parents are somewhat problematic, we only observe three events that prefigure triangular strategies, that is, affect signaling. They are moments when Tom distinctly orients in succession toward one parent and then the other. The three events concern moments of stress not only between him and his parents, but also between the parents themselves.

We find indications pointing to an infant's early triangular competence in many families we have observed. However, variability between families and between infants is considerable, and it appears necessary to seek recourse to stricter and more controlled conditions of observations to better delimit the possibility of early triangular competence. At the time of this writing, two observational paradigms appear promising.

The first one is a modified version of the LTP that we are studying with four-month-old infants. It includes a still-face condition. Practically, it is made of four parts: (1) a three-together, (2) a two-plus-one, (3) a two-plus-one with the previously active parent displaying a still face, and (4) a three-together.

We ask the infant the following question. Given that you have experienced a three-together interaction (Part I) followed by a two-plus-one with your mother (Part II), will you appeal to your third party father for help in regulating your affects during the stressful still-face (Part III)? Likewise, will you appeal to your father at the time of reconciliation with your previously still-faced mother (part IV)? We assume that an infant with triangular competence would demonstrate strategies that prefigure triangular affect sharing, affect signaling, and social referencing.

Another promising paradigm has been designed by H. Tremblay-Leveau (personal communication, December 1997). It consists in observing infants (three to six months old) in a triadic setting with two adult experimenters. They alternately interact with the infant and then look at each other, starting a conversation that momentarily leaves the infant in a third party position.

These studies are in progress. Preliminary results indicate that this issue is worth researching. Needless to say, it may pose a considerable challenge to current developmental theories.

Discussion

We have presented a new method to study the triad as a whole rather than a collection of dyads. The data from Tom's family already show that the LTP situation provides observations that are rich, original, and relevant developmentally as well as clinically. The conjoint clinical, structural, and developmental readings provide a global perspective on the triad's internal and external functioning—its family and working alliances. They also enlighten the interplay of influences between subsystems, in particular between the parental party and the parent-infant dyads. Furthermore, they allow approaching the development of triangulation between the infant and his parents in a new way.

Let us stress the importance of elaborating the three readings in parallel. The clinical perspective helps to keep sight of the global, subjective view that is so essential in dealing with human affairs. The structural reading forces systematic coverage of the domains that work as well as those that do

not work. It is not possible to overemphasize the importance of bringing to light strengths as well as weaknesses. Finally, only a microreading allows exposing triangular strategies that unfold in split-second moments.

We trust that our measures of family alliances may have tapped into an important property of the triad that is relatively stable over the first year, yet amenable to change. More precisely, out of the 12 families, 10 sustained the same type of family alliance, and 2 showed an evolution that was positive (Frascorolo et al., in preparation). We interpret the stability of the alliance in families like Tom's as indicating that the family has sufficient internal and external resources to manage the enormous challenges of the first postnatal year, namely affording a place to the infant, investing in coparenting in addition to the marital relationship, realigning the relations with origin families, and adjusting to the infant development. In contrast, in problematic alliances, this stability would manifest the rigidity of the family's dysfunctioning.

Likewise, the microanalysis of triangular strategies opens up new avenues to the development of family process beyond the dyad. Not only does it extend the well-acknowledged domain of triadic interactions to relations with two persons, but it poses anew the question of triangular process before the advent of secondary intersubjectivity (Trevarthen & Hubley, 1978). Likewise, it poses the question of an infant's eventual preprogrammed triangular competence (Tremblay-Leveau & Nadel, 1995; Fivaz-Depeursinge, 1998).

Conducting research observations in a

clinically oriented context allows directly envisioning preventive or therapeutic interventions. Note that many volunteer families use the research program as a resource. For instance, we have clinical indications that, in spite of their defensiveness, Tom's parents were seeking guidance to substitute for the weak and somewhat confusing support they were getting from their origin families. Indeed, during the reviewing of the videotapes with us, a moment that provides opportunities to approach the parents' preoccupations, they were extremely attentive. On several occasions they mentioned that the research situations had given them the opportunity to think over issues they had not envisioned themselves.

Thanks to the multiple perspectives provided by the readings, were we to work with Tom's family in therapy, we would know precisely on which resources to rely and on which difficulties to work. The resources are the readiness to engage and play by the rules. The difficulties are the fragmentation of interactions owing to the fear of not being up to it and the accumulation of tensions between the parents. The goal would be to help the family establish joint attention and affective contact in the face of conflict and uncertainty as well as pleasure. In general, depending on the family's propensity to reflect versus to act, we might suggest work with videotaping, examining the actions that worked well and those that worked less well. We might seize opportunities to work with the family directly in the LTP setting by creating new contexts that would naturally trigger changes in their interactive patterns (Cor-

boz-Warnery & Fivaz-Depeursinge, 1994; Stern, 1995). The reader will recognize the similarity of this approach to that of others in this field, such as interactional guidance (McDonough, 1993) or the treatment procedure designed by B. Beebe (Beebe, Lachman, & Jaffe, 1997).

New Studies on Triangular Relationships in Infancy

This research being explorative, the obvious question that comes to mind is whether these results can be replicated on other larger and representative samples. How will they relate to known outcome measures, such as the child's socioaffective development, relationships with peers, and attachment patterns, the parents' marital relationship, and the family's functioning? Fortunately, all of these issues now enter into a new network of studies by the group Trilogie, so that the validity of the LTP model will be put to the test. This group has nourished the thinking on the LTP model during these last years. It is constituted of teams who have started longitudinal studies on the father-mother-infant triad in the 1990s and have included the LTP procedure in their protocol. Of particular interest is the diversity of perspectives they represent, from psychodynamics, with two studies on triangular representations (D. Bürgin and K. von Klitzing in Basel; S. Lebovici and M. Lamour in Paris), to human ethology (J. Gottman and A. Shapiro in Seattle) to family systems (M. Hedenbro in Stockholm; the authors in Lausanne).

Moreover, this network has also designed a multicultural study that compares early triadic interactions at three months in the United States, France, Sweden, and Switzerland.

Results from the study by D. Bürgin and K. von Klitzing in Basel are already available. It focuses on the relationship between prenatal characteristics of personality/relationships and the child's postnatal relationship development. Interestingly, their first results on a sample of 38 nonclinical families showed that there was a close connection between prenatal representations and postnatal interactions. More precisely, there was a significant correlation between the parents' relationships measured prenatally by means of the Basel Parent Interview, a standardized interview conducted with both parents, and the parent-child relationship as observed in the LTP at four months (Bürgin & von Klitzing, 1995; von Klitzing, Bürgin, Antusch, & Amsler, 1995). It is in particular on the basis of these results that we designed the prenatal LTP, expecting perhaps even stronger relationships between prenatal and postnatal interactions.

Preliminary results from Gottman's teams are also available. Their special interest is in the transfer of marital conflict to both the dynamics of the triadic interaction as a whole and to the regulatory ability of the infant within the triad. Previous results by these same teams on these relations at later ages have demonstrated this relation (Gottman & Fainsilber Katz, 1989; Katz & Gottman, 1993, 1997). Thus, they trace the characteristics of the marriage from the first few months of marriage, through pregnancy and the postnatal period. They observe the family in the LTP situation when the infant is three months old. They hypothesize that for families where there is marital discord, interaction between the members of the triad will be less positive than in families with happily married parents. Further, they propose that infant emotional regulation abilities, as reflected by physiological measures, will be greater in infants of families with happily married parents than in families with marital discord. Preliminary results indicate that it is a "plausible hypothesis that the roots of the young child's emotion regulation ability lie in early infancy and in how the nature of face-to-face play is affected by marital discord" (Fearnley, Shapiro, et al., 1997, p. 26). Again, linking infant regulation abilities with the longitudinal course of the parents' marital relationship is essential in bridging infant development and family process.

On several occasions, we mentioned the study group on the interfaces between the intrapsychic, interactional, and intergenerational in the primary triangle. This group provided major incentives for revisiting triangulation (Byng-Hall, 1995; Fivaz-Depeursinge et al., 1997; Fivaz-Depeursinge et al., 1994; Stern, 1995)

The importance of the triad beyond the first year is also increasingly acknowledged. The 1996 publication of a New Direction volume on family-level variables attests to that (McHale & Cowan, 1996). This volume's main focus is the influence of the coparenting relationship (in contrast to the marital one) on the child's development. Observed in the context of the triad, the coparenting relationship was considered a family-level variable, although one might object that observing a dyad without taking into account the contribution of the third partner falls short of tapping a triadic variable. Perhaps Tom's story is a good illustration of how an infant participates in the makings of the coparenting party. In any case, the results of these studies showed that this type of method "adds uniquely to understanding individual differences in children's adaptation" (McHale & Cowan, 1996, p. 95). Moreover, many of the concepts used by the authors either to build their hypotheses or interpret their results borrowed from the clinical field of family process. Thus, the volume was a major contribution to bridging child development with family process. In conclusion, the importance of studying the triad as a whole cannot be overemphasized, be it for the benefit of our knowledge of the fundamentals of child and family development or for clinical purposes. Moreover, it poses a new question concerning the infant's triangular competence before the intersubjective stage, a challenge indeed for developmental psychology. Finally, this new pathway to the triad is only the first step toward bridging child development and family process (Emde, 1991).

References

Ammaniti, M. (1991). Maternal representations during pregnancy and early infant-mother interactions. *Infant Mental Health Journal 12*, 246–255.

Bakeman, R., & Adamson, L. B. (1984). Coordinating attention to people and objects in mother-infant and peer-infant interaction. *Child Development 55*, 1278–1289.

Bates, E. (1979). *The emergence of symbols.* New York: Academic.

Beebe, B., & Lachman, F. (1994). Representation and internalization in infancy: Three principles of salience. *Psychoanalytic Psychology, 11*(2), 127–165.

Beebe, B., Lachman, F., & Jaffe, J. (1997). Mother-infant interaction structures and presymbolic self and object representations. *Psychoanalytic Dialogues, 7*(2), 133–182.

Belsky, J., Rovine, M., & Fish, M. (1989). The developing family system. In M. R. Gunnar & E. Thelen (Eds.), *Systems and development* (Vol. 22; pp. 110–165). Hillsdale, NJ: Erlbaum.

Broderick, C. B. (1993). *Understanding family process.* Newbury Park: Sage.

Bruner, J. (1990). *Acts of meaning.* Cambridge, MA: Harvard University Press.

Bruner, J. S. (1978). From communication to language: A psychological perspective. In I. Marlova (Ed.), *The social context of language* (pp. 17–48). New York: Wiley.

Bürgin, D., & von Klitzing, K. (1995). Prenatal representations and postnatal interactions of a threesome (mother, father and baby). In J. Bitter & M. Stauber (Eds.), *Psychosomatic obstetrics and Gynaecology* (pp. 185–192). Bologna: Monduzzi.

Byng-Hall, J. (1995). *Rewriting family scripts: Improvisation and systems change.* New York: Guilford.

Cohn, J. F., & Tronick, E. Z. (1987). Mother-infant face-to-face interaction: The sequence of dyadic states at 3, 6 and 9 months. *Developmental Psychology, 23*, 1–10.

Corboz-Warnery, A., & Fivaz-Depeursinge, E. (1994). L'observation du "Jeu Triade

Lausanne" et son utilisation thérapeutique. *Perspectives Psychiatriques, 43*(3), 142–147.

Corboz-Warnery, A., Fivaz-Depeursinge, E., Gertsch-Bettens, C., & Favez, N. (1993). Systemic analysis of father-mother-baby interaction: The Lausanne Triadic Play. *Infant Mental Health Journal, 14*(4), 298–316.

Emde, R. N. (1991). The wonder of our complex enterprise: Steps enabled by attachment and the effects of relationships on relationships. *Infant Mental Health Journal, 12*(3), 164–173.

Emde, R. N. (1994). Commentary: Triadification experiences and a bold new direction for infant mental health. *Infant Mental Health Journal, 15*(1), 90–95.

Emde, R. N., & Buchsbaum, H. K. (1990). "Didn't you hear my mommy?" Autonomy with connectedness in moral self emergence. In D. Cicchetti & M. Beeghly (Eds.), *The self in transition: Infancy to childhood* (pp. 35–60). Chicago, IL: University of Chicago.

Fearnley Shapiro, A., Gottman, J., Lubkin, S., Swanson, C., Burgess, P., & Murray, J. (1997). *The transfer of marital conflict to the developing infant: Examining dynamics within the father-mother-baby triad and the roots of emotion regulation.* Paper presented at the Conference on Affects and Systems: The Affective Foundations of Therapy and Counseling, Zurich.

Fivaz-Depeursinge, E. (1989). Vers une théorie de la triade familiale. In S. Lebovici (Ed.), *Précis de psychopathologie du bébé* (pp. 99–106). Paris: Presses Universitaires de France.

Fivaz-Depeursinge, E. (1991). Documenting a time-bound, circular view of hierarchies: A microanalysis of parent-infant dyadic interaction. *Family Process, 30*(1), 101–120.

Fivaz-Depeursinge, E. (1998). Infant's triangulation strategies: A new issue in development. *The Signal, 6*(2).

Fivaz-Depeursinge, E., & Corboz-Warnery, A. (1995). Triangulation in relationships. *The Signal, 3*(2), 1–6.

Fivaz-Depeursinge, E., & Corboz-Warnery, A. (1999). *The primary triangle. A developmental systems view of fathers, mothers and infants.* New York: Basic Books.

Fivaz-Depeursinge, E., Cornut-Zimmer, B., Borcard-Sacco, M., & Corboz-Warnery, A. (1997). *The GETCEF: A grid for the analysis of triadic interactions* (Second version, Research Report 67). Center for Family Studies.

Fivaz-Depeursinge, E., Frascarolo, F., & Corboz-Warnery, A. (1996). Assessing the triadic alliance between father, mother and infant at play. In J. P. McHale & P. A. Cowan (Eds.), *Understanding how family-level dynamics affect children's development: Studies of two-parent families* (Vol. 74; pp. 27–44). San Francisco: Jossey-Bass.

Fivaz-Depeursinge, E., Stern, D., Corboz-Warnery, A., & Bürgin, D. (1997). *When and how does the family triangle originate: Four perspectives on affective communication.* Paper presented at the Affects and Systems: The Affective Foundations of Therapy and Counseling, Zurich.

Fivaz-Depeursinge, E., Stern, D. N., Bürgin, D., Byng-Hall, J., Corboz-Warnery, A., Lamour, M., & Lebovici, S. (1994). The dynamics of interfaces: Seven authors in search of encounters across levels of description of an event involving a mother, father, and baby. *Infant Mental Health Journal, 15*(1), 69–89.

Frascarolo, F. (1997). Les incidences de l'engagement paternel quotidien sur les modalitiés d'interaction ludique père-enfant et mère-enfant. *Enfance, 3,* 381–387.

Frascarolo, F., Fivaz-Depeursinge, E., & Corboz-Warnery, A. (in preparation). The evolution of the family alliance over the first year.

Gertsch Bettens, C., Favez, N., Corboz-Warnery, A., & Fivaz-Depeursinge, E. (1992). Les débuts de la communication à trois. Interactions visuelles triadiques entre père, mère et bébé. *Enfance, 46*(4), 322–348.

Gottman, J. M. (1994). *What predicts divorce? The relationship between marital processes and marital outcomes.* Hillsdale, NJ: Erlbaum.

Gottman, J. M., & Fainsilber Katz, L. (1989). Effects of marital discord on young children's peer interaction and health. *Developmental Psychology, 25*(3), 373–381.

Kasari, C., Sigman, M., Mundy, P., & Yirmya, N. (1990). Affective sharing in the context of joint attention: Interactions of normal, autistic, and mentally retarded children. *Journal of Autism and Developmental Disorders, 20*(1), 87–100.

Katz, L. F., & Gottman, J. M. (1993). Patterns of marital conflict predict children's internalizing and externalizing behavior. *Developmental Psychology 29,* 940–950.

Katz, L. F., & Gottman, J. M. (1997). Spillover effects of marital conflict: In search of parenting and co-parenting mechanisms. In J. McHale & P. Cowan (Eds.), *Understanding how family-level dynamics affect children's development: Studies of two-parent families* (Vol. 74; pp. 57–76). San Francisco: Jossey-Bass.

Klinnert, M. D., Campos, J. J., Sorce, J. F., Emde, R. N., & Svejda, M. (1983). Emotions as behavior regulators: Social refer-

encing in infancy. In R. Plutchik & H. Kellerman (Eds.), *Emotion: Theory, research and experience* (pp. 57–86). New York: Academic.

Lauretti, A., & McHale, J. (1997, April). *Shifting patterns of parenting styles between dyadic and family settings: The role of marital quality.* Paper presented at the Society for Research in Child Development, Washington, DC.

Lewis, J. M., Owen, M. T., & Cox, M. J. (1988). The transition to parenthood: III. Incorporation of the child into the family. *Family Process, 27,* 411–421.

McDonough, S. C. (1993). Interaction guidance: Understanding and treating early infant-caregiver relationship disorders. In C. Zeanah (Ed.), *Handbook of infant mental health* (pp. 414–426). New York: Guilford.

McHale, J., & Cowan, P. (Eds.). (1996). *Understanding how family-level dynamics affect children's development: Studies of two-parent families* (Vol. 74). San Francisco: Jossey-Bass.

Minuchin, S., Baker, L., Roseman, B. L., Milman, L., & Todd, T. C. (1975). A conceptual model of psychosomatic illness in children. *Archives of General Psychiatry, 32,* 1031–1038.

Papoušek, H., & Papoušek, M. (1987). Intuitive parenting: A dialectic counterpart to the infant's integrative competence. In J. D. Osofsky (Ed.), *Handbook of infant development* (2nd ed.; pp. 669–720). New York: Wiley.

Papoušek, H., & Papoušek, M. (1993). Early interactional signalling: The role of facial movements. In A. A. Kalverboer, B. Hopkins, & R. H. Geuze (Eds.), *Longitudinal approach to the study of motor development in early and later childhood* (pp. 136–152). Cambridge, UK: Cambridge University Press.

Parke, R. D. (1988). Families in life-span perspective: A multilevel developmental approach. In M. E. Hetherington, R. M. Lerner, & M. Perlmutter (Eds.), *Child development in life-span perspective* (pp. 159–190). Hillsdale, NJ: Erlbaum.

Parke, R. D., Power, T. G., & Gottman, J. M. (1979). Conceptualizing and quantifying influence patterns in the family triad. In M. E. Lamb, S. J. Suomi, & G. R. Stephenson (Eds.), *Social interaction analysis: Methodological issues* (pp. 207–230). Madison, WI: University of Wisconsin Press.

Pedersen, F. A. (1985). Research and the father: Where do we go from there? In S. Hanson & F. Bozett (Eds.), *Dimensions of fatherhood* (pp. 437–450). Beverly Hills: Sage.

Reiss, D. (1981). *The family's construction of reality*. Cambridge, MA: Harvard University Press.

Scheflen, A. E. (1964). The significance of posture in communication systems. *Psychiatry, 27,* 316–331.

Stern, D. N. (1974). The goal and structure of mother-infant play. *Journal of the American Academy of Child Psychiatry 13,* 402–421.

Stern, D. N. (1995). *The motherhood constellation.* New York: Basic Books.

Stern, D. N., Hofer, L., Haft, W., & Dore, J. (1985). Affect attunement: The sharing of feeling states between mother and infant by means of inter-modal fluency. In T. M. Field & N. A. Fox (Eds.), *Social perception in infants* (pp. 249–268). Norwood: Ablex.

Tremblay-Leveau, H., & Nadel, J. (1995). Young children's communication skills in triads. *International Journal of Behavioral Development, 18*(2), 227–242.

Trevarthen, C., & Hubley, P. (1978). Secondary intersubjectivity: Confidence, confiding and acts of meaning in the first year. In A. Lock (Ed.), *Action, gesture and symbol: The emergence of language* (pp. 183–229). New York: Academic.

Vogel, E. F., & Bell, N. W. (1960). The emotionally disturbed child as the family scapegoat. In N. W. Bell & E. F. Vogel (Eds.), *A modern introduction to the family* (pp. 382–397). New York: Free Press.

von Klitzing, K., Bürgin, D., Antusch, D., & Amsler, F. (1995). Enfant imaginaire, enfant réel et triade. *Devenir, 7*(4), 59–75.

Yogman, M. W. (1981). Games fathers and mothers play with their infants. *Infant Mental Health Journal, 2*(4), 241–248.

Author Index

Subject Index

Subject Index

Breinigsville, PA USA
25 April 2010
236693BV00007B/2/A